Watering the Revolution

Watering the Revolution

An Environmental and Technological History of
Agrarian Reform in Mexico *Mikael D. Wolfe*

Duke University Press | Durham and London | 2017

Printed in the United States of America on acid-free paper ∞
Interior designed by Courtney Leigh Baker
Typeset in Garamond Premier Pro by Typesetter, Inc.

Library of Congress Cataloging-in-Publication Data
Names: Wolfe, Mikael, author.
Title: Watering the Revolution : An Environmental and
Technological History of Agrarian Reform in Mexico /
Mikael D. Wolfe.
Description: Durham : Duke University Press, 2017. |
Includes bibliographical references and index.
Identifiers: LCCN 2016058123 (print) | LCCN 2017004587 (ebook)
ISBN 9780822363590 (hardcover : alk. paper)
ISBN 9780822363743 (pbk. : alk. paper)
ISBN 9780822373063 (e-book)
Subjects: LCSH: Land reform—Mexico—Laguna Region—
History—20th century. | Water-supply, Agricultura—Mexico—
Laguna Region—History—20th century. | Agriculture—Mexico—
Laguna Region—History—20th century. | Agricultural
innovations—Mexico—Laguna Region—History—20th century. |
Agriculture—Environmental aspects—Mexico—Laguna Region—
20th century.
Classification: LCC HD1333.M62 L38 2017 (print) |
LCC HD1333.M62 (ebook)
DDC 333.9100972/41—dc23
LC record available at https://lccn.loc.gov/2016058123

Duke University Press gratefully acknowledges the support of
Stanford University's School of Humanities and Sciences, which
provided funds toward the publication of this book.

Cover art: Diego Rivera, *Water, Origin of Life* (Water reservoir),
1951. Lerma hydraulic works, Chapultepec Park, Mexico City.
Photo: © 2017 Banco de México Diego Rivera Frida Kahlo
Museums Trust, Mexico, D.F. /Artists Rights Society (ARS),
New York/Schalkwijk.

To my parents

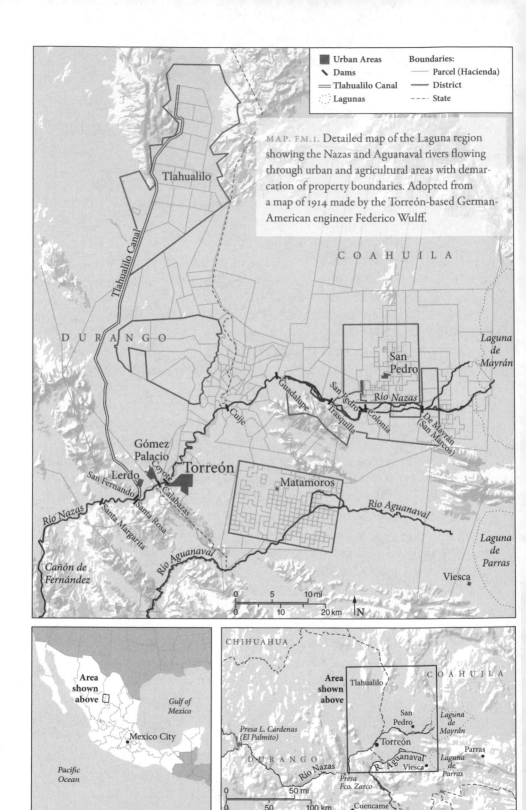

Urban Areas
Dams
Tlahualilo Canal
Lagunas

Boundaries:
Parcel (Hacienda)
District
State

MAP. FM.I. Detailed map of the Laguna region showing the Nazas and Aguanaval rivers flowing through urban and agricultural areas with demarcation of property boundaries. Adopted from a map of 1914 made by the Torreón-based German-American engineer Federico Wulff.

Tlahualilo

C O A H U I L A

D U R A N G O

Laguna de Mayrán

San Pedro

Rio Nazas

Cuije

Guadalupe

San Pedro Colonia

Trasquila

De Mayrán (San Marcos)

Gómez Palacio

Coyote

Torreón

Matamoros

Lerdo

San Fernando

Calabazas

Rio Aguanaval

Santa Rosa

Santa Margarita

Rio Nazas

Laguna de Parras

Cañón de Fernández

Rio Aguanaval

Viesca

0   5   10 mi
0   10   20 km   N

Area shown above

Gulf of Mexico

Mexico City

Pacific Ocean

CHIHUAHUA

Area shown above

Tlahualilo

C O A H U I L A

San Pedro

Laguna de Mayrán

Presa L. Cárdenas (El Palmito)

Torreón

D U R A N G O

Rio Nazas

R. Aguanaval

Viesca

Parras

Laguna de Parras

Presa Fco. Zarco

Cuencame

0   50 mi
0   50   100 km

Contents

Acknowledgments | ix   Abbreviations | xi

Introduction | 1

PART I. El Agua de la Revolución
(The Water of the Revolution)

1. River of Revolution | 23

2. The Debate over Damming and Pumping El Agua de la Revolución | 59

3. Distributing El Agua de la Revolución | 95

PART II. The Second Agrarian Reform

4. Life and Work on the Revolutionary Dam Site and Ejidos | 131

5. (Counter)Revolutionary Dam, Pumps, and Pesticides | 163

6. Rehabilitating El Agua de la Revolución | 191

Epilogue. The Legacies of Water Use and Abuse in Neoliberal Mexico | 219

Appendixes | 231   Notes | 239   Bibliography | 287   Index | 305

Acknowledgments

This book started as a dissertation more than a decade ago at the University of Chicago. My dissertation chair, Emilio Kourí, was an exemplary mentor, always supportive but also giving me the pointed criticism I needed. I thank him and my other dissertation committee members Claudio Lomnitz, Dain Borges, and Christopher Boyer for their critical support as I made the transition from graduate student to assistant professor. As a fellow environmental historian of Mexico, Chris has been both a mentor and collaborator over the years. I also thank my cohort of graduate students, postdoctoral fellows, and colleagues at the University of Chicago; University of Notre Dame; University of California, San Diego (UCSD); University of California, Los Angeles (UCLA); and Stanford University, among others, for their critical feedback on the dissertation or the book manuscript. If I tried to list here the dozens and dozens of you, I am afraid I would inadvertently fail to include everybody, so I prefer to express my gratitude to all of you collectively.

I am grateful to the archivists and librarians of the following who helped me locate a wide variety of primary sources: Archivo General de la Nación, Archivo Histórico del Agua, Archivo Agustín Espinoza de la Universidad Iberoamericana, Archivo Municipal de Torreón, Archivo Marte R. Gómez, Archivo Calles-Torreblanca, U.S. National Archives and Records Administration, Archives Center of the Museum of American History (Worthington Corporation Records), the Rockefeller Archive Center, Biblioteca Lerdo de Tejada, Hemeroteca Nacional, Hemeroteca El Siglo de Torreón, and Hemeroteca La Opinión de Torreón. I express special thanks to two Mexican colleagues and friends: Luis Aboites and Sergio Corona Páez. Luis piqued my interest in *los usos sociales del agua.* His pioneering scholarship on Mexican water history was an inspiration for this book. Sergio's prolific scholarship was crucial to my understanding of the Laguna as a region with a history and identity since at least the late sixteenth century. Over the past decade, he has provided me with invaluable feedback and materials, including maps and photos for this book, and, more important, close friendship.

I thank my editor at Duke University Press, Gisela Fosado, for her professionalism and enthusiasm as she shepherded my book manuscript through the long peer review and revision process. My two anonymous peer readers helpfully and constructively critiqued my manuscript, helping me improve it immeasurably.

I acknowledge support from the Fulbright García-Robles Fellowship in Mexico, the Quinn Family Foundation Fellowship through the University of Chicago's Department of History, the Visiting Fellowship at the Kellogg Institute for International Affairs at the University of Notre Dame, the Visiting Fellowship at the Center for U.S.-Mexican Studies at UCSD, and the Mellon Visiting Assistant Professorship at UCLA. I also thank Debra Satz, senior associate dean of the humanities and sciences at Stanford, who helped defray publishing costs.

My late father, Alan S. Wolfe, would have been proud to see this book in print. He encouraged me to pursue a career in academia, and although he did not live to see how it turned out, his spirit lives on. My *maman,* Marie-Pierre; sister, Marika; and brother-in-law, Peter Hohn, gave me much love and encouragement over the many years of researching and writing this book. Peter read through the entire dissertation and book manuscript and did a superb job of thoroughly editing the latter.

My wife, Yovanna Pineda, helped me in myriad ways with much love, advice, and patience to complete this book. Our daughter Vivianne was born soon after I submitted the manuscript for peer review, her delightful little smile bringing me great joy as if she approved every revised line of the manuscript.

AHA	Archivo Histórico del Agua (Historical Water Archive)
CCM	Confederación Campesina Mexicana (Mexican Peasant Confederation)
CEMEX	Cementos Mexicanos (Mexican Cement Company)
CFE	Comisión Federal de Electricidad (Federal Electricity Commission)
CNA	Comisión Nacional del Agua (National Water Commission)
CNC	Confederación Nacional Campesina (National Confederation of Campesinos)
CNI	Comisión Nacional de Irrigación (National Irrigation Commission)
CROM	Confederación Regional Obrera Mexicana (Regional Mexican Labor Confederation)
CTM	Confederación de Trabajadores de México (Workers' Confederation of Mexico)
DDT	Dichlorodiphenyltrichloroethane
GDP	gross domestic product
ISI	import substitution industrialization
LALA	La Laguna Dairy Company
NAFTA	North American Free Trade Agreement

PAN	Partido Acción Nacional (National Action Party)
PNR	Partido Nacional Revolucionario (National Revolutionary Party)
PPACL	Pequeña Propiedad Agrícola de la Comarca Lagunera (Small Landholders of the Laguna Region)
PRD	Partido de la Revolución Democrática (Revolutionary Democratic Party)
PRI	Partido Revolucionario Institucional (Institutional Revolutionary Party)
SAF	Secretaría de Agricultura y Fomento (Ministry of Agriculture and Development)
SAG	Secretaría de Agricultura y Ganadería (Ministry of Agriculture and Livestock)
SEMARNAP	Secretaría de Medio Ambiente, Recursos Naturales y Pesca (Ministry of the Environment, Natural Resources, and Fisheries)
SEMARNAT	Secretaría de Medio Ambiente y Recursos Naturales (Ministry of the Environment and Natural Resources)
SEP	Secretaría de Educación Pública (Ministry of Public Education)
SF	Secretaría de Fomento (Ministry of Industry and Development)
SRH	Secretaría de Recursos Hidráulicos (Ministry of Hydraulic Resources)
UNAM	Universidad Nacional Autónoma de México (National Autonomous University of Mexico)

Technology was lacking; from the beginning it was not understood that merely shifting the title to the land could not produce the miracle of greater profits from labor that operated under exactly the same physical, economic, and technological conditions. No serious effort was made to discover what changes in methods and in crops could best overcome the unfavorable conditions in which our agriculture has always existed.

DANIEL COSÍO VILLEGAS, "La crisis de México"

We opened our mouths to say that we didn't want the plain, that we wanted what was by the river. From the river up to where, through the meadows, the trees called casuarinas are, and the pastures and the good land. Not this tough cow's hide they call the Plain.

But they didn't let us say these things. The official hadn't come to converse with us. He put the papers in our hands and told us,

"Don't be afraid to have so much land just for yourselves."

"But the Plain, sir—"

"There are thousands and thousands of plots of land."

"But there's no water. There's not even a mouthful of water."

JUAN RULFO, *They Gave Us the Land*

This book investigates how people managed their water—via dams, canals, and groundwater pumps—in a great crucible of the Mexican Revolution, the arid north-central Laguna region. In so doing, it demonstrates how Mexican federal engineers, also known as *técnicos,* were not merely passive implementers of large-scale state development schemes such as agrarian reform. Instead, to implement it, they actively mediated knowledge between state and society, identifying what they thought was technologically possible and predicting its environmental consequences. The book also explains how técnicos encountered an intrinsic tension between farmers' insatiable demand for water and the urgency to conserve it. Not only are these two intertwined processes largely overlooked in the literature of postrevolutionary Mexican state formation, but also in Latin American environmental history, Latin American history of technology, and even global development studies. By closely examining how the Mexican state watered one of the world's most extensive agrarian reforms, this book tackles a global question that, of yet, has not been convincingly answered: how and why do governments persistently deploy invasive technologies for development even when they know those technologies are ecologically unsustainable?

The problem of unequal land distribution has been a grand motif throughout Mexican history but especially since the Mexican Revolution and its Magna Carta, the 1917 Constitution, mandated in Article 27 agrarian reform for the entire country. Appropriating the powerful symbolism of the agrarian revolutionary martyr Emiliano Zapata and the battle cry of "land and liberty" his movement made famous during the Revolution, from 1917 to 1992 the postrevolutionary Mexican state distributed nearly half of the country's arable land and 60 percent of its rural property to some thirty thousand *ejidos* (communal land grants worked and managed by state agricultural cooperatives or collectives), and thousands of small private landholders.[1] Yet Article 27 also mandated water distribution and conservation as indispensable to agrarian reform, which the postrevolutionary state pursued by building grand hydraulic infrastructure that rapidly expanded irrigation for agriculture. Accounting for 77 percent of all water used, Mexico's agricultural sector historically has been, and continues to be, the nation's largest water consumer, especially in some of its most productive land: the arid and semi-arid central and northern areas that cover two-thirds of the country.

Nowhere was this dependence on water more pronounced than in the Laguna, the fertile region that straddles the northern states of Durango and Coahuila. Short for Comarca Lagunera, or "region of lakes," the Laguna's relationship to its largest river, the Nazas, is like Egypt's relationship to the Nile—the sustenance for human habitation in the region. Historically, Laguna farmers exploited the Nile of the Laguna's torrential flow through a technically sophisticated flood-farming, or *aniego,* method of irrigation. Their extensive use of the aniego method transformed the Laguna into Mexico's leading cotton-producing region by 1900 and the Nazas into one of the nation's most important rivers. Because of the economic and geostrategic value that the cotton-rich Laguna attained during the autocratic rule of Porfirio Díaz, the Porfiriato (1876–1911), the region emerged as a bloody battleground during the military phase of the Mexican Revolution from 1910 to 1920. Until the advent of motorized groundwater pumping on a large scale and high-dam building in the 1930s and 1940s, aniego was ecologically sustainable but socially inequitable. From the 1950s, an even more water-intensive dairy industry largely led to the demise of aniego via state-sponsored modernization projects, chief among them the lining of earthen canals with concrete. The industry's success culminated with the formation of the LALA (short for "La Laguna Dairy Company") in the 1970s (now Mexico's largest), and with it the old "white gold" of cotton fell to the new white gold of milk.[2]

Since the late nineteenth century, Laguneros have not only initiated and embraced large-scale change at home; they have also spread it nationally. For instance, the "apostle of democracy" and Lagunero Francisco I. Madero was the first to publicly advocate building a high dam on the Nazas River in 1906. Exactly four years to the day later, in 1910, he would call for something far more dramatic: the revolution that would oust Díaz and sweep him into the presidency. Just as he left Mexico for exile in France, Díaz purportedly remarked, "Madero has unleashed a tiger. Now let's see if he can tame it."[3] Unfortunately, Madero was not only unable to tame the tiger; he further provoked political destabilization and social crisis by failing to implement the agrarian reform he had promised and was tragically assassinated barely fifteen months later. Although he shelved the Nazas dam project during his crisis-ridden presidency, it would live on and a quarter-century later, in 1936, become the key technological component—indeed, the "revolutionary" dam—of massive agrarian reform by the far more radical president, Lázaro Cárdenas, in the Laguna.

Cárdenas's progressive reforms of the 1930s, like the dam, were in spirit the progeny of Madero, but their substance and evolution over time bore the imprint of the tiger Madero could not control during the 1910s. In the Laguna, the tiger took the form of two decades' worth of mass-mobilization and unionization of campesinos and workers that culminated in the great agrarian reform of 1936. Yet while ordinary campesinos and workers deserve the greatest share of credit for generating the political will for the reform, Cárdenas assigned the actual execution of it to three hundred técnicos, many of them students. It was they who hastily redistributed 500,000 acres from 226 expropriated cotton and wheat estates to approximately 1,700 small landholders and nearly thirty thousand campesino families in three hundred newly created ejidos—all in a record six weeks, three weeks of which Cárdenas even personally supervised.

Sympathetic American observers, including the journalist Marshall Hail of the *Washington Daily News* (the predecessor of the conservative tabloid *Washington Star News*), called the Cardenista agrarian reform in the Laguna "probably the most advanced social experiment in the Western Hemisphere."[4] The *reparto de tierras* (distribution of the land) was fast and relatively easy. The *reparto de aguas* (distribution of the water) for this new land regime proved to be a far greater technical challenge that was never fully overcome. As a result, it left the majority of reparto beneficiaries to tragically suffer severe contamination of, and unequal access to, scarce and fragile water supplies for decades. An unintended, de facto "water apartheid" regime still exists in the region today, and some local critics refer to the dilemma as an *acuifundio,* or a water-hoarding neo-latifundio, between water haves and have-nots.[5] The haves are generally private landholders who can afford to install and maintain their own motorized pumps that reach deep down to perennially available but harder-to-access groundwater, pumps whose use the government—pretense aside—has seldom regulated. The have-nots are generally ejidos who are unable to afford pumps in the same quantity and quality. Instead, they must rely on what was supposed to be the technological linchpin of Cárdenas's agrarian reform in the Laguna: the dam that bears his name. Dedicated in 1946, and named to commemorate the president who decreed the great reparto de tierras exactly ten years before, the dam, since its inauguration, has remained a woefully inadequate solution to the technical challenges of the reparto de aguas. Yet in stark contrast to their unwillingness to enforce restrictions on groundwater use, federal técnicos, like their counterparts throughout the world, have strictly regulated reservoir water over the same period.

Watering the Revolution tells the story of how and why this happened from the late nineteenth century to the late twentieth century and what it means for the present and future. Part I, "El Agua de la Revolución (The Water of the Revolution)," contains three chapters spanning from the late Porfiriato to the end of the long Mexican Revolution (1910–40). Chapter 1 begins with Francisco I. Madero's ill-fated effort shortly before the Revolution to unite his fellow landowning, riverine Laguneros to lobby the government for a high dam on the Nazas River—a project President Díaz already supported. In the process, it describes the longer-term historical ecology of the Laguna since the colonial period, how land tenure and water rights fit into and affected that ecology through irrigated cotton growing, and the emergence of agrarian reform as a broad process of social, environmental, and technological change during the late Porfiriato and the Revolution. Chapter 2 tells the story of the controversial Nazas River Dam project's postrevolutionary revival and the burgeoning growth of motorized groundwater pumping, and how, in the 1920s and 1930s, both played an important role in the tumultuous sociopolitical transformation of the region. It details how a shifting kaleidoscope of local and national actors transcended class and political divisions to form coalitions that lobbied for and against the dam. Chapter 3 reveals the environmentally and technically complex and sociopolitically charged tasks that federal técnicos encountered trying to make the 1936 reparto de tierras compatible with the reparto de aguas. Facing a series of difficult tradeoffs, they reengineered the Laguna's irrigation system to rely on an unbuilt dam—and, to their growing alarm, on groundwater pumping they long knew depleted and contaminated the aquifer. The chapter demonstrates how the incompatibility between the two repartos compromised the Cardenista agrarian reform's long-term sustainability even before sociopolitical factors such as endemic corruption and implacable opposition severely weakened and then undermined the reform.

Part II, "The Second Agrarian Reform," composed of three more chapters, continues the story beyond the Cárdenas presidency through the 1970s. Chapter 4 turns to the work and life of técnicos and their employees and families—many of them *ejidatarios* (members of ejidos)—on the Nazas River Dam construction site from 1936 to 1946. It describes how the government tried to make the site into an exemplary, though socially stratified, "company town," one with striking parallels to their water-deprived ejidos. Chapter 5 examines the postwar and post-dam transformation of the region's water regime, characterized by a sharply rightward sociopolitical turn in Mexico, severe drought, and profligate use of chemical pesticides and groundwater pumps in the late 1940s and 1950s. As a case study, it focuses on how the politically well-connected técnico, former secretary of agriculture (1928–30, 1940–46), and self-styled Zapatista and agrarista Marte R. Gómez helped to facilitate this transformation by creating the U.S. subsidiary Worthington de México in the late 1940s and expanding it into Mexico's largest pump manufacturing company by the 1960s. The company's growth flew in the face of numerous government prohibitions on pumping that began in the 1940s and were meant to stem the crisis of aquifer depletion and contamination—a crisis that Gómez had been fully aware of as agriculture secretary. Chapter 6 tells the paradoxical story of the short-term technical success of the federal government's grand rehabilitation plan for the Laguna in the 1960s and 1970s. It shows how, even while they enthusiastically implemented it, técnicos accurately predicted the negative medium- and long-term social and ecological consequences the plan would have on the region.

In the epilogue, I discuss Mexico's current water crisis since President Carlos Salinas de Gortari's controversial revision of Article 27 in 1992 terminated seventy-five years of agrarian reform as sacrosanct national policy. I illustrate how recent debates over damming the Aguanaval River, considered the little sister of the Nazas,[6] in the 2000s were remarkably similar to those surrounding the Nazas in the 1920s and 1930s—an unfortunate testament to the fact that, despite the inclusion of environmentalist language in government hydraulic development plans and a greater public awareness of their social and ecological costs, it is a story in need of telling.

Definitions: Envirotech(nical)

What is envirotech history and how is it crucial to understanding the story of the Nazas River Dam project and its broader significance to Mexican, Latin American, and world history? Envirotech history was a natural outgrowth of historians' doing environmental history and history of technology.[7] In the 1990s, several of them combined their work and formed the single hybrid field of envirotech history. Its premise is that throughout history people have consistently blurred the "illusory boundary" between nature and technology by modifying the former with the latter to create "new natures."[8] Exemplifying the approach is Timothy Mitchell's description of the Nile before the building of the Aswan High Dam: "The Nile was already as much a technical and social phenomenon as a natural one," its waters "channeled, stored, raised, distributed, and drained by the interaction of mechanical, human, animal, and hydraulic power." He thus remarks, "It would have been difficult in describing these arrangements to say where natural forces ended and technology began, or to draw a line between ingenuity and nature."[9]

Surprisingly, environmental historians and historians of technology of Latin America in general have yet to embrace the premise behind envirotech history. Part of the reason for this may simply be that the two fields emerged more recently in Latin America (in the past two decades) than in Europe and the United States, where they are longer established. Another possible reason is the legacy of European and U.S. imperialism for Latin American historiography, which perpetuated a narrative that technology was "imported magic" unsuited to the "backward" conditions of the region's society, culture, and environment.[10] Technology, in that narrative, therefore appeared foreign to both Latin American peoples and their environments. While Latin American historiography definitively revised and repudiated this imperialist narrative decades ago, the illusory boundary between nature and technology that the narrative presupposed generally persists. To be sure, environmental historians and historians of technology of Latin America acknowledge and cite each other's works, but generally they have yet to fully engage with, much less incorporate, each other's foci and methodologies.[11]

This book, the first such envirotech history of agrarian reform in Mexico, aims to fully integrate the two. It shows that by the late nineteenth century the

Laguna's system of small diversion dams, dikes, and canals, all of which were designed to serve human agricultural needs, also created artificial oases of nutrient-rich waterways that became important habitat on which local flora and fauna depended. Envirotech, and especially the adjective "envirotechnical" that I use throughout this book, thus denotes an interdependence between human ingenuity and nonhuman nature in this relatively sustainable hybrid ecosystem. By interdependence, however, I do not mean that the technology people deployed to modify natural processes was ecologically harmonious or functioned sustainably—although proponents of technological progress argued (and still do) precisely this, especially in the case of dams.

Like their European and American counterparts whom they sought to emulate, creole and then Mexican técnicos have been among the most conspicuous proponents of technological progress since the late eighteenth century. Indeed, their education and professional training focused largely on acquiring the theoretical and practical skills to develop and deploy technology to "improve" nature, often by subduing or conquering it, for human use.[12] For example, in a speech to the Association of Mexican Engineers and Architects in 1938, at the height of radical Cardenismo, the Comisión Nacional de Irrigación (National Irrigation Commission; CNI) engineer César Jiménez—much as his predecessors had going back centuries—proclaimed:

> The struggle against nature is a matter of life in Mexico, and it is precisely for this reason that it is absolutely necessary to count on capable men to dominate nature, in other words, engineers. . . . The development of this country is in the hands of engineers. The country needs engineers in all the senses of the word; not simply virtuoso or accredited engineers, but engineering men [*ingenieros-hombres*], instilled with the idea of professional and social responsibility that directs all efforts, sacrifices, and energies into the gigantic task with which they are entrusted for the building of a Grand Mexico.[13]

The CNI's logo visually expressed his sentiments: a large dam with an eagle and a serpent above the boldfaced motto "Por la grandeza de México" (For the grandeur of Mexico). In that same year, the logo also appeared in a mural sponsored by the CNI that was exhibited at an agricultural fair, which portrayed técnicos and campesinos patriotically partnering to build a large dam (see figure Intro.1). It was thematically similar to the contemporaneous murals of Diego Rivera, who celebrated motifs of putative harmony among humanity, nature, and technology, depicting técnicos adroitly executing land distribution *and* installing hydraulic infrastructure (see figures Intro.2–4).

FIG. INTRO.1 A hydraulic engineer, facing the viewer with blueprint scroll in hand, and a campesino, with face unseen and back toward the viewer, shake hands on top of a dam under construction. Bringing the two together behind them is the Mexican Angel of Independence. *Irrigación en México* 18, no. 3 (November–December 1938).

FIG. INTRO.2 An engineer and representative of the revolutionary government, pointing to and holding a land survey, explain how the land will be redistributed to armed campesinos gathered around them. Diego Rivera (1886–1957) at Artists Right Society, New York. Distribution of the Land (Dotación de Ejidos o Reparto de la tierra). 1923–1928. Center panel, part of three connected panels, 4.15 m × 2.38 m; 4.15 m × 2.38 m; 4.15 m × 2.35 m, detail. Court of Fiestas, Level 1, South Wall (Secretaría de Educación Pública 105–6). Courtesy of Schalkwijk/Art Resource, New York.

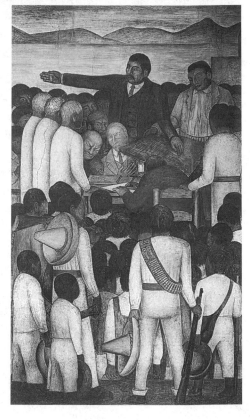

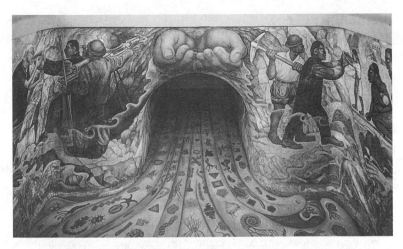

FIGS. INTRO.3–INTRO.4 (*top*) The Hands of Nature offer water for the building of the Lerma hydraulic works that brought water outside of Mexico City into the city. An engineer drills through the bedrock while two government representatives provide water to thirsty residents. (*bottom*) On the other side of the mural, painted on the actual basin through which water flowed into the pumping sump regulated by several doorways, Rivera positively and optimistically depicts the engineers and architects who designed the grand hydraulic work. Diego Rivera (1886–1957) at Artists Right Society, New York. *Water, Origin of Life* (Water reservoir), 1951. Fresco in polystyrene and rubber solution. Courtesy of Schalkwijk/Art Resource, New York

By featuring técnicos so prominently, these and other muralists of the time highlighted the human agency behind technological progress. They even intuitively grasped Merritt Roe Smith and Leo Marx's nuanced analysis of technological determinism in their influential edited volume *Does Technology Drive History?:* "Once [a technology] has been developed, its determinative efficacy may then become sufficient to direct the course of events. . . . In that case technological determinism has been redefined: it now refers to the human tendency to create the kind of society that invests technologies with enough power to drive history."[14] In addition, the kind of society that técnicos sought to create—or re-create, as it were—varied according to the unique circumstances of their countries, and regions within them, during the time they worked.

Superficially, postrevolutionary Mexico seemingly epitomized the "high modernist" authoritarian state, able and willing to impose its developmental schemes on a "prostrate" civil society, with tragic, unintended consequences. In his seminal work *Seeing Like a State,* James C. Scott argues that this dynamic occurred not only in the Soviet Union but also in Brazil, Tanzania, and other places, and in each case engineers generally appear as unquestioning executors of state blueprints for remaking nature and society into "legible" subjects of rule.[15] But this was not the case in "soft authoritarian" Mexico, something Scott himself acknowledged several years before publishing *Seeing Like a State:* "The postrevolutionary Mexican state, though surely a child of the Enlightenment and of nineteenth-century views of scientific progress, was far less determined, it seems, than was Lenin to force a high-modernist, centralized, utopian grid on society at no matter what cost."[16] Similarly, Mitchell employs the term "technopolitics" to describe the relationship between expertise and development worldwide during the twentieth century. With it he means to describe how political and economic demands within a liberal capitalist and colonial order affected supposedly objective, impartial experts, such as engineers and social scientists. Such demands impelled them to presume not only that nature and peasant agriculture were inherently defective but that the wider society and economy were, too. Yet in applying technopolitics to Egypt, Mitchell includes an important caveat: although experts portrayed nature and society as passive and needing improvement, or as forces merely to be acted on, a concrete understanding of the relationship of science to development came into being only by *working with* natural and social forces.[17]

In recent years, historians of Latin America have highlighted the "middling" roles técnicos played between state and society, much like the roles that teachers and artists played in the cultural sphere.[18] Mark Carey, in particular, describes government-employed glacier experts in Peru as generally "mediating" between various competing social groups as well as the physical environment.[19] As Bruno Latour makes clear, mediators and intermediaries are not interchangeable: intermediaries convey meaning or force without modification, whereas mediators "transform, translate, distort, and modify the meaning or the elements they are supposed to" convey.[20] Intermediaries, like conduits, merely transmit messages between social groups while mediators both translate and complicate those same messages by introducing their own agendas. In this book, unlike Scott's and Mitchell's portrayals in other countries, Mexican técnicos-cum-government employees were decidedly mediators and not mere intermediaries, for they actively shaped and transformed a developmental agenda ostensibly imposed by the state. They did so not only from their offices in Mexico City, but, as was the case in the Laguna, also as troubleshooters sent out by the government to resolve local land and water issues. There, they mediated, in this Latourian sense, envirotechnical knowledge between the soft authoritarian Mexican state and a deeply divided but very active and far from prostrate civil society.

As a group, Mexican técnicos exhibited a puzzling combination of traits: the mundane and the imperfect, yet also the ambitious and the fair-minded. They certainly had their limitations, for as informal mediators of envirotechnical knowledge, técnicos were partial to the state not only for the understandable reason that they were, at the end of the day, state employees seeking promotion or just to keep their jobs. Several of them with high-level political appointments went further and took advantage of business opportunities that their privileged positions opened up, creating conflicts of interest. Yet whether they were high-, mid-, or low-level government técnicos, their professional ethos nevertheless required, in the historian Richard White's phrase, "getting to know nature through labor."[21] By labor, White meant hard, manual labor, such as fishing or canoeing, on the Columbia River. Two Lagunero muralists in the 1940s similarly depicted such a relationship between labor and the Nazas, but they differed starkly according to their class ideologies. Figure Intro.5, for instance, is an *agrarista* depiction of bare-chested mestizo men doing the hard, physical labor of maintaining irrigation canals while a mestiza woman sits at their side with a vessel of water. They look out reverently at the cresting Nazas within a desolate landscape. By contrast, figure Intro.6 is a landowner's depiction of nicely dressed, and light-skinned, men and women joyously harvesting cotton and fruit while the Nazas flows through a bountiful landscape.

FIG. INTRO.5 An agrarista depiction of agricultural workers revering the cresting Nazas. Author's photograph of public mural painted in the 1940s in Torreón, Coahuila, Mexico, 2006.

Whereas workers and campesinos got to know nature through their physical labor, técnicos did so through the *envirotechnical* labor of reconnoitering, measuring, and modeling natural processes (hydrological cycles, soil quality, climate, and so forth) for fairer water distribution before the Revolution and, in its wake, fairer land and water distribution. Yet even while they did so wholeheartedly, some técnicos rapidly discovered and openly admitted the large discrepancy between the hubristic attitude their formal education had instilled in them toward nature and the reality of its finite and fragile boundaries. Thus técnicos primarily concerned with spurring development in Mexico— arguably the vast majority—occasionally became what I term "incidental conservationists." That is, they came to realize conservation was not a luxury that could wait until Mexico achieved "developed" status, as Mexican and other "developing" nation politicians insisted (and often continue to). Instead, they saw conservation as an urgent necessity to ensure the long-term viability of key developmental objectives such as agrarian reform.[22]

FIG. INTRO.6 A landowner's depiction of nicely dressed, and light-skinned, men and women joyously harvesting cotton and fruit while the Nazas flows through a bountiful landscape. Author's photograph of public mural painted in the 1940s in Torreón, Coahuila, Mexico, 2006.

Incidentally Conserving El Agua de la Revolución

Generally, Mexican técnicos' incidental conservationism was primarily utilitarian, similar to the U.S. Progressive "wise use" of natural resources, but it could vary, both individually from one técnico to another and according to the resource (surface water, groundwater, forests, minerals, soil), its location, and how it was extracted and exploited.[23] Conservation of forests, for instance, as Christopher Boyer and Emily Wakild's recent environmental histories of Mexico have shown, morphed from utilitarian conservationism before the Revolution into a more deliberate policy of "social and political landscaping" after the Revolution, a policy exemplified by the forty national parks that Cárdenas founded in the 1930s. Government foresters, some of whom had trained as civil engineers, sought to accomplish the revolutionary goal of more equitable distribution of natural resources through joint state-community management of forests that would balance preservation of their biological integrity and sustainable use of their resources.[24]

Yet unlike old or second growth forest conservation (as distinct from tree plantations), which was a response to overcutting with increasingly powerful technologies, water conservation initially played handmaiden to the advent of modern and invasive hydraulic technology. As Donald Worster explains in his classic *Rivers of Empire,* in early eighteenth-century England, before the Industrial Revolution and the age of technological dominance that it ushered in globally, conserving a river had long meant letting it flow and the fish it supported, swim free. But by the late nineteenth century and early twentieth century, conservation "had nothing to do with protecting rivers from harm, with preserving their integrity, or with saving them for posterity's enjoyment." Instead, it signified the opposite: conserving water meant damming rivers and creating "reservoirs," or large artificial lakes, for human water supply, flood control, power, and even recreation. This newer understanding of "conservation" sought to prevent "wasting" water, even at the cost of dramatically altering the integrity of natural hydrological cycles.[25]

The Mexican technical elite in the late nineteenth century embraced these principles and helped set national water policy on a historical trajectory distinct from forest conservation.[26] The case of the French-educated civil engineer Miguel Ángel de Quevedo is instructive in this regard. Nicknamed the "apostle of the tree" during his long career from the late nineteenth century to the 1940s, he lobbied successive presidents to adopt a policy of "ecological paternalism." In his view, the state had a moral obligation to protect forests from the depredations of campesinos by replacing—as he saw it—their antiquated, unsustainable agricultural practices with more modern, profitable, and sustainable ones.[27]

One of Quevedo's major achievements toward this end was successfully lobbying for a conservationist provision in the revolutionary Constitution of 1917. In his memoir, he describes how his many years of advocating for conservation legislation began with his "alarm" at Mexico's rampant deforestation while he worked on a hydroelectric plant as a young engineer. The plant could not perform at capacity because of a low water level that he attributed to clear-cutting in the nearby hills, and when he researched what laws existed to stop such reckless deforestation, he discovered none in the Constitution of 1857. He then mistakenly assumed that the government could only apply the colonial Law of the Indies and a few inefficient and ineffective state and local government laws. Through his personal connection to future President Venustiano Carranza's secretary of agriculture, the engineer Pastor Rouaix, he created an opportune historical moment during the Revolution, inviting Carranza and the secretary of the Constitutional Congress of 1917 to his home in Mexico City.[28]

While he hosted these two powerful revolutionaries, Quevedo impressed on them the need to remedy Mexico's deficient conservation laws by inserting a provision in the new Constitution for "Conservation of National Biological

Resources of Flora and Fauna" modeled on resolutions approved by the North American Natural Resource Conservation Convention, held in Washington, DC, in 1909. Representing Theodore Roosevelt, Gifford Pinchot, the chief U.S. forester, invited Mexico to the convention, which Quevedo and the agricultural engineer Rómulo Escobar attended as representatives. Yet the Mexican government under Díaz, who favorably received Quevedo and Escobar's report when they returned from the convention, was unable to match the conservation efforts of the United States and Canada, for Quevedo believed it lacked legal authority to pass a federal conservation law under the 1857 Constitution. The promulgation of the new 1917 Constitution—with its incorporation of the conservationist provision in Article 27—explicitly enabled congressional passage of a comprehensive forestry code in 1926.[29] As a result, Mexico's new Constitution surpassed that of the United States as the first charter in the world to combine social and environmental rights.[30]

Although Quevedo successfully persuaded revolutionaries to incorporate the provision in the new constitution, the language they used for Article 27 was contradictory and vague. On the one hand, the article affirmed the collective right of the Mexican populace to use and exploit water, woods, and pasturelands and to develop agriculture on state-granted or redistributed lands. On the other hand, it also obligated the "Nation" (the citizens of Mexico represented by their state) to conserve, and prevent the destruction of, those same natural resources in the public interest. It did not specify how the government would simultaneously satisfy the popular demand for agricultural development and enforce the right of the nation to impose conservation of natural resources. Even more elementally, it failed to stipulate precisely what the nation's relationship to its natural resources was.

In particular, the wording that a certain resource "originally belongs [*corresponde originariamente*] to the Nation" and is "the property of the Nation," suggested that the article's goal was complete nationalization of natural resources. But in the very same clause it also clearly upheld private ownership of natural resources except when the state determined they were of "public utility."[31] This vagueness and contradictoriness reflected several factors, including the eclectic property regimes that independent Mexico inherited in 1821; the violent fractiousness of the Revolution; and Quevedo's conception of conservation as a combination of preserving natural resources for biological, aesthetic, and health reasons and Pinchot-inspired wise use of them for long-term economic development.[32]

Revolutionaries' approach to water resources, however, was more confusing than vague, as Article 27's authors included surface water and not groundwater, which they defined as "water extracted from mines."[33] The historian Luis Aboites used "El agua de la nación" (the water of the nation), also the title of his influential 1998 book, *El agua de la nación*, to conceptually denote the process by which an inexorably "centralizing/federalizing" Mexican state defined water as national property from 1888 to 1946. He chose 1888 to start this periodization because Díaz pushed a law through Congress that year placing most navigable rivers under federal jurisdiction to grant water from the (actually non-navigable) Nazas River to the Laguna-based Tlahualilo Cotton Company. The end of his periodization, 1946, was a watershed event: the Mexican government replaced the subministerial CNI with the Secretaría de Recursos Hidráulicos (Ministry of Hydraulic Resources) and in so doing created the only ministry of its kind in the Western Hemisphere. The replacement symbolized both the importance of hydraulic resource development to the postrevolutionary Mexican state and the increasing power the state had amassed over water management throughout the country. Indeed, the CNI, founded by President Plutarco Elías Calles in 1926, for twenty years had been charged with spurring formation of a prosperous class of Mexican farmers, whether small individual landholders as envisioned by Calles or ejidos by Cárdenas, through irrigation and colonization schemes.[34] These historical developments reflected Aboites's thesis of inexorable centralization/federalization of water in Mexico and the "social uses" of water that it subsumed in an array of contexts and regions. He defined social uses of water as "the concrete forms which human labor oriented toward controlling, storing and distributing water, as well as its diverse forms of appropriation and regulation, assumes."[35] Although each historical period (Porfiriato, Revolution, postrevolutionary reconstruction) would have its defining features, Aboites's goal was to make federal appropriation of water resources an essential and enduring component of Mexican political history during the late nineteenth century and twentieth century.

Toward that end, Aboites and several other historians drew on the rich repository of the Archivo Histórico del Agua (Historical Water Archive; AHA) to pioneer water history in Mexico, long a subfield of agrarian history.[36] Established in Mexico City in 1994, this unique archive has made tens of thousands of documents—correspondence of engineers, water user concessions, petitions and complaints, reports, analyses, contracts, maps, diagrams, photos, and other sources—from government water agencies at all levels easily accessible to researchers. Since the publication of *El agua de la nación*, water historians of Mexico have produced many detailed historical case studies focused on specific cities, regions, states, and river basins of Mexico. These studies elucidate the complex relationship between land and water policies, the changing technologies of water use, and the often confusing and overlapping jurisdictions—municipal, state, and federal—for managing the social uses of water. This continuously growing literature, including Aboites's sequel *La decadencia del agua de la nación* (The Decadence of the Water of the Nation), has revised *El agua de la nación*'s overarching framework, demonstrating that the federalization of water resources was less inexorable, top-down, and far-reaching than Aboites first argued.[37]

Aboites's initial work and the revisions it inspired made crucial and innovative contributions to Mexican history but are insufficient. For this book, I searched the AHA along with numerous national, state, regional, local, and U.S. archives from an envirotechnical perspective (seeing environmental and technological processes as intertwined and overlapping) and concluded that there is a need for a new and more precise paradigm: the term "El agua de la nación" should be replaced with what I call "El agua de la Revolución" (the water of the Revolution). El agua de la Revolución reflects the reality that water, in Mexican history, was not just an abstract resource over which the state claimed jurisdiction for economic development and growth but also a tangible necessity the state would have to actively manage and supervise—indeed, engineer—*as a matter of social justice.*

Specifically, the old paradigm of El agua de la nación encapsulates the process of the federalization of water in Mexico beginning with the Ley sobre aprovechamientos de aguas de jurisdicción federal (Law on the Use of Waters under Federal Jurisdiction), passed in December 1910 under Díaz, and for good reason: the 1910 law expanded federal jurisdiction over far more waterways than the 1888 water law by stating that *all* rivers were of the "public dominion and common use, and in consequence, inalienable and imprescriptible."[38] In *El agua de la nación*'s linear narrative, the 1910 water law set the stage, seven years later, for Article 27 to build on the continuous progress that Mexico had made in water matters since 1888. Indeed, both the 1910 water law and Article 27 empowered the state to distribute water as a public good at its discretion. Yet Article 27 went further by defining water as unequivocally belonging to the Mexican people and not merely to an ownerless public dominion managed by the state, per the 1910 water law. Key to this new definition in Article 27 was also making popular *access* to water into a social right. As a resource scarcer than land, water in Mexico was equally valuable and generated powerful interests invested in it. By stipulating that all citizens have access to land *and* water, Article 27 mandated, in practical terms, redistribution of wealth to the poor agrarian majority, whereas the 1910 law, as progressive as it was for its time, did not explicitly mandate redistribution. Instead, it only allowed the federal government to grant use of water under its jurisdiction to "private individuals, companies constituted according to national laws, and Mexican private or public corporations which have the legal capacity to obtain such concessions."[39] In contrast, Article 27 empowered the nation with the "right to impose on private property the modalities that the public interest dictates . . . *in order to equitably distribute public wealth as well as to conserve it.*"[40] The difference between the wording of the two regarding distribution of resources, with one not mentioning it at all and the other making it central, could not be more evident.

Therefore, the term "El agua de la Revolución" in this book describes two distinct, but interrelated, historical processes that converged juridically, socially, and politically shortly before and during the Mexican Revolution: the authority of the Mexican state to regulate water within its widening jurisdiction per the 1910 water law *and* the mandate to redistribute and conserve it per Article 27 of the 1917 Constitution. After all, it was only thanks to the Revolution that the conservative upper-middle-class landowner Carranza's victorious faction could constitutionally define water as the "property of the Nation" that could legally be, but was never—not even at the height of Mexican authoritarian state power in the 1950s–70s—completely federalized. Although Carrancistas defeated their more radical Zapatista archrivals on the battlefield, Carrancista constitutional delegates largely incorporated Zapata's 1911 Plan of Ayala demanding large-scale agrarian reform. In 1917, they understood that Zapatismo and allied Villismo had transformed the Revolution into a true social and not merely political revolution.[41] To reflect the fact that the Revolution was a social revolution, in this book I use the more precise paradigm of El agua de la Revolución to refer to Mexico's postrevolutionary water resources, especially the Nazas River. The "Nazas question," as it was called from the late nineteenth century to the 1930s, had the largest influence on Mexican federal water law during this critical period.[42]

It is difficult to ascertain how aware Mexican técnicos were of Article 27's conservationist provision, and, if they were aware, how they thought it was applicable to water conservation.[43] For his part, Quevedo felt that his fellow civil, agricultural, and hydraulic engineers did not sufficiently appreciate the connection among intact forests, water supply regeneration, and soil quality— or what is known today as "desiccation theory."[44] He thus made numerous efforts during his long career to educate them on the important role that forests played in the hydrological cycle, as he understood it. Despite advocating this more holistic approach to engineering, Quevedo persisted with the work he began early in his career, during Díaz's presidency, of continuing the *desagüe* (the centuries-long project of draining Mexico City's lakes), an indicator that he had no qualms about grand hydraulic infrastructure building—provided it was economically feasible, technically sound, and truly necessary. He believed that the criterion of necessity should be assessed case by case, including the case of the Nazas River Dam. Notably, after closely examining it, he concluded the dam was unnecessary.

More far-sighted than his peers on many fronts, Quevedo also linked forest conservation to a healthy groundwater supply, arguing that reforested hillsides attracted more precipitation, retained more water, and was therefore a cost-effective way to recharge aquifers. Yet conserving surface water and conserving groundwater were different beasts. Whereas conserving surface water primarily meant damming and creating reservoirs that made great rivers such as the Colorado into "a river no more,"[45] conserving groundwater—especially as farmers installed more and more motorized pumps running on fuel or electricity in the 1920s and 1930s—increasingly entailed regulating pumping and preserving the natural integrity of aquifers. Unlike deforestation, however, which is visible to the eye and quantifiable (though before the advent of satellites, not always easily), accurately measuring groundwater volume was nearly impossible before the late twentieth century. When the government finally decided to do it, its measurements were a matter of educated guesswork. Not until the 1940s and 1950s, two decades after motorized groundwater pumping had commenced on a large scale in Mexico, did federal engineers estimate a total national groundwater supply, and even then their estimates ranged widely: from 180,000 to 350,000 cubic megameters, depending on the different methods they employed.[46] But to any farmer who had to drill deeper and deeper for water that was progressively contaminated with salt and toxic substances such as arsenic, it was obvious, even in the absence of a reliable measurement of total volume, when an aquifer was overexploited.

In the history of conservation in Mexico—as well as globally—there are sharp distinctions in how people deployed technology that must be highlighted, for, as this book shows, the distinctions become more consequential over time: clear differences between conserving forests and water, as well as subtler, but no less important, differences between conserving surface and subsurface water. When técnicos and others advocated conserving water by regulating rivers via dams, they imagined technology dominating an unruly nature, transforming the latter into a productive force for humanity. By contrast, when they called for conserving groundwater, it was in response to humanity's excessive technological invasion of finite and fragile aquifers. Técnicos wanted the conservation of surface and groundwater to be two distinct tasks, requiring two different technologies, but nature—no matter how much technology modified it—made no distinction; surface and subsurface water could not be conserved separately in the Laguna. The irony was that Laguneros who employed a much simpler human technology implicitly recognized this and had already created a sustainable— albeit erratic—irrigation system. For generations through aniego, they diverted the Nazas floodwaters into an extensive earthen canal network that was an important source for recharging overexploited aquifers. While a dam reservoir would conserve water, it could also impede aquifer recharge by reducing the free flow on which aniego depended.

Mexican técnicos who understood the delicate and interconnected hydro-logical cycle between surface water and groundwater did not miss the irony that by building a dam on the Nazas to "conserve" water, they would be damag-ing an equally important source of water: the aquifer. And this damage would disproportionately affect ejidatarios, the intended beneficiaries of Cardenista agrarian reform. On balance, however, most técnicos, according to the massive documentation they left behind, were convinced that the perceived economic and political benefits of dam building far outweighed its predictable social and environmental costs. Whatever envirotechnical problems they expected de-ployment of their hydraulic technology to create, they had unbridled faith that more advanced technology could solve them later. By and large, they would remain, far past the point any responsible scientist should have been even be-fore the rise of environmentalism beginning in the 1970s, negligent, at best, and callous, at worst, about how invasive deployment of their technology would prove to be. In this respect, they were no different from their counterparts throughout the world.

Part I. El Agua de la Revolución
(The Water of the Revolution)

1. River of Revolution

¡Ni un verdecido alcor, ni una pradera!	[Neither a verdant hill nor a field
Tan sólo miro, de mi vista enfrente,	I simply look, the view in front of me,
la llanura sin fin, seca y ardiente	at the endless plains, dry and very hot
donde jamás reinó la primavera.	Where spring never reigned.
Rueda el río monótono en la austera	The river rolls monotonous in the austere
cuenca, sin un cantil ni una rompiente	bed, with neither a cliff nor a shoal
y, al ras del horizonte, el sol poniente,	and at the edge of the horizon, the setting sun
cual la boca de un horno, reverbera.	Hovers, like at the mouth of an oven.
Y en esta gama gris que no abrillanta	And in the gray array there glows
ningún color; aquí, do el aire azota	not a single color; here, where the air whips
con ígneo soplo la reseca planta,	with a burning breeze the desiccated plant
sólo, al romper su cárcel, la bellota	only the acorn, upon breaking free of its prison,
en el pajizo algodonal levanta	amidst the cottony hay raises
de su cándido airón la blanca nota.	The white note from its candid crest.]

MANUEL JOSÉ OTHÓN, "Una estapa del Nazas" (Steppe of the Nazas)

Francisco I. Madero wondered why his fellow riverine landowners were so indifferent to what he believed were the obvious benefits of building a high dam on the unwieldy Nazas. He had convinced the ten most prominent of them, both upriver and downriver, to meet on November 20, 1906—exactly four years to the day before he would call for a national revolution to overthrow the dictatorship of Porfirio Díaz by force of arms—to discuss the "transcendent" matter. He had even published an announcement as a reminder one month before the event. Yet when the day came, only a few attended, and among the absent majority only one had the courtesy to excuse himself. Madero provided an explanation for this failure of a meeting: although he "hated to say it," a "ridiculous egoism" and "extreme apathy" reigned among Laguneros. As Madero saw it, this culture of selfishness and pride was so endemic that large landowners could not even agree to form an agricultural chamber to lobby for their common interests and prevent textile producers in Mexico's central cities from unilaterally lowering the price of raw cotton. The "white note" rising from its irrigated land—as Manuel José Othón described it in his famous poem—cotton was the Laguna's chief crop, and with the advent of the railroad in the 1880s, the region became the nation's leading domestic producer of raw cotton. To add insult to injury, when the meeting convened Madero remarked that the few Laguneros who had bothered to appear "wanted to sell the bear's skin before having killed it" (or "to count their chickens before they hatched"). In short, they accomplished nothing except an anemic agreement to form a committee that would revisit the matter at a later, unspecified, time.[1]

Madero persevered after the failed meeting. Drawing on both his own training in agronomy in the United States and France and his considerable experience as a Laguna riverine farmer, he closely studied earlier surveys of the river. From 1901 to 1903, as part of the Nazas River Inspection Commission, federal engineers had completed preliminary technical and reconnaissance studies for a dam on the river. Díaz had established this commission, financed by users and managed by federal engineers, in 1891 to design federally enforceable regulations for distributing the Nazas waters in conformity with the first-ever federal water law passed in 1888. Shortly thereafter, federal engineers began recording flow volumes and within a few years examined the feasibility of building a storage dam in the Fernández Canyon just southwest of the Laguna's principal city, Torreón. They hoped that such a dam would facilitate more equitable distribution of water and resolve the perennial conflicts between upriver and downriver users over limited and uneven allocation.

In 1907, Madero self-published a study of his own, drawn extensively from the earlier federal studies, in which he sought to persuade his fellow Laguneros of how advantageous damming the Nazas would be. In his study, Madero challenged his fellow Laguneros to imagine how much their region would augment its wealth if the Nazas were dammed: "[After all,] if with this currently defective [river] regime so much capital has been raised leading to such a fast developmental boom of cities such as Torreón, which only fifteen years ago was a miserable village and now is one of the principal cities in the border states—how great it will be when the better use of the Nazas waters increases annual production to its maximum and our farms and ranches triple or quadruple in value?"[2]

Madero's glowing assessment of the engineers' studies was partial and selective, however. Although he tried to reassure riverine landowners that there was nothing to fear and everything to gain from the dam, he did not reveal—or, perhaps, was unaware of—the concerns of the Nazas River Inspection Commission engineers about building a dam in the Fernández Canyon.[3] Therein lay the irony of Madero's proposal: although Laguneros relied on a "defective" river, they had *already* developed Mexico's most technologically advanced irrigated agriculture reliant on the river. Indeed, the Laguna boasted a dense, intricate, and vast network of small diversion dams, canals, secondary canals, and *acequias* (irrigation ditches) that channeled the river's flow to highly fertile lands. Laguna farmers and their tenacious laborers had tapped into the transformative force of the free-flowing torrential Nazas current with a combination of labor, technology, and capital to create one of Mexico's most prosperous agricultural regions. Yet the Nazas delivered water seasonally and, occasionally ruinously— hence, landowners' relationship to the river was tense and unstable; it defied their desire for predictability. Madero would strive, as he saw it, to rectify that deficiency.

Region of Lakes

The Laguna, short for "La Comarca de la Laguna" (the region of the lake) or "La Comarca Lagunera" (region of lakes),[4] is a large arid and semi-arid, roughly rectangular zone that occupies significant portions of northeastern Durango and southwestern Coahuila. Its soil is generally of sedimentary origin from millennia-long accumulation of mud, gravel, and sands arriving with the torrential flows of the Nazas and Aguanaval rivers in a great valley surrounded in all directions by small mountain ranges, or sierras.

Other Mexican rivers drain into the Pacific or the Gulf of Mexico but not the Nazas and Aguanaval.[5] The average yearly regional rainfall is a scant 20 centimeters, and most of the rain arrives between June and September in irregular intervals; these two highly variable currents created sporadic lakes millennia ago as the seasons alternated between dry and wet. These lakes might remain intermittently but more often evaporated or filtered underground to recharge the region's aquifers. Until the late nineteenth century and early twentieth century, the region's regularly visible and identifiable lakes were those of Mayrán in the east and northeast, Tlahualilo in the northwest, Laguna Seca in the south, and Laguna del Álamo (present-day Viesca) in the southeast. Where they did not pool, the rivers formed divergent, and frequently shifting, branches or offshoots known as *derramaderos* (wash or dry stream beds) that constituted *vegas* (fertile lowlands).[6]

Together, the Nazas and the Aguanaval rivers currently drain a watershed that nourishes an enormous expanse of nearly five million hectares of alluvial soil. Topographically, this expanse has the peculiarity of being extraordinarily flat, with minimal sloping toward the north or west. It has given the Nazas flow a northeasterly direction after it meanders down from its origin at the confluence of the Oros and Ramos rivers in the Sierra Madre Mountains of Durango. Since the founding of Mexico's modern state boundaries in the 1820s and 1830s, the Nazas has flowed through Durango State (considered the "upriver region") before reaching Coahuila State (the "downriver region"). It then serves as a rough north-south boundary between the two states for about fifty kilometers before veering east entirely into Coahuila and draining into the Laguna de Mayrán.[7]

Rain and temperature heavily influenced the character of life in the Laguna, as it still does to this day. During the dry season, primarily the winter months from November to February, temperatures average in the teens Celsius during the day and fall a little below zero at night, while in the wet season, primarily during the summer months from May to September, average temperatures reach 37 degrees Celsius or higher during the day, with comfortable lows in the teens at night.[8] Between these extremes, nestled among river-fed lakes, native grasses, rush, and ditch reed (*carrizo*) once offered refuge for brown and white herons, as well as ducks, killdeer birds (*tildíos*), and many others that would enliven their surroundings with their song. The lakes were richly populated with fish, especially the *matalote* (a ray-finned freshwater fish), *bagre* (catfish), sardines, and trout, all important protein sources for local native peoples.[9] Indeed, the name "Nasas" for the region's principal river, later changed to Nazas, signified an implement—a kind of net—for catching and storing fish.

At present, ecologists classify the Laguna as part of the Mapimí ecoregion, a large endorheic basin characterized by closed-basin streams and spring environments.[10] Isolated and insular, therefore, the region's streams feed an environment that has a relative paucity of species but high endemism; of the region's twenty-six fish species, for instance, thirteen are found nowhere else.[11] Yet as striking as this insularity appears, it may not have always been the case. According to a recent hydrogeological study of the nearby Cuatro Ciénegas region, in north-central Coahuila, designated a United Nations World Biosphere area for its naturally occurring (and endangered) crystal blue wells and ponds in the middle of the Chihuahuan desert, the system of lakes and their connection to the Nazas River flow may in prehistoric times have constituted part of a far larger hydroecological region encompassing a broad swath of the present-day Mexican north. The study's authors surmise that below ground, an enormous regional aquifer system "may have linked the Río Nazas and Aguanaval of the Sierra Madre Occidental to the Río Grande via the Cuatro Ciénegas Closed Basin and other large, currently dry, upgradient lakes." They hypothesize that this system once formed a large catchment of groundwater wholly or partially occupying some 91,000 square kilometers across five northern states (Coahuila, Durango, Chihuahua, Zacatecas, and Nuevo León). Meanwhile, above ground, over this enormous area "an extensive lake system may have existed connecting the Nazas, Cuatro Ciénegas and the Río Grande (through its tributary the Río Salado) until the late Holocene [about ten thousand years ago], when either regional climatic drying or uplift in the eastern Sierra Madre Oriental severed the connection."[12]

Recent ecological and scientific investigations reinforce a fact clearly indicated by colonial accounts and maps that date as far back as Spanish colonization and penetration of the northern frontier in the late sixteenth century and carry through to independence in the early nineteenth century (see figure 1.1): the Laguna's historical ecology had always been dynamic. As early as 1787, Dionisio Gutiérrez, a historian and secular parish priest of the Hispano-Tlaxcalan pueblo of Parras, the Laguna's economic and cultural center at the time, remarked that the Nazas had various branches that sometimes drained in one area and sometimes in another.[13]

After independence, the Mexican state gradually began compiling more precise geographical and scientific data throughout the country. Even with the more precise data, the direction of the Nazas River's flow and the locations of the corresponding lagoons it fed were a source of confusion until the late nineteenth century. The Nazas had two principal branches once it reached the present-day interstate boundary between Durango and Coahuila: one flowed north to the Tlahualilo basin in Durango, and the other flowed east to the Laguna de Mayrán in Coahuila. The former's flow progressively decreased before it ceased altogether sometime between 1829 and 1845. This natural phenomenon, typical of torrential rivers like the Nazas, left the erroneous impression that the river had completely shifted course from north to east rather than having momentarily (in geological time) extinguished one of its two principal branches. Despite their frustrations with the river's irregular flow, Laguneros appreciated its effects on the soil. Parras, where Gutiérrez lived, drew its name from the prosperous viticulture that made it the colonial Laguna's principal town. He observed there that "with water all types of grains, vegetables, cotton and flax are produced with good results."[14]

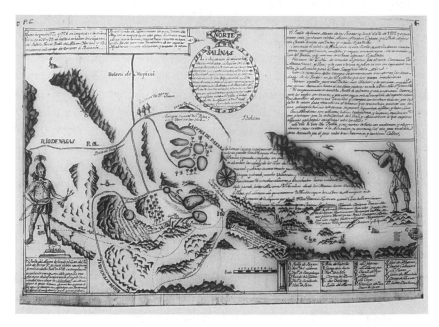

FIG. 1.1 In this 1787 map drawn by the Spanish explorer Melchor Núñez de Esquivel, the "Río de Nasas" (Nazas) is the river beginning from the west above and the "Río de Buenhabal" (Aguanaval) from the south. Here they are portrayed as merging through a spillway, which was intermittent and eventually disappeared in the nineteenth century. The map also depicts the "Laguna de Parras" as a cluster of lakes into which the rivers drained (and that in turn regenerated the region's aquifers and fertilized the alluvial plains before the building of high dams and installation of motorized groundwater pumps). On the right side of the map, a Spanish soldier stands with a rifle seemingly aimed at an "Apache" on the left side standing with bow and arrows. From Archivo General de Indias, Seville, Spain.

Similarly, in his famous account of his visit to New Spain in 1803–4, Alexander von Humboldt, wrote optimistically about the potential for cotton production in the soon-to-be-independent Spanish colony. He noted that in 1791, New Spain exported six times more cotton than the United States. By 1800, these figures had changed dramatically. Eli Whitney's invention of the cotton gin (short for "engine") in 1793 and its subsequent adoption eliminated the constraints formerly imposed by the need for manual separation of seed and lint. The United States surged ahead with a 2,300 percent increase in raw cotton production. By 1810, that had increased by 6,000 percent.[15] Widespread diffusion of the cotton gin contributed significantly to the social and economic transformation of cotton production by revitalizing slavery in the southern United States. The deployment of this new technology enabled supply not only to satisfy but also to significantly increase demand in the early stages of the transatlantic Industrial Revolution.[16] Predicting that New Spain would eventually catch up, Humboldt remarked: "When we consider the physical positions of the United States and Mexico, we can hardly entertain a doubt that these two countries will one day be enabled to produce all the cotton employed in the manufactures of Europe."[17] Among the northern regions of New Spain that Humboldt identified as particularly promising was the intendancy of Durango, in which the Laguna was located. He anticipated that northern Mexico could "one day rival Galicia and the Asturias in the production of flax."[18]

The Origins of Mexico's White Gold in the Laguna

Etymologically, the English word "cotton" derives from the old French *coton,* a modification of the Arabic *kutn* originating from Sanskrit, Greek, and Latin and the source of the Spanish *algodón.*[19] Cotton is the fruit of the plant that produces the fiber so valued for making textiles. Before describing its cultivation in the late nineteenth-century and twentieth-century Laguna using the flood-farming irrigation method known as aniego, I offer a brief historical overview of the cotton plant's morphology, botany, and geographical lineage that demonstrates cotton's global importance.[20]

Recent DNA analyses suggest that the *Gossypium* cotton genus diverged from its closest relatives 10–15 million years ago during the Miocene geological epoch to originate as a distinct species 5 million–10 million years ago.[21] Three principal centers of diversity developed during the early evolution of *Gossypium:* Australia, northeast Africa and Arabia, and west-central and southern Mexico. Since the agricultural revolution began some ten thousand years ago, humans have grown cotton in all these world regions. It was the species *Gossypium hirsutum* that originated in Mesoamerica, however, that would come to dominate world cotton cultivation and provide more than 90 percent of the world's annual cotton crop in more than forty countries by the late twentieth century.[22] New World genomes include the largest number of cotton species in the world—eighteen—compared with a total of forty-nine for all other regions combined. Overall, New World species are "agronomically superior," according to leading experts on the crop, and most of the modern *Gossypium hirsutum* cultivars are based on the upland variety developed in the southern United States from the introduction of the Mexican highland stock in 1806.[23]

For three millennia, India was the center of the world's cotton handicraft industry until British colonialism during the nineteenth century forcibly displaced it to favor Lancashire's cheaper mass-produced cotton goods.[24] Nevertheless, with the highest-quality genus endemic to their lands, Mesoamericans valued cotton greatly and developed advanced textile production capabilities, as well as trade networks through which they exchanged cotton cloth far and wide. Archaeologists of Mesoamerica have found that "cotton cloth had no pan-Mesoamerican rival as the most widely esteemed fabric." Mesoamericans indicated its economic value at the time of the Conquest by using it "as one of a few widely accepted media of exchange or 'proto-money,'" alongside cacao beans. In the Mexica/Aztec period in particular, "Raw cotton and cotton textile were the most widely demanded materials for trade and tribute and entailed the most pervasive involvement of people."[25] Scholars estimate that indigenous peoples annually produced 50,000 metric tons, or approximately 300,000 bales, of cotton before the Conquest. If this is at all accurate, the volume would be unequaled in post–Conquest Mexico until the late nineteenth century.[26]

For the most part, cotton in Mesoamerica was a lowland crop requiring a rather constant warm temperature (19–25 degrees Celsius) and a heavy rainy season followed by a warm sunny period. Veracruz and the Gulf and Pacific coasts met these climatic requirements. Mesoamericans could also grow cotton, however, in inland valleys below 1,000 meters in elevation, provided there was sufficient water to support irrigated agriculture. According to Bernardino de Sahagún's Nahua (Aztec) informants after the Conquest, "The good cotton, the precious . . . [in the Tlatelolco market in Mexico City] comes from irrigated lands."[27] Archaeological evidence indicates that the extensive trade network of the Mexica reached present-day northwestern Mexico and the southwestern United States, where the Pueblo peoples had grown cotton using sophisticated irrigation techniques for centuries. However rare the trade may have been, it is thus possible that some of the "good, precious" cotton available in the Tlatelolco marketplace came from the area.[28] Cotton production overall continued at a reduced level under the Spanish, who, beginning in Florida in 1556, were the first non-native people to experiment with cotton culture in the New World.[29]

Reflecting this geographical diffusion, the cotton genus also demonstrates impressive botanical diversity, from herbaceous perennials to small trees.[30] Cotton fibers accordingly range from nearly nonexistent to "short, stiff, dense brown hairs that aid in wind dispersal" and the most desired, improved cultivars typified by long, fine white fibers. After elongating for up to thirty-nine days, a particular cultivar will yield fiber of varying length and thickness depending on its age and the temperature, water stress, soil nutrients, diseases, and insects of the environment in which it grows.[31] Water is, of course, essential to cotton plants;

their seeds do not begin to germinate until they have absorbed a quantity of water equal to at least half the plant seed's weight. Germination is generally slow, owing to water scarcity in the surface layer of soil in warm climates. With sufficient moisture in the soil, however, the plants can absorb enough water within a few days. The optimal conditions for this to occur are after a warm rain shower supplies an abundance of water for rapid germination.[32]

In Mexico, the Laguna was ideally suited to cotton growing, which began on a significant scale as early as 1813 in the upper Nazas River basin of Durango.[33] By 1830, the area had the potential to supply much of Mexico's domestic raw cotton to textile mills. According to the cotton farmer José Leonardo Flores, who responded to a survey conducted by a Durango bank in 1830–31, of the two cottonseed types that were widely planted in the Laguna—black (*Gossypium barbadense,* known as "Sea Island Cotton," introduced from Peru and the Barbados to South Carolina in the late eighteenth century) and green (the native Mexican *Gossypium hirsutum,* adopted in the U.S. southern cotton belt)—black seed fetched seven pounds sterling per *arroba* (twenty-five pounds, or eleven kilograms), while green fetched six. In husking the black seed type, Flores wrote, the "cottonseed pops out easily, and stays very clean without any fiber. By contrast, the green seed type resisted a clean separation of the fiber from the cottonseed, making the process more laborious." Likewise, another survey respondent, José de Matos, described the greater prevalence of black seed over white seed (the latter a southern U.S. variant of the original Mexican green seed) since "the [black seed's] bud is more abundant."[34]

The irrigation methods Matos described to cultivate the cotton were very rudimentary since the *rancherías* (small farms and ranches) could all abundantly produce cotton "without doing much more than sowing it, removing the fodder which it creates, and weeding it; and then watering it when the plant needs it." Moreover, the "land is so fertile, that I've seen a vast extension of land in which plants grow to 1.6 meters in height, and thus yielding an abundant harvest." The "benign climate" also helped the plant's growth. Besides this detailed survey of 1830, few published sources exist that investigate cotton growing in this zone of the Nazas basin where river flow was constant. The downriver zones of the later Torreón-centered Laguna of the 1880s, where the flow was comparatively inconstant, received much more attention.[35]

Interestingly, these Durango planters preferred the black or long staple Sea Island variety of cotton to the green or varied staple length Mexican variety that had been adapted for cultivation in the U.S. cotton belt. This preference contrasted with the reports of Lucas Alamán, an important conservative statesman and prolific historian, in the 1840s. He claimed that cotton cultivation had been initiated with the Mexican variety known as "del país" (of the country), which consisted of permanent stalks that reached double the height of a man.[36] These conflicting reports suggest the genetic interdependence of cottonseed varieties between the United States and Mexico: first with the exportation of the Mexican green (*hirsutum*) to the United States, where it proved to be more suited to machine ginning, and then with the subsequent reimportation to Mexico of new varieties derived from the green, including white and gray seeds, in the 1880s.

In 1885, the Secretaría de Fomento (Ministry of Industry and Development; SF) published a manual by the Laguna farmer Donato Gutiérrez of Durango on how to grow the "fig tree" (*higuera*) cotton plant. In the manual, Gutiérrez referred to a reimported Mexican variety from the United States. As he described, "Its large leaves are divided into five lobes, joined to the branch by a petiole. The large, white flowers turn purple a day after blossoming on exposure to sunlight, and the calyx of the flower divides into three parts, with its round or conic fruit, which when opened at perfect maturation, reveals its bright white cotton balls. The seed is covered by the cotton (fruit), to which it is adhered or separated, depending on the species of plant." Once the flower blossomed, it needed sixty days for the fruit to mature perfectly, give or take eight days, depending on the rigors of drought or excess humidity.[37]

Gutiérrez hoped the higuera would become the Laguna cotton plant par excellence. So named because of its enormous black leaves, the plant was "elegant and pyramidal." More important, it bore regular fruit that produced sixty-six buds per pound. Gutiérrez and his fellow cotton farmers believed that, with time, this plant could withstand summer droughts with minimal watering yet still produce abundant yields. Nevertheless, as of 1885 when he wrote, the roots of the cotton plant needed soft and deep soil to prosper, for the deeper the plant roots could grow, the thicker they became. Planting cotton, he warned, was a "very delicate operation," for "if the owner of the finca cannot plant the seed on his own in the soil, it's important to have the most honorable men you can find to rely on." Even though the cottonseed conserved its germinating properties for many years, it could lose them easily because of humidity; any mishap at planting time could lead to "fatal consequences," as the chance to plant came only once a year.[38]

Gutiérrez described three methods of planting cotton in the Laguna: by scattering the seeds in the air (*al vuelo*), planting them in rows (*en rayas*), or planting them in chessboard-like patterns (*ajedrezado*). Each method had its advantages and disadvantages. The first method left the plants misaligned, making it impossible to cultivate them using draft animals. The second, planting cottonseed in rows, was "the best for us [planters]," for they could calculate their location according to the distance required by the terrain. The third, the chessboard pattern, was "pretty, no doubt, but the prettiest isn't always the best." The challenge with the third method was the need to plant cottonseed in precise spots, and with "indolent workers" the results could be uncertain.[39] No matter the method, the best time to plant was generally in mid March or earlier, when destructive worms could not imperil the delicate crop.[40]

Gutiérrez pointed out that worm infestation was beyond human control but that chlorosis, a yellowing of leaves from deficient chlorophyll, resulted from overwatering and inadequate cleaning. Humans therefore could prevent the disease: "Prudence in watering and cleaning, careless sirs, is the only thing that the plant can ask for so it can give you good yields." Gutiérrez hoped for improved cultivation of Mexican green seed cotton. In the Laguna, green seed cotton consisted of permanent stalks that grew for several years with just a light watering and could be replanted where necessary. Farmers commonly planted this Mexican variety in soft soil where the roots could penetrate deeply, but in the hard mud and clay common on many haciendas, they began planting a tougher, rebred American variety of (originally Mexican) green seed stock known as *chinchilla,* which required annual replanting.[41]

Rafael Arocena, a tenant on and then the owner of the Santa Teresa hacienda on the Durango side of the Nazas, was apparently the first to use the American chinchilla variety and disseminate it among other farmers. Its use brought about an important change in the region, for the Mexican del país, or green seed, variety had yielded 54 kilograms per hectare of cotton while the chinchilla variety yielded 250 kilograms per hectare. Whereas planters could cultivate the former with light irrigation, they had to cultivate the latter using the aniego, or flood-farming, irrigation method, which required much greater quantities of water.[42] All along the river, increasing water consumption led to intensification of water conflicts that had been brewing since the late 1840s, especially between upriver and downriver farmers. The conflicts effectively pitted the states of Durango and Coahuila against each other. By the late 1880s, the escalating disputes challenged the nation with the seemingly intractable "Nazas question," in which the federal government felt compelled to intervene.[43] It did so by granting a major water concession from the Nazas to a newly formed and politically well-connected Mexican company named Tlahualilo. The first-ever federal water law, which Congress hastily passed in 1888, granted formal recognition of the concession. The government then entrusted the Nazas question to federal engineers. Their reports, along with contemporary anthropological and hydraulic engineering studies, furnish the knowledge from which I histori-cally reconstruct the aniego method of irrigation that was so indispensable to cotton growing in the Laguna but that would become a bane for Francisco I. Madero by 1906.

The Laguna Way of Irrigation: Aniego

The modernization and expansion of Laguna irrigation capacity in the late nineteenth century did not fundamentally alter the hydrological cycle of the Nazas—or, in engineering discourse, its "torrential river regime." Rather, plant-ing the new, higher-yielding seeds prompted a transition to a more technologi-cal and capital-intensive agriculture than the lower-tech one that had existed for decades. Farmers extended irrigation to their lands by diverting irregular river flow through an elaborate network of small diversion dams, earthen ca-nals, acequias, dikes, and levees; the method hinged on channeling and captur-ing the nutrient-rich flow of the Nazas in embanked lots. Yet their objective in employing this method was less about retaining large pools of water that easily evaporated than conserving moisture in the soil until climatic conditions were favorable for planting and harvesting.

The Spanish name for this was *aniego* or *entarquinamiento,* terms that con-note purposeful flooding or impounding of water. The English equivalent is flood-farm irrigation, of which there are various types: canal, complementary water table farming, pot, and, in combination with wells, wells and furrow ir-rigation, among others.[44] Until the 1920s, the Laguna's irrigation ecology ap-peared to consist of canal and complementary water table farming, the nature and scale of which varied according to location along the Nazas River. For in-stance, in the upriver area in Durango, thanks to first-use rights and a stronger flow, more water was accessible; however, since soil conditions were poorer than in the lower region of Coahuila, more water was necessary for cultivation. Consequently, in the downriver area, farmers constructed a more intensive hy-draulic infrastructure to conserve water as much as they could, whether they grew cotton, wheat, or corn.

As late as 2005, some Laguna farmers still used aniego, if in a very limited capacity. This allowed the hydraulic engineer Carlos Cháirez Araiza, of Lerdo, Durango, to study this historical irrigation method. He found the aniego prac-tice to be beneficial, productive, efficient, and ecologically sustainable when farmers carefully employed it in times of least evaporation. When they did so, aniego enabled plants opportunely to absorb enough water to satisfy their needs from the aquifers, from the little precipitation afforded the region, from supplementary irrigation provided by deep wells, and from the May–June river flows. Far from being "wasted," as nearly all engineers claimed, the unused water from flooding filtered back underground into the subterranean water supply.

Farmers also adopted aniego according to season and crop, the most important being not only cotton but also wheat. After flooding their fields from September to November, they could choose between them. They would plant wheat from November to December. The plant's germination and growth would then normally occur from the conserved moisture in the soil that the aniego method produced. In March and April, after the dry winter months, the fully flowering cotton crop planted between February and March required a supplementary watering to remoisten the soil. Since river flow was insufficient, farmers relied on groundwater, but the technology to extract it in mass volumes was not generally available before the 1920s.[45] Although farmers planted cotton later, from mid-February to mid-March, they still relied on aniego. In many cases, during full blossoming, when the flows of the Nazas and Aguanaval rivers were insufficient, they were obliged to extract groundwater from wells.

The irrigation ecology created by practicing aniego in the Laguna included oases of vegetation that attracted flocks of aquatic birds, primarily in the winter, when they would migrate from Canada and the United States. The birds included various species of ducks, cranes, geese, and others that would feed on a great variety of large fish such as catfish, matalote, and *mojarra* (a common prey and baitfish in Latin America). These fish flourished in the naturally fertilizing, sediment-rich Nazas, which farmers then diverted into embanked lots, creating pools up to three feet deep.[46] Root-eating earthworms lived in the moistened soil of these embanked lots, but farmers protected their crop through the nonchemical pest control method of *apisonado,* or having their workers kill the worms by trampling on both sides of each furrow near the cotton plants. In addition to storing diverted floodwaters from the Nazas, the embankments, especially those erected around small check dams along the river course, also served to prevent floods from penetrating the central areas of the haciendas and the housing of hacienda peons.[47]

In 1892, amid heated disputes between the Tlahualilo Company and downriver users, Díaz received the investigative reports of the Nazas River Inspection Commission proposing how to resolve them. The Commission was composed of J. Ramón de Ibarrola, the head civil engineer; Manuel Marroquín y Rivera, Álvaro Rodríguez, and Manuel Serrato, the assistant engineers of roads, bridges, and canals; and Eduardo de la Huerta, the site manager. Ibarrola and Marroquín y

Rivera in particular were among the leading engineers of the Porfiriato. A few months later, four clerks (*mozos*) and an agronomist (*ingeniero agrónomo*) named Agustín Colizza joined them.[48] In their reports, they explained that because of unstable river flow, Laguna farmers tried to divert large volumes of water as rapidly as possible, for which it was essential to build large canals. From the San Fernando hacienda in Durango to San Pedro in Coahuila, they counted twenty-seven small dams feeding twenty canals along both sides of the Nazas River (figure 1.2). Canal builders had clustered them in groups according to geographical location along the Nazas—namely, upriver and downriver (and, occasionally, mid-river)—and each canal supplied water to one or more haciendas. In turn, many landowners then subdivided their canals among sharecroppers and tenants (see map 1.1).

Marroquín y Rivera observed that farmers used large quantities of water for intensive watering that each lasted up to a few days. As a result, the soil could conserve moisture a little below the ground surface for nearly a year. Marroquín y Rivera was certain that the Nazas was a source of the Laguna's fertile soil: "It's an indisputable fact that the material forming the present terrain in this region was to a great depth deposited by the waters [of the Nazas]." In addition, he emphasized the recent nature of the sediment buildup. For instance, in the Yucatán hacienda three miles past San Pedro on the right bank of the Nazas, a "layer three or four meters thick of sediment" had accumulated over fifteen years.[49] He observed rich fertilizing properties in the sediment: "The sand interposed between the mud has the effect of producing very porous grayish soil that crumbles easily from light pressure, rendering it a fine dust. This soil is of the best class—just to give an idea of its fertility we need only mention the extraordinary yield that was obtained in one harvest of the Yucatán, which within a 30–33 hectare area, produced 6,000 arrobas [69,000 kilograms] of cotton."[50] In other nearby areas where the Nazas had crested, he likewise found soil of "amazing fertility," to which each new flow would add.

Farmers in all areas of the Laguna practiced some form of aniego. Because of a combination of less water, smaller landholdings, and more fertile soil, however, planters in the downriver region in Coahuila used the technique more adeptly. They invested in hydraulic works that made it as efficient and profitable as possible. For example, in 1919, Gil Ornelas, a Laguna farmer and engineer, observed that the works in the downriver region were far more efficient than the upriver region—an observation that surely reflected his partiality as a downriver user resentful of upriver users' water hoarding. Yet it also reflected sheer necessity, as less secure and unpredictable flow compelled downriver users to conserve more through whatever techniques available.[51]

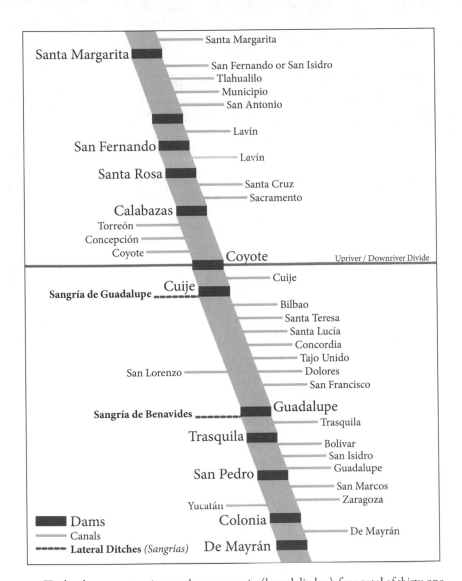

Santa Margarita

Santa Margarita
San Fernando or San Isidro
Tlahualilo
Municipio
San Antonio

Lavín

San Fernando

Lavín

Santa Rosa

Santa Cruz
Sacramento

Calabazas

Torreón
Concepción
Coyote

Coyote   Upriver / Downriver Divide

Cuije
Sangría de Guadalupe   Cuije

Bilbao
Santa Teresa
Santa Lucía
Concordia
Tajo Unido
San Lorenzo   Dolores
San Francisco

Sangría de Benavides   Guadalupe
Trasquila

Trasquila
Bolívar
San Isidro
San Pedro   Guadalupe

San Marcos
Zaragoza
Yucatán

■■■ Dams   Colonia
— Canals   De Mayrán
■ ■ ■ Lateral Ditches (Sangrías)   De Mayrán

FIG. 1.2 Twelve dams, twenty-nine canals, two *sangrías* (lateral ditches), for a total of thirty-one intake points as of 1929 (expanded from twenty-seven in 1892). This diagram displays the Nazas River in cascading vertical form, with Santa Margarita the foremost upriver area and De Mayrán the foremost downriver area along the river course. Through the Nazas River Inspection Commission the federal government regulated this stretch of the river flowing west to east, or from Durango, becoming the interstate boundary, and then into Coahuila. The canals on the right are the left bank of the Nazas, or the Durango side until the Cuije canal, below which they are in Coahuila. All of the canals on the left of the diagram are on the right bank of the Nazas, or in Coahuila from the Torreón canal onward. Each diversion dam would supply one or more canals, which in turn would supply secondary canals and acequias spreading grid-like out throughout the vast hacienda fields. Adapted and modified from Carlos Cháirez Araiza, "El impacto de la regulación de los ríos en la recarga a los acuíferos: El caso del acuífero principal de la Comarca de la Laguna," Ph.D. diss., Colegio de Postgraduados, Chapingo, 2005.

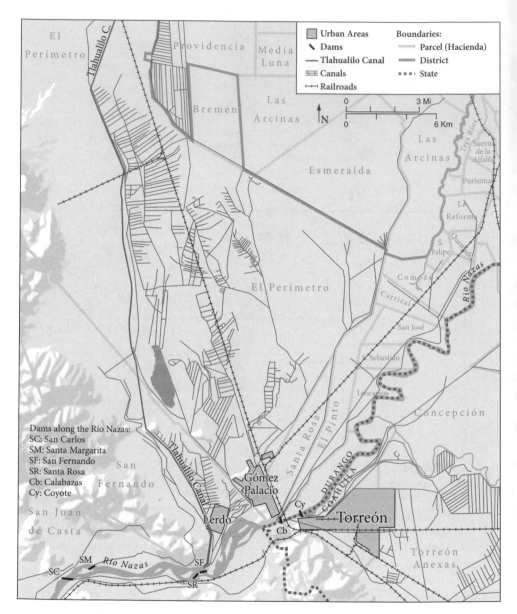

MAP. 1.1 The map shows the canal network, including the forty-mile-long Tlahualilo, or Sacramento, Canal, in the upriver region of Durango north of Lerdo and Gómez Palacio, as well as some of the network east of Torreón.

To apply aniego, planters would divide a principal canal receiving water directly from the river and divert it among various secondary canals. They would, in turn, subdivide the secondary canals according to the importance of the property or section of property until the smallest subdivided canals became "watering acequias." In each of them, farmers could cultivate one or two square kilometers of land, as well as dig other smaller "counter-acequias." They then divided them in spaces called *tablas* (water tables). The number of counter-acequias and the distance farmers placed between them depended on the slope of the terrain; the counter-acequias would always cross through the highest terrain unless topographical conditions forced their path through the lower terrain. Farmers thereby ensured that they located essential terraces at the lowest elevation possible. When the terrain was primarily flat with little incline, the most effective practice for farmers was to place the terraces 200–300 meters apart and in nearly parallel directions. Farmers in turn subdivided tablas via embankments perpendicular to the direction of the counter-acequias, in spaces called *tendidas* (little water tables). They placed the tendidas between the embankments in flat terrain and at a mostly horizontal distance from 250 meters to 335 meters (see figure 1.3).[52]

Marroquín y Rivera remarked that the most productive haciendas applied aniego, but not every year, especially those that had already been cultivating for some time. Instead, they applied it every four or five years when they planted new crops. In the intervening years, simple watering would suffice, allowing just enough water to flow into a tendida so it could run across to the next one. Farmers would thus rearrange tendidas according to the particular ecological conditions of the terrain. This rearrangement would conserve water and prevent plants in the lower-level areas from remaining flooded, which, as Donato Gutiérrez noted as early as 1885, could cause them to contract chlorosis or other fatal diseases. Marroquín y Rivera also remarked that the volume of water Laguna farmers consumed with aniego, compared with similar irrigation methods in France and Italy, was not excessive, as some detractors had alleged. For instance, in the arid Laguna, a farmer might consume 16,000 cubic meters per hectare annually, the same amount that his counterpart typically consumed in certain areas of more humid France and not much more than the 14,000 cubic meters farmers typically consumed in Lombardia.[53]

Aniego was an ingenious irrigation method with deep colonial roots in the region that grew and expanded as the arrival of the railroad helped bring modern development during the late nineteenth century. The railroad was the symbol during the Porfiriato of Mexico's economic and political modernization:

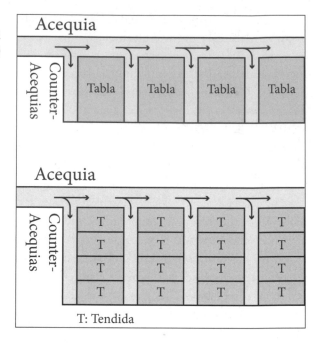

FIG. 1.3 The arrangement of *tablas* (water tables) and *tendidas* (little water tables) for aniego irrigation.

economically for creating a national market for the supply and demand of various agricultural and industrial goods and politically for the newfound stability that ended a half-century of civil strife since independence, including pacification of the northern frontier, which terminated the threat of the "indio bárbaro."[54] More than the railroad, however, for all its ingenuity as a human adaptation to the Nazas, expanding aniego generated intense conflict among users because of the river's unpredictable annual flow volumes. For this reason, the engineers of the Nazas River Inspection Commission deemed the method inefficient and wasteful despite their admiration for it. (For the variability of river flow, see appendix 1.) There was simply too little water for too many users, as individual owners erected hydraulic works to maximize scarce water for themselves. Thus, when the cresting river overwhelmed the capacity of a small diversion dam, the floodwaters surged toward a lateral exit, "very possibly undermining the terrain which supports the foundations of the [diversion] dam." In the case of a dam constructed near a hill in Villa Lerdo in the upriver region, the river could not find a lateral route and routinely flooded the area.[55] Although federal engineers in the 1890s tried to distribute water more equitably, they did not take into account the quantities of water "lost" because of the formidable challenges of accurately measuring river flow.

It is in this context that the legal history of water in the Laguna had major implications for Mexican water law, beginning with the Ley sobre vías generales de comunicación (Federal Law on General Means of Communications) of 1888. This law expanded federal jurisdiction over roads and railroads to various waterways, among them navigable and floatable rivers including those that served as international or interstate boundaries. Only the SF could concede private rights to such waterways, provided the concession did "not produce or threaten to produce a change in the course of the rivers or canals [under federal jurisdiction] or deprive use of their waters to downriver users."[56] It is clear from this provision, which perfectly described the situation of the Nazas, that the Congress, under Díaz's sway, had this particular river in mind when it passed the law for the entire nation. Congress then passed new regulations specific to the Nazas in 1891, 1895, and 1909. Each was the product of more precise river flow measurements and hydrological understanding of the river regime, as the Porfirian state developed a cadre of elite policy makers known as *Científicos* steeped in French positivism.[57] Although not considered reliable by U.S. standards in the late 1920s, these measurements were far more accurate than Marroquín y Rivera's efforts to quantify volume through the historical memories of local river users before 1893. In compiling such oral testimonies covering the years from 1867 to 1892, for example, Marroquín y Rivera took such terse notes as "very scarce, first flow came down August 13th" (1867), "scarce years" (1870–74), "medium" (1880 and 1881), "extremely dry" (1883), "exceptionally scarce" (1891), and "abundant" (1892). He sprinkled these with other notes on what months or on specific dates the river may have flowed down or there was no flow.[58]

For agriculture, the Nazas River Inspection Commission engineers remarked that land without water might be worthless, especially in an arid region, but water without good land was certainly not worth much either.[59] In the Laguna, securing both ensured a good crop when the Nazas flowed, but farmers also needed access to sufficient capital, labor, and technology to transform riverside properties into irrigated oases. As the historian Sergio Corona Páez and archaeologists and anthropologists of the colonial Laguna have shown, by independence in 1821 two centuries of Hispano-Tlaxcalan colonization of the nearby colonial pueblo of Parras had produced New Spain's greatest viticultural center using both subterranean and surface irrigation from springs and streams hydrologically connected to the Nazas and Aguanaval rivers.[60] Building on the long-standing farming techniques of descendants of these

Hispano-Tlaxcalans (who provided much of the local workforce), labor-, capital-, and technology-intensive irrigated cotton production emerged in several stages over the course of the nineteenth century and early twentieth century preceding the Revolution. Although they make little or no reference to this rich colonial history or its historical ecology, the seminal works of the Laguna historians Manuel Plana and William K. Meyers provide detailed studies of how domestic and foreign entrepreneurs, their hired laborers, and the federal government all contributed to radically altering the region's socioeconomic and political structures and land tenure patterns—especially during the Porfiriato, when the pace of change accelerated greatly.[61]

The first stage, from the 1840s to the 1860s, consisted of the partial sale of the colonial-era latifundio to the first post-latifundio generation. The agricultural "pioneers" Leonardo Zuloaga of Coahuila, owner of the Torreón ranch, and Juan Ignacio Jiménez and Juan Nepomuceno Flores, property owners on the Durango side of the river, dominated this generation but failed to convert their properties into profitable enterprises because of the confluence of three mutually reinforcing factors: the economic and political impact of the Mexican and U.S. civil wars, devastating losses from Apache and Comanche raids and local agrarian revolts, and increasing indebtedness. A second stage, from around 1870 to the mid-1880s, witnessed the transfer of these first-generation properties to a second generation of primarily northern, and especially Monterrey-based, entrepreneurs through subdivision of the first generation's lands, mortgage buyouts, debt retirement, and land leases to tenants and sharecroppers. The first and second phases occurred as the liberals, led by Benito Juárez, defeated the conservatives. The victorious Juárez expropriated significant portions of the conservative Zuloaga's lands to found the villas of Matamoros in 1864 and San Pedro in 1871, where small individual parcels and agricultural colonies were the dominant landholders.[62]

By the 1880s, increasing federal involvement, both to spur greater economic activity and to resolve bitter water disputes, brought about a third stage, characterized by the arrival of the railroad and an overhaul of fiscal policies. Regional, national, and international investors capable of taking advantage of new economies of scale, capital-intensive technologies, and extra-regional migrant wage labor vastly expanded irrigable areas in the Laguna. During this third stage, a new agrarian bourgeoisie consolidated more modern, highly rationalized, and well-capitalized cotton estates marked by highly concentrated landownership patterns. Many members of this agrarian bourgeoisie also owned industries and urban property in the Laguna, making it the fastest-growing Mexican region during the Porfiriato. As Madero (who was a member of this class) boasted in his 1907 study promoting construction of a Nazas high dam, during this stage Torreón emerged from a devastated, inundated "miserable village" in 1868 to become a bustling rail entrepôt with the designation of town (*villa*) in 1893 and then city (*ciudad*) in 1907. Along with the neighboring cities of Lerdo, Gómez Palacio, and San Pedro, Torreón and the Laguna as a whole underwent tremendous demographic growth.

In 1871, the Laguna had an estimated population of 20,000; by 1910, it had grown to 172,000. The Coahuila portion of this grew from 10,000 to 105,000 people, while the Durango portion grew from 10,000 to 67,000. Both rural and urban populations grew rapidly, with the rural population 55 percent of the total and the urban 45 percent by 1910. Torreón in particular tripled its population just from nearly 4,000 in 1895 to nearly 12,000 in 1900, only to triple it again by 1910. In a record twenty years, it became the second most populated city after Orizaba, Veracruz, without being a state capital. The rural population of haciendas and ranchos in the Coahuila portion of the Laguna increased from approximately 8,000 to 53,000. Most of the increase occurred in ranchos located within large properties rather than individual ranchos typical of San Pedro and Matamoros. Overall, the population of Laguna haciendas remained fairly constant between 1,000 and 1,500 residents from 1878 to 1900, with slight increases from 1900 to 1910, particularly in the El Coyote, La Concha, Avilés, Sacramento, Noé, and Zaragoza haciendas.[63]

In all, by 1900 the Laguna was one of the most densely populated rural areas of the north. The demographic process, according to Plana, was already evident between 1878 and 1881 in the region, or before the arrival of the railroad and just as the latifundio was being subdivided. Nevertheless, from about 1895 to 1936—with the exception of the convulsions of the military phase of the Revolution in the region (1910–17)—land tenure patterns remained relatively consistent. Properties changed hands frequently, but, along with water, stayed in concentrated holdings until Lázaro Cárdenas's large-scale expropriation of the region's 226 medium and large estates in 1936.

By 1910, twenty-four landowners were cultivating 100,000 hectares of cotton, the majority on irrigable land. Each landowner possessed an area between 1,000 hectares and 15,000 hectares, which in turn was subdivided into lots varying from 100 hectares to 1,000 hectares. By contrast, although small properties initially dominated the downriver region of Matamoros and San Pedro, a wave of buying and selling transformed them into new, larger farms averaging between 500 hectares and 1,000 hectares. For example, after establishing themselves in Parras in the 1850s and reviving the old colonial era Hispano-Tlaxcalan vineyards of Rosario and San Lorenzo into a highly profitable enterprise, the

Madero family entered the San Pedro real estate market by acquiring various ranchos from the 1870s.[64] They subsequently subdivided them into cultivated lots and leased them to tenants and sharecroppers. Altogether, the Madero family's patchwork of ranchos amounted to the area of a large hacienda in 1914.

Nationalist Water Law and Engineering versus the Tlahualilo Estate

Another major estate that entered the crowded and risky, but highly profitable, Laguna cotton market was the Tlahualilo Company. In 1885, sixteen Mexican shareholders met in Lerdo, Durango, and invested 250,000 pesos each in the company.[65] In the same year, they also requested permission to build an irrigation canal, but the petition did not advance, as a law on the matter was still pending in Congress. In 1887, the company sent the petition directly to SF Minister Carlos Pacheco, who approved it. Then, in an effort to secure federal intervention, Pacheco and the company turned the petition into a request to colonize, even though the shareholders did not actually intend to colonize on a large scale.[66] On June 5, 1888, Congress passed the Law on General Means of Communications, by which it extended federal jurisdiction over rivers such as the Nazas. In so doing, it legitimized the Tlahualilo Company's colonization contract. The contract permitted the company to construct a wide canal to conduct an unspecified volume of water for more than 60 kilometers along the course of the extinguished northern Nazas branch to irrigate 46,000 hectares (twenty-six *sitios de ganado mayor*) in the former Tlahualilo lakebed once intermittently filled by the branch. This hastily devised solution to the Nazas question would cause the Díaz regime major legal headaches for the next two decades.[67]

Once Tlahualilo bought the upriver San Fernando hacienda and took possession of the diversion dam of the same name from the hacendado Juan N. Flores, the company became a riparian owner with first access to Nazas water. As a result, it was endowed with rights "as both concessionaire and riparian owner."[68] In the meantime, sixty-nine downriver owners furiously lobbied the government for confirmation of their preexisting water rights.[69] The overriding problem, as the legal scholar Martín Díaz y Díaz comments in a detailed juridical analysis of the case, was that though the 1888 law tried to create one, neither Castilian law nor indigenous practices had developed a normative system that could be applied ex post facto to the distribution of water within irrigable basins.[70] Among other things, the law inaccurately designated the Nazas as a navigable stream by which the federal government could regulate it as an interstate boundary. The 1888 law, therefore, effectively became both a private contract *and* a federal statute. Previously, vague colonial laws originating in the royal concessions to the latifundio of the Marqués de San Miguel de Aguayo, owner of much of the Laguna's land at the beginning of the eighteenth century, loosely regulated water use in the region. Back then, the land had been designated for grazing, and water for cattle troughs (*abrevadero*) was the primary concern. In the late nineteenth century, with the exception of viticultural Parras and its offshoots of Viesca and San Pedro, land and water use in the region changed from grazing to growing cotton and wheat.

The 1888 law did not make any specific provisions for these changes in land and water use. This compelled Pacheco to try to forge a consensus among Laguna riverine landowners for fairer distribution of water at the meetings he convened. His efforts did not succeed, however, and he subsequently resigned, leaving his successor to try, in Díaz y Díaz's words, a state-imposed "vertical distribution of water" in the regulations of 1891, 1895, and, finally, 1909. All three regulations largely failed to resolve the vituperative legal disputes over the Nazas. The disputes escalated into a lawsuit between Tlahualilo and the Mexican government that, from 1909 to 1911, the Mexican Supreme Court adjudicated. The origins of the lawsuit began with the 1891 regulations, which reduced Tlahualilo's original concession in 1888 of 440 million cubic meters of water to a yearly fixed volume of 200 million—sufficient to irrigate about 20,000 hectares—in addition to rights to 95 million cubic meters acquired by the company's purchase of the upriver San Fernando hacienda. The government would distribute the remainder of the Nazas water to all other downriver users. At the time of this regulation, the company was not equipped to cultivate more than 10,000 hectares. Nevertheless, it considered the 1891 regulation a "major sacrifice" in terms of economic security and moral principle and only reluctantly agreed to it on condition Díaz would find a permanent solution to the controversy—with the understanding the solution would be in its favor.[71]

The new 1895 regulation, however, upset the company further. Although it was allowed to consume its share of water as a riparian owner with priority over all other downriver users, as a concessionaire the company could only take water that remained *after* all other claimants had consumed their allocated shares. This drastically reduced its total volume from 200 million to 22 million cubic meters.[72] The government hoped the regulation would establish more proportional and balanced distribution of the Nazas waters, which downriver users considered a significant victory. For a time, the implementation of the regulation seemed to have resolved disputes between upriver and downriver users. By 1900, however, the Tlahualilo Company began to ignore the regulation and claimed 28 percent of the Nazas flow for its needs when it used an average of only 12 percent. Meanwhile, downriver users had erected technologically superior hydraulic works and expanded cultivation onto more fertile land, spurring even more demand for scarce water.

In 1903, a group of British and American investors gained control of Tlahualilo after investigations revealed that the original shareholders had defrauded them by falsely declaring that the company had increased sixfold in value from 1885 to 1895 to secure a loan of 350,000 pounds sterling from the group. Renaming the company the Mexican Cotton Estates of Tlahualilo, Ltd., the new Anglo-American ownership and management revitalized its operations. It increased capitalization, installed new hydraulic technology, built a private railroad network that connected to national rail lines, and expanded its labor force to eight thousand workers, two thousand of them permanent and six thousand temporary. Altogether, it cultivated 44,000 hectares subdivided into thirty-one individual 1,700 hectare ranchos. Although geographically within the upriver zone, Tlahualilo held a distinct position as the first corporation in the region operating as a single unit according to the "most advanced principles of engineering and modern management to maximize cotton production."[73]

While tensions remained high in the Laguna, record strong river flows and strong demand for cotton in the years 1905 to 1907 prompted a hiatus in disputes over water rights. But when economic crisis sparked by a financial panic in the United States struck the region in 1907, compounded by devastating drought, the simmering conflicts burst into flames anew. After downriver users petitioned him, the new SF Minister Olegario Molina issued an executive order in July 1908 forbidding upriver users from diverting any river flow during September so downriver users could use the entire flow. His order provoked vehement protests from upriver users, but Molina held firm. Backed by the Durango state authorities, upriver users then took their case to a Durango state court and lost. Supported by the British foreign minister to Mexico, Tlahualilo subsequently decided to file its own lawsuit in 1909 primarily to uphold the principle of first-use and foreign concession rights in Mexico, but not because it was actually suffering from water shortages. Rather, imbued with a late Victorian imperialist mentality, the Anglo-American estate's goal was to teach the Mexican government a lesson, alleging the government had reneged on contractual obligations made twenty years before, even though British officials imposed and enforced similar water laws in their rule over Egypt.[74]

In 1902, the impending change of ownership from Mexican to Anglo-American hands aroused nationalist opposition in the Laguna. The prominent landowner and cotton merchant Feliciano Cobián, for example, called on his fellow Laguna landowners to buy the Tlahualilo mortgage, which he claimed the federal government would support; this would be "the way we will save ourselves and get the Yankee element off our backs, in addition to thereby making us the owners of Tlahualilo."[75] The Historical Water Archive (Archivo Histórico del Agua) is replete with complaints filed by downriver users about Tlahualilo's actions in the 1890s and 1900s, quite apart from its better-known imperialist obstinacy vis-à-vis the Mexican government. Complaints include a user appealing to the Nazas River Inspection Commission to prevent the company from expanding its canal into his property, hoarding of rainwater by not allowing it to flow into a neighboring canal, refusing to build bridges over its canals so neighbors could cross, and opening its diversion dam sluicegates without authorization.[76] Yet when the company was not angering its neighbors, it appears to have been manipulating them. For instance, according to the commission, a request made by a group of colonists on Tlahualilo property in 1898 for a new, additional water concession that was not included in the original contract/statute of 1888 "makes one suspect that these colonists are acting at the suggestion of the Tlahualilo Company."[77]

In the summer of 1909, after convening numerous meetings with all riparian owners through the Nazas River Conference except Tlahualilo, which refused to attend, the government approved and published a new regulation. It effectively reaffirmed the basis of the 1895 regulation with some modifications, while specifying that the Mexican government could not modify the new distribution scheme without gaining the consent of all Nazas riparian owners.[78] The 1909 regulation would remain in effect until 1938 after Laguna riverine landowners, including Tlahualilo, lost much of their lands and virtually all preexisting water rights with Cárdenas's agrarian reform of 1936.

Madero's Dam Proposal

It is in the context of the Tlahualilo lawsuit and the double blow of drought and a U.S.-originated recession that Madero's advocacy for a high dam on the Nazas appealed to Díaz—both as an envirotechnical solution to the legal and diplomatic woes that the lawsuit was causing and as a means to help stabilize the region and his regime sociopolitically and economically. Furthermore, building the Nazas and other large dams would respond to a growing call during the Porfiriato among the Mexican elite, including técnicos, for a national irrigation policy to solve an acute agricultural crisis that forced Mexico to import agricultural goods, including (most worryingly) food. The Laguna, however, though not a significant food producer, was one of the few bright spots in the bleak picture of agriculture that many analysts were otherwise painting. The region supplied a yearly average of 76.5 percent, or 142,000 bales, of Mexico's domestic cotton supply from 1897 to 1909.[79]

Madero published his study after the failed meeting on November 20, 1906, that began this chapter to publicize two mutually reinforcing goals of his personal lobbying campaign: first, to pique the interest of a high-level federal official ("one who rules our destinies," as he described it) to bring the Nazas Dam to fruition; and second, to unify Nazas users all along the river behind the project to do their part and cooperate. Madero added that Díaz already backed the project but wanted local and regional support before pursuing it.[80]

Madero's public advocacy sought to disprove various ecological, technical, financial, and legal arguments against the project and assuage the fears they generated among many Laguneros. On the ecological side, riverine landowners feared that water would be lost from filtration and evaporation from the reservoir. Even more seriously, the dammed Nazas current would cease to deliver the nutrient-rich sediment that fertilized the Laguna soil. On the technical side, they worried the dam might not be strong enough to withstand a sudden influx of water during one of the Nazas's torrential flows. And financially, they questioned whether a costly investment in the dam could truly pay off, presuming, as they did, that they would foot the bill. Last, but certainly not least, they were afraid any change in the river regime would adversely affect existing water rights and concessions secured in the 1895 federal regulation.

Madero began his case for the dam by enumerating the principal inconveniences of the Nazas River regime, as he perceived them. Chief among them, the great economic hardship caused by inopportune river flows that did not coincide with the planting and harvesting seasons in the spring and fall, respectively. According to the technical and reconnaissance studies of the Nazas River Inspection Commission that he cited, the dam at the Fernández Canyon site would be 55 meters high, require 685,000 cubic meters of masonry, have a storage capacity of 1,187,000 cubic meters in its reservoir, and cost 5.6 million pesos to complete. Although this was a relatively large sum at the time, he proposed a novel financing plan by which riverine landowners would take out a government-backed mortgage and repay the interest and depreciation at a "not very onerous" rate of 900,000 pesos annually.[81] As shareholders of the dam, they would be assigned an amount of water from it (according to a new regulation that would be devised after the dam's completion) and pay proportionately to their assigned amount. Per user agreement, a special commission of engineers charged with fairly and equitably distributing reservoir water would withhold or reduce water as a penalty for delinquent or late payment. Water rights, however, would be secured as part and parcel of existing land titles. Madero was confident the dam would pay for itself many times over. The storage capacity of the reservoir, he asserted, would enable retention of summer floodwaters through December. The reservoir would therefore increase irrigated land area as much as 50 percent by reducing reliance on the generally less abundant, and always random, winter floodwaters, which would in turn forgo costly preparations for them. Retention of summer floodwater through the winter would thus make more cash available to hire migrant laborers for the autumn cotton harvest and boost profits substantially.[82]

Madero minimized the potential ecological harm from the dam to the natural fertilizing function of the river that so concerned his fellow landowners, yet he nevertheless proposed that should soil quality deteriorate, chemical fertilizers would be available. He claimed that they had considerably improved agricultural productivity in Europe and the United States, where they could be acquired cheaply and then prepared in Mexico. It was not the only alternative, however; he also proposed letting the land lie fallow, alternating crops, and using cottonseed as fertilizer. He argued that the dam would facilitate all of these alternatives by making watering times during the agricultural calendar more opportune for all.[83]

In the same paternally benevolent manner he was known to care for his workers and peons, Madero (whose nickname was "Don Panchito") described the hardship both landowners and laborers endured from the unstable river regime. In particular, he empathized with the plight of the thousands of migrant laborers who flocked to the Laguna for the annual cotton harvest "at great sacrifice." Because of the usurious rates the railroads charged and the inability of farmers to provide work during years of no or low river flow, "There have been years in which many of these unfortunate souls have died of hunger or thirst on the roads that they have tried to travel on foot or by mule for lack of rail transportation."[84]

Imbued with the prevailing view of conservation regarding free-flowing rivers at the time, he asserted that from 1901 to 1906 878,642,244 cubic meters of summer floodwater had been lost to the Laguna de Mayrán. If used, such a volume could have irrigated 187 square kilometers of land, producing about 187,000 bales (62,000 metric tons); at a price of 137.50 pesos per bale, this amount would have sold for 24,145,000 pesos. What is more, if all the water lost to the Laguna de Mayrán had been used, he estimated an increase of nearly 400,000 bales of cotton amounting to 53,762,500 pesos in sales. According to government estimates, the highest production figure until that time in the Laguna was the improbable yield of 618,000 bales in 1905, or the vast majority of 645,000 bales nationally, and three times the national average from 1897 to 1909.[85]

Madero wrote passionately in his study, envisioning a new political economy for the entire nation: the dam would help reduce cotton prices by greatly augmenting cotton supplies and allowing textile factories to manufacture cheap cloth from which all classes, but especially the lower ones, would benefit. Although Madero was unable to unify Laguna landowners behind the dam project in 1906 and 1907 and thereby mobilize local support for Díaz, the president nevertheless proceeded to hire the British engineering firm S. Pearson and Son to conduct further studies of the proposed dam site in 1909. According to the U.S. Department of Commerce and Labor, Díaz budgeted $240,000 at the time for the survey work, and had $7 million available to build the dam.[86] Evidently, Díaz was optimistic that once the dam was built, it would supply plentiful water to all Nazas users. Indeed, SF Minister Molina announced during the negotiations with Tlahualilo and all other Nazas water users that "the government is working to provide more water to all through the study of a dam and diverting water from other rivers to the Nazas. We will postpone a definitive solution until these plans can be realized, while in the interim a satisfactory agreement for all will be made."[87]

Unfortunately for Díaz and Madero alike—and as the Nazas River Inspection Commission had determined as early as 1895—S. Pearson and Son concluded that the geological formation of the Fernández Canyon dam site would be unable to withstand dam construction.[88] Yet like Madero, the British and Mexican engineers on the reconnaissance team for S. Pearson and Son severely criticized aniego in their report: "It is nearly impossible to estimate the total monetary loss which the country, property owners, and workers suffer owing to the little development of agriculture, a result of the current irrigation system, which is so irregular, and to the unequal distribution of water that it occasions." They compared and contrasted the Nile of the Laguna to the Egyptian Nile, with which the British engineers were intimately familiar.[89]

Although the hydraulic engineering of the Nile could not be transplanted to the Nazas, in the absence of a high dam S. Pearson and Son recommended building a "master" canal to distribute water to a network of new diversion dams and dikes. Barring that possibility, the company endorsed the view that a high dam would be beneficial only if it was built in a more appropriate site than the Fernández Canyon. They proposed several other sites, including one just above the hamlet of El Palmito, located 120 miles from the principal urban centers of the Laguna, at the confluence of the Oros and Ramos rivers from which the Nazas River originates. Díaz probably expected that the endorsement of a reputable British firm would greatly enhance the appeal of the Nazas dam project, but a number of esteemed Mexican engineers, among them Roberto Gayol, Manuel Vera, and Manuel Marroquín y Rivera, cast doubt on the firm's findings in 1911, leaving the matter of whether and where to build the dam indefinitely unsettled.[90]

In the meantime, Mexican water law advanced through two separate, but interrelated, legal processes—one legislative, and the other juridical. Legislatively, in December 1910, Congress passed the Ley sobre aprovechamientos de aguas de jurisdicción federal (Law on the Use of Waters under Federal Jurisdiction). It greatly expanded federal authority over far more waterways than the 1888 law and articulated that authority through articles specifying the rights and obligations of governmental, social, and private concessions and their uses. No longer did rivers need to be navigable or floatable to fall under federal jurisdiction; now they needed only to be of "public dominion and common use, and in consequence, inalienable and imprescriptible."[91]

Juridically, in March 1911 the Mexican Supreme Court ruled in favor of the government and against Tlahualilo solely as a breach-of-contract case. The ruling was narrow in scope and did not consider the 1910 law or other regulations. The detailed and passionate argumentation on both sides of the case, however, helped to elucidate the complex, confusing, and eclectic French, Spanish, Roman, and Arabic origins of Mexican water law partially codified in the 1910 water law.[92] Furthermore, the favorable verdict was a Pyrrhic victory for Díaz: in the subsequent two months, his federal army lost critical battles to revolutionary forces in Chihuahua nominally led by Madero. These losses compelled the autocrat of thirty-five years to finally resign and leave for exile in France.

The Nazas Question and El Agua de la Revolución

During the Revolution that ravaged much of the north from 1910 to 1917, the Laguna, and Torreón in particular as its rail center, became the site of numerous bloody battles and military occupations, most famously that of Pancho Villa from April 1914 to September 1915.[93] Ecologically, the unstable Nazas river regime indirectly affected these regional dynamics while socially and politically the long juridical struggle over its control during the Porfiriato directly influenced the legal status of the nation's water resources (see figure 1.4). These intertwined and overlapping processes played a key role in forming a national agrarian reform program during and after the Revolution for which irrigation would be indispensable.

FIG. 1.4 This photograph dated September 1917 is of the cresting Nazas flowing under the electric tram bridge that once connected Coahuila and Durango states. Laguneros would flock to the riverbanks and onto the bridge to watch the infrequent flow. Fondo "Beatriz González" of the Archivo Agustín Espinoza de la Universidad Iberoamericana.

The relationship between land and water use was also important to Mexico's most famous revolutionary, Emiliano Zapata, whose casus belli was return of land unjustly taken from villages since 1856. In that year, the ascendant liberals decreed the Lerdo Law mandating expropriation of church and village corporate landholdings. Although they were effective fighters against federal and rival revolutionary forces, the Zapatistas were largely constrained by their local agricultural calendars. They were thus unable to travel far from their villages to expand politico-military power outside their central-south strongholds of Morelos and parts of Guerrero, Tlaxcala, Puebla, Estado de México, and the Federal District, lest their fields lie fallow and their subsistence crops rot. Yet Zapata's Plan of Ayala of 1911—the Magna Carta of Mexican *agrarismo* (agrarianism)—called for access to land and essential natural resources (water and woods) as a "traditional and historic" right of *all* Mexicans, without any mention of conserving and protecting these resources. Zapata's Agrarian Law of October 1915 not only reiterated the Plan of Ayala's demand for this right. It also, in its eighth article, empowered the Secretaría de Agricultura y Colonización (Ministry of Agriculture and Colonization, which would replace the existing SF) to form commissions for carrying out land surveys and provided for a national irrigation and construction service (Servicio Nacional de Irrigación y Construcciones) that the ministry would manage. Zapata's demands reflected the particular social and ecological conditions of Morelos, a state with a varied but generally semi-humid climate and abundant water resources. Irrigation was nevertheless critical for water-intensive sugar-dominated expansion of the state's agricultural frontier by 1910.[94]

Zapata's ally Villa eventually accepted the Plan of Ayala after some persuasion, but the more heterogeneous social composition of Villa's División del Norte army, reflecting as it did the particular social and ecological conditions of Chihuahua and Durango, allowed him to be less constrained by agricultural cycles. He could thus field his army far beyond its regional stronghold, and by winning major battles and successfully governing the territory he controlled, Villa projected his politico-military power onto the national level.[95] Nevertheless, in those regions he did control, his army was not immune to local ecological conditions. The arid Laguna was no exception: as a major railway hub located midway between the Mexico-U.S. border and Mexico City and the country's foremost producer of cotton, it was a crucial strategic and economic region. Occupying it thus required maintaining both cotton cultivation and the rail lines to supply domestic and international markets.

Toward that end, Villa confiscated a number of cotton haciendas for emergency production and forced owners to finance military operations through sales of cotton to buyers in the United States. Specifically, he charged an office of "Confiscated Cotton" (Algodón Decomisado) to select which haciendas to occupy and distribute among his men. He then charged the agricultural commission of the Laguna to manage the haciendas and ship and sell their cotton. Answerable only to Villa's headquarters, the commission nonetheless respected preexisting contracts between tenants/sharecroppers and owners, and, in effect, replaced the landowner to whom a percentage of crops had to be ceded. The majority of confiscated haciendas belonged to a few individuals or families who had been large Porfirian landowners and alleged Huerta partisans; in particular, Villa distributed the property of the Luján family, the 15,000 hectare irrigated hacienda of Sacramento, among eleven heirs, while he distributed other properties among his generals, or, as was the case with the Concha and San Sebastián haciendas, among tenants and poor sharecroppers.[96]

Although Villa's policy overall during his occupation appeared to leave private property intact, there were signs as early as 1911, before the Plan of Ayala, that revolutionaries had inchoate plans and ideas for agrarian reform in and around the Laguna. Those plans were, according to Alan Knight, "inevitably chaotic, arbitrary and transient." One example was Cheche Campos, who "clearly espoused a form of de facto agrarian reform," as he "encamped with 1500 men among the haciendas around Mapimí, Durango" and allowed "sharesmen and peons on all the ranches" to retain their harvested crops for their own uses or for sale.[97] Manuel Plana documents another case from 1912 in which the mayor of San Pedro, Madero's base in the Laguna, submitted a petition to the federal government signed by fifty of the city's inhabitants requesting a local agrarian reform program. Tellingly, with regard to the Nazas, one of its articles stipulated that should landowners fail to irrigate their lands properly, the government could order agricultural experts to subdivide the land among the landowner's workers. If implemented, the article would have placed Laguna landowners completely at the whim of the Nazas River regime. That is, if the river delivered insufficient water with which to irrigate, landowners could face seizure of part or all of their lands.[98]

Meyers has shown in this context the relationship between cotton production—so crucially dependent on the Nazas River flow—and the dynamics of rebellion in the region from 1910 to 1916. According to U.S. consular and other records he examined, there was a close correlation between revolutionaries' political and military successes in the Laguna and the ebb and flow of the Nazas. In low-flow seasons, unemployed migrants were ideal recruits for revolutionary armies, while in high-flow seasons, there was sufficient employment to keep the economy running and revolutionaries supplied with necessary provisions. Since the fickle behavior of the Nazas had a direct impact on the profitability of cotton production, Meyers argues it was a determining factor in Pancho Villa's shifting fortunes in the Laguna and, by extension, nationally.[99] It would be an exaggeration to claim that Villismo literally sank or swam in accordance with the erratic Nazas flow. It is likely, however, that from a strictly military, let alone developmental, standpoint, Villa would have regarded stabilizing agricultural cycles via damming the Nazas and other rivers under his control quite favorably.

Yet Villa was slow to put forth a national program that addressed the agrarian question. When he finally decreed his own General Agrarian Law in May 1915, months after his archrival Venustiano Carranza had decreed his own law in January 1915, his military fortunes were waning dramatically. Carranza's law was incorporated in Article 27 of the 1917 Constitution and partially written by the attorney Luis Cabrera (who had represented the Tlahualilo Estate in its lawsuit against the Porfirian regime) and Cabrera's intellectual mentor, Andrés Molina Enríquez. Drawing on the language of the Plan of Ayala, the Carrancista agrarian law declared that all pueblos, communities, and ranchos whose "fields, timber and water" had been despoiled since 1856 could have them restored. The "Nation" would then recognize the "traditional and historic rights" of these groups to possess and administer communal land—namely, ejidos.[100]

Villa's law also decreed an end to large landed properties, but it differed significantly from Carranza's and Zapata's by empowering state governments rather than the federal government to fix the maximum area of land *and quantity of water for irrigation* that a single landholder could own—an area and quantity the law never specified, even in the form of guidelines. Significantly, Villa's law called for application in conformity with "local necessities," including "the variety of the soils and the agronomic conditions of each region." Like the local agrarian reform decreed in San Pedro in 1912, two years before Villa occupied the Laguna, the law's Article 6 stipulated that "waters from springs, dams, and from whatever other source will be expropriated in the quantity that an owner of a finca to which it belongs cannot use whenever such waters may be used in another [finca]. If the owner of these waters does not use them even when able to he will be granted a term for their use under the penalty that if he does not [make use of them by the term's end] the said waters will be subject to expropriation."[101]

When Carrancista forces retook Torreón from Villa in October 1915, they established their own local Oficina de Bienes Intervenidos (Office of Confiscated Goods) and assigned it the task of returning confiscated agricultural and urban properties and textile factories to their original owners. Nevertheless, Carranza delayed their return to seize all the revenues from sales of the 1914–15 cotton crop to central Mexican textile mills that the Villistas had not yet harvested. Indeed, Espinosa Mireles, the Carrancista provisional governor of Coahuila, published a federal decree that empowered the government to acquire all of the Laguna's cotton and to expropriate any properties whose owners refused to cooperate. When Carranza took the capital in early 1916, he established a federal office of confiscated goods that supplanted state, local, or military offices. This forced expropriated hacendados to deal directly with him to recover their property. Meanwhile, Laguneros unsurprisingly experienced deep misery—empty store shelves, scant harvests, and wandering, hungry people as rival revolutionary factions continued to assault rail cars. In December 1916, Villa briefly reoccupied the Laguna, forced property owners to lend him one million pesos (reduced from two million after he discovered Laguna landowners did not hold that much money in cash), and grabbed a number of rail cars before Carrancistas definitively reoccupied the region in early January 1917.[102]

A month later, to secure his still precarious position vis-à-vis his Villista and Zapatista rivals, Carranza promulgated the 1917 Constitution, which, as previously mentioned, incorporated his agrarian law into its Article 27. Article 27 declared ownership of lands and waters within the Mexican territory "vested originally in the Nation." It bestowed on the nation the right to create private property through the authority to transmit property titles to private persons as well as to expropriate property with compensation for "public use." This national ownership included all land, bodies of surface water (lakes, rivers, streams, springs, estuaries, basins of all kinds, and so forth), and subsoil minerals (coal, petroleum, iron ore, precious stones and metals, salt, and so on), without explicitly mentioning groundwater.[103] The article also reaffirmed the right to communal use of surface water granted in the January 1915 law, including, like the Nazas, "those intermittent currents which run through two or more States by their principal branches, the waters of rivers, arroyos or ravines when they serve as boundaries for the national territory or for the states." Unlike the Villista (which delegated to the states and localities) and Zapatista (which centralized power in the federal government) agrarian laws, however, Article 27 assigned *both* the federal Congress and the state legislatures responsibility for fixing a maximum area of rural property that a single individual or association could use or possess.

Regarding the legal status of water, Article 27 went far beyond the prerevolutionary Water Law of 1910. That law, as I discussed in the introduction, was quite progressive for its time by declaring federal waters to be part of an ownerless public dominion to which the government could grant use to "private individuals, companies constituted according to national laws, and Mexican private or public corporations which have the legal capacity to obtain such concessions." (It could also abrogate these concessions in the public interest.) By contrast, Article 27 stipulated that the nation has the "right to impose on private property the modalities that the public interest dictates . . . *to equitably distribute public wealth as well as to conserve it*" (emphasis added). In this phrasing, much as in the Zapatista and Villista conceptions, public wealth derived from the collective ownership and use of natural resources.

Although the rival Villistas and Zapatistas undoubtedly influenced the agrarian and hydraulic provisions of Article 27, perhaps equally influential— but less well known—were the revolutionary decrees by the erstwhile Maderista Emilio Vázquez Gómez in February 1913 during and shortly after the Ten Tragic Days mutiny that took the lives of Madero and his vice-president José María Pino Suárez. Although Vázquez Gómez lived in exile in San Antonio, Texas, after he turned against Madero in 1912, his followers continued to draft and publish his decrees (or did so in his name) from their "Provisional Government of the Revolution" headquarters in Paloma, Chihuahua. They sent the decrees to all of the "revolutionists of the Republic" and foreign consulates, including the U.S. Consulate, which translated and archived them for posterity. They declared Vázquez Gómez provisional president of Mexico and General José Inés Salazar, an engineer, commander of the revolutionary forces of the North. In addition to embracing agrarian reform, Vázquez Gómez's followers produced a decree devoted to "storing up of waters and works of irrigation" by the future revolutionary government. Its preamble declared that "one of the most important and transcendental ideals that the present revolution has the ambition to realize for the benefit of all the inhabitants of the country, whether natives or foreigners, is the storing up and control of the numerous quantities of water that, temporarily or permanently, run throughout the extent of the Mexican territory, including in this project subterranean waters, which also exist in considerable quantity." Immediately after the preamble, the first article of this ideal water law established "all water courses, lakes, and lagoons existing or which may be formed within the territory of the Republic" as the "property of the Nation." Unlike the 1917 Constitution, however, it called for a "Public Labor Corps" composed of twenty thousand prisoners throughout the country to do irrigation work in exchange for reduced sentences and receipt of a small annual cash allowance. The prisoners would thereby learn the "habit of labor" as the "most powerful and effective instrument of regeneration and moralization" on their release.[104]

The conservationist provision in Article 27 absent in the prior agrarian laws and decrees of all revolutionaries was incorporated at the behest of the civil engineer and conservationist Miguel Ángel de Quevedo. Carranza felt compelled to accept the draft of Article 27 written by his own radical delegates—including his most capable general, Álvaro Obregón, who had defeated Villa on the battlefield—at the Constitutional Convention. He implemented relatively little agrarian reform or conservation during his short-lived presidency, from 1917 to 1920. It would take another decade before passage and promulgation of new laws, decrees, and regulations breathed life into Article 27's provisions. In the case of conservation, however, these were primarily for forestry. "Conserving" water signified damming waterways to create reservoirs, yet for a decade or more groundwater seemed so abundant, as it gushed forth from newly installed motorized pumps, that few showed any concern for its conservation. The Nazas River and the principal aquifer it recharged was Mexico's preeminent case of El agua de la Revolución, but for its waters to serve revolutionary purposes, the new postrevolutionary state needed to implement agrarian reform in the region. Most of its técnicos saw building a high dam on the Nazas as indispensable to this formidable envirotechnical task, which would continue to cause conflict among Laguneros of all social classes.

2. The Debate over Damming and Pumping El Agua de la Revolución

I believe and sustain that land distribution without irrigation is absurd, inconvenient and dimwitted.

PASTOR ROUAIX, engineer

In this chapter I tell the story of the postrevolutionary Nazas River Dam project and the burgeoning growth of motorized groundwater pumping. It is a story that was integral to the initiation and form of agrarian policy in the Laguna from 1917 until Cárdenas's landmark decree of October 6, 1936, that expropriated the region's estates and replaced them with ejidos and small landholdings. Eventually, the controversial dam that Francisco I. Madero first publicly advocated in 1907 came to symbolize a revolutionary envirotechnical modernity for Mexico—one that reflected the rapidly changing local and national historical dynamics of the 1920s and 1930s. Advances in science, technology, engineering, and law, along with the contradictory attitudes toward nonhuman nature that they helped shape, played a key role in bringing about both the agrarian reform and the dam. Cárdenas viewed them as complementary in the Laguna, yet his conviction did not emerge in a vacuum. Rather, his historic decision to decree a massive agrarian reform was, in part, the product of nearly three decades of active lobbying and counter-lobbying over the Nazas River regime's fate—efforts that, together with mass-mobilization of campesinos and workers, generated competing local and national discourses on Article 27's applicability to the Laguna. As the Six-Year Plan of 1934, which guided Cárdenas's presidency, stipulated, "Irrigation works are considered by the National Revolutionary Party as a mandatory *complement* of the policy aimed at achieving the agricultural progress of the country."[1] Among those irrigation works listed in the plan was the Nazas River Dam.

The dam project was not only integral to the complementarity of agrarian reform and modernizing water control at the federal level. From the local campesinos, workers, and técnicos who generally embraced the technology as liberating to the powerful landowners who, for the most part, deemed it a threat to their privileged socioeconomic status and existing irrigation ecology, a diverse and active civil society was invested in the project. The history of the project also shows that, in contrast to the generalizations that much recent global environmentalist literature has made, socially disadvantaged communities did not always oppose large dams.[2] Therefore, the deployment of hydraulic technology for Cardenista agrarian reform in the Laguna also fulfilled, albeit imperfectly and incompletely, the promise of El agua de la Revolución: applying Article 27's mandate to more equitably distribute federal waters and conserve them. To fulfill the promise, however, Mexican and foreign técnicos, landowners, campesinos, and politicians engaged in a prolonged and heated debate about building the dam. Recurrent questions arose: would it truly work technically? How would it affect the natural fertilizing properties of the Nazas flow? Would chemical fertilizers be an effective substitute? Was it worth the cost, given the increasingly available option of installing imported motorized groundwater pumps? If the dam worked as promised, would it facilitate a moderate or radical agrarian reform, or none at all?

The Laguna's Postrevolutionary "Plagas"

Carranza's Agrarian Law, decreed in January 1915 during the Revolution, sent shudders down the spines of Laguna landowners. As the historian María Vargas-Lobsinger aptly describes their reaction, it hung over them like the "sword of Damocles."[3] Indeed, as devastating as the fighting and Villista occupation of the Laguna was during the Revolution, the prospect of having their lands legally taken from them was even more disconcerting. As a result, the long-divided Laguna landowners finally united on the matter of forming their own regional chapter of the National Agricultural Chambers of Mexico in April 1916. An executive committee of seven managed the chamber and elected Pedro Franco Ugarte, a wealthy tenant farmer who successfully worked on various large Porfirian-era haciendas for absentee landowners, as its first president. One of the chamber's priorities was to publish a regular newsletter to disseminate important information to farmers, such as on cotton sales, credit, purchasing modern machinery, combating pest infestations, and announcing agricultural achievements. The newsletter, which began publishing in September 1917, also served as a medium of communication with federal authorities, primarily the

Secretaría de Agricultura y Fomento (Ministry of Agriculture and Development; SAF), in 1917. It thus helped to encourage the kind of solidarity among Laguna farmers that had been sorely lacking before the Revolution.[4]

In 1920, as the Revolution's military phase wound down, the chamber's February issue reported that, much as during the Porfiriato, tenants and large sharecroppers cultivated 60 percent of Laguna landholdings.[5] The September issue then starkly enumerated several so-called *plagas* that landowners perceived to be adversely influencing regional agriculture: the pink bollworm infestation, the volatility of cotton prices, drought, the Nazas River regime, and unions.[6] The word "plaga" perfectly encapsulated how besieged the Laguna agroindustrial elite felt by sociopolitical and envirotechnical processes largely out of their control.

The first of these plagas, the pink bollworm infestation, posed an existential threat to cotton growing, as it did in many other areas of the world, including across the border in the United States. The pink bollworm, or *Pectinophora gossypiella,* is distinct from the more commonly known boll weevil, or *Anthonomus grandis grandis.* The boll weevil devastated large swaths of the southern U.S. cotton belt. Its entry, according to cotton experts, was "probably the single most important entomological event to have occurred in cotton." The infestation was so severe that it was a major factor driving the westward shift in cotton production toward New Mexico, Arizona, and California and away from the U.S. South, which diversified its crops in the early twentieth century.[7] Although the boll weevil originated in Central America and Mexico, entomologists know little about its history before the discovery in Texas in 1892. However, documents from an archive in Monclova, Coahuila, indicate that farmers there nearly abandoned cotton growing in 1848 possibly because of the weevil. The U.S. entomologist Edward Palmers collected a specimen he described as very similar to the weevil in 1880. He claimed that it had destroyed Monclova's "large supply of cotton" for which the city was once famous.[8] By 1894, this pest had spread throughout northern Mexico and into Texas.[9] In 1903, the weevils were discovered in cottonseed en route to the Laguna, but, according to an entomological report to the Senate by the U.S. Department of Agriculture in 1912, "Effective measures were taken by the Mexican authorities, and the infestation was suppressed. Since that time the weevil has never been recorded from this important cotton region."[10]

The pink bollworm, however, would soon become for the Laguna what the boll weevil was to the southern U.S. cotton belt. In 1842, the British entomologist W. W. Saunders received insect specimens found to be "very destructive to cotton" in India in 1842, to which he gave its Latin name. The bollworm spread from India to Southeast Asia and Africa, and then to Egypt in 1907, where it had an impact on the country's entire cotton crop. In 1911, it arrived in long-fibered cottonseed shipments from Egypt and the government allowed them into Mexico, despite having received reports of the Egyptian cotton infestation. Shortly thereafter, a cotton farmer from San Pedro in the Laguna and another from Monterrey ordered the cottonseed in which pink bollworm larvae were incubating. Within a few years, the pink bollworm's infestation of Laguna cotton had become devastating. The amount of damage it inflicted varied from 1–2 percent to more than 25 percent of the crop from year to year. Although the SAF formed an Infestation Inspection Commission to combat the pest, it met with mixed success through the 1920s and 1930s owing to insufficient federal resources and farmers' lack of compliance with regulations. It would take massive use of chemical pesticides in the late 1940s to reduce the pink bollworm to a relatively minor problem (while causing a host of new problems).[11]

The volatility of cotton prices was the second plaga Laguna planters faced, as they had before the Revolution. Prices declined during the first few years of the Revolution but then rose dramatically, from 317 pesos per ton in 1915 to more than 1,000 pesos per ton in 1920, only to drop to 601 pesos per ton by 1921.[12] Prices gradually increased again through most of the 1920s as the postwar global economy grew, but the crash on Wall Street in 1929 and the Great Depression caused prices to plunge through the early 1930s. The Nazas's variable flow aggravated this volatility in prices. In 1919–20, the river delivered a record 3.3 million cubic meters from the Sierra Madre of Durango, enabling cultivation of 225,000 bales of cotton, tying the record for second-best harvest during the Porfiriato.[13] A mere three years later, river flow dropped to less than 300,000 cubic meters, with which farmers harvested a scant 31,000 bales. This 7:1 ratio within only three years devastated not only cotton farmers but also, especially, migrant workers, for the workers bore the brunt of the downturns as farmers cut their costs by shedding workforces, mechanizing, and cutting wages. For example, in November 1923, the plight of unemployed migrant workers in San Pedro was so dire—some of them "nearly dying of hunger" and without money to leave the region to look for work elsewhere or return home—that the government sent an agent to the Laguna to distribute free rail passes to 3,255 men, women, and children fortunate enough to get one before they quickly ran out.[14]

It was in this context that the fourth perceived plaga emerged for Laguna farmers: unionization. Although the Laguna had experienced labor organizing and revolt before and during the Revolution in the form of Magonismo and

Villismo,[15] Article 123 of the 1917 Constitution legally mandated labor rights, including the formation of unions. As a result, beginning in 1918 the Confederación Regional Obrera Mexicana (Regional Mexican Labor Confederation; CROM), founded in Saltillo under the auspices of Coahuila's Governor Gustavo Espinosa Mireles, organized openly in the region. The labor-based Communist Party, founded in 1919 in Mexico City by Mexicans and foreigners inspired by the Russian Revolution, also began organizing, albeit clandestinely.[16] By early 1920, unionization had advanced sufficiently that after a poor harvest, 150 unionized workers launched a strike in the Santa Teresa hacienda of the Arocena family, located in the upriver Durango area. The strikers demanded better working conditions, including limiting hard labor to five hours per day. The strike spread to other nearby haciendas before it ultimately fizzled. Another strike led by CROM in that same year lasted one month and involved ten thousand peons on thirty-five haciendas demanding a daily wage of 3 pesos (prevailing wages were 1–1.5 pesos), a reduction in work hours, and recognition of their unions. As campesinos formed unions throughout the Laguna, attaining 2,450 members in thirty-five haciendas by 1923, they laid the groundwork for nearly fifteen years' worth of mass labor mobilization, which reached a crescendo during the first two years of the Cárdenas presidency (1934–40).[17]

Since before the Revolution, the Laguna's agricultural labor force was semi-proletarianized, reflecting the region's agroindustrial economy.[18] Although semi-proletarianized agricultural workers primarily demanded better wages and working conditions, some also demanded land for ejidos according to the general provisions of Article 27 and the subsequent regulatory laws passed during the presidency of Álvaro Obregón (1920–24). The CROM supported agrarian reform, calling for distribution of large cultivable private or federal lands, but it never mentioned restoration or granting of communal property, whether for ejidos, pueblos, or communities. It did, however, emphasize "free use of waters no matter the rights that businesses or individuals try to maintain over them via concessions that monopolize the liquid and harm small farmers, as decreed in Article 27."[19] In response to this agrarista organizing, the federal government granted several petitions for land on the Durango side of the Laguna. Every grantee received 1,755 hectares of generally poor-quality land.[20]

Thus, within a few years after 1917, the general contours of a new social and ecological landscape were discernible as the pink bollworm infestation exacerbated the socioeconomic effects of variable cotton prices and river flow. These developments in turn deepened the sociopolitical divisions surrounding agrarian reform and working conditions and wages between the region's agroindustrial upper classes and rural and urban lower classes.[21] As we shall see, the lower classes generally struggled for better working conditions and wages, including some kind of agrarian reform program. For their part, the upper classes generally resisted agrarian reform and were reluctant to significantly improve working conditions and wages in their haciendas and factories. The lower classes appeared generally in favor of the Nazas River Dam project. They saw it as technological progress that would liberate the region from the destabilizing vagaries of the free-flowing Nazas by improving working conditions and wages, boosting employment (including by providing jobs during its construction), and facilitating some kind of agrarian reform program through more equitable water distribution. By contrast, the upper classes were generally determined to defend the region's existing irrigation ecology and water rights. Doing so required conserving the free-flowing Nazas on which the productive but unstable aniego method relied.

Integrating Water and Agrarian Reform

Under Obregón, the federal government signaled an interest in reviving the Nazas River Dam project. The challenge, however, was assessing the extent to which impounding river flow would require adjustments in water redistribution that would then affect the Laguna's land-tenure structure. Pro-dam farmers and their federal supporters sought to find ways to modernize the Nazas river regime (synonymous with damming it) without making any major changes to the land regime. Article 27 stipulated that "centers of population that at present either have no lands or water or that do not possess them in sufficient quantities for the needs of their inhabitants shall be entitled to grants thereof, which shall be taken from adjacent properties, the rights of small landed holdings in operation being respected at all times."[22]

In the Laguna, the problem was the availability not of land but of *irrigable* land. Yet not all irrigable land was equally fertile. For large landholders, sacrificing some land for agrarian reform was tolerable provided that the federal and state governments respected existing water rights and concessions, principally the 1909 regulation that had provoked the epic lawsuit by the Tlahualilo Company. In the 1920s, the separation between land and water rights became more difficult to sustain as the federal government gradually integrated land and water policies by passing new laws for both that applied Article 27's general provisions in specific circumstances. Obregón believed that agrarian reform was necessary, but only at a gradual pace and only for large landowners who had not modernized or made efficient use of new production methods. Although he did not object to creating ejidos from hacienda lands, he believed that agricultural modernization should emphasize development of small individual landholdings. He reassured landowners that agrarian reform would not involve large-scale expropriation, provided they committed themselves to mildly redistributive policies, such as improving the social conditions of dispossessed villagers. As a group, landowners interpreted his policy to mean respect for private property.[23]

At the state level, Coahuila and Durango passed laws in 1921 and 1922 restricting landholdings to a maximum area: 2,000 hectares for irrigated lands in both states and for lands without irrigation, Coahuila, where "possession of latifundio" was proscribed by law, allowed 35,000 hectares, while Durango allowed 10,000 hectares of grazing land and 20,000 hectares of forest lands. In April 1922, Obregón decreed a federal agrarian regulation (*reglamento agrario*) of Article 27 that streamlined the process of ejido land grants via two important novelties: it fixed the extension of ejidal parcels, in the case of *dotación* (concession or grant), to three to five hectares of irrigated or humid lands, four to six for semiarid lands, and six to eight for lands of other classes. In addition, the regulation established a maximum extension for small property of 150 hectares for irrigated and humid land, 250 hectares in regions with regular and abundant rainfall, and 500 hectares for all other classes of seasonal land. It exempted from expropriation "any property which by its very nature forms an industrial agricultural unit in exploitation" (but "in such a case the owner must substitute an equal quantity of good land as nearby as possible"), including its waterworks and canals for irrigation. Furthermore, the decree exempted estates that grew commercially important crops such as coffee, cocoa, vanilla, and hule. To the chagrin of Laguna farmers, it did not include cotton, to which they continuously lobbied the federal government to extend an exemption through the 1930s.[24]

When Obregón's former interior minister, Adolfo de la Huerta, who had also served as interim president for a few months in 1920, rebelled with the support of two-thirds of the military in December 1923, Obregón maintained much campesino support, thanks to the various agrarian reform laws that he had passed and partially implemented since he took office.[25] Shortly before the rebellion in August 1923, moreover, he decreed a "homestead law," or colonization scheme, for citizens older than eighteen to possess uncultivated or federal lands (*terrenos baldíos*) to a maximum area of 25 hectares with irrigation, 100 hectares with temporal rainfall, and 500 hectares with "wild" lands (*terrenos cerriles*) or pasture, provided they worked the lands for two years and did not take them illegally from ejidos or private property. In November 1923, Obregón reformed the 1922 agrarian regulation for the third time by decreeing who may solicit and obtain lands by restitution or grant of ejidos, with preferred right to the use of federal waters.[26] With regional exceptions, these laws and decrees remained in place until 1927, when Calles abrogated them and replaced them with a law more explicitly integrating land and water concessions (discussed later).

The Laguna appeared to be one such significant exception because of its unstable river flow. As a case in point, after the banner year of 1919–20, the region experienced yet another plaga: that of a devastating three-year drought. Rural workers, from resident and part-time hacienda peons (*acasillados* and *eventuales*) to temporary migrant workers (*bonanceros/migratorios*), all bore the brunt of such drought-induced downturns. Landowners did nevertheless try to provide some unemployment relief through dead work (*obras muertas*) such as repairing and cleaning canals. When the Nazas delivered a large flow in 1923, however, and cotton harvests recovered by mid-1924, agraristas became more active, as well, invading the lands of forty-five haciendas and ranchos.[27]

Seeking relief from their metaphorical plagas of a resurgent agrarismo, new agrarian laws and decrees, and volatile river flow and commodity prices, members of the agricultural chamber of the Laguna personally delivered a petition to Obregón in Mexico City. They claimed that his agrarian laws were not applicable to the Laguna, since no colonial-era villages had ever existed in the area. As a result, they purported that Laguna properties, primarily worked by tenants and sharecroppers, were not actually haciendas and thus not subject to expropriation. The chamber also accused agraristas of stealing valuable irrigation works, causing landowners to stop installing them, given the cost in time and money in litigation to recover them and the alleged partiality of state judges to agraristas. Appealing directly for federal favor, the petitioners pointed out that they had always cooperated with the federal government. For instance, they had funded the Nazas River Inspection Commission since its establishment in 1891, as mandated in Porfirio Díaz's federal water law of 1888. They also reminded Obregón that the Laguna accounted for 40 percent of Durango's and Coahuila's economic production in spite of the region's small size.

In response to Obregón's agrarian regulation in 1922 and its revision in 1923, the petitioners also claimed that the particularities of the Nazas River and its irrigation ecology exempted them from the regulation's "Federal Zones" by which land grantees could secure preferred rights to federal waters under state management: "This decree maintained that the legal concept of Federal Zones could not be applied to regions like the Laguna. Since its origins as a region were by formation from alluvial deposits, the rivers easily change course and it takes only a large flow for the waters to spill out of irrigated lots and flood an enormous area of land. This [river regime] would make it absurd for all of the Laguna to be declared a Federal Zone."[28] Recalling this petition in his memoir, the manager of the Arocena estate remarked that the 100 meters of prime riverine land on each side of the river to be ceded for Federal Zones would be distributed to "agrarista elements." His fear was that the zones would "serve as a base" for such "undesirable people," who always "constituted a danger" for his hacienda.[29] (On the other side, the CROM-affiliated Federation of Worker and Campesino Syndicates of the Comarca Lagunera, based in Gómez Palacio, complained to Obregón that several haciendas purposefully wasted water by not using as much as 50 percent of their allocations from the Nazas. They called it a "criminal maneuver" designed to harm campesino unions.)[30]

Laguna landowners thus argued for a kind of envirotechnical exceptionalism, consisting of a mythohistory—a region with no significant colonial past and land-tenure patterns distinct from indigenous areas of the center-south—shaped by the idiosyncratic Nazas River regime.[31] Both were incompatible with the technological direction in which the postrevolutionary government was moving as it promulgated a slew of new national agrarian and water laws, decrees, and regulations for implementing Article 27 in the late 1920s and 1930s.[32]

The Tlahualilo Company and the Formation of a Pro-Dam Lobby

The Tlahualilo Company's continuing legal battles with federal and local authorities demonstrates the challenges of merging hydraulic technologies imported and adopted in Mexico and the land and water concessions arising from the Laguna's irrigation ecology in the 1920s. The company faced legal problems with not only water rights—it had lost its case in the Supreme Court decision of 1911—but also with its lands. In April 1913, the neo-Porfirian regime of Victoriano Huerta (1913–14) had negotiated a new contract with Tlahualilo and the U.S. and British governments. In the contract, the company renounced all claims to compensation for water lost since the 1895 regulation and all legal fees as a result of the 1909–11 litigation. For this compromise it obtained a secure but reduced water concession.[33] The post-Huerta revolutionary government nominally led by Venustiano Carranza considered this concession illegitimate. Carranza nevertheless effected a general revalidation of the concession in a circular of November 1915 that retroactively reaffirmed the company's federal water rights from February 1914 to August 1915. In September 1916, however, Carranza's Minister of Agriculture Pastor Rouaix unilaterally rescinded the 1913 contract without referencing the circular and without allowing the company to defend itself. Tlahualilo powerlessly complained in a formal response

FIG. 2.1 The unpaved and eroded Tlahualilo Canal. Courtesy of Archivo Histórico del Agua, *Vista mostrando la erosión del canal de Tlahualilo cerca de Bermejillo,* 1941, Lerdo, Durango. CONAGUA-AHA, Fondo Aprovechamientos Superficiales, box 3067, file 42425, 44.

of November 1916 that "no authority, neither judicial nor administrative, can change the facts [of the case]."[34] To make matters worse, the company had to contend with the possible forced subdivision of its riverine San Fernando hacienda in the city of Lerdo, Durango, where a small dam diverted Nazas water into the company's forty-mile canal and, ultimately, to its fertile lands (see figure 2.1).

In the 1920s, Lerdo petitioned the State of Durango to expropriate part of San Fernando's land for agraristas demanding an ejido. Tlahualilo argued that, as a city, Lerdo was ineligible to confiscate land for ejidos, as stipulated by the circular of June 30, 1916, that Carranza decreed to weaken his own January 1915 agrarian law. The circular's authors excluded cities from ceding land to ejidos by designating them "population centers," since they anticipated that such concessions would stymie future urban growth.[35] Months and years of litigation could not convince Durango state judges, whom the company referred to as "Bolsheviki," of the justice of their appeal. Unable to fend off expropriation of San Fernando hacienda land through state courts, Tlahualilo's Mexican attorneys advised accepting its subdivision. In response, the company ceded land for five hundred families, but by April 1922, the project failed after most recipients abandoned it. Anticipating more forced land concessions as inevitable, however, Tlahualilo from then on turned primarily to protecting its remaining water rights. In December 1922, it commented that "after all [water] is the life blood," and in January 1923, that "if we save the water we can keep operating, and although the loss of the land hurts, it is not fatal. . . . The loss of water would be."[36]

Two years later, in January 1925, following one setback after another to the Durango State Agrarian Commission's demands for land, Tlahualilo representatives lost faith in litigation. They hoped instead that a direct appeal to the newly elected (in 1924) president, Plutarco Elías Calles, would bear more fruit. As the leading presidential candidate in 1923 to succeed Obregón, Calles emulated his mentor regarding agrarian reform. He declared that it should be gradually implemented to prevent the collapse of agricultural production, which he argued would mostly harm those whom the reform was intended to help. He advocated compensation for land expropriated from latifundio to grant ejidos, and that expropriations proceed only after "careful study and meditation." After his election in 1924, Calles was in the delicate position of having to reconcile his promise to grant ejidos to agraristas and his conviction that only a prosperous agrarian middle class of small individual landholders, not communal land grants, could boost agricultural production. During visits to France, Germany, and the United States, where he perceived such an agrarian middle class, his conviction only deepened.[37]

T. M. Fairburn, Tlahualilo's treasurer and secretary, assessed the new political situation for his company president in London under Calles: "We think the moment a propitious one approaching directly this new Government, which has expressed itself so strongly in favor of doing everything in its power to further agricultural production throughout the country, and have better hopes of obtaining a settlement in this way than by fighting through the courts. . . . Better to deal directly with Fomento [SAF] and the President. . . . It all goes to show that one has little hope of obtaining justice through the Mexican courts." A month later, he noted that the U.S. ambassador to Mexico had observed that the "agrarian question" is the "toughest nut to crack," as the federal government was still too weak to control local agrarian committees. Another month hence, in a memo to the company office in Mexico City, Fairburn lamented that Calles was uninformed of all the "outrages" committed in the name of ejidos. Not only was it "impossible" for the president to keep abreast of events on the ground, but, Fairburn bemoaned, "In this country everyone has to run and see the president." Regretfully, he concluded that Tlahualilo was not as adept politically as downriver landowners in organizing domestic pressure groups and lobbies that could capture the ear of the president. Rather, the company had relied excessively on the support of the British and U.S. governments, a strategy that badly backfired in 1911.[38]

While Tlahualilo unsuccessfully fought land expropriation and tried to retain its water rights, in December 1922 *El Siglo de Torreón* published an op-ed by the engineer Ignacio López Bancalari, director of the Center of Mexican Engineers. He advocated resumption of the Nazas dam project following S. Pearson and Son's 1911 recommendation of the El Palmito site at the origination point of the Nazas 120 miles west of Torreón. He emphasized the earlier study's central selling points: the dam reservoir in that location would capture 80 percent of the river's flow volume, enabling an increase of irrigation capacity of up to 50 percent in the Laguna as well as hydroelectric potential.[39] An internal SAF memo soon after reiterated his arguments. It favorably referred to the S. Pearson and Son Report prepared for Díaz in 1911 and asserted that damming the Nazas "*guaranteed* that current cultivated area would be doubled to at least 100,000 hectares and that *undoubtedly* the total cost of the project would not much exceed the sum of 25 million pesos budgeted by S. Pearson and Son."[40]

Unlike before the Revolution, when landowners were largely indifferent to Madero's advocacy effort, many of them now organized into an agricultural chamber vehemently opposed to the dam's postrevolutionary revival. In a letter to his superior, Luis Arturo Romo, director of land, colonization, water, and irrigation within the SAF, the federal engineer Gumaro García de la Cadena emphasized that the prerevolutionary 1909 regulation of Nazas water had turned user "interests" into "true privileges." He spoke of an unspecified commission that consisted solely of "enemies of the project," which led him to "logically conclude" that the strongest capitalists in the Laguna were opposed to it. At the last meeting of the agricultural chamber he attended, "These oppositionists requested in an insistent manner that [the 1909] regulation not be touched, and that the SAF make an explicit declaration to that effect."[41]

Although land tenure patterns and water distribution had not substantially changed since before the Revolution (see tables 2.1–2.2), the irrigation system had expanded considerably by the mid-1920s. Farmers had installed two more diversion dams, for a total of nine, and increased primary canals from twenty-two to twenty-nine. If the Laguna's canals were combined into one long canal at the time, they would total thousands of miles in distance. In addition, the global hydrocarbon revolution, which oil-producing Mexico helped supply and which fueled the spread of automobiles, trucks, tractors, harvesters, and cultivators throughout the region, also powered the advent of motorized pumps.

TABLE 2.1. Laguna properties and corresponding land extensions in hectares by municipality, 1926

Cities	Less than 100	100–500	500–1,000	1,000–5,000	5,000–10,000	More than 10,000	Total
Torreón	4	12	4	8	1	1	30
San Pedro	40	24	16	38	4	10	132
Matamoros	0	2	1	11	1	0	15
Gómez Palacio	0	2	10	7	7	2	28
Lerdo	0	0	2	3	4	5	14
Mapimí	0	0	0	1	0	1	2
Total	44	40	33	68	17	19	221

SOURCE: Enrique Nájera, Manuel López Portillo, and Estanislao Peña, *Informe general de la comisión de estudios de la Comarca Lagunera, designada por el secretario de Agricultura y Fomento* (Mexico City: Editorial Cultura, 1930), 48–53.

TABLE 2.2. Aggregate of Laguna lands in hectares and their cadastral values, 1926

Cities	Irrigated	Grazing	Total	Cadastral value (pesos)
Torreón	15,596	55,499	71,095	5,639,330
San Pedro	91,985	930,930	1,022,915	31,937,901
Matamoros	16,712	14,818	31,530	5,967,539
G. Palacio	39,788	86,245	126,033	5,363,121
Lerdo	8,757	196,776	205,533	2,336,028
Mapimí	18,430	29,956	48,386	4,365,825
Total	191,268	1,314,224	1,505,492	55,609,744

SOURCE: Enrique Nájera, Manuel López Portillo, and Estanislao Peña, *Informe general de la comisión de estudios de la Comarca Lagunera, designada por el secretario de Agricultura y Fomento* (Mexico City: Editorial Cultura, 1930), 48–53.

Tied to this technological revolution, the majority of haciendas also acquired their own cotton ginning machines and private telephone lines to rapidly communicate with the cities.[42]

Federal engineers estimated that the value of all hydraulic works in the Laguna amounted to 35,575,413 pesos. The majority (31.6 million) was for works within the federally regulated zone between the San Fernando and San Pedro diversion dams covering 189,154 hectares of irrigable lands. They estimated that the works outside the regulated zone toward the river's terminus were worth 876,484 pesos, the embankments from the Guadalupe dam downriver were worth 593,886 pesos, and the works to capture and distribute subterranean water (primarily groundwater pumps) were worth 2.5 million pesos.[43] Because of the high value and productivity of the Laguna's land and water regimes, landowners understandably regarded any proposed changes to either land tenure or water distribution with extreme suspicion. Accordingly, García de la Cadena explained the two-pronged nature of their opposition to the proposed Nazas Dam:

1. Those most opposed received large volumes of water that exceeded their needs, enabling them to divert this excess water on a moment's notice to nonriverine areas through long canals, such as the Santa Teresa hacienda in the upriver zone in Durango. Its four major canals (El Cuije, Santa Teresa, Bilbao, and Los Desfogues) could divert a total of 400 cubic meters of water per second.
2. They were strongly resistant to the creation of new water users, who they felt would become competitors if more water were made available with a dam.

García de la Cadena also noted that Spanish investors, the largest foreign capitalists in the region, had begun to withdraw their money to express their opposition in a discreet, even sly, manner. He identified Fernando González Fariño and the future antigovernment conspirator General Gonzalo Escobar as two prominent "Spaniards" ridiculing the project and planning to communicate their disparaging opinions to the president.[44]

Judging from available federal documents, by the end of 1925 momentum seemed to be slipping away from dam proponents, yet in January 1926 Calles started what would become a revolution in Mexican water policy when he promulgated a new Law of Irrigation, creating a new agency within the SAF, the Comisión Nacional de Irrigación (National Irrigation Commission, or CNI). In doing so, he sent a clear signal of his determination systematically to engineer the nation's waterways through what the historian Luis Aboites termed "revolutionary irrigation"—a socially transformative federal policy that would nonetheless bypass more radical approaches to agrarian reform, such as distributing prime hacienda land to create or restore communal landholdings. In other words, hydraulic technology would bring social liberation to the agrarian masses without the government radically altering existing land-tenure patterns. The CNI pursued its mission by encouraging colonization of unpopulated northern areas by building irrigation works through public financing as well as to increase irrigation capacity in densely settled regions.[45]

The objective of Callista revolutionary irrigation was to create a prosperous American-style agrarian middle class that would be a source of sociopolitical moderation and advanced technical agricultural skills for Mexican campesinos. Calles's experience in his home state of Sonora, where California-style agriculture was prevalent, influenced his thinking on land and water matters. Like his Porfirian predecessors, he believed irrigation was essential to an evolutionary transformation of land tenure that would both revive agricultural production and, from a postrevolutionary perspective, reduce the likelihood of another bloody agrarian revolution. In the late 1920s, the CNI proceeded to hire engineers from the New York–based White Engineering, many of whom had worked for the U.S. Bureau of Reclamation, to tutor their Mexican counterparts. These Mexican engineers would then "Mexicanize" their technical ability and reduce reliance on foreigners.[46]

Given that as early as 1917, the government could grant little irrigable land without extensively subdividing large properties, it was unclear how the government should implement the irrigation law in the Laguna without provoking conflict between agraristas and landowners. In his 1919 treatise on irrigation, the distinguished federal engineer José Herrera y Lasso lamented the scant development of irrigation in Mexico, as compared with the mostly arid and semi-arid U.S. West, and California in particular. He described California as "overrun barely seventy years ago . . . by searchers and adventurers looking for gold, who joined into groups to defend themselves from Redskins [*Pieles Rojas*] by founding insignificant villages around which they would plant small extensions of land, whenever water could be stored. Today many of those villages are great cities—among the most beautiful in the Union—and the earth of California has been transformed into an immense garden." The exceptional example he used to demonstrate Mexico's California-like irrigation potential was the "cotton oasis" created in the Laguna in less than thirty years: the torrential Nazas, "useless for centuries," had created, through aniego, the "miracle" of three active cities, a dozen important towns, and 80 percent of the domestic cotton used by national industry. This success contrasted to other areas, especially in the center and east, 80 percent of which had been artificially irrigating lands since colonial times. Herrera y Lasso maintained that the task of the Revolution was to do the "social" work of irrigation in cooperation with "capitalist elements."[47] Although Calles's new irrigation policy reflected Herrera y Lasso's moderation, Laguna landowners were not generally enthusiastic about it, for proponents of the Nazas River Dam, among them a vocal minority of landowners, used it as a golden opportunity to urge Calles to build the dam quickly.

In the summer of 1925, even before passage of the 1926 irrigation law, the Mexican American entrepreneur Juan Brittingham, owner of the soap company La Esperanza and an important shareholder in Cementos Hidalgo, a cement company founded in Gómez Palacio in 1906 that later morphed into the behemoth Cementos Mexicanos (CEMEX), received Calles in his home in the Laguna. The assistant manager of Tlahualilo, T. M. Fairburn, was also present during the president's visit, which he described in some detail in correspondence to his superior in London. He noted that "absolutely no attention was paid to any schedules" for the president and that there "were probably three or four hundred people tagging along, including all of the Hacendados, and goodness knows how many Generals and other Military Officers." General Nájera in particular, after speaking at length with Fairburn about Tlahualilo's "ejido problems" with its water rights, managed to include Fairburn in a personal meeting with Calles in Brittingham's home. Fairburn hoped to raise Tlahualilo's travails with the president "for upwards of an hour" during which the president chatted with three or four other people. Instead, to Fairburn's chagrin, "The conversation was almost entirely confined to the construction of a dam on the Nazas River. Various plans were discussed. The question of raising funds also. Details of the additional acreage possible, assurance of crops, etc. were gone into, also how much a quintal the Hacendados could contribute towards the cost, etc."[48] According to Brittingham's account of the same meeting, Calles approved of the dam and promised its completion by the end of his term in 1928. Believing he had thereby secured federal support, Brittingham announced the fait accompli in the region without consulting Nazas riverine owners. Although Brittingham claimed the project would be of general benefit to the region and nation, his private correspondence reveals how much he anticipated construction of the dam spurring a massive increase in federal cement procurements, to the benefit of Cementos Hidalgo.[49]

This self-serving individual initiative having failed, on February 2, 1926, shortly after the irrigation law's promulgation, the fifth National Convention of Engineers met during the annual Cotton Fair held in Torreón and requested the construction of the dam "to spare agriculture the random nature of the Nazas." A small group of prominent Laguneros then formed the Asociación para el Fomento de la Presa sobre el Río Nazas (Association to Promote the Nazas River Dam), with an elected board, and announced that their principal objective was "to convince the public (*llevar al convencimiento público*) of the necessity of constructing the dam."[50] The association held its first meeting in Torreón's Casino de la Laguna on February 14, which a hundred of the Laguna elite, including the governors of Coahuila and Durango, the mayors of Torreón and Gómez Palacio, state assembly representatives, and representatives of the regional chamber of commerce attended. Key speakers were the association's President Plácido Vargas (a downriver medium-size landowner), the federal engineer Francisco Allen, the downriver landowner and engineer José de la Fuente, the attorney Celso A. Enríquez, and the accountant Salvador Valencia. All presented the principal legal, financial, and envirotechnical arguments in the dam's favor. They tried to reassure landowners that any major changes to the river regime brought about by the dam would not adversely affect them; if any agrarian reform were implemented, the association members promised, it would only be minor and, undoubtedly, compensated. They tried to further persuade landowners that regulating the Nazas would benefit the region economically and offset any potential losses from minor land concessions since stabilizing the cotton growing cycle would greatly boost profits.[51]

As things stood, the year 1926 augured well for the region. The Nazas was flowing strongly, and cotton had become the third-largest Mexican agricultural export after henequen and coffee now that the government allowed Laguna farmers to export 200,000 bales of cotton over the previous two years. Domestic textile producers, in a reversal of their advantageous prerevolutionary position of being able to manipulate prices more easily, had lobbied Obregón to reduce tariffs on imported cotton to make up the shortfall.[52] Torreón, which had increased from forty thousand inhabitants in 1911 to fifty-one thousand in 1920 and then jumped again to become the second largest in the north after Monterrey at sixty-five thousand by 1926, used the revenue from sales of the Laguna's white gold to beautify the city. Proponents of taming the mighty but fickle Nazas at the 1926 meeting thus discursively framed their cause in terms of human "progress," "evolution," and the "struggle for life" that the region's "psychological forces" over the years had unleashed; building the dam was a "transcendental matter." The attorney Celso A. Enríquez in particular referenced Article 27 of the 1917 Constitution and its conservationist provision, claiming that its "principles and tendencies have just been crystallized in the Irrigation Law." Like the civil engineer and forest conservationist Miguel Ángel de Quevedo, who likely wrote the provision, he thereby interpreted the mandate for conservation in Article 27 as creation of dam reservoirs when applied to water resources.[53]

Diagnosing the historic question of the Nazas, the engineer Allen reprised S. Pearson and Son's 1909 study in his presentation, reiterating the statistic that the proposed El Palmito site could capture—and thus conserve—80 percent of the Nazas flow with the creation of a dam reservoir there. S. Pearson and Son had calculated the figure from the Nazas River Inspection Commission's flow records from 1891 to 1910, but highly esteemed Porfirian-era Mexican engineers who had a deep knowledge of the Nazas, including Manuel Marroquín y Rivera, found the number questionable. Allen and pro-dam federal engineers continued citing this figure repeatedly for years, despite the widespread skepticism of many powerful Laguna landowners and engineers, who were conspicuously absent from the 1926 meeting. Three of these landowners—Carlos González Fariño, Jesús Pamanes, and Pedro Franco Ugarte, the president of the agricultural chamber—explained that "while in principle we consider that the dam is a factor of progress, we are not convinced that in the Laguna it would be beneficial." Before they could support it, they demanded to see far more recent data and evidence demonstrating its technical soundness.[54]

In response to such demands over the next few years, the CNI outsourced new technical studies to the American engineer F. F. Smith of the U.S. Bureau of Reclamation, through its cooperative agreement with White Engineering. The agreement enabled the CNI to hire White engineers in Mexico to serve as technical advisers and trainers. After two years of study, Smith issued a long report more or less corroborating the 80 percent figure, estimating it at a slightly lower 73 percent.[55] The report's publication in the CNI newsletter and in local and national newspapers enhanced the project's legitimacy in the face of vehement attacks by Manuel Lorenzo Pardo, a well-respected Spanish "hydrographer."[56] He participated in the 1909 survey by S. Pearson and Son as a young assistant to the British engineers, but then distanced himself from their recommendations. Writing in Mexican national newspapers in the late 1920s and 1930s, Pardo argued that a major storage dam would harm the Laguna economy, since river flows would be insufficient to increase irrigation capacity. Rather than a technically questionable and financially costly dam that would produce an uncertain outcome, one likely to harm campesinos most, he recommended increasing the capacity and quantity of motorized pumps to extract groundwater. Armed with F. F. Smith's study as ammunition, pro-dam engineers countered that Pardo's pump option as an alternative to a high dam, which they claimed was based on faulty calculations, would primarily benefit large landowners, given its prohibitive cost for campesinos.[57]

Nevertheless, in private correspondence, both sides expressed reservations about their arguments. In one revealing letter, Smith wrote to Andrew Weiss, an American engineer of White Engineering hired by the CNI who later became a naturalized Mexican citizen. Smith admitted that Nazas flow records from 1891 to 1910 were "accomplished at *poorly selected* gauging stations by *primitive* methods and were therefore judged to be *entirely unreliable* for use as an indication of actual river discharge. . . . It is reported that an explanation was not given in the text of the report of why these years were omitted from the river supply study, as it leaves a point of attack for those so minded."[58] Although Smith's observation cast into doubt the basis of the 1909 regulation still in effect, it seemed to arouse very little consternation among high-level federal engineers and politicians.[59] In private, Allen and his assistants corroborated Smith's assessment in their analyses. They casually remarked, "It can be concluded that the hydrometric observations which cover the period from 1890 to 1931 with data calculated from the volume [of water that] passed through the Coyote Dike [located midway between the upper and farthest downriver zones] are *not worthy* of confidence during the *whole of the period* indicated. [For the reasons enumerated above] they are *unacceptable.*"[60] Moreover, the high degree of uncertainty that these engineers expressed in private apparently never colored their public claims. Notably, among numerous examples, in a response to a personal memo written by Allen countering his criticisms of the dam's technical and financial feasibility, Pardo conceded that his own data and methodologies were flawed. Yet this concession failed to persuade Pardo, the foreign-based anti-dam técnico par excellence, to desist from his scathing public attacks on the project, which he continued to level even after the completion of the dam in the late 1940s.[61]

In 1925, while engineers (publicly and privately) debated water flows and the government still considered the dam site in the Fernández Canyon near Torreón viable (as Madero did before the Revolution), Quevedo raised a different, but no less important, issue. He expressed his opposition to the dam at the fourth national convention of engineers held in Torreón in September 1925— just a few months before the same convention would declare its resolute support for the dam. Quevedo was apparently unable to convince the majority of his fellow engineers of his principal contention: rather than building a costly dam that could impede the flow of nutrient-rich sediments to Laguna fields, the government should reforest the badly denuded hills and mountains of the Nazas River basin near its origination point to ensure continued conveyance of such sediments. He argued that deforestation diminished not only the volume of these sediments to the Nazas as it flowed down from the mountains but also local evapotranspiration. That is, deforestation reduced precipitation, in turn leading to less evaporation of water from forests that could attract clouds and regenerate the hydrological cycle. Quevedo cited the studies of the Hydrological Forestry Station of Nancy, France, that "had demonstrated an increase of 28 to 60 percent in pluvial precipitation [in sufficiently forested land] compared with identical neighboring agricultural or sparsely forested lands." Quevedo also cited statistics from Ignacio Ruiz Martínez, chief of the Mexican Commission of Forest Exploration, in 1923. Ordered by the SAF to inspect the Nazas basin, Martínez found that 104,000 hectares of forest had been clear-cut while only 34,000 hectares remained forested. Two years later, Martínez found the trend continued with even more forest disappearing. Regarding groundwater, Quevedo exhorted his fellow engineers that it was imperative to view the basin's mountainous forests as "the principal supplier of the subterranean waters" since they helped to regenerate the Nazas surface flow. The flow in turn recharged the aquifer through filtration. Deforestation, he warned, threatened the supply of groundwater Laguneros enthusiastically exploited—not unlike in the Valley of Mexico, where he claimed the level of artesian waters was dropping from rampant deforestation in the surrounding mountains.[62]

Interestingly, Quevedo was so focused on the relationship between forests and water supply that he missed the proverbial forest for the trees with respect to the larger picture of groundwater conservation: over-pumping. In other words, even if reforested mountains could restore and maintain a healthy hydrological cycle, nature simply could not keep recharging the aquifers at the rate at which farmers withdrew water from them—a fact engineers would discover only a few years later.[63]

Controversial Dam, Uncontroversial Pumps

Quevedo's and Pardo's advocacy of groundwater pumping to increase and stabilize irrigation reflected its growing significance as a new technology introduced to Mexico in the 1900s. Indeed, the growth of unrestricted pumping from the early 1920s in the Laguna was emblematic of Mexico's arid north-central agricultural regions, the most productive in the country, as well as of a global trend. Engineers, politicians, and farmers of all stripes first welcomed the advent of motorized pumps for deep-water wells with euphoria. According to the newspapers, memoirs, journals, private correspondence, and reports they produced, Laguneros widely expected that a major expansion of groundwater pumping would reduce reliance on irregular river flow for irrigation, thereby increasing the flexibility of watering times. The improved flexibility would in turn reduce the exposure of the cotton plant to the pink bollworm and other destructive pests and weeds. As soon as it began publishing in 1921, the Laguna's principal daily, *El Siglo de Torreón,* featured articles describing the various

brands of European and American pumps and drills available and their capabilities for drawing up groundwater.[64]

At the Rotary Club of Torreón in 1923, a presentation by Dr. Juan Castillón
exemplified the euphoria and pump-as-savior fervor that was pervasive in the
region for decades. Castillón described the Laguna as sitting on a "subterranean lake the dimensions of which I cannot calculate." He called it a matter of
"providence" that practicing aniego with the Nazas River's torrential flows
would eventually filter 150 meters deep into the aquifer. The summer river
flows helped "maintain this subterranean lake, always supplied with water,"
thereby enabling "abundant harvests," but this was nothing compared with
what farmers could expect if they "knew how to use natural resources." The first
well for agricultural use in the Laguna, he noted, was drilled in 1893. The well was
still in use in the 1920s, but, with the addition of a motorized pump, it was now
able to water three times as much land. Every day, he remarked enthusiastically,
farmers sunk more and more pump-equipped wells and installed power plants
to run them.[65]

The cost of well drilling varied, Castillón explained, and depended on subsoil conditions. Water could be tapped at 12, 37, or more meters in depth. Once
tapped, however, a well could last indefinitely, since "not a single well has run
out of water to the point of becoming unproductive." As of August 1923, when
Castillón spoke, eighty pumps were extracting 6,000 liters of water per second
from the aquifer. By the end of the year, he anticipated, twenty more would be
installed: "The development of this new industry—that is, pump irrigation
here—has increased greatly and there is a veritable fever to drill more wells." He
boldly predicted that these hundred pumps "will realize the wealth of the region"
by supplying 7,500 liters of water per second. Looking forward to 1924, he anticipated the number of pumps doubling, increasing available groundwater to
366,000 cubic meters at a rate of 15,000 liters per second over nearly a year—a
volume that exceeded the entire Nazas flow of 293,000 cubic meters in 1910. In
economic terms, he concluded, an investment of 12.5 million pesos in five hundred pumps would boost the value of agricultural production by 18 million
pesos over what farmers could earn using surface irrigation only.[66]

Castillón's predictions about increased groundwater pumping capacity were
largely accurate: in 1924, the agricultural chamber's memorial to Obregón,
with similarly great expectations, declared that eighty-four pumps had been
installed; by 1928, there were 160, with the number increasing tenfold over the
following decade. In particular, the discovery of a mostly salt-free aquifer in the
Torreón-Porvenir-Florencia zone, extending 6–20 kilometers on each bank of

the Nazas including the Santa Teresa hacienda, spurred the increase in pump acquisition. Other aquifers, in and around San Pedro and the Tlahualilo lands, were saturated with salt and thus of little use.[67] However accurate their predictions of pump installations were, time would soon prove Castillón and the chamber far too optimistic with regard to pumping's ecological impact on the regional aquifer.

As tensions heightened among agraristas, unions, and haciendas, Calles sent a commission of three federal engineers in 1928 to investigate the social and economic conditions of the Laguna and make a recommendation on implementing an agrarian reform program. The commission noted that some farmers had improved irrigation by connecting gasoline- or diesel-powered motors to their pumps, but the cost of purchasing and installing the pumps, tubes, and motors could be prohibitive for all but the wealthiest haciendas.[68] The cost of each unit varied between 20,000 pesos and 40,000 pesos, but drilling several wells in the same lot and installing a central power plant could substantially reduce the cost per unit. As more and more well-drilling companies began competing for customers, farmers could secure for between 8,000 pesos and 10,000 pesos everything necessary for pumping groundwater except the 75–80 horsepower motor. Once installed, farmers with motorized pumps could irrigate as many as 100 hectares and make the pumps last between eight and ten years, provided they maintained them well. This was sufficient time for farmers to repay loans with interest from the significant increase in agricultural productivity, thanks to additional water from pumping. The engineers observed that the most efficient means of employing pump-installed wells on the same lot (about 1 square kilometer) was to combine pumped groundwater with surface water obtained through special canals. If a farmer with one pump-installed well could extract 100 liters of groundwater per second to flood one lot 22 centimeters deep in forty days, one with five pump-installed wells extracting 500 liters per second could irrigate five lots at the same depth in thirty days. The pro-dam advocate Plácido Vargas in Torreón, for instance, cultivated a maximum of 150 hectares on his Las Vegas hacienda before 1920; from 1920 to 1924, he drilled six wells and installed pumps in them that augmented his cultivable land area to nearly 880 hectares.[69]

The continued proliferation of these pumps, however, required farmers to use electrical current rather than gas or diesel motors, for which an American company proposed to install a grand central electric plant with a capacity of 50,000–70,000 horsepower. In addition to pumps, this supply of electricity could power ginning machines, small industry, and lighting for the entire region. The principal obstacle to installing the plant was the indefinite status of agrarian policies in the region, which made long-term investment difficult.[70] Though not the panacea that farmers had hoped, the pump option could simultaneously help them reduce reliance on surface irrigation, yield better harvests less harmed by the pink bollworm, and reduce social tensions by stabilizing employment for thousands of their workers.[71] Furthermore, by 1925 pump-installed wells partially liberated farmers from near-exclusive reliance on cotton and considerably boosted wheat production during the cotton off-season as other regions began or increased their cotton production (see tables 2.3–2.4).

As mentioned earlier, American and European companies quickly moved to capture this booming pump market revolutionizing irrigated agriculture not just in the Laguna but also in much of Mexico and the world. Two that stood out in engineering and newspaper reports and advertisements were the Texas-based Layne and Bowler Pump Company and the New York–based Worthington Pump and Machinery Corporation. The 1928 engineering report commissioned by Calles highlighted installation and use of Layne and Bowler, while Worthington appeared in far more newspaper stories and advertisements.

By 1932, Laguneros possessed 365 pumps, and as increased sales reduced the price of units, CNI geologists began to detect the ecological impact of their burgeoning use.[72] The leading CNI geologist was a naturalized Mexican of Austrian origin, Paul Waitz, a geochemist by training whom the Porfirian-era National Geology Institute hired shortly before the Revolution. Waitz remained to become one of Mexico's leading figures in the emergent field of geohydrology.[73] Defining geohydrology as "the study of the presence, distribution, movement, quality and rational use of subterranean water," the Mexican hydraulic engineer and historian José P. Arreguín Mañón credits Charles V. Theis of the U.S. Geological Survey for effectively creating the field in 1935. In that year, Theis employed the vital analogy between groundwater flow and heat transfer to formulate the first transient solution for groundwater flow toward a well. The Theis transient pump test solution thereafter became the standard for geohydrologists globally for well-test interpretation.[74]

Even before global dissemination of Theis's formula, Waitz published numerous studies on Mexico's groundwater resources in the CNI's new quarterly journal *Irrigación en México,* describing how to detect, measure, and extract them. He observed that in the Laguna during the year 1930, groundwater exploitation with "pumps of a great diameter" had increased to such an extent that farmers extracted "great quantities of water" at "very deep levels" from the filtration of Nazas River flow deposits into the alluvial plain.[75] Underlying his studies was a sense of caution about the potential consequences of

TABLE 2.3. Cotton and wheat production in Laguna, 1926–1935

	Cotton		Wheat	
Years	Hectares	Bales	Hectares	Tons
1925–26	119,733	212,415	11,062	na
1926–27	52,492	95,933	36,848	na
1927–28	94,480	137,121	15,973	na
1928–29	76,950	105,588	26,650	na
1929–30	78,844	62,000	6,148	na
1930–31	68,870	41,456	31,849	53,088
1931–32	43,731	59,340	27,629	32,784
1932–33	78,839	175,853	45,073	50,005
1933–34	60,751	132,350	30,016	33,958
1934–35	66,468	146,412	18,295	22,202
Total	874,258	1,441,957	286,791	243,977
Average	79,478	131,087	26,071	40,663

SOURCE: María Vargas-Lobsinger, *La Comarca Lagunera: De la Revolución a la expropiación de las haciendas, 1910–1940* (Mexico City: Universidad Nacional Autónoma de México, 1999), 209.

TABLE 2.4. Mexican cotton production and area by region, 1925–1934

Region	Production (%)	Area (%)
Laguna	54.48	45.35
Valle de Mexicali	22.69	25.61
Matamoros (Tamaulipas)	9.16	12.77
Juárez	4.71	4.99
D. Martín	1.38	1.65
Yaqui	1.19	1.21
Conchos	0.69	0.76
Pacific	2.99	3.55
Gulf	.30	.36
Other areas	2.41	3.75

SOURCE: María Vargas-Lobsinger, *La Comarca Lagunera: De la Revolución a la expropiación de las haciendas, 1910–1940* (Mexico City: Universidad Nacional Autónoma de México, 1999), 209.

profligate groundwater exploitation. A fellow geologist and student of Waitz, Gonzalo Vivar, made this sentiment explicit in a 1934 study: "It is desirable that in the case of drilling in the [Laguna] plain in search of water under pressure there exist adequate regulations on behalf of everyone. So far a true anarchy reigns with regard to the exploitation of groundwater: there is no technical direction in the distribution of drillings, or in the extraction of water from each drilling."[76]

At the time Vivar recommended that the agricultural chamber regulate drilling, but this proved fruitless; farmers jealously guarded their precious water resources and were loath to cooperate with the federal government lest it expropriate their lands. In the meantime, *El Siglo de Torreón* continued to run ads for Worthington pumps, one of them by an engineer named W. S. Hessel. Hessel's slogan was "The Great Pump for the Laguna," illustrated by the Worthington trademark eagle.[77] On October 1, 1936, just five days before Cárdenas decreed the Laguna's historic agrarian reform, Hessel had formed his own company, Técnica del Norte, with two partners and become a distributor for Worthington in Torreón.[78]

Whereas Pardo advocated the pump option as a viable alternative to the dam and Quevedo argued that reforestation in the Sierra Madre along with the pump option could augment water supplies without the high financial and ecological costs of a dam, Waitz, Allen, and other CNI engineers countered that a dam reservoir would actually help recharge the aquifer and improve groundwater quality.[79] Unlike for pumps, however, the task of convincing regional public opinion and the federal government to support the dam project remained unfinished in the late 1920s.

Federalizing the Nazas to Dam(n) It

While engineers sparred over the merits of building a dam, the pro-dam downriver landowners Plácido Vargas and José de la Fuente immediately provoked controversy as they launched their lobbying campaign. For months after the February 1926 inaugural meeting of the Association for the Promotion of the Nazas Dam, Torreón's other newspaper, *La Opinión,* ran front-page articles accusing them of doctoring official declarations to bolster their case. For instance, on March 7, 1926, members of the agricultural chamber opposed to the dam formed a commission retorting that "the 'rabble-rousing liberal' system adopted by the pro-dam gentlemen is not the most adequate to inspire confidence in the public. The use of the label 'conservative' [to describe their position] is meant to harm us in the eyes of the authorities. The dam may appear magnificent, but really it is harmful. . . . Our cotton will be replaced by chili, alfalfa, barley." In an editorial a few days later, the newspaper claimed that 90 percent of Laguna landowners opposed the dam, as they believed it would bring ruin to the region. Nevertheless the editorialists looked forward to a "scientific duel" on its merits.[80] Although *La Opinión* scathingly criticized the project, the editorialists carefully reiterated their support of Calles's national irrigation policy but argued that the Laguna was not an appropriate site for it.

In contrast, *El Siglo de Torreón's* favorable coverage throughout the 1920s and 1930s reflected its cautious support for the dam. Occasionally, however, it published the views of dam "skeptics," though it portrayed them in the minority rather than as the majority, as the rival *La Opinión* claimed. For instance, in late 1929, *El Siglo de Torreón* ran a piece by the dam skeptic José de San Román, who explained his opposition in a sometimes rambling missive. He pleaded that skeptics like him needed to see statistics showing that if the dam had been built three decades before, there would never have been drought or economic crisis in the Laguna. In addition to regularizing river flow, therefore, he remarked, "It would be necessary to regularize the atmosphere, weather, infestations, cotton pickers at harvesting time, and, finally, the cotton stock exchange." He persisted, ever more philosophically: "There is nothing more random than the cultivation of land; for that reason farmers spend their lives contemplating the [agricultural] cycle and concocting fantastic calculations which never come to fruition. If you take chance away from all efforts in any struggle, if everything has to be regular, mediocre, systematized, standard; if success has to be shared by all in equal portions, even in politics, there would be no heroes. . . . Economic, social and political crises are inevitable, like natural phenomena; otherwise boredom would make life intolerable."

He even argued that the economic and ecological crises that arose from severe drought in the Laguna in 1907, 1921, and 1922 "ended up being advantageous for the advent of pumps." San Román repeated the Laguna's mythical narrative of envirotechnical exceptionalism by reminding readers of the "strong men" who had broken out the virgin lands of the colonial latifundio, erected twenty-nine diversion dams on the Nazas, miraculously created "an agricultural center that is so envied," and founded the two "great cities" of Gómez Palacio and Torreón. He continued proudly that "not even on the margins of the Usumacinta, of the Grijalva, the Papaloapan and the Pánuco [all ocean-bound rivers with much greater and regular flow] from Independence to the present day has a village, let alone a city been founded." After all, he observed, the largest national rivers flowed freely and unimpeded; seldom had the government tampered with them. For all his exuberance, San Román was careful, as skeptics had been since the early 1920s, to identify himself as a progressive who was not against high dams in principle. He merely felt that the Nazas was already sufficiently engineered. Yet he conceded that if the government and dam proponents took "appropriate and transparent legal, technical, and economic measures," regional support for the dam would quickly materialize.[81]

The commission report by Calles's engineers, published in 1930 and based on their painstaking surveys of the land and water regimes from 1926 to 1928, corroborates *La Opinión*'s contention that opinions such as San Román's were in the majority. More than that, they were rather moderate, for while San Román was skeptical, the commission found outright hostility among many landowners toward any government effort to control the Nazas flow. They surmised that this opposition derived from two fears landowners harbored: one was losing their advantageous legal and economic position vis-à-vis distribution of Nazas water, and the other was the possibility of a "maximum subdivision [*fraccionamiento*] of lands owned by large companies or individuals, a subdivision that can be of an ejidal nature or colonization, without their being able to predict to what degree creation of small properties in the [Laguna] would harm their private interests."[82] The engineers agreed that a large-scale subdivision of latifundio into ejidos would undermine the Laguna's economy. Instead, they recommended a more moderate agrarian reform that would fix a maximum extension of 300 hectares per landowner, or double what the agrarian law authorized, while remaining areas would be sold to the "discontented rural middle class" to form small landholdings.[83] On the whole, its recommendation reflected Calles's stated policy of gradually transforming concentrated landownership into a small landholding class.

Although landowners' opposition to the dam centered on a fear of large-scale agrarian reform and a desire to preserve existing landholdings and water rights, the commission engineers reported a strong and articulated envirotechnical component to it as well, which is worth quoting at length:

By being impounded in the dam, the waters will tend to deposit all of the sediments and fertilizing materials that they convey [downstream], which will be detrimental to the present fertility of the lands on which cotton is cultivated; by doing preparatory watering at times later [in the season] than it is currently done and doing a supplementary watering of the plants, there is an imminent danger that the *plagas* that at present infect the fields, and that so far haven't flourished to the point of making cotton cultivation unaffordable, could be exacerbated, especially the pink bollworm, due to the greater moisture and climatic changes that [damming the river] would produce. . . . Supplementary irrigation [groundwater pumping], even when done opportunely, only benefits medium-quality lands, such that for lands of great fertility this kind of irrigation primarily develops the leafy part of the plant to the detriment of cotton production.[84]

The engineers' commission detected a palpable fear among many farmers that the dam could alter the delicate cycle of irrigated cotton growing in the La- guna. One farmer, Ramón de Belausteguigoitia, the manager of the Santa Te- resa hacienda in the upriver zone of Durango, described his position similarly in his memoirs by explicitly linking the sociopolitical and envirotechnical grounds for his opposition, also worth presenting in full:

> In the first months of 1926, there emerged a grave issue of much danger to the interests of the estates of the Laguna including Santa Teresa and San Ignacio. There had arisen in the Laguna the idea of constructing a dam on the Nazas River, in Durango, in order to capture its waters and distribute them methodically. Dr. Juan Brittingham, Aymes, and other elements full of enmity toward the privileged situation of Santa Teresa were pushing the project. They were owners of dry lands wanting to take the Nazas waters in order to vary the system of canals and irrigation. The dam's construction was to have been at the landowners' expense, making one suppose that for Santa Teresa and San Ignacio it would have required [shouldering] an enormous proportion of the total cost.
>
> Moreover, the dam's effectiveness seemed very doubtful in that the organic elements that constitute the basis of the Laguna's fertility would be lost. In addition, the dam [reservoir] would end up empty since nearly all the water that flows down is used for irrigation. It was plausible, thus, that the dam project constituted a sleight of hand by elements with dry lands conspiring against the present state of affairs.

Belausteguigoitia added that, after careful study, he felt the project was enor- mously expensive and its proponents were "wickedly" pushing it—hence, his "resolute opposition."[85]

One such proponent was the engineer José Bonilla, who questioned in a paper published by *El Siglo de Torreón* whether the Nazas truly enriched La- guna lands with natural fertilizers from nutrient-rich sediments upstream. He argued that even if the river acted as a natural fertilizer, it could be substituted for chemical fertilizers. In response, the agronomist Rafael B. Narro argued that Bonilla's assertion was not only unsubstantiated but also amounted to a politicized effort to promote the dam. One long-standing concern since before Madero's public advocacy of it in 1906 was that damming the Nazas might well impede the flow of natural fertilizers to Laguna lands through aniego. Reaffirm- ing observations by the engineer Marroquín y Rivera from the early 1890s, Narro restated Bonilla's own self-refuting admission that "the riverbed of the

Nazas, as a mechanical agent, is an improver of great value for the soils." Substituting the free-flowing river for chemical fertilizers, Narro added, would be harmful because the fertilizers were "scientifically doubtful" and "economically costly," and, more to the point, "never could human procedures equal the security and efficiency of those of nature."[86]

Despite the contentiousness of the dam project as illustrated by the wrangling over its costs, technical feasibility, potential ecological harm, and impact on existing water rights, the federal government announced on November 27, 1929, that it would decree "regularization of the torrential waters of the Nazas of public utility" on December 5. It then ordered a detailed study of how to implement it, which, as previously noted, the CNI outsourced to the American engineer F. F. Smith. The CNI framed the decree's language in terms of "definitively" ridding the region of a persistent defect: "radically correcting (*corregir*) the random character of crops due to the *insecurity* of the Nazas flows." It also reassured landowners that it would not confiscate existing irrigation works and that the dam would enable cultivation of larger land extensions, encourage diversification away from cotton monoculture, and lead to the settlement of the region's large migratory population. Secretary Marte R. Gómez of the SAF weighed in by assuring that the dam would not affect the flow of nourishing sediments to Laguna lands and would even help reduce the damage caused by the pink bollworm. Coahuila's Governor Manuel Pérez Treviño telegrammed Gómez to express his support for the project and to suggest users themselves finance it to "liberate" the region.[87]

The decree thus paved the way for the river's full federalization in accordance with the new Water Law of August 1929, enacted by President Emilio Portes Gil (1928–30). An update of the prerevolutionary 1910 Water Law, the 1929 law restated and amplified Article 27's broad definition of national waters by stipulating that the nation's dominion over its lands and waters is "complete . . . inalienable . . . and inherent . . . to the exclusion of every other political or private entity whatever." It also empowered the nation to grant concessions for the use of its waters to private or public persons in the public interest while taking every regulatory precaution to guard against any monopoly or unfair use of national waters for any purpose (and thus giving the nation the power to revoke concessions). To this end, it provided that all concessions in existence before August 1929 were subject to review and confirmation.[88] This last provision particularly unnerved Laguna landowners determined to preserve the water rights granted them in the Porfirian-era 1909 regulation and affirmed in the 1910 Water Law. They had reason to worry, for the December 1929 decree announced that building one or more storage dams for more "economical" and "efficient" use of the river, which would otherwise require a review and confirmation of existing water rights, was in the public interest.

Pro-dam lobbyists cited both the National Water Law of August 1929 and the December decree on the Nazas to try to push the project forward by appealing to President Portes Gil and then to President Pascual Ortiz Rubio (1930–32). They also appealed to Calles, who continued to wield considerable power behind the scenes as the "Jefe Máximo de la Revolución" during 1928–34, a period known as the "Maximato."[89] In his numerous telegrams and communications to national leaders, Plácido Vargas, co-founder of the pro-dam association, tried to appeal to Calles's irrigation policy. Part of his efforts stemmed from his concern that the project did not seem to interest the Jefe Máximo because the Laguna did not neatly fit into the CNI's social mission of cultivating new colonized lands with government irrigation works.

If Vargas was confused, he had a good reason. Calles had sent mixed signals regarding his position on the dam as he pushed for passage of these new laws; on one hand he told industrialists such as Juan Brittingham that the project would be completed forthwith, and on the other he assured the agricultural chamber that he was not seriously considering it.[90] This ambivalence may have stemmed from the fact that unlike other Callista projects of irrigation and colonization in Tamaulipas, Aguascalientes, Sonora, and other northern arid states and regions, the Laguna was already too densely populated to provide much more land for colonization without expropriation of existing properties.

This density complicated the region's case for colonizing lands with government irrigation works. The Irrigation Law of 1926, which mandated the creation of the CNI, was, according to Aboites, after all a "combination of a fiscal policy and an agrarian policy, since lands open to irrigation with federal money would be colonized with small property owners."[91] By contrast, the Callista Law of Dotation and Restitution of Lands and Waters, which replaced Obregón's agrarian regulation of 1922, explicitly stated in its first article: "Every populated place (*poblado*) which lacks lands and waters or which does not possess these elements in amounts sufficient for the agricultural needs of its inhabitants, has the right to a dotation of them in the amount and under the conditions set forth in this law."[92]

The 1927 law, however, did not include resident laborers on haciendas (*peones acasillados*) as eligible, and they constituted much of the Laguna's agricultural population. After the publication of F. F. Smith's report in 1932 recommending building the dam at the El Palmito site, there was fresh momentum for the project, with the governors of Durango and Coahuila personally encouraging the federal government to build it forthwith. Both governors established study commissions composed of Nazas water users and government engineers. The commissions would report directly to the governors, who in turn would use the findings to try to get all stakeholders to reach a consensus. But amid the persistently uncertain state of agrarian reform programs, reaching a consensus proved difficult. As the agricultural chamber's 1924 memorial and Tlahualilo's legal struggles with agraristas exemplified, landowners desperately sought to exempt themselves from creating ejidos and thought they had found the solution in 1930: offering the government marginal lands that lacked sufficient water for its "ejidal districts."[93]

In late 1929, during a trip to New York City, Calles seemed to call for an end to agrarian reform (especially with the advent of the global Depression). In 1930 and 1931, Ortiz Rubio supported state and federal decrees and resolutions that greatly restricted ejido grants, if not terminating them altogether.[94] His actions sparked protest throughout Mexico, particularly from federal agronomists. They had carried out the first comprehensive postrevolutionary national agrarian census in 1930, concluding from it that agrarian reform should not be slowed or terminated but, rather, accelerated and expanded.[95] From 1930 to 1932, the economic crisis devastated the entire country, and the Laguna was no exception. In 1931, the price of cotton plunged to $5.87 per quintal (11 kilograms) from an average of $20 during the 1920s. With unemployed migrants staying put, expatriate Mexicans returning or deported from the United States, and no prospects for economic betterment, cotton farmers turned to the government for emergency loans. They obtained them through the newly founded Banco Refaccionario de La Laguna (Laguna Loan Bank), an institution that received cash infusions from the Bank of Mexico and the treasury secretary. In spite of the moribund economy, land prices did not decline since the "agrarian problem" seemed to have been resolved.[96]

By 1933, after much lobbying and publication of numerous engineering studies concluding that the dam was technically sound and economically viable, Calles came on board more vocally. In particular, Plácido Vargas wrote in an adulatory manner to Calles:

> The Governor of Coahuila informs us of your enthusiasm for the Nazas Dam and invites you to come and convince users to construct the magna obra. Such an act would crown your high prestige as statesman. 170,000 people depend directly or indirectly on the Nazas waters in this region and there is an urgent humanitarian need to improve the conditions of

40,000 campesinos and families so they can sustain themselves. If such a grand work were completed, your memory would forever endure in the Comarca.[97]

Echoing this, national newspapers reported that building the dam was a "fact," declaring that it enjoyed virtually unanimous support in the Laguna and the SAF's full backing.

In private correspondence among pro-dam landowners, federal engineers, and the governors, however, the outlook was not so sanguine. Two major obstacles still stood in the way of building the dam: how to finance it and to finally resolve the agrarian problem. Despite their hopes, Laguna landowners found that ceding marginal lands in ejidal districts had not prevented agraristas and campesino unions from demanding better-quality land (meaning, with reliable access to water), as well as higher wages and improved working conditions. The resulting tensions caused considerable violence in the region.[98] In an open letter to Calles published in *El Siglo de Torreón* in 1933 that illustrates the persistent need to pressure the federal government to intervene from the bottom up, the private engineer and downriver farmer José de la Fuente described his quest of more than a decade as an effective lobbyist for the cause:

> Since late 1922 I, a user of the Nazas, alone began a campaign of persuasion through articles and talks with users of this river and with members of the agricultural chamber to complete the impounding of the torrential waters of the Nazas.
>
> In early 1926, Mr. Plácido Vargas and other users joined me to form the association for the promotion of a dam on the Nazas. Apart from our work of persuasion and illustration, the association obtained the necessary financing for the work in Canada by means of suitable legislation for a contract, construction, etc., as we demonstrated to the federal government.
>
> In 1929 these same users formed a company, which the SAF recognized, called Nazas River Dam, Inc., and obtained from the government a declaration of public utility for the impounding of the waters of the Nazas River for their improved use.
>
> The agrarian problem of the Laguna is about to be resolved, and few obstacles remain to achieve the wellbeing and prosperity of the region by the only means possible: IMPOUNDING THE WATERS.[99]

On November 4, 1933, the pro-dam lobby achieved something of a coup when Abelardo Rodríguez approved the Nazas dam project for its inclusion in the National Revolutionary Party's Six-Year Plan of 1934. The plan's most important plank reaffirmed the continued viability of Article 27 of the Constitution as "the axis of Mexican social matters so long as the needs of all the campesinos of the country for land and water, in all their integrity, are not satisfied." In a change from previous law, the new agrarian code, which the plan authorized deputies to draft, legalized land petitioning for hacienda peons; until then they had been barred from acquiring land to join ejidos. Nevertheless, a schism erupted between Callistas and newly empowered Cardenistas such as Ramón Beteta. The former saw agrarian reform and creation of ejidos as a step toward small individual private land ownership. The latter viewed them as the foundation for a new socialist economy characterized by land collectivization.[100]

El Siglo de Torreón's editorialists pointed out that the delegates to the National Revolutionary Party's convention in Querétaro had to be prodded to support, and the public had to be reminded of, the dam's importance:

> [The Six-Year Plan] dedicates its best articles to the expansion of agriculture and specifies that in order to increase production it is necessary to construct many irrigation systems; and it enumerates several that are necessary but forgets one of the most important, namely, the Laguna. This region produces like few other agricultural regions of the country and for that reason it needs, more than other regions, a stabilization of its wealth by liberating it from the random character of its agriculture that now distinguishes it. It was necessary that the Coahuila and Durango delegations propose in the Querétaro Convention that the construction of the dam be included in the Six-Year Plan, so that it be *recalled* that this project is one of the most important within the program for agricultural development.[101]

Yet the general public did not need reminding, for federal engineers, landowners, industrialists, and state and local politicians did not exclusively set the terms of debate over the dam. Campesinos, tenants, sharecroppers, peons, agricultural and industrial laborers, and smaller landowners—indeed, the majority of the Laguna's population—also held and expressed their own opinions on modernizing the river regime by damming it. Unfortunately, archival sources have far fewer documents indicating what they thought of this important matter. Nevertheless, transcriptions of a few union meetings, newspaper reports, and correspondence to state and federal authorities indicate strong support for the construction of the dam among rural and urban labor union and party representatives.

For instance, at the seventh Convención de Obreros y Campesinos del Estado de Durango (Convention of Workers and Peasants of Durango), held on

April 1, 1927, in Gómez Palacio, the local union number 24 of the hacienda La Flor of Torreón asked that "a campaign be started in favor of a great dam on the Nazas River so that the storage of great quantities of its waters guarantee irrigation and thus the well-being of campesinos. A letter to this effect shall be sent to the federal government."[102] In December 1929, the secretary-general of the Liga Socialista de San Pedro (Socialist League of San Pedro) wrote a long piece published in the paper supporting the dam on behalf of "small farmers, workers, commerce and industry." He argued that small farmers "played a game of dice" when they irrigated with the uncontrolled Nazas. As a result, in some years the region enjoyed prosperity while in others it suffered misery and desolation. Without the dam, he claimed, the region would never achieve "economic independence" from the vagaries of nature, harming industry and workers alike. He ended the piece with the Socialist League's slogan of "proletarian emancipation."[103]

A few years later, in February 1932, *El Siglo de Torreón* reported on an "important new development." The commission that Coahuila's Governor Nazario S. Ortiz Garza appointed to study the merits of building the dam had solicited input from a committee of the Confederación Sindicalista de Obreros y Campesinos (Syndical Confederation of Workers and Peasants). The committee declared that,

> in the name of more than sixty groups which together represent twelve thousand agricultural and urban workers, this executive committee humbly declares that, after informing itself of this comprehensive and conscientious study of the Nazas River Dam, and for which a regional committee has been established to assess the merits of its completion, the organization Obrera del Municipio de Torreón, fully supportive of the said project, will immediately offer its cooperation for the construction of this wonderful work sure to be beneficial to the Comarca Lagunera.[104]

A year later, Antonio Gutiérrez, an agrarista senator from Durango, sent a declaration to newspapers, which *El Siglo de Torreón* published. In it, he expressed a more elaborated view on what organized campesino constituencies in the region might have thought. Although Gutiérrez favored the dam, he emphasized that individual Nazas water rights acquired by landowners since the late nineteenth century should be nullified or else substantially modified. "I believe," he wrote, "that the Nazas problem should be considered of public utility; local and federal governments intent on resolving the problem should absolutely renounce any individual interests which selfishly always look to take advantage of such problems." He then advocated that the dam's benefits should be spread out among many, not just those most able to take Nazas water through expensive irrigation works, which would undermine the revolutionary ideal of better land distribution.[105]

Without calling for outright expropriation of large properties, Gutiérrez seemed to recommend an envirotechnical middle ground in which the dam could help provide more land for most, less land for a few, but more water for all. His agrarista advocacy and thinking about land and water distribution in the Laguna soon found expression in the person of Lázaro Cárdenas.

3. Distributing El Agua de la Revolución

In brief, we distributed the land among men, but if you ponder a bit, it is clear that it was preferable to distribute men on the land.

LIGA DE AGRÓNOMOS SOCIALISTAS (League of Socialist Agronomists)

The massive Cardenista agrarian reform of the 1930s was one of the most ambitious and far-reaching social experiments of its kind in Latin America, if not the world. Nationwide, it distributed a total of 45 million acres of land to eleven thousand ejidos populated by nearly a million people. Although in the decades thereafter his successors mostly neglected or undermined the ejido as the central institution of Mexican agrarian reform, collective memory has kept the legacy of Lázaro Cárdenas alive. Nowhere is this more the case than in the Laguna's ejidos, where Cárdenas remains a secular saint whose efforts continue to be venerated to this day.[1] This veneration reflects the fact that Cárdenas crafted his new nationwide agrarian reform by drawing on policies and institutions in gestation or development since the Revolution, such as the Banco Nacional de Crédito Agrícola (National Agricultural Credit Bank), the Comisión Nacional Agraria (National Agrarian Commission), the Departamento Agrario (Agrarian Department), and the Comisión Nacional de Irrigación (National Irrigation Commission; CNI), and by choosing the most extensive and (historically, at least) economically important commercial agricultural regions.[2] He sought to secure the economic independence of "collective" ejidos by cooperatively integrating work, production, and credit under government auspices, for he believed that, in the long run, ejidos would prove more socioeconomically viable than the expropriated haciendas they replaced.[3] As a result, the Laguna, with its 226 medium-size and large cotton and wheat estates and impressively organized agroindustrial workforce, was the model for transforming Mexico's agrarian structure.

On October 6, 1936, the government announced the resolution (*acuerdo*) for the Laguna, incorporating various components of the evolving and often confusing agrarian and water legislation passed since 1917.[4] It warned landowners that agrarian reform was irreversible, and instead of resisting, it was in their best interest and the nation's to cooperate with the authorities so that their agricultural workers (soon to be transformed into ejidatarios) could lawfully enjoy the region's economic development. Unsurprisingly, landowners were stunned, but their protests by then were futile.[5]

The government executed the decree swiftly and decisively. It sent three hundred técnicos to the region, many of them students, to survey and demarcate the land. Time was of the essence, for if they did not distribute the land rapidly enough to prepare for aniego, sowed fields would not retain the moisture necessary for plant growth. By October 18, from six to twenty ejidos were receiving land daily. Despite the reduction of paperwork to expedite land petitions, implementation of the decree began to flounder in late October. Cárdenas thus personally traveled to the region, arriving in San Pedro on November 9, and installed his office in a modest house once owned by Francisco I. Madero. Seated at a desk in front of a portrait of Emiliano Zapata, he spent three weeks working twelve to fifteen hours daily supervising the distribution of estates to newly created ejidos, small properties, and colonies. He also spent much time personally appealing to and persuading hacienda peons to join ejidos.[6]

A military and civilian contingent of five state secretaries, engineers, doctors, lawyers, economists, professors, and students joined Cárdenas in this massive mobilization effort, including Secretary Saturnino Cedillo of the Secretaría de Agricultura y Fomento (Ministry of Agriculture and Development; SAF); Carlos Peralta, director of the new Banco Nacional de Crédito Ejidal (National Ejido Credit Bank); Gabino Vázquez, director of the Agrarian Department; Interior Subminister Agustín Arroyo Ch.; Ramón Beteta, director of the Laguna Study Commission and Cardenista ideologue; and the governors of Coahuila and Durango.[7] During the mobilization, Cárdenas highlighted the leading role of engineers to the general secretaries of the campesino unions gathered to hear him speak in San Pedro:

> When the personnel of the Agrarian Department present themselves, the honorable engineers responsible for distributing the land will assemble the ejidatarios of each community [*poblado*] so that in the Assembly they can inform the ejidatarios of the available resources for which

they will be responsible for ejido crops. [They will do this] while expecting the sincerity and comprehensive spirit which animates you, resolves your differences and lets you live going forward as a single family; in this way you will be provided the best proof of solidarity from a government that has fulfilled its obligation to give you the necessary land and credit.[8]

Just as he spoke, however, Cárdenas's engineers belied his confidence in them in reams of confidential documentation that they produced. In those documents, they urgently warned him that they had not resolved the principal challenge on which the entire enterprise of his reparto de tierras hinged: the reparto de aguas, or supplying the new land regime with a clean, reliable, and regular supply of water. How they confronted this challenge under circumstances largely out of their control follows.

The Hydraulic Complement to Agrarian Reform

In November 1934, Cárdenas, a reformist general and former governor of Michoacán, was inaugurated president under the shadow of Plutarco Elías Calles. Calles expected to continue acting as powerbroker behind the scenes, as he had done to varying degrees during the three previous short-lived presidencies.[9] Cárdenas, however, categorically rejected this role and exiled his erstwhile mentor, purged most Callistas from positions of power and influence, and proceeded to implement nearly six years of what, among other terms, scholars have variously described as "radical," "populist," "missionary," "utopian," "socialist," and "bourgeois-democratic" rule. The numerous narratives have long characterized the Cárdenas presidency as fulfilling the promises of the Revolution inscribed in the 1917 Constitution via transformative policies on agrarian reform, labor rights, socialist education, nationalization of oil, and other controversial issues. Cárdenas was the first postrevolutionary president with the mettle to carry out the will of the "masses" and to build the political structures that would represent and sustain them in a hegemonic party system—a process that Chris Boyer has aptly termed "regimented empowerment."[10]

When Cárdenas began his term in late 1934, the Laguna had recovered significantly from the nadir of the Great Depression in 1932. From 1932 to 1934, cotton prices modestly recovered and stabilized, and cultivation was exceptionally good, thanks to large river flows enabling farmers to water their lands liberally through aniego and supplementary pump-installed wells. In 1932–33, they cultivated 175,000 bales of cotton and 50,000 tons of wheat. Nevertheless, postrevolutionary labor organizing and mobilization intensified during the 1930s, led by the Communist Party's Confederación Socialista Unificada de México (Unified Socialist Confederation of Mexico), which was a founding member of the Comité Nacional de Defensa Proletaria en México (National Committee of Proletarian Defense in Mexico) in June 1935. The committee's aggressive organizing efforts, along with the noncommunist Confederación Federal del Trabajo (Federal Confederation of Work), Liga de Comunidades Agrarias (League of Agrarian Communities), and Federación de Sindicatos de Obreros y Campesinos de la Comarca Lagunera (Federation of Worker and Campesino Unions of the Comarca Lagunera), began to bear fruit. As a result, some large landowners formed reactionary "white unions" and "white guards" among their loyal resident peons to fight such "red unions."[11] In this polarized environment, the Laguna appeared headed for civil war for the third time in a generation (General José Gonzalo Escobar's uprising of 1929 and the Revolution of the 1910s being the previous two times).

As labor and campesino mobilization reached an unprecedented level in the Laguna by mid-1935, with Cárdenas's acquiescence or approval, many landowners saw the writing on the wall and prepared themselves for major expropriation. They included Plácido Vargas, who moved to Mexico City in 1935 in anticipation of losing his land but continued to lobby for the Nazas dam from afar. Even without his land, he held the conviction that the dam was the solution to virtually all of the region's problems.[12] Yet the largest landowners, primarily in the upriver zone, still contested the project. They considered it little more than government engineering of the river regime to serve radical agrarista ends.

The informal representative of these upriver landowners, Mario Blázquez, represented dam skeptics in intensive negotiations with dam proponents and CNI officials. The skeptics appeared to accept the dam as inevitable, and in February 1935 the two sides reached a binding agreement. The agreement included federal guarantees that the dam would be technically and financially feasible, that existing water rights would be protected, and that the agrarian problem would be promptly settled before its construction. In addition, the two sides created a "mixed committee," consisting of Nazas water users and CNI engineers, to oversee the engineering studies and project completion. In a gesture of sycophancy, they also voted to name the dam "Lázaro Cárdenas." After years of persistent lobbying and negotiations among various groups beginning with the Porfirian-era Nazas River Inspection Commission, this unprecedented agreement appeared to embrace and codify a private-public partnership and local-federal cooperation. For the skeptics, the agreement ensured that the dam's ultimate social purpose was to complement and not radically alter the Laguna's existing land and water regimes.[13]

Despite the agreement, however, Cárdenas began to send mixed signals as agrarian and labor militancy greatly intensified in mid-1935. At that time, red unions launched a strike in Gómez Palacio's Manila hacienda over wages and working conditions but said nothing regarding land or water. The strike spurred greater unionization throughout the Laguna, including a rural unionization drive that developed ties to larger national groups who reached out to both workers and campesinos and who explicitly defended the Cárdenas administration. As strikes spread through the summer and fall of 1935, urban unions in Torreón and Gómez Palacio actively supported their rural counterparts in acts of rural-urban "proletarian solidarity," blurring the boundaries between the two.[14]

Major strikes in Monterrey emboldened the Confederación de Trabajadores de México (Workers' Confederation of Mexico; CTM) founded by the Marxist intellectual and labor organizer Vicente Lombardo Toledano in February 1936, and its local Communist Party organizer in the Laguna, Dionisio Encinas, to spread strikes further in the region. Unlike before, however, the strikers explicitly demanded agrarian reform. In June 1935, Lombardo Toledano had called for subdividing haciendas into maximum extensions of 200 hectares and granting ejidos to agrarian communities and hacienda peons, but Cárdenas and the Confederación Campesina Mexicana (Mexican Peasant Confederation; CCM) of the Partido Nacional Revolucionario (National Revolutionary Party; PNR) opposed the CTM's demand for land; they wanted to keep the rural and urban workers' organizations separate lest they become too powerful and undermine the ruling party. Nevertheless, in the Laguna a temporary "worker-campesino alliance" formed in May 1936 when both agrarian and urban unions began to call broadly for land distribution and for land grants to hacienda peons in fulfillment of the 1934 Agrarian Code.[15]

Along with the threat posed by rural and urban labor mobilization, the impending construction of a high dam on the Nazas ominously occupied the minds of Laguna landowners. As they perceived it, the two went hand in glove: Tlahualilo representatives remarked, for instance, in September 1935 that "the planters know from very reliable sources that the government has decided to undertake construction of the dam, and in that case they are very much afraid that the water will be distributed among the ejidos and 'pequeñas propiedades'; therefore we will probably be despoiled of the largest part of our property and the corresponding water rights. . . . If the government builds the dam, it makes it more imperative for us to subdivide our property."[16] They also recounted a personal meeting between Blázquez and Cárdenas in December 1935 regarding construction of the dam. At the meeting, Blázquez communicated the concerns of Laguna landowners, including Tlahualilo, over unilateral changes the president had made to the February 1935 agreement. The president's changes effectively downgraded the landowners' role in the cooperative venture, as they understood it. Blázquez nevertheless expressed, perhaps out of desperation, the landowners' continued "enthusiasm" to cooperate with the president. The president made it clear, however, that he intended to change the agreement, since the more favorable economic climate that year enabled the government to undertake all the studies and finance dam construction itself. The president's message was thus loud and clear: the government would build the dam unilaterally. He then asked Blázquez whether his insistent offer of cooperation derived from a fear that existing water rights would be revoked. Blázquez replied affirmatively, but the president reassured him that Laguna landowners' water rights were safe and he should relay that reassurance to them.[17]

In July 1936, as tensions mounted over land and labor issues, Cárdenas planned a visit to the Laguna. In anticipation of his arrival, the region's two principal newspapers sent him questionnaires about his plans for the region, indicating the importance of the dam and pumps to their readers. Indeed, of the sixteen questions *El Siglo de Torreón* asked him, the first few were about building the dam and powering groundwater pumps, followed by questions about labor and land reform. Specifically, the paper asked: "Do you propose to finish the dam on the Nazas during your presidential term? Will the government complete this 'magna obra' directly, or will you outsource it to some special company? Given the necessity to continue extracting groundwater in the region, even after the dam is built and taking into account the fact that the CFE [Comisión Federal de Electricidad/Federal Electricity Commission] refuses to connect new pumping plants, will the government take some measure to remedy this deficiency?"

By contrast, *La Opinión,* which opposed the dam in the 1920s, asked a total of ten questions. Only the last two were about the dam, but both indicated the editors' continued skepticism toward it: "Will not the construction of the Dam on the Nazas River in 'El Palmito' cause future problems for distributing water between the upriver and downriver regions of the Laguna resulting from existing water rights? From a technical point of view, will not the construction of the Nazas Dam diminish the quality of Laguna lands for the lack of alluvium in its [Nazas River's] flow?"

Cárdenas gave a generic answer to the questions, identical to the propaganda of dam proponents, especially his CNI técnicos: "The construction of the Palmito Dam to store the waters of the Nazas River will bring greater prosperity to the Laguna region because it will normalize and ensure irrigation. [Moreover] the reservoir in itself will enable the generation of power to expand regional cultivation to 100,000 hectares. When added to the 200,000 that will be irrigated with the reservoir [water], it will ensure that we can cultivate more than 300,000 hectares."[18]

A few weeks later, from August 18 to September 3, 1936, twenty thousand unionized peons launched and sustained a general strike on 104 haciendas in Coahuila and Durango, increasing to more than 150 haciendas (out of 226) by its end. Most of their demands were for higher minimum wages, housing, drinking water supplies, and medical attention, but one did include a call for land in the form of plots (*lotes de tierra*). During these fifteen days that shook Mexico, Cárdenas informed the Laguna Strike Committee, including prominent Communist Party members, that he would authorize subdivision of hacienda lands among fifteen thousand eligible peons in exchange for the strike's termination. On August 31, the Federación de Trabajadores de la Región Lagunera (Workers' Federation of the Laguna Region) agreed to the arrangement and ordered its members to resume work.[19]

For the next month, between the end of the strike and the expropriation decree, landowner associations and campesino and worker unions accused each other of sabotaging agricultural production, particularly by neglecting to irrigate sowed fields while the Nazas River flowed. For example, Mariano Padilla, secretary of the Federation of Worker and Campesino Unions of the Comarca Lagunera, telegrammed Cárdenas to request his intervention "to prevent the majority of haciendas from wasting water by letting it flow into the vegas [low-lying areas] and down the river course to the Mayrán lagoon." He claimed that the subchief of military operations in Torreón had instructions to give hacendados guarantees that they could do as they pleased on their property with complete freedom.[20] Noting that the investigative commission had not arrived, Benigno Martínez, secretary of the Sindicato de Comerciantes en Pequeño y Trabajadores de la Federación de la Región Lagunera (Laguna Federation of Small Merchants and Workers), also complained to Cárdenas in a telegram that an unnamed hacienda was "maneuvering" to hoard water in vegas where it could not flow out or otherwise to let it inundate areas with roads and paths.[21] By contrast, Pedro Suinaga Luján, secretary of the Comisión de Agricultores Pro Resolución al Problema Agrario de la Comarca Lagunera (Farmers' Commission for the Resolution of the Laguna Agrarian Problem), wrote that landowners had spent large sums of money to prepare for aniego as the Nazas flowed, despite the threat the CTM posed to them. They reported that engineers from the Agrarian Department and the Ejido Bank had surveyed their land for subdivision, but without any guarantees that they would be able to cultivate their crops on their still intact properties, they could not obtain financing for the expensive preliminary work required for cultivation.[22]

Cárdenas appeared aware of the situation, for a few weeks earlier, during the general strike, he telegraphed the governors of Coahuila and Durango that he had ordered the Agrarian Department and the Ejido Bank to each designate an engineer to send to the Laguna. The engineers were to investigate the wasting of the Nazas flow and report back to him on what urgent measures the government should take to ensure its use for immediate cultivation of the land. The director of the Agrarian Department replied that he would send Román Ayluardo, chief of the Water Office, and Inspector J. Trinidad Rangel Carrillo.[23] Local actors on all sides looked to these técnicos as mediators of envirotechnical knowledge, if not troubleshooters, who could help resolve the water problem amid the growing land and labor conflicts. J. Isabel García, secretary of the Federation of Workers in the Laguna, had accused the owners of the La Palma, La Victoria, Santa Lucía, Filipinas, and San José del Viñedo y California haciendas of wasting water by dumping it in the vegas and dismantling their pumps. He claimed this water wasting was part of a planned strike (*paro*) that landowners had threatened in late August 1936 in retaliation for the impending workers' strike. He hoped the engineers responsible for surveying land for the forthcoming subdivision that Cárdenas announced after the workers' strike would halt these hacienda "maneuvers" (*maniobras*).[24] Another Lagunero, E. Rojas Miranda, asked Cárdenas for "absolutely trustworthy" people, presumably engineers, to review campesinos' charges that landowners were wasting water, to determine who exactly was right.[25]

Responding to accusations from the campesino union that hacendados confiscated mules, pumps, and machinery to disemploy campesinos, Governor Enrique Calderón R. of Durango personally traveled to the ranchos and haciendas on the Durango side of the Nazas, including Sacramento and Tlahualilo, to investigate. He concluded that most charges were "unfounded," as the general situation was "normal" and labor conditions were "correct." At worst, only two smaller property owners had taken away a motor and mules from their campesinos. Perhaps to show his solidarity with campesinos after effectively corroborating the landowners' views, the governor also mentioned that he supplied a group of campesinos from San José del Viñedo with generous relief aid after the river crested and left them stranded on its bank.[26]

The counsel (*consejero*) of the Agrarian Department and future governor of Coahuila, Pedro V. Rodríguez Triana, reported in late September 1936 that neither landowners nor campesinos took advantage of the flowing Nazas.

This gave landowners the pretext—"with some justifiable exceptions," in his judgment—that they could not harvest their cotton since striking unionized workers prevented bonanceros (nonunionized migrant workers, many of whom had been hired as scabs) from entering the haciendas. For their part, campesinos also feared the consequences of wasting water and were determined to irrigate the land, or demand that landowners let them do so. Rodríguez Triana revealed to Cárdenas that the Laguna Ejido Unión had assembled on September 18 and named a special commission charged with water management and labor organizing to collaborate with government representatives.

Most notable among the government representatives was the Nazas River Inspection Commission, which reported it was allocating existing water concessions without verifying whether they were actually being used. The commission warned that the Nazas would flow for only twenty more days, delivering an average of 60,000 cubic meters per second.[27] Lombardo Toledano also telegraphed Cárdenas on behalf of the Torreón branch of the CTM that hacendados continued to waste water and dismantle pumps, and that he should intervene to make the "dangerous number" of bonanceros remaining in the region leave.[28] The danger to him arose from the sheer number of bonanceros; there were an estimated ten thousand more of them than the average migrant yearly population in the Laguna.[29]

As the Nazas flowed past land left unprepared for aniego, and Cárdenas adopted a more radical agrarista position toward the Laguna conflict under his adviser Beteta's influence, Manuel Gómez Morín—the lawyer, banker, one-time rector of the Universidad Nacional Autónoma de México (National Autonomous University of Mexico; UNAM), and future founder of the opposition rightist Partido Acción Nacional—proposed his own "considerations on the Laguna problem." As a former adviser to the Laguna Cotton Loan Bank, he knew the region well, and a couple of weeks before the reparto de tierras, he critiqued the two policies he expected Cárdenas to choose from: application of the 1934 Agrarian Code to all hacienda peons in the Laguna or the collectivist route, something he believed had failed in other countries (he had worked for the Soviet embassy in Mexico).[30]

Both would lead to disaster, he argued, since they would lower productivity and there was no government money to offer proper compensation to landowners. Instead, he recommended a "third way," one that was similar to the engineers' commission of inquiry of 1928 under Calles: construction of the dam and completion of the ejidal districts, indispensable for dividing the surplus land of large haciendas into 100–150 hectare lots in accordance with the Agrarian Code. Landowners were unable to sell surplus land, not because of a lack of desire, but because prospective buyers, familiar with the Laguna's irrigation system and fearing a radical agrarian reform, refrained from making large land purchases. Being the laissez-faire "revolutionary" that he was, Gómez Morín proposed that peons be allowed to share in the haciendas' profits. He believed the Laguna campesino would "prefer the security of this type of contract with a reasonable work day and the advantages of participating in the profit generation of the boss" rather than risk facing the Nazas river flow's instability, the dangers of pest infestations, and cotton price volatility alone.[31]

Gómez Morín, however, was apparently unaware that Cárdenas had already ordered construction of the dam, on which engineers had been busy at work since January 1936. Ten months later, on October 6, and nearly thirty years after Madero's unsuccessful meeting to launch a lobbying campaign among sympathetic Laguna landowners, Cárdenas had made the dam-in-progress the indispensable hydraulic complement to his massive reparto de tierras. He left it to his anxious engineers, however, to solve just how the reparto de aguas dependent on an unfinished dam would actually complement this grand social experiment.

Reparto de Tierras versus Reparto de Aguas

On November 28, 1936, the national press announced the end of the "agrarian problem" in the Laguna, and two days later, from a radio studio in Torreón, Cárdenas broadcast to the nation that the Laguna's reparto de tierras was complete and had fulfilled the legal mandates of both Article 27 of the Constitution and the 1934 Agrarian Code. Indeed, the reparto was a historic achievement. According to a census the Agrarian Department rapidly conducted in October 1936, there were forty-one thousand mostly landless agricultural workers in the region, of whom ten thousand were former strikebreakers, fifteen thousand were migrant workers, and sixteen thousand were hacienda peons. Six weeks later, the government had transformed twenty-eight thousand of them into ejidatarios. By 1938, a total of thirty-eight thousand heads of families within ejidos had received 67 percent, or 146,000 hectares, of the region's total irrigable land area of 218,000 hectares. Thirty-one percent, or 67,000 hectares, of the remainder went to small landholdings and 2 percent, or 5,000 hectares, went to colonists. These figures, however, translated into 3.8 hectares, 16.7 hectares, and 39.3 hectares per capita for ejidos, colonists, and small landholders, respectively. The Ejido Bank organized ejidos into 312 collective associations (*sociedades colectivas*) and had the task of distributing credit, seed, fertilizer, and machinery to all of them. In addition, the government promised every ejido a school, recreation area, plaza, gardens, markets, social service buildings, nurseries, and a host of other amenities and facilities.[32]

An intrepid American journalist, Marshall Hail of the *Washington Daily News,* provided a generally sympathetic outsider's account of the several days he spent in late November 1936 covering "probably the most advanced social experiment in the Western Hemisphere." Quoting Cárdenas that "the Mexican Revolution . . . is resolved to settle the problems of land, water, financing and education in the Laguna," Hail noted the high stakes involved, for "if the Laguna experiment fails, there could be a Spanish-like Civil War," given the similarities between the two countries' agrarian reforms.[33] With some exaggeration, he reported that "in the Laguna, workers and campesinos suffer from over-organization rather than lack of organization . . . the peon has fared so well in collective bargaining through union activity that he is dubious about being a prosperous landowner under the government's scheme." Moreover, "Like the peons, the landowners are divided in their reactions to the expropriation program. Most of them—when assured that they will not be quoted—curse the government. But none has any serious thought of fomenting armed resistance." Hail even found one hacendado supportive of the reform:

> The attitude of Antonio Juambelz, young publisher of *El Siglo de Tor-reón,* the leading newspaper in the region, is remarkable. Juambelz is a dispossessed hacendado himself, the government having separated him from a farm valued at a quarter of a million pesos. "It saddens me greatly to lose my land," smiled Publisher Juambelz, cheerfully puffing at a cigar. "The expropriation program is so big that no human beings, however expert, could put it into effect without creating a difficult transition period. It has to be done quickly, because of the peculiar irrigation and land cultivation conditions. Time is against the government. So far it has had a disastrous effect on business in the region. It has hurt my newspaper business. But basically I believe that agrarian reform is just. I did not work my land myself. I merely collected rentals from it. Why shouldn't it go to those who work it? You see, I was brought up during the revolutionary period."[34]

Others were simply puzzled as to how the government could even carry out the reform. T. M. Fairburn, assistant general manager of the Tlahualilo Estate, corresponding with his superiors in London and New York about the threat of expropriation after the promulgation of the 1934 Agrarian Code, wondered aloud: "As far as I know we do not propose to subdivide the property until it is forced upon us by law. The property does not lend itself to subdivision on account of water distribution and the tremendous distance from headgates to the property. Let us suppose that the property was divided up into 10 or 20 units and that Zaragoza [one of the Tlahualilo ranches] was one of these units. What in the world would the other units do for domestic water when their tanks went dry?"[35] Two-and-a-half years hence, when the dreaded reform finally materialized, Tlahualilo's manager John Holby defended the company's labor record, telling Hail:

> We believe that our workers have received a better deal from us than they could have got anywhere else. We give them free medical service. For 30 years we have provided schools for our employees and paid the teachers. We taught up to the sixth grade, though the law required only to the fourth. We have always paid better wages than the average. Since August 1935, the minimum wage was advanced from 1 peso to 1.5 pesos a day (50 to 75 cents), and later the seventh-day payment made it 1.75 a day. But our laborers here make as high as 3 and 4 pesos a day. Because of the uncertain water supply we have lean years. One year we raised only 200 bales of cotton. But in the bad years we have cared for our employees. During the revolution we brought in trainloads of food for our people.[36]

These property owners' reactions pointed to the principal challenge of the reparto de tierras: making it compatible with a reparto de aguas that the government had yet to engineer. Productivity, employment, and wages depended directly upon the availability of water in the Laguna; as hacendados had long argued, with substantial disingenuousness to be sure, it was nature's fault if there was no work or they had to pay low wages, and not because the prevailing social relations of production prioritized profits over workers.[37]

When Cárdenas arrived to personally supervise the reparto de tierras in November 1936, hydraulic engineers fretted. How would they harmonize it with the reparto de aguas? Although the fanfare over the Palmito Dam's groundbreaking in late 1936 and early 1937 highlighted how many in the region and the nation expected it to be the technological panacea for the water issue, what they overlooked in their celebration was a simple but important question: what was the government's plan in the three- to four-year interim until the expected completion of the dam?

The existing regulatory framework for apportioning water that Porfirian-era engineers had painstakingly devised in 1895, and modified in 1909, continued to function fairly effectively, but after a quarter-century of tumultuous change in the region and the country, Cardenista técnicos increasingly felt that

TABLE 3.1. 1909 regulation

Region	Dams	Canals
Upriver	Santa Margarita	Santa Margarita
Upriver	San Fernando	San Fernando, Tlahualilo, Municipio, San Antonio
Upriver	Santa Rosa	Santa Rosa
Upriver	Calabazas	San Ramón, Relámpago, Sacramento, Santa Cruz
Upriver	Coyote	Torreón, Concepción, Coyote
Downriver	Cuije	Cuije
Downriver	Guadalupe	Bilbao, Santa Teresa, Santa Lucía, Concordia, Tajo Unido, San Lorenzo, Dolores, San Francisco, Trasquila
Downriver	San Pedro	Bolívar, Sangría de Benavides, San Isidro, Guadalupe
Downriver	Colonia	San Marcos, Yucatán, Zaragoza
Downriver	De Mayrán	De Mayrán

SOURCE: Carlos Castañón Cuadros, "Una perspectiva hidráulica de la historia regional: economía y revolución en el agua de La Laguna," *Buenaval*, no. 3 (Winter 2006): 20.

the 1909 regulation was outdated and preserved privilege by benefiting the largest landowners, such as Tlahualilo, Santa Teresa, Lavín, and Luján. Not coincidentally, these large landowners had all also stridently opposed the dam for years. Some engineers thus maligned the prerevolutionary regulation as "onerous" and even "semi-feudal." Negotiated between Díaz's SF Secretary Olegario Molina and Nazas water users, except the Tlahualilo Company (which was then suing the government), the 1909 regulatory framework had divided the Laguna agricultural cycle into three periods: June 1–August 20, August 20–October 20, and October 20–June 1 of the following year. Engineers were to distribute water by *tanda,* or allocation round, according to the location of canals along the river course, thereby allowing users of each canal to take from "normal" to "maximum" amounts of water depending on river flow volume. (For lists of the canals within the "regulated zone" from the San Fernando canal to the river terminus at the Laguna de Mayrán, see tables 3.1–3.2.)

The first five diversion dams listed in table 3.1 sat in the upriver zone, primarily in Durango, while the next four were located in the downriver zone, primarily in Coahuila. Engineers allocated the upriver zone an average of 64 percent of yearly river flows, while the lower zone received 36 percent. The downriver zone's far greater soil fertility largely offset the 2:1 ratio in favor of upriver users, and the downriver zone produced on average 60 percent of total

TABLE 3.2. Capacity of water consumption of principal canals in regulated Nazas River zone (all from upriver zone)

Canals	Normal (cubic meters per second)	Maximum (cubic meters per second)
Santa Margarita	3,000	6,000
San Fernando	3,670	7,340
San Antonio	4,080	8,160
Santa Rosa	12,830	25,660
Santa Cruz	10,933	21,866
Sacramento	16,500	33,000
Relámpago	5,467	10,934
San Ramón	500	1,000
Coyote	21,180	42,360
Concepción	12,330	24,660
Torreón	7,620	15,240
Tlahualilo	27,720	55,440
Total	125,830	251,660

SOURCE: Carlos Castañón Cuadros, "Una perspectiva hidráulica de la historia regional: Economía y revolución en el agua de La Laguna," *Buenaval*, no. 3 (Winter 2006): 20.

harvests, compared with 40 percent for the upriver zone. Gil Ornelas, a downriver landowner and engineer, boasted in 1919 that "in no other area of the country that I've visited have so many advances been made" in measuring, diverting, capturing, and using water—an observation that the more impartial Callista engineers' commission of 1928 corroborated. Specifically, Ornelas explained, "In effect, here we go to every expense and sacrifice to acquire and use all classes of the most advanced implements from the United States and even from some parts of Europe for cultivation and irrigation. Thus not only are the principal canals and dams well designed for the methodical distribution of waters; every hacienda also has a complete and practical system internally for profitably using the water corresponding to each. The cultivation system here breaks completely with the ordinary methods used all over the country."[38] Ornelas irrigated his lands using the Trasquila diversion dam located in the downriver zone. He boasted that thanks "to its construction and system [it] is the second[-largest] in [Latin] America, since the first one was built in Chile a little before. I should make it clear that I conceived of this entirely modern system of German origin as the desideratum in diversion dam materials for torrential rivers."[39]

The increased reliance on new technology in the form of pump-installed wells played a role in making the 1909 regulations work so well for years thereafter, but so, too, did the advent of organizational factors. The formation of a national irrigation policy in the 1920s led to the creation of a commission that gradually assumed the distributive and measuring tasks of the 1891 Nazas River Inspection Commission. A new reparto de aguas thus entailed more than just redistributing water; it also involved creation of new bureaucratic actors and power configurations on the basis of differing ideologies and policies, under the umbrella of the ruling PNR (founded in 1929).[40]

The October 6, 1936, resolution expropriating the Laguna's landed estates stipulated that the new water regime would accompany the new land regime in due course, but it left the specifics for a later time. In the interim, Cárdenas founded a Comisión Mixta de Aguas (Mixed Waters Commission) to serve as an ad hoc body for making recommendations to the president on designing new water regulations. It was composed of representatives from the SAF (under which the CNI was housed), the Ejido Bank, the National Agricultural Credit Bank, and the Agrarian Department.[41] All except the Ejido Bank were Callista creations from the 1920s whose jurisdictions were not always clearly defined and that were thus given to internecine dispute.

Cárdenas sought to fuse both his administration and the PNR into an overarching corporatist system. In his crosshairs was the agency most naturally fit to take charge of designing a new water regime: the CNI, which was not yet a fully Cardenista agency ideologically. It retained bureaucrats committed to Callista goals of colonization through irrigation and a gradual breakup of latifundio to create an agrarian middle class of small individual landholders. They regarded the creation of ejidos as a temporary expedient to achieving this goal rather than as the central institution for agricultural modernization that Cardenistas planned. It would thus take Cárdenas time to change personnel or imbue them with his conviction that irrigation should be the indispensable complement for a radically transformative ejido-centered agrarian reform.[42]

The Mixed Waters Commission produced voluminous documentation in the form of memoranda, reports, studies, and correspondence reflecting the inherent complexities in, and the confusion over, reengineering the Nazas River regime to achieve this Cardenista goal for the Laguna. In January 1937, more than a month after Cárdenas announced the completion of the reparto de tierras, it drafted an executive summary of the work on the reparto de aguas completed since October 6, 1936. The summary conveyed the hydraulic engineers' alarm for the reparto de tierras's prospects without resolution of the "delicate" and "very complicated" water problem. In one of its entries, it described a meeting on November 10, 1936, at which surveyors gathered data for all thirty of the Laguna's principal canals by traversing six thousand miles through the vast irrigation network. The report combined these data with a review of the work of several agencies and numerous técnicos and starkly warned that no agrarian reform could succeed without an adequate supply of water.[43]

The engineers concluded as a consequence of the meeting that it was "absurd to change the current regulations" since it would seriously disrupt regional agriculture. For one, the irrigation system relied on specialized technical and administrative personnel from the defunct Nazas River Inspection Commission, which landowners stopped financing right after the October 6 decree. These personnel were the only ones capable of continuing the smooth distribution of water. The commission's engineers thus did all they could to retain these personnel who had "identified themselves with the ideology of the Supreme Government" and not abandoned their posts. Abandoning their posts would have surely provoked intense conflict over water distribution. Even with these personnel still at their posts, the summary described the status of the Laguna's reparto de aguas in dire terms. It warned that the success of the ejido program depended on a new distribution of water that should be swiftly implemented in a "dictatorial manner" by "perfectly capable and extremely honest men" in order to avert anarchy. Moreover, it called for engineers to implement it strictly according to a law "not dictated by men . . . but rather one IMPOSED BY NATURE" to avoid wasting precious water.[44]

In December 1936, the commission unsuccessfully attempted to meet personally with Cárdenas regarding the reparto de aguas. Instead, it met with Gabino Vázquez del Mercado, assistant secretary of the SAF and director of the Agrarian Department. In that meeting, they agreed that the commission would be dissolved and its duties transferred to the CNI. In the meantime, the commission would accept responsibility for devising new regulations for land and water distribution in accordance with presidential resolutions.[45] Consequently, nature would not impose the law as they had initially sought; men would dictate it after all. Although it was not necessarily averse to acting dictatorially, the CNI simply did not have the power to do so; rather, Article 77 of the Federal Water Law of 1934 allowed water users to make "well-founded complaints" about a new regulation or modification thereof within two years so that the ministry in charge could "resolve [it] as appropriate."[46]

The CNI confronted two daunting challenges beginning in January 1937 when it assumed management of the Nazas River regime. The first was that since the regulation of 1895, which the regulation of 1909 modified to the advantage of downriver users, the number of large diversion dams grew from seven to twelve, and the number of canals grew from twenty-two to twenty-nine (thirty, including a *sangría,* or smaller drainage ditch), and, much more significant, the number of motorized pumps installed by farmers rapidly grew. As a result, irrigated area increased from a maximum capacity of 60,000 hectares before the new hydraulic infrastructure to 200,000 hectares (but in practice rarely exceeded 160,000 hectares) after it. Second, according to a report by the engineer Joaquín Serrano, director of the Regulatory Section of the Mixed Waters Commission, addressed to the chief of the Geography, Meteorology and Hydrology Section of the SAF's Department of Water Regulation, in the nearly thirty years from Díaz's decree of the regulations just before the Revolution up to 1937, the government had never carried out a comprehensive cadastral survey of irrigated lands.[47]

Serrano explained that the first 1895 regulation had authorized Nazas users to sell or transfer their water allocations independently of federal authority once water flowed into their canals. The result was that tandas did not correspond to the actual needs of landowners. Some received far more water than they needed, and others received far too little, making for "great complication in the distribution" of water and "lack of equity." Moreover, in the downriver region, the 1909 modifications to the 1895 regulation rendered distribution highly "defective," as they were based on distribution by diversion dam and not by canal.[48] That is, as the tables earlier in this chapter indicate, one diversion dam could serve various canals. Consequently, no fixed volume of water was allocated to each property; rather, fixed volumes were allocated to *groups* of properties. This regulatory arrangement created a kind of watering free-for-all in the downriver region, particularly for the Guadalupe Dam because it served nine canals.

To be sure, Serrano observed that subdivision of landed estates to create ejidos in the Laguna complicated an already intricate water regime, but this further complexity only made changes in the existing water regulation all the more urgent, and not just for greater simplicity and equity. It was also critical to bring water distribution into compliance with presidential resolutions that in some cases had arbitrarily, and often incorrectly, classified land as irrigated, pasture, or barren. In spite of the urgency with which the Mixed Waters Commission produced its report in November 1936, Serrano judged that the CNI was less eager to assume responsibility for designing new regulations in January 1937. The CNI countered that the reparto de tierras had to be completed before it could be harmonized with a new reparto de aguas, both directly from the river and within all the canals. However, the CNI did agree that since, according to its data, "90 percent of irrigated lands" belonged to ejidos, a new distribution prioritizing ejidos as the largest group of water users was imperative.[49]

Serrano believed the government should preserve the old irrigation system by tanda and keep existing water allocations to each canal. Importantly, he recommended that the CNI maintain limits on water transfers between one diversion dam and another to conserve water. However, he urged that new regulations allow distribution of water *within* the canals. As a result, he believed, the best option with the time available (March–May 1937) was for the CNI—as the agency with sufficient resources at hand—to formulate a general plan for the region that included a long-overdue cadastral survey to demarcate property boundaries. The CNI accepted his view and based the new reparto de aguas on this plan, which included a survey. Without a proper survey, the government would have to rely on far more unreliable sources, such as private maps and presidential resolutions that arbitrarily fixed ejido land areas. With one, it could more easily devise a general plan by studying the kind of hydraulic works necessary to "counteract" the natural conditions of the Nazas River's current and facilitate more equitable distribution of river flow.[50]

More than a year later, the CNI engineer Francisco Allen observed in a memo to SAF Secretary José G. Parres that although the reparto de tierras changed the property regime, "it did not alter the river regime one bit."[51] Allen was instrumental in lobbying the government to build the dam in the 1920s and 1930s, and under Cárdenas he became president of the Mixed Regulatory Commission for the Nazas and Aguanaval rivers, which replaced the Mixed Waters Commission. By "river regime," Allen clearly referred to the unregulated river, but Serrano had observed alarming environmental changes in his report that did in fact indicate a changed river regime: the riverbed had increased its permeability due to the over-pumping of groundwater.[52] On November 16, 1936, while Cárdenas was still in the Laguna expediting land petitions to ejidos, the Mixed Waters Commission warned that excessive drilling of new wells should be halted, and drilling in general should be regulated. Unregulated pumping was drawing down the regional aquifer and diminishing the irrigable land area being distributed to ejidos.[53] The presidential decree of December 15, 1936 (discussed later), subsequently ordered the CNI to study and propose a regulation for well-water usage and its legal basis.

In April 1937, the CNI geohydrologist Paul Waitz followed up on the Mixed Waters Commission's memo in a long report on how profligate pumping in the region depleted the aquifer. In 1932 and 1934—both years when the flow of the Nazas was low and drilling common—he remarked, there was a marked drop in the water table. Depending on the area and well, the level dropped to between 7 meters and 15 meters. By 1935, the levels around Torreón, he explained, had dropped further to between 15 meters and 20 meters. He concluded that continuing extractions from the aquifer would ultimately affect "every well throughout the region," even beyond zones where pumping was most intense.[54]

The "absolute limit," he continued, of possible extractions would be reached when they equaled the volume that underground aquifer levels received from rainfall, river flow, or artificial recharge, but before this would even occur, Waitz predicted, farmers would hit a "practical economic limit." In other words, it would become too expensive to pump groundwater. With an estimated 900–1,000 pumps already installed in 1937, a tenfold increase over 1926, and 550 more planned, over-pumping would only accelerate, with potentially "disastrous" consequences. Drilling and pumping deeper, Waitz warned, not only disrupted irrigation in the region but required more energy. Already, there had been a shortage of electricity from the CFE since 1933. Local power plants could not provide sufficient energy to power pumps penetrating so deeply underground.[55]

Waitz's proposed solutions included strict regulation of pumping after carefully measuring how much water each pump extracted, prohibiting it in the most exploited zones, and increasing overall extractions only in zones where pumps were already installed and the water table was still high enough—provided that deep well pumps were located at least 500 meters apart. Concerned that salt deposits and other naturally occurring noxious substances contaminated so much of the deeper groundwater, he also encouraged regular chemical analyses. Perhaps most significant, he recommended a thorough juridical study of groundwater pumping to effect a "convenient legalization of groundwater use, not only in the Comarca Lagunera but in the entire country."[56] With a legal framework in place, the government could regulate groundwater and implement the measures he advocated. Echoing Waitz, Allen also expressed his concern for the proliferation of pump-installed wells in a review of the progress of the reparto de aguas. In meetings in June 1938 with his superiors Governor Pedro Rodríguez Triana of Coahuila and Gabino Vázquez, director of the CNI, he recommended that pumping should be merely a "supplementary" means of irrigating wheat and cotton fields. He remarked candidly, "every day [extracting water from wells] becomes more random and costly."[57] The process of legalizing groundwater pumping to regulate it, however, would take ten years to complete.

Motorized pumps nevertheless presented something of a dilemma for técnicos. As Serrano wrote in a riposte to Allen, since the early 1920s, when they spread in large numbers throughout the region, the pumps had become a veritable savior for regional agriculture in the face of devastating infestations, especially the pink bollworm. Without the pumps, he asserted, the Laguna region in general would have been in "ruins." This was already the case in some downriver areas, where during low flow years the salt concentrations rose so high that farmers could not extract groundwater and helplessly watched their crops die. Furthermore, by the late 1930s pumping was so intense in the upriver region that it dried up 95 percent of the wells of urban dwellers in Lerdo, Durango, thereby halting potable water service in the town for several months during the year.[58] Overall, despite the repeated warnings of técnicos beginning in the 1930s, well drilling persisted unabated as construction of the Palmito Dam continued into the 1940s.

What is more, pump-installed wells were not evenly distributed among most ejidos and small landholders, an inequity that the resolution of October 6, 1936, in part created anew and in part exacerbated from preexisting technological and financial conditions. Although the resolution mandated subdivision of estates to create both ejidos and private landholdings no larger than 150 hectares, it was rife with ambiguity and outright contradictions, subjecting it to legal disputes over the meaning of its stipulations. For instance, the third clause of the decree simply stipulated that regulations for water distribution between ejidos and landholders would be forthcoming, while the fourth clause stated that the "agricultural unity" of productive land areas necessary for viability of cultivation would be kept intact. For the third and fourth clauses to concur, strong and precise regulations were necessary to ensure that water distribution did not break up the unity of new land subdivisions. The seventh clause, however, allowed properties reduced to 150 hectares or less of irrigable land, from surface or subterranean sources, to choose the areas they wanted to keep within their properties. This clause effectively undermined the CNI's ability to devise new water regulations that would maintain agricultural unity of productive land areas.

As the League of Socialist Agronomists explained in an oft-quoted passage of its book on the Laguna reparto, by "distributing the land among men rather than men on the land," ejidos and small landholders could not maximize productive land units. The problem, as the agronomists saw it, was the existing agrarian legislation that the October resolution incorporated, which specified that to form an ejido land had to be taken from a circumference of seven kilometers around a population nucleus. It thus encouraged divisions of productive hacienda units or fragmented parcels from a number of haciendas. In addition, former hacendados naturally kept the most productive areas, which were the *cascos* forming the administrative hub as well as the most valuable equipment of the hacienda, including water pumps, installations, and warehouses; or they chose the most irrigable land along canals or communication routes. They could sell the remaining land to relatives, who would acquire the best parcels, leaving, on many occasions, the land of lowest quality to ejidos.[59]

If former hacendados had to give up any valuable equipment, especially pumps, the resolution required compensation from the CNI. Indeed, after completion of the reparto, the engineer Carlos Peralta, director of the Ejido Bank, announced to the "Señores Hacendados" of the Laguna (evidently addressing expropriated small landholders) that the bank would assess the value only of properly functioning pumps and motors ceded to ejidos, not of dismantled pumps that were exempt from compensation. The latter could be repaired and reassessed without penalty of expropriation if completed within ten days, provided hacendados informed the bank of their intention to do so within five days and thereby become eligible for compensation.[60]

Although ejidos did nevertheless obtain some of the best land in the region—and the best land of any other area of the country that Cárdenas targeted for agrarian reform—the inherent contradiction and ambiguity regarding water distribution led to much recrimination and discord between the ejido and small landholding sectors. The Agrarian Code of 1934, on which basis Cárdenas decreed the October 6, 1936, resolution for the Laguna, specified that ejidos had priority access to water sources for agriculture over any and all private landholders after domestic and public uses. Yet this priority of water distribution for ejidos preceded creation of "small landholdings," categorized as possessing 20 hectares or less. These post-agrarian reform small landholders in possession of 20 hectares or less demanded parity in government prioritization of water allocations between themselves and ejidos.

In the year and a half between the October 6 resolution and the new preliminary water regulation that the CNI decreed in April 1938—the one intended to replace the earlier regulations of 1909 until the Palmito Dam was completed—ejido and smallholder representatives lobbied state and federal authorities amid the legal confusion and ambiguity to secure the best possible water allocations for their constituents. Although creation or restitution of ejidos on a massive-scale was the agrarian developmental ethos of the Cárdenas administration, small landholders held considerable advantages in resources, organization, and unity to impress their claims on decision makers, including the president. In the new preliminary regulation, the CNI addressed the concerns of small landholders with 20 hectares or less by ordering priority in water distribution from the Nazas and Aguanaval rivers this way: (1) domestic and public use; (2) proportionality between use on the part of ejidos and small landholdings of 20 hectares or less; (3) use for landholdings between 20 hectares and 150 hectares; and (4) use by all other landholders.

Despite the second clause, which was a victory for very small landholders, the preliminary regulation alarmed other small landholders, especially those who owned as many as 150 hectares, and they also tried to blunt the ejidos' relative advantage in surface water allocations. In July 1938, the newly created civil association Pequeña Propiedad Agrícola de la Comarca Lagunera (Small Landholders of the Laguna Region; PPACL) wrote to SAF Secretary Parres to express surprise on seeing publication of the new preliminary water regulation in May 1938. In their meeting with Cárdenas that same month, PPACL members claimed that the president had not mentioned that he considered the issue of water distribution "resolved." Given the importance of the small landholding sector to the economy, and the government's expectation of an important proportion of agricultural production from it, the PPACL emphasized the need for a more equitable water supply, one in compliance with, per their judgment, the 1934 Agrarian Code and 1934 Federal Water Law.[61] At a meeting in June, Parres and the PPACL representatives met and exchanged views on the impending overhaul of the 1909 regulation. Turnout was high, at about ninety people, and the agenda item they all focused on was a new resolution on water distribution that could satisfy the needs of all sectors, not just ejidos. Attendees requested that people express their opinions in a "practical" and "nonideological" fashion for most effective resolution to the problem.[62]

Agustín Zarzosa, the leader of the PPACL, declared that Laguna landowners had put the past behind them (referring to the 1936 reparto) and were prepared to return to work as they always had. But to do so, they needed the government's recognition of their preexisting water rights, since so many lacked pumps for their wells. Even those landholders fortunate enough to possess pumps could not consistently use them for agriculture because of the enormous cost they incurred, and without crops to grow, they could not afford to hire agricultural workers. Unable to work their land in the previous agricultural cycle of 1937–38, small landholders, Zarzosa pleaded, were in a "distressing" situation. The only measure that could provide small landholders more equitable distribution of water, he continued, was to reinstate the 1909 regulation, "since this regulation takes into account all of the technical aspects of a correct distribution." In other words, as Serrano had also remarked, engineers could distribute water by canal, which Zarzosa argued would be just and equitable, and proportional between the ejido and small landholding sectors.[63]

As the April 1938 regulation on the Laguna's river water made clear, the crux of the issue was one of equity. Who would benefit: thirty-eight thousand ejidatarios or approximately a thousand small landholders? Although the answer appeared obvious to CNI técnicos, Zarzosa reminded them that there were more than ten thousand campesinos working for small landholders who were not ejidatarios, and they, too, had "the right to live." Only reinstating the 1909 regulations, he argued, could prevent the wasting of precious water resources.[64] Yet because they owned more pumps, and despite all of Zarzosa's objections to the contrary, small landholders in general enjoyed better supplies of water than ejidos. For instance, in 1937–38, the first full agricultural cycle after the reparto, the ejido sector cultivated 100,000 hectares, 50,000 hectares of which were irrigated by river flow, 20,000 hectares by a combination of river flow and supplementary groundwater pumping, and 30,000 hectares by pumping only. In all, small landholders possessed approximately five hundred pumps while ejidos possessed six hundred, amounting to 70,000 hectares for small landholders and 140,000 hectares for ejidos. But averaged out, there were 140 hectares per pump for small landholders and 233 for ejidos (per capita, the disparity was even larger).[65]

In addition, because the reform subdivided more or less well-demarcated land units, the relatively few pumps that ejidos acquired were often located in wells at long distances from irrigable lands or in terrain that was too high or too low to irrigate effectively. Much of the pumped water was also of poor quality. The two organizations in charge of ejido affairs, the Collective Ejido Associations and the Ejido Bank, tried to mitigate ejido water shortages by brokering agreements with small landholders to divert groundwater pumped out of their better-located wells into the same canals. Furthermore, the ejido organizations allowed the small landholding sector to sell ejidos their surplus water, of generally superior quality, to reduce unequal distribution. As it was, pump irrigation was considerably more expensive. For example, according to the League of Socialist Agronomists, the bank lent 20,822 pesos to cultivate 100 hectares of cotton with river water and 23,822 pesos with groundwater. The league remarked that despite the scarcity of groundwater—and its high price—ejidos remained overly optimistic in their use of pumps: "Ejidos don't pay much attention to how much water they consume and don't worry about it until [their pumps] cease to function. Many pumps are found completely dismantled and out of use."[66]

In a more precise and less normative assessment, the Mixed Regulatory Commission engineers counted 363 pump-installed wells in Coahuila ejidos, 266 of which ran on "induction" motors, or those supplied from electric current generated in small local power plants, and 97 on internal combustion motors powered by gasoline or diesel. Several of the plants, they remarked, had "very deficient service, due as much to the lack of fuel as to the antiquated state of machinery and recurrent breakdowns, which means regular interruptions for 30 pump installed wells." They stressed that "it is indispensable given the gravity of the situation that the problem of opportunely supplying lubricants and fuel to irrigation wells in the ejido lands be addressed; any delay or deficiency in this supply service delays planting and irrigation, and is strongly reflected as losses in ejido accounts." Moreover, in fifty-one ejidos in Coahuila, they reported, there were problems supplying potable water. As a result, most of these ejidos were obliged to get their water from completely unsanitary troughs, sometimes containing large quantities of salt that endangered public health by causing a high rate of infant mortality. To the commission's engineers, sinking new wells to pump groundwater was not a solution for these fifty-one Coahuilan ejidos because they were located in the downriver area where salt saturated the groundwater. Thirty-four of the ejidos thus each paid small landholders an average of 100 pesos per month for potable water service. "Frequently," the commission engineers observed, "there are difficulties with this arrangement since the small landholders for the most trivial reason threaten ejidos with suspension of water supplies."[67]

Because they could generally obtain more groundwater, small landholders enjoyed more access to credit than ejidos and thereby enjoyed more economic stability. The practical effect was to create a kind of de facto "water apartheid"— that is, by force of undesirable circumstances, ejidos suffered greater insecurity from cheap but fickle river water while small landholders could enjoy the relative security of expensive groundwater as supplemental supply in years of little or low river flow. The Cárdenas administration rejected the PPACL's call in 1938 to reinstate Porfirian-era regulations as a transparent plan to weaken the ejido sector. Yet Cardenista engineers, as before, faced a continuous conundrum, given the limited alternatives with which they had to work: they could either establish a new equitable system that was unworkable without completion of the regulatory Palmito Dam or maintain an outdated system that was the only one they knew to be capable of reducing tensions over the interim reparto de aguas. By devising the new preliminary water regulation in 1938, they chose to do the former.

For ejidos, in contrast to small landholders, the regulation was too little, too late. Insufficient surface water not only impeded the cultivation of crops but also made it more difficult to obtain credit, which increased unemployment. For instance, members of the Águila ejido wrote a letter published in *El Siglo de Torreón* claiming that forty-six campesinos and their families lived in "complete misery." Due to a lack of water, they could plant wheat on only a few hectares of irrigated land, and consequently the Ejido Bank would not provide them with pre-harvest credit. "You cannot imagine how sad our situation is," the letter writer pleaded. "There are days when we don't even have a tortilla for our children, who cry of hunger, driving us to desperation. We don't even have water to slake our thirst." Furthermore, they claimed that they had been unable to drill wells necessary for irrigation and potable water, forcing them to rely on contaminated water supplies.[68]

Nearly a year after the 1938 regulation was promulgated, the representatives of the ejido E. Viñedo of Durango similarly wrote to Cárdenas that they were about to lose their wheat crop for lack of water because they did not have pumps and because engineers had unfairly distributed the last tandas allocated from the Nazas River; they alleged that the tandas had gone to the colonists (*fraccionistas*) of the small landholding sector who possessed many pumps, and no local authority would do anything about it.[69] By contrast, in a memo expressing its "points of view" on the "flawed" 1938 regulation, the PPACL argued that the regulation that prioritized ejidos and landholdings no larger than 20 hectares had no legal basis and "could in no case be applied in the Laguna while the 'El Palmito' Dam was not built," because "it can never be known when there will or will not be water scarcity."[70] As *El Siglo de Torreón* reported in article after article in 1937 and 1938, unemployment and economic hardship cast a shadow over most ejidos and small landholders in the first two years after the reparto de tierras.

According to the economists Iván Restrepo and Salomón Eckstein, who together spent decades analyzing the economic performance of ejidos, however, Laguna cotton production maintained its overall 1930 level in 1940 (but lower in terms of bales harvested per hectare), while wheat production increased substantially (see table 3.3).

The Regulatory Commission that analyzed Coahuila ejidos of the Laguna corroborated these figures: it calculated that in 1936–37, the year of the reparto, Coahuila ejidos cultivated 70,500 hectares—66,000 hectares in cotton and 4,500 hectares in wheat—leaving 32,000 hectares of potentially irrigable land uncultivated. The following year, the Nazas and Aguanaval rivers watered 49,000 hectares, with 25,500 irrigated by pumps, leaving 28,000 hectares uncultivable among irrigable ejido lands. Cotton production dropped to 48,000 hectares; wheat increased to 24,000 hectares; alfalfa came next at 2,000 hectares; and the subsistence crops of maize, beans, and fruit combined for 1,800 hectares. The commission predicted a better year in 1938 agriculturally for the ejidos,

TABLE 3.3. Cultivated Area of Laguna by Decade, 1930–1970

	1930		1940		1950		1960		1970/1	
Crops	Hect	%	Hect	%	Hect	%	Hect	%	Hect	%
Total	127,405	100	166,388	100	158,022	100	144,580	100	153,469	100
Cotton	81,018	63.6	80,277	48.2	94,795	60	106,222	73.5	87,986	57.3
Wheat	26,950	21.1	73,208	44	42,438	26.8	23,591	16.3	13,390	8.7
Corn	11,296	8.8	7,238	4.3	6,058	3.8	7,259	5	7,850	5.1
Green alfalfa	6,929	5.4	3,322	2	4,208	2.6	3,805	2.6	12,278	8
Grapes	235	0.1	279	0.1	1,085	0.6	2,109	1.4	5,786	3.8
Other	977	0.7	2,064	1.2	9,438	6.0	1,594	1.1	26,179	17.1

SOURCE: Restrepo and Eckstein, *La agricultura colectiva en México: la experiencia de La Laguna*, 66.

and it praised their skills: "The preparatory work for cotton cultivation, which is the principal crop, has been done following refined methods over many years of practice in every one of the regions, which will ensure the success of the crops, except in unforeseen circumstances beyond human control. In general terms, one could say that there is not a single cultivable area in the Coahuila portion of the Laguna that has been lost." In particular, they declared that the wheat crop was in "unbeatable" (*inmejorables*) condition; they particularly encouraged growing subsistence crops by each individual family for domestic consumption "when it did not harm the crops of collective labor" because it would improve family nutrition and thereby make the ejidatario feel more rooted and the exclusive beneficiary of his small parcel.[71]

Other aggregate figures (see appendix 1) also show a relative decline in harvested bales from 1936 to 1940, but not a precipitous decline. Given that the flow of the Nazas was large for three of those years (more than two million cubic meters), however, the difficult transition and coordination from the old land regime to new, and then the old water regime to new, certainly took a toll on production and socioeconomic well-being. But this was to be expected, as Cárdenas argued at the time and continued to do years later: "The ejido shoulders a double responsibility—as a social system, it must free the campesino from the exploitation to which he was subject under both the feudal and the individualistic regimes; and as a mode of agricultural production, it must yield enough to furnish the nation with its food requirements." The social intention would come first; production, second.[72]

Unfortunately for Cárdenas, the country's economic reality demanded that production would have to come first. In addition to the Laguna, Cárdenas sought to create a new irrigated cotton zone in Matamoros and expropriated the rich cotton lands of Mexicali, largely at the expense of the American Colorado River Land Company. By 1937, the government was in control of more than half the cotton producing zones of the country thanks to the implementation of its agrarian reform decrees. It thus faced the formidable task of financing, coordinating, and commercializing the cotton crop. The Houston-based Anderson Clayton Company was the world's largest cotton distributor and marketer and had been doing business in Mexico since 1921. By the early 1930s, it financed much of Mexico's crop in these northern regions, and Cárdenas turned to the company to finance and market ejido cotton production. Anderson Clayton obliged, seeking growth in foreign countries to offset New Deal mandates for decreases in U.S. cotton production. Luis Montes de Oca, president of the Bank of Mexico, and William Clayton, the owner of Anderson Clayton, met to forge agreements according to which Clayton's company would finance Mexican ejido cotton through the Ejido Bank.[73]

Since the mid-1920s, Laguna cotton farmers and Anderson Clayton had endured a sometimes tense relationship. In 1925, in a letter published in *El Siglo de Torreón*, J. Paul King, the company's representative in Mexico, informed Laguna farmers that the company had marketed and sold some of their cotton in Europe. King wrote that Europeans were generally "very satisfied" with the crop, but that its fibers were a little short for optimal ginning, which made them harder to use with their looms than Texas cotton. Because this was an "easily correctable challenge," however, he had decided to take the liberty to inform Laguna farmers publicly so they could address the issue and make their cotton even more desirable to foreigners.[74]

A few years later, the company angered Laguna cotton farmers by taking out a patent on the *paca redonda* (round bundle) that it made with its own cotton press. The farmers considered this an attempt to create a monopoly, since they did not possess the press to make their own bundles, and the company would not sell the presses to them. As a result, the agricultural chamber of the Laguna, which included representatives from Santa Teresa, Tlahualilo, and other large cotton estates, agreed unanimously to boycott the company by refusing to sell any cotton to it and encouraged the other Mexican cotton-growing regions of Mexicali, Matamoros, and Ciudad Juárez to join them.[75] A few weeks later, Anderson Clayton responded with a full-page newspaper advertisement calling its detractors sore losers who conducted a defamation campaign of false accusations against the company because they did not want the competition, not because the company sought to create a monopoly. It reminded farmers that cotton merchants were not speculators; rather, they "serve[d] as intermediaries between the producer and the consumer, delivering a double-service." Indeed, "We [Anderson Clayton] do not seek profits at the expense of the planter, industrialist, OR THE COMPETITOR."[76] A few days later, the company took out another, more conciliatory advertisement that simply enumerated the advantages of the new packaging method, including cleaner fibers and easier transportation. It also stated that all farmers could use Anderson Clayton's presses for a small fee, and anyone who purchased one could make his own bundles free of charge.[77] Soon thereafter, Laguna farmers and the company reached a modus vivendi along the lines proposed in this second advertisement, and the chamber ended the boycott.

Barely a year later, however, Anderson Clayton clashed with the state government of Coahuila over alleged tax evasion. When the state confiscated one hundred bales out of thirty thousand as forced payment, the company sought an injunction from a state judge, arguing that it paid all of its taxes in Mexico City. The judge rejected the company's plea.[78] A few months later the company and the governor of Coahuila reached an agreement on taxes, and the governor returned to the company two hundred bales of confiscated cotton.[79] By 1932, Anderson Clayton's importance to Mexico's cotton production had reached impressive proportions. For instance, in a dispute between Mexican textile industrialists and cotton farmers over allowing cotton imports, farmers claimed that Anderson Clayton's stockpiles along with their own crop would meet domestic demand without imports.[80] The CNI also turned to Anderson Clayton in 1933 as financier of last resort when a group of colonists under its supervision were unable to obtain forty tons of cottonseed worth five thousand pesos in time for planting.[81]

In January 1937, four months after the October 1936 reparto, the company extended a credit of 140,000 pesos for 550 bales of ejido cotton from the Durango area of the Laguna. The engineers representing the agricultural banks and the Agrarian Department participated in this successful "operation," and within a week the ejidos received the profits.[82] In another such operation a year later, Anderson Clayton and two other cotton brokerage firms bought the entire ejido harvest of 85,000 bales of cotton.[83]

Not all participants, however, were satisfied with these arrangements. The owner of the Esmeralda hacienda, A. Menéndez, wrote an open letter to *El Siglo de Torreón* in March 1937 stating that the Banco Mexicano Refaccionario (Mexican Loan Bank) had falsely accused him of fraud for allegedly failing to deliver all of the hacienda's cotton to the bank. If any cotton was missing, Menéndez claimed it was because the bank "obliged us to sell our products to Anderson Clayton at the time and price that they fixed."[84] The Ejido Bank used the revenue from these arranged sales to help finance the sinking of new water wells in ejidos. One of the ejidos was also named Esmeralda, likely itself created from lands Menéndez had to cede from his hacienda in the 1936 reparto.[85] Indeed, as much as access to financing was critical for successful cotton production, it was not possible to grow at all without water. Unsurprisingly, inequitable access to water generated continuous conflicts in the post-reparto Laguna.

Water Conflicts in Former Tlahualilo Lands

The new provisional water regulation of 1938 that Cardenista técnicos painstakingly devised, although more equitable on paper, did not correspond to the natural hydrological cycle of the Nazas. By contrast, the Porfirian-era técnicos who had devised the supplanted 1909 regulation carefully adapted it to the river's flow cycle, but in a form that perpetuated socioeconomic inequality between classes and privileged certain landowners within the upper classes. The Tlahualilo Company's case is instructive in this regard. Because it was the largest foreign-owned estate in the Laguna with a long history of conflict with the Mexican federal government and downriver users, Cárdenas targeted it for a major subdivision: of the company's 18,000 hectares, he distributed 12,222 hectares to twelve ejidos for the benefit of three thousand campesinos out of a population of six thousand.[86] In addition, he granted some land to colonists, many of them members of Legión de Veteranos de la Revolución (Legion of Veterans of the Revolution), a group of veterans from Pancho Villa's División del Norte. Cárdenas provided the legion's 782 members with 16,633 hectares on both banks of the river in the upper and lower Laguna regions. Sixty of the legion's members received 950 hectares of the Tlahualilo Company's land in a colony named San Juan de Tlahualilo. (For the demarcations of the Tlahualilo subdivisions as of 1914, see the upper-left-hand corner of map FM.1.) In 1938, they signed a contract making them de facto sharecroppers who had to pay 15 percent of their harvest to a small landholder.[87]

In March 1939, the veterans sent Serrano a request to legalize their diversion of water from the Tlahualilo Canal. The government asked the veterans to provide it with titles to their property and water rights. Instead, the veterans attached a copy of a request they had made to divert more water from the canal and a map of property boundaries they had demarcated themselves, which they claimed totaled nearly 900 hectares. Since the government had still not officially demarcated any boundaries, the veterans did not know which land belonged to them, obliging them to remain as colonists with insecure land and water rights.[88] With their informal property demarcations, they moved to strike a deal with the German Mexican Bernardo Weckmann, who represented Emilia Muñoz. Muñoz was owner of the land known as Fracción de San Juan de Tlahualilo, totaling 1,098 hectares, presumably before the 1936 reparto. Complying with the reparto, she sold 898 hectares to the veterans and retained the rest. The representative of the veterans, Froylán Sandoval, accepted the offer of sale from Muñoz to irrigate the land with water from the Tlahualilo Canal to which he expected the government to grant the veterans rights.[89]

The transaction soon went awry, for this purchased land, known as La Colonia, originally belonged to the liquidated Tlahualilo Company through a concession the government made to the company in 1888 to colonize and irrigate the area. Since the company never colonized the land, it reverted to Bernardo Weckmann's father, the German-born Luis Weckmann. Bernardo submitted a document showing that his family had irrigated La Colonia for a long time with water diverted from the Tlahualilo Canal. Although the water concession for La Colonia belonged to the Tlahualilo Company, the document, Bernardo argued, recognized his family's and Muñoz's right to a portion of the canal's water, even though it referred to unauthorized pasturelands (*eriazo*) rather than irrigable lands. From Serrano's perspective, Weckmann therefore had no rights whatever to use even insufficient water from the Nazas, for if the government prioritized users like him with preexisting rights, no water would remain to establish new water rights for ejidos. Allowing the veterans and Muñoz (via Weckmann) both to claim allocations would only aggravate the situation, Serrano argued, since in normal years of river flow it was nearly impossible for the government to satisfy concessions for ejidos. Serrano determined that the veterans were taking water "fraudulently, without legal authorization, and if they're giving water to Muñoz, that use is also fraudulent." His recommendation was stern: Muñoz and the veterans should be denied their petitions and prohibited from taking water. He even ordered the local office of the Irrigation District to criminalize their actions if they tried to continue taking water.[90]

Weckmann responded by defending his water concession and insisting it was legal. He proudly stated that his father had worked the land since 1892 and that he had been working the land since 1922 using aniego.[91] Implicit in his spirited defense was that the 1938 regulation, which the *Diario Oficial de la Federación* finally published in August 1939, in effect terminated two generations of sustainable water use by granting ejidos priority in water concessions in the name of social equity. Weckmann tried to acquire title to his long-standing land and water rights as a newly designated small landholder, but as he possessed more than 20 hectares, he could count on water being available only *after* ejidos and landholders that possessed less than 20 hectares took enough water for their needs. Although the new preliminary regulation of 1938 clearly distinguished between these two sets of different-size landholders, there was considerably more ambiguity regarding distribution between ejidos and landholders possessing less than 20 hectares, each of which was to receive a proportional amount of water. From 1939 through the early 1940s, the small landholders and ejidos of Tlahualilo bitterly contested water allocations, prompting the government to take forceful measures.

In one emblematic instance, Tlahualilo ejido representatives sent a short telegram in December 1939 to Cárdenas stating they did not recognize the Tlahualilo colonists: "We ejidatarios will take our water, satisfy ejidal necessities/ hope not to surprise you. Colonists agitated." In other words, they refused to release water to non-ejido lands and requested an interview with Cárdenas to sanction their action.[92] Six months later, toward the end of May 1940, the conflict persisted, and the SAF received reports that ejidos would continue to refuse releasing water during cresting of the Nazas. The local manager of the Irrigation District run by the CNI expressed his worries to his superiors that these small landholders could suffer another year without water due to ejido obstruction. By July 1940, the situation had become serious enough that Serrano referred the matter to the secretary of national defense, explicitly requesting the assistance of the armed forces to enforce the water regulation. The secretary declined his request and recommended that the CNI clearly demarcate lands belonging to colonists and ejidos and assign corresponding volumes of water to each.[93]

As this example of the Tlahualilo ejido case demonstrates, the sheer complexity of the 1938 regulation confused many people. It grew from three principles defined in the water legislation of the time: the system of Irrigation Districts, management by a group of organized users, and distribution according to a system of those users' preferences, and *not* of rights acquired prior to the 1936 reparto. The regulation also authorized the "public authority"—that is, the CNI—to be in charge of the Irrigation District's management, the assigned number for which was seventeen out of seventy-five districts nationwide.[94] Accordingly, the 1938 regulations empowered the CNI to organize users into associations of local water boards. The boards would then administer and execute maintenance and improvement works for the irrigation systems through user fees and monitor distribution of water through all of the diversion dams along the river. The CNI appointed the boards of canal users who served for a one-year term and represented three distinct types of water usage: public and domestic, ejidatarios, and small landholders. The selection of the ejidatarios would be the responsibility of the official ejido representative, usually from the Ejido Bank, while the other two would elect a member from one of their own. Each board would include a president, a secretary, a treasurer, and other posts.[95]

Serrano pointed out that the 1938 regulations, though an improvement over the 1909 regulation, nevertheless fixed only the water allocation of each authorized canal, not distribution among *users* of all the canals. He recommended that authorities allocate and distribute canal water to groups of ejidos and small landholders according to clearly specified land areas. The CNI had already received the surface water volumes and rights of Tlahualilo ejidos from the manager of the Irrigation District. The problem was thus not a matter of insufficient information, Serrano believed. Rather, it required redressing serious ejido noncompliance with the regulation in the Tlahualilo area. The ejidos were openly defying the government by preventing small landholders from exercising their water rights.[96] In the meantime, the CNI convened a meeting in August 1940 to create a water board consisting of two representatives of ejidos, small landholders, the municipality, the CNI, and the zone. Ejido representatives subsequently complained that small landholders were overrepresented, but the articles of the board's constitution upheld the proportionality of representation.[97]

The water board's constitution evidently did not sway these ejido representatives. In September 1940, for instance, SAF Secretary José Parres reported to the Irrigation District's manager that ejidos continued to refuse to release water under their control to small landholders of Tlahualilo, jeopardizing the small landholders' well-being. Parres pleaded with the manager to authorize the use of armed force, when necessary and requested, to ensure that ejidos complied with the regulations.[98] His request went unheeded, and several months later, in January 1941, the Grupo de Pequeños Fraccionistas del Perímetro del Tlahualilo (Group of Small Colonists of the Tlahualilo Perimeter) sent a memo directly to the recently elected president, Manuel Ávila Camacho, requesting direct executive intervention to reform the 1938 regulations. It wrote, "It's been three years since we cultivated our lands, during which time we've suffered more economically here than at any time in 40 years. We have never before experienced the misery through which our families are now living. This is due to the unfair distribution of water, since we cannot conceive that we are suffering misery as property owners. We had a better situation as salaried workers; nor can we conceive how water is provided to one group while the other goes hungry."

The group's members added that they had been unable to irrigate their land, even though they had acquired it by presidential decree in November 1936 and their ownership was confirmed by a subsequent decree in August 1940. They complained that the ejidos had not only satisfied their watering needs but also retained half a hectare's surplus of water for individual use. They noted wryly that their long experience and technical skills in drilling wells, producing cottonseed oil, and employing all types of agricultural machinery had become a stain on them since they were "completely forgotten by [our] supreme government." They even accused the Ejido Bank of connivance with local "communist agitators" to take away their land. They protested that despite the ample documentation for claims they submitted to the president and the SAF, and even the arrival of the military to enforce water distribution, water deprivation persisted. The group concluded the memo requesting stronger laws to guarantee its members' access to water and expressed their desire for a more authoritarian solution by requesting that a CNI engineer manage water distribution instead of the elected water board.[99]

In March 1941, a CNI engineer reviewed the case and concluded that, from a strictly legal standpoint, these small landholders had no grounds for redress: they possessed more than 20 hectares, which made them lower than ejidos in order of priority access to river flow from the canal. In the relatively low flow year of 1939–40, ejidos' preferential concession was insufficient, despite the increase of watering tandas from a yearly average of ten to thirteen. The CNI dedicated a special tanda exclusively to small landholders in 1939 over the bitter opposition of ejidos, prompting the use of armed force to "overcome the resistance." This CNI engineer diagnosed these colonists' predicament as symptomatic of the larger problem that small landholders faced in the region: inadequate water allocations to irrigate the entire land area designated for ejidos. This inadequacy made small landholders who possessed more than 20 hectares unable to receive any water save during exceptionally large river flows.[100] The conflict would continue on well after the Cárdenas presidency.

In the meantime, however, dozens of técnicos and thousands of workers, many of them ejidatarios, were busily constructing the Palmito Dam under the scorching Durango desert sun. The dam-in-progress loomed large in the minds of Laguneros who eagerly anticipated it to be the ultimate envirotechnical solution for their water woes.

Part II. The Second Agrarian Reform

4. Life and Work on the Revolutionary Dam Site and Ejidos

Water is the origin of life and necessary element for human life that the efforts of técnicos and workers provide to Mexico City and to all social classes which comprise its population.

DIEGO RIVERA

In 1940, when Lázaro Cárdenas left office, Mexico was far more polarized socially and politically than it had been in 1934 when he started his presidency. After 1938, he moved toward the political center from the left in part because he feared that Mexico would meet the same fate as Republican Spain. As a result, his initial commitment to radical agrarian reform—and the collective ejido as its central institution—began to wane long before there was sufficient time to overcome numerous challenges to its viability, among them inadequate financial resources, endemic corruption, low morale, and outright sabotage by its enemies.

The new president, Manuel Ávila Camacho, announced in early 1941 that he would continue his predecessor's more moderate agrarian policies. In practical terms, this meant the ejido would remain intact but, at best, benignly neglected and, at worst, purposely undermined depending on the president in power. Although this generalization accurately describes overall national trends, as numerous studies have shown, it does not take into account the envirotechnical continuities at the local level, especially regarding water access. Viewed from this perspective, there was more continuity than discontinuity in agrarian policies from the pre-1938 Cárdenas administration to the post-1940 administration of Ávila Camacho than has met the eye of many students of Mexican agrarian reform. Indeed, an important reason supporters and critics alike judged the Laguna agrarian reform model unsuccessful was that the Nazas River Dam remained incomplete. Thus, the new preliminary water regulation of 1938, which replaced the prerevolutionary 1909 regulation, could not be fully implemented; this lack of implementation delayed, perhaps fatally, the predictable and equitable reparto de aguas that Cardenista técnicos regarded as indispensable to the long-term success of the reparto de tierras.

The Cárdenas administration's later rightward sociopolitical shift indelibly weakened support for the ejido experiment, but the fact that the same técnicos and many of the same workers, including ejidatarios, still labored on the dam that Cárdenas broke ground on in 1936 complicates the general narrative of rupture in 1940. After all, beneficiaries of agrarian reform looked to the dam's completion as the comprehensive solution to the problem that seemed to exacerbate, if not cause, nearly all others for them: the lack of water. Without water, they could not grow crops or raise livestock of any quantity or quality, and, especially given how inefficient and corrupt ejido governance could be, they had little means to obtain credit and maintain an agricultural livelihood. Moreover, técnicos of the Comisión Nacional de Irrigación (National Irrigation Commission; CNI) ostensibly designed the 1938 regulation and the dam to prioritize ejidos overall with respect to water distribution.

The dam building on the Nazas was a nodal site where técnicos, workers, and ejidatarios metaphorically, and sometimes literally, swam the murky waters between environment and technology. The actual dam site, which accommodated dozens of técnicos and thirteen thousand workers and their dependents and others at its population peak, was a revolutionary experiment in and of itself that reflected the social and environmental conditions of everyday life in ejidos during the late 1930s and 1940s. The Palmito Dam project on the Nazas River was one of five large dams in mostly arid central-northern states that Cárdenas launched included in the National Revolutionary Party's Six-Year Plan of 1934. In addition to Palmito, there were also the Solís Dam on the Lerma River in Guanajuato; the Sanalona Dam on the Tamazula River in northwestern Sinaloa; the Angostura Dam on the Yaqui River in northeastern Sonora; and the Azúcar Dam on the San Juan River in northeastern Tamaulipas.[1] Of the five, the Palmito, Angostura, and Azúcar dams were the flagship high dams. The federal government, through the General Credit Bureau of the Treasury Ministry under the direction of Eduardo Suárez, began soliciting bids for their construction from individuals and private companies between January 1 and March 31, 1936.[2] The CNI constructed campamentos (encampments) on the dam sites that functioned as company towns replete with modern amenities, including housing, schools, hospitals, and sports and cultural facilities. As on the ejidos, however, living conditions and access to amenities varied greatly according to the social class and occupation of the campamento inhabitants. Such inequities affected how people experienced the inclemency of nature, especially the unwieldy Nazas.

Engineering Trials and Tribulations in an Unstable Environment

In August 1923, Manuel Favela wrote a brief note, published in *El Siglo de Torreón*, that the "Padre Nazas" was "pouring" its "magnificent gift" on the Laguna region. The arrival of its torrential flow at the Coyote dike early in the morning was a regular spectacle for local Laguneros, who would gather on the riverbanks by the thousands to watch it in gratitude. Favela went on to call the river the "venerated deity" of Laguneros for the "promise of prosperity, well-being, and abundance" that its flows would "scatter" about. Moreover, since this late summer flow was strong, it portended many more for the fall.[3] In a similar vein, an editorial in July 1929 titled "The Very First Flow of the Laguna Nile" described the river's social, economic, and ecological importance to the region in such reverential terms that they deserve to be quoted in their entirety:

> Probably by the time these words have been printed, the very first flow of the Río Nazas will have arrived at one of the diversion dams in the upriver region of the Comarca Lagunera, a flow which the agricultural workers have always received joyously and which all Laguneros have received as a blessing in general. No matter how random, the very first flow acts like the leader of subsequent flows, which are not only of more importance, but also largely determine the success of the region's agricultural efforts for the next year.
>
> The very first flow of the Laguna's Nile will always be seen as symbolic—just like the first bale of cotton that is harvested is also viewed as symbolic. For this reason, it will always generate enthusiasm and jubilation in the Laguna. Indeed, older agriculture workers would go to the banks of the Padre Nazas so that they could uncork a bottle of champagne and make a toast in reverence to the foamy content of the turbid waters, which are rich in lime, i.e., that deeply layered substance that fertilizes Lagunera lands and makes it produce white gold, notwithstanding its [rapid] depletion.
>
> It is here that the first flow revives the enthusiasm and the optimism of the people, both of which seem to disappear in the region during the months prior to the cotton season. In fact, [the first flow] signifies the apex of all business matters—both agriculturally and industrially—as

well as that of its by-products. This means that the era of small transactions and big business deals has now finally arrived; it is the beginning, too, of a brief spate of continuous activities characterized by indefatigable labor, and by happiness, which in the rest of the country is commonly known as the "Lagunera Bonanza."[4]

Although Laguneros could revere the Nazas as a father and even a deity, it was an extremely unstable divine father. Indeed, instability largely defined life in the Laguna. Proponents of the Nazas Dam argued it would stabilize the region's economic and social life. Yet planning and building the dam under unstable environmental conditions presented daunting technical challenges for engineers, whose blueprints assumed a high degree of predictability, and especially their workers.

Although the postrevolutionary revival of the Nazas Dam project was highly controversial, and it was thus far from certain that it would be built, the federal Nazas River Inspection Commission nevertheless sent a directive on April 23, 1921, to all of its members to obtain more reliable flow data for the potential Palmito Dam site by modernizing their gauging methods. Particularly at the confluence of the Ramos and Oros rivers, where the headwaters of the Nazas formed, the chief of the commission deemed it "indispensable to get as much data as possible." He added, "Do whatever it takes to get this done in terms of methods, equipment, etc." There, three days later, the commission had installed windlasses (machines for raising weights by winding a rope or chain upon a barrel or drum driven by a crank or motor), but more than a year later, little had been achieved. The area was difficult to reach and unsafe, so the commission proposed a gauging area more accessible than El Palmito where someone could monitor the measurements full time. Consequently, the commission installed a meter in the hacienda of Rincón de Ramos, located at the Nazas headwaters. On March 25, 1923, the commission received a report that Guadalupe Guerrero, a nearby farmer living on the hacienda, earned 0.5 pesos (about 25 cents) daily for supervising the station. The trip to the station from Indé, the nearest town accessible by automobile, took one day on horseback.[5]

In 1924, the Department of Land, Colonization, Water, and Irrigation of the Secretaría de Agricultura y Fomento (Ministry of Agriculture and Development; SAF) complained that there was "no descriptive plan for the station and a lack of measurement records in October and half of November 1923." The department demanded the missing records forthwith from Guerrero. In response, he wrote, "Due to the re-concentration of ranches in the San Jerónimo hacienda by order of the military division commanded by Marcelo Caraveo,

I find myself [stuck] in this hacienda, having left my house abandoned and closed up. For this reason, they are not allowing anybody to enter El Rincón and it is impossible for me in this hacienda to get the little book that you are referring to." The department's engineers noted in exasperation that Guerrero made excuses whenever they asked him for the missing records, which raised suspicion that he was not doing his job. As a result, they recommended that he be suspended from his duties.

By early 1925, the department detected errors in the measurements from the Rincón de Ramos station and demanded that the station manager be replaced. For the next two years, no one correctly read river flow measurements. In November 1926, the regional chief of the Third Water Zone, charged with the Laguna region, requested reinstallation of the "third class" gauging station in El Palmito. The new station manager, Gregorio Medina, was a local farmer and manager of a meteorological station in Concepción, Durango, approximately sixty miles on horseback from El Palmito. On October 20, 1926, Medina reported on the installation of a windlass: given how hard it was to install, he placed it in the "least bad" location. He furnished detailed instructions to the gauge reader: "Take daily readings at the intervals of six, twelve and eighteen hours recording each in the registration book, and then transfer these observations to the cards and send them to the Third Water Zone Office weekly. In the season of river cresting make extra observations of the intervals according to its variations."

Although engineers stressed the importance of "exact and continuous measurements" for a "definitive projection" in case the Palmito Dam was built, they frequently reinstalled gauges over the next three years, yielding less than satisfactory results. In September 1929, a report stated it was possible to reach El Palmito in twelve hours by car from Lerdo, an improvement over the full day it previously took on horseback. By May 1930, engineers had installed more numerous and sophisticated instruments and entrusted them to an observer whom they paid three pesos per day (a sixfold increase from 1923 and twofold from 1926), and to an assistant peon whom they paid one peso per day. The following year, in October 1931, they reinstalled another first-class gauge. As of September 1934, there were hydrometer stations in nine locations along the river, enabling engineers at last to measure flow volume precisely.[6]

Without waiting even for a few months to collect more precise flow data using the newly installed gauges, the CNI was sending specialist engineers by the end of 1934 to carry out reconnaissance and geological surveys of potential dam sites in and around El Palmito.[7] Until then, they had been relying largely on the comprehensive, but incomplete, geological and topographical surveys of British and American engineers from twenty-five years and five years before, respectively. The CNI was anxious to complete the surveying and preliminary drilling so the project could begin as soon as Cárdenas ordered it. This anxiousness, revealed in correspondence, placed considerable pressure on the reconnaissance team, which consisted of two Mexican drilling specialists, their assistants, and the CNI's geohydrologist, Paul Waitz, as a consultant. Their lack of reliable equipment in difficult environmental conditions only made matters worse.

On a tour of the El Palmito area in early April 1934, for example, Waitz sent a report on the equipment needed to begin drilling and gather soil samples for local construction material and road-building conditions. He noted an abandoned railroad track wide enough to be reconstructed or readapted as a highway to facilitate transportation and considerably reduce costs. The arrival of high flow in April would delay work for two months, so his intention was to commence drilling in the riverbed and left bank of the Nazas as rapidly as possible before it became unfordable.[8]

Waitz expected the work to begin the following day, but two weeks later, in late April 1934, an assistant to Jorge Blake, the lead drilling engineer, sent a report to the director of the CNI, the engineer Alfredo Becerril Colín, describing the arduous trek they had experienced from Ciudad Juárez, Chihuahua, to El Palmito, Durango. On the first leg of their journey, from Delicias to Parral, Chihuahua, they were struck by a combination of rain and sand storms that caused creeks to overflow and muddy the road. Their truck got stuck three times, and at nine o'clock one night they were obliged to leave it on the road and walk back seven miles to the nearest village, Boquilla. The next day, with local help, they managed to dig the truck out but had to wait another day because the road was impassable. With much difficulty they reached the town of Indé, Durango, within twenty-five miles of La Concepción, the embarkation point to El Palmito. But from Indé to Concepción, no cars could pass, so they rode on horseback for seven hours.[9] Their ordeal led Becerril to comment that a better route would have to be found for transportation of materials to the dam site.

No work could begin, however, until the drilling engineers could arrive by truck from Chihuahua with their equipment. Inclement weather continued to create very rough road conditions that postponed the drilling well into the following year. In March 1935, Blake submitted a budget for his work for April of the same year (see table 4.1).[10] Yet in late July, Blake reported to Waitz that he was using human porters to carry equipment because the roads had washed out. "Under these circumstances it's very difficult to fix a date by which I can

TABLE 4.1. The engineer Jorge Blake's monthly budget for April 1935

Expenses	Pesos
Salary for driller and operators	984.00
Purchase of 1,500 liters of gasoline at 0.2 pesos/liter	300.00
Purchase of 55 liter drum of oil	29.70
Freight charges for gas and oil	46.65
Wage for *peons*	150.00
Cost of pump repair	40.00
Reimbursement of transport cost from Culiacán, Sin., to El Palmito for Rafael Herrera	126.50
Cost of repair of the Chevy truck	26.70
Purchase of Ford motor engine parts	16.35
Other costs	8.50
Total	1,728.50*

* About $480 at the 1933 exchange rate.
SOURCE: Blake to CNI Accounting Department, Archivo Histórico del Agua, Consultivo Técnico, March 19, 1935, box 142, file 1129, 137.

finish all this work," he explained. "I'll do whatever I can and I'm even working Sundays, but understand that I cannot make miracles. I am anxious to leave this exile especially as I find myself a little ill."[11] A few days later, Waitz nevertheless responded, "I deplore these delays in the receipt of these important documents now more than ever because I am constantly being asked what drillings are still needed." But then he ended on a sympathetic note: "I can imagine the difficulties you are faced with now that it has rained so much and I am surprised your wife is there with you in that desert and exile."[12]

Nearly a month later, Blake asked Director Francisco Vázquez del Mercado of the CNI for a leave of two or three months to take care of his sick family, which Vázquez del Mercado granted him after he finished his work and returned the machinery.[13] Three weeks later, however, Blake had still not left El Palmito. Instead, he reported that the machinery was in bad condition and unable to drill to the required depth of 80–100 meters. In one spot, he had managed to carry machinery across the river at low flow only to find it suddenly rising. He had to leave the machinery on the other bank where the river current soon washed it away, along with a number of other tools. In other areas, the water level rose so high—nearly seven meters—that it became impossible to complete the drilling. When Blake sent back supplies by truck, the drivers had to return in two days without making it even halfway to Indé; instead, the truck remained stuck for a night in a creek that overflowed and submerged the vehicle. This particular creek, Tizonazo, would not allow even a horse to pass. Blake ended his letter with, "I find myself in a desperate situation unable to leave, since my family is sick and we still don't have fuel."[14]

The trials and tribulations to lay the foundations to build the dam convinced the CNI to construct a major highway connecting the Palmito Dam site with the town of Mapimí. The town was accessible via a good road to Bermejillo, a town on a rail line linking it to Ciudad Juárez and Mexico City, and by road to Torreón (map FM.1). The hundred-mile road from Mapimí to the dam site was needed to haul an anticipated 200,000 tons of machinery, equipment, and construction materials. Workers began clearing the highway's path in May 1936 in Bermejillo and some ten days later started clearing the entire path in four segments, which they completed in August 1936. It then took until May 1937 to pave the road. The total cost of the road was 2,166,891.15 pesos (about $600,000), or 21,600 pesos ($6,000) per mile.[15] Building the road, however, was only the beginning.

Taming the Nazas: The First Four Years (1936–1940)
Northern Durango's ecologically diverse landscape consists of a vast arid and semi-arid desert punctuated by mountains that occasionally resemble craters. Wildlife such as turtles, hares, doves, boars, coyotes, mountain cats, deer, and reptiles live in this ecosystem full of prickly pear (*nopal*) cacti and vivid rocks. The Sierra Madre Occidental in this area is composed of rhyolite, a very acidic volcanic rock, and of limestone, which supports the terrain of massive cliffs. Both types of rocks were common at the Palmito Dam site. Before the eruption of volcanoes millions of years ago, the former andesitic rock formations underwent a period of intense erosion and were gradually replaced by rhyolite and limestone, which entirely modified the regional topography. As the Nazas runs through this topography allowing for lush vegetation to grow on its banks, rain-formed torrential currents uproot the vegetation, carry it downriver, and deposit it into the Laguna's alluvial plains hundreds of miles away—thereby turning some of this vegetation-turned-organic detritus into sediment-rich fertilizer for farming.[16]

It was in these spectacular natural surroundings that CNI técnicos and workers toiled for ten years to complete the Palmito Dam. It was a huge undertaking, requiring an unprecedented level of technical and logistical organization for the CNI. The CNI hired the American engineer Henry Van Rosenthal Thorne—who first came to work in Mexico when Calles hired White Engineering of New York to train CNI técnicos in the late 1920s—as superintendent of the project. He performed his duties proudly and energetically. Thorne had worked on two previous Mexican dams, the El Pabellón Dam in Hidalgo and the ill-fated Don Martín Dam in Tamaulipas, the reservoir of which dried up shortly after it was constructed. Lacking qualified engineering assistants, Thorne and his immediate subordinate, Roberto Salas Álvarez, had to supervise workers personally. Thorne enjoyed a good working relationship with Cárdenas, who approved the use of new and more modern equipment than was ever before employed in Mexico on dam projects. The use of the equipment enabled building the Nazas Dam "with ultramodern procedures which served as practice for the técnicos and training for the employees."[17]

A little more than a year after the agrarian reform decree of October 1936, the CNI took Mexican and foreign visitors to observe the dam construction in progress. The visitors were, according to effusive newspaper coverage, "impressed with the perfect systematization of work and order at the charge of Thorne and Salas, and of the skill of Mexican workers." Two foreign diplomats remarked that their visit to the dam site dispelled the views they had of Mexico as "disorderly and uncultured"; instead, they came "to appreciate the Mexican government's enormous effort to produce new sources of wealth and cultivate vast new areas of land." A Mexican senator then expressed his desire that all Mexicans become aware of public works such as El Palmito, for through them, he proclaimed, "The Revolution demonstrates its program of effective economic recovery and better distribution of wealth." Another Mexican visitor, echoing Cárdenas, observed that the dam and other irrigation works would help improve the governance of ejidos, which, in his mind, should be the principal objective of the revolutionary government.[18]

Newspaper coverage that relied on official sources unduly stressed the positive, but some of it was corroborated by private correspondence. For instance, in a confidential progress report submitted in October 1940 to the CNI's director, Arturo Sandoval, and reviewed by eight other engineers—among them the American consulting engineer Andrew Weiss—the CNI engineers Armando Riemann and Ernesto Biestro provided detailed and precise information about the flow of the Nazas River and the Laguna region. Their report reflected significantly increased understanding and advances in data gathering and analysis of hydrological processes during Cárdenas's term. They observed that isolated samples collected from 1908 to 1927 indicated a yearly average of 6.5 grams of sediment per liter of water, or 0.66 percent solid materials, flowing down the Nazas. In 1938, by contrast, they broke their samples down by monthly and ten-day intervals during high flow season and demonstrated a clear correlation between volume of water and amount of organic detritus.[19]

For decades, anti-dam landowners feared that damming the river would prevent its rich fertilizing sediments from bathing their lands via the aniego irrigation method. The CNI engineers, however, were convinced that these natural fertilizers would not only continue to flow after they dammed the river but that they would be *enhanced* because they would be able to release reservoir water, sediment and all, at more opportune moments—moments that actually corresponded to agricultural cycles. Unlike a few pro-dam engineers in the 1920s who tried to downplay the river's fertilizing prowess, CNI engineers in 1940 affirmed that the "soils of the region are of recent alluvial formation," but the irregular conveyance of the nutrients caused by unpredictable flows led to varying quality in the Laguna's soils depending on their location along the Nazas River's course. For instance, in the San Ignacio, La Concordia, and Tlahualilo areas (the first two in the downriver region in Coahuila, the third in the upriver region in Durango) the lands were, engineers declared, "agriculturally of the first class," and, they continued, not "excessively permeable for conducting irrigation water, and the necessary volumes for irrigation are small." Engineers provided detailed information on their soil characteristics, which varied according to depth. Yet, overall, they concluded that all the region's soils had "uniform profiles."[20]

The question of *where* to build the dam was nearly as controversial as that of whether to build it. Francisco I. Madero had initially believed that the Fernández Canyon thirty miles upriver from Torreón would be an appropriate site in 1907, but the British engineering firm S. Pearson and Son concluded in 1911 that the Palmito site far upriver was much more suitable for dam building due to stronger bedrock that could withstand the weight of concrete demanded of it. Although S. Pearson and Son estimated that the Fernández Canyon could nevertheless capture 100 percent of pluvial discharge, as opposed to 90 percent for Palmito, the CNI estimated the cost per thousand cubic meters of stored waters at 6.17 pesos for Palmito and 8.52 for Fernández, a considerable difference. Estimates by the engineer F. F. Smith of White Engineering in 1930 placed the dam curtain at Palmito in the lower area of the canyon, but the CNI engineers elected to move it to the upper area. They also chose to raise the curtain because a later economic study concluded it would be less costly to elevate it than to dig deeper at the original location.[21]

S. Pearson and Son and F. F. Smith had already done much of the reconnaissance work for the Palmito site (though by no means all, as Blake's and Waitz's trials and tribulations in laying the dam foundations testifies), but the CNI had to do all of the preliminary work for the proposed hydroelectric plant. By installing a 2,000 horsepower plant, Smith calculated, there could be a 35 percent savings in cost per hectare for powering pump-installed wells throughout the Laguna. However, the CNI considered electrical generation "secondary work" to the dam's principal purpose of storing and regulating river flow for irrigation.[22]

According to Riemann and Biestro's timeline, the work to lay the foundations for the dam took four years, beginning in December 1936, soon after Cárdenas announced the completion of the reparto de tierras in Torreón on November 30. Workers began taming the temperamental Nazas at Palmito first by digging access ways for tunnels that would divert the river as they erected the dam. Next, in January 1937, workers commenced excavating a six-meter-high diversion canal followed, in February, by a smaller diversion canal. In March, they dug the tunnel exits and completed the diversion canal, and in June they cleared the lateral routes. By August, they were ready to install a telephone line from the former Noé hacienda to Bermejillo, which, along with the opening of the Bermejillo-Palmito road in May 1937, greatly sped up communication.[23]

Although engineers and workers progressed considerably in taming the Nazas over the first year and a half, the river remained the dominant force, for they had to suspend their work when it crested in September and October 1937. Consequently, engineers relocated the tunnels, diversion canals, and ditches or changed their depths. Finally, in December they ordered workers to clear the riverbed to install the hydroelectric plant. For the next three months, construction advanced as workers carved the rock walls and cliffs into terraces and continued the diversion structures. In April 1938, the month in which Cárdenas decreed new water regulations that overhauled the 1909 regulations, engineers and workers diverted the Nazas into the diversion canal. This enabled them to move the rocks from the quarry onto the riverbed to build the dam curtain. Nevertheless, they still had not tamed the Nazas: from July to September 1938, its flows destroyed 2,000 cubic meters of diversion canal materials. It took three months, until the end of the year, to replace the material destroyed by the 1938 flow. In early 1939, engineers and workers began waterproofing the curtain, and in the spring and summer they prepared the second and third diversion tunnels and lined them with concrete. In the fall they installed a protective structure over the tunnel entrances and completed the entrances one by one— and this time, they appeared to have tamed the Nazas. By April 1940, they had lined all of the diversion tunnels with concrete (see figure 4.1).[24]

They had yet to erect the curtain, however, and completion of the dam was already past due as Cárdenas's presidency neared its end in late 1940. The numerous reasons for the delay included inclement weather conditions, trouble

FIG. 4.1 A worker drilling into a diversion tunnel at the Palmito Dam site. *La obra de la Comisión Nacional de Irrigación*, 1940, 149.

TRABAJOS DE PERFORACION
en uno de los túneles de la gran presa de
El Palmito, Dgo.

with material procurement, financial constraints, and the need for improvisation and experimentation when things did not turn out as planned. Riemann and Biestro's detailed report covering the years 1936–40, on which much of this narrative is drawn, was only one of dozens that CNI engineers filed from the beginning of construction until completion in 1946. The lively details they convey show the ingenuity of engineers and workers toiling in difficult environmental conditions, but it came at a high price. Already by June 1940, the unfinished Palmito Dam had cost 17,412,700 pesos (about $4.5 million), a number close to the initial estimate for its total cost on *completion*.[25]

Cárdenas's expropriation of foreign oil companies on March 18, 1938, had a crippling effect on the economy, including dam building, and was another major, nearly fatal, challenge to the Palmito project. The British and American oil giants, backed by their governments, responded to Cárdenas's bold nationalist move by boycotting Mexican oil, so Mexico turned to the Axis powers to compensate for the lost markets.[26] Similarly, to continue construction on its dam projects, the CNI had to turn to Axis suppliers. In the case of Palmito, engineers required numerous machines and replacement parts for them to quarry clay and other earthen material for construction of the ninety-five-meter-high curtain and to truck in domestically produced concrete. Soon after the oil nationalization, with uncertainty about Mexican government finances growing, Thorne proposed various options to the CNI for how to proceed with construction. Options included investing completely in finishing the cofferdams, excavating and lining diversion tunnels with concrete, or a combination of both, without any guarantee that they could be completed with existing funds.[27] As a result, a private Mexican construction company proposed to the CNI that it could take over the work and complete it in two years through a six-year financing plan, but the CNI rejected the proposal and continued the work itself.[28]

Through 1938, the CNI had procured nearly all of its machines and machine parts not manufactured in Mexico from the United States, but after 1938, this became much more difficult. In a letter to M. Levitt of Joshua Hendy Iron Works in the United States regarding his orders for butterfly valves, Andrew Weiss wrote, "Personally, I am sorry that owing to the trade relations which are forced upon this country by the oil sales to Germany, we must admit them as competitors in these manufactures." Having little choice, the CNI placed orders with a German competitor, the machinery company Bach y Dorsch, in February 1939.[29]

After Adolf Hitler invaded the Soviet Union in 1941, however, German supplies were no longer available, and the military buildup in the United States began to make Mexican procurement more difficult. In June of that year, Thorne commented in a memo that he had some trouble acquiring lubricating oils.[30] Shortly after Pearl Harbor, he anxiously awaited the release of twelve Mack trucks the U.S. government had held up for quite some time at the Laredo border crossing. In April 1942, engineers drew up a long list of supplies for conductors, isolates, towers, accessories, and other materials for transmission lines for the hydroelectric plant. They planned to procure all of the items from American companies, including General Cable of New York, American Bridge and Brown Knox and Company of Pittsburgh, and Bethlehem Steel of New York. The commission's chief executive engineer commented that the CNI was having "serious difficulties in obtaining the necessary equipment for the completion of this work; the lack of tires and brakes for the Mack trucks" forced it to use small trucks, which slowed work considerably. Wartime conditions also affected rail transportation in Mexico. Insufficient rail cars for transportation of cement and steel left both the Nazas River Dam and the Azúcar Dam, in the State of Tamaulipas, "in danger of being paralyzed due to lack of materials."[31]

It was in this context that Thorne worked shrewdly with Mexican diplomats. By framing the dam as essential to the Allies' war aims, they obtained an aid package directly from the U.S. government to ensure construction could continue. The golden opportunity came when the U.S. Department of Agriculture announced an anticipated forty-eight-year low for the 1943 cotton yield, a 5.6 percent drop from the previous year and a potentially serious problem for the war effort.[32] In exchange for Mexico's agreement to increase cultivation by 3.3 million acres to provide food and agricultural material for the war effort, the U.S. government diverted from war production trucks, tractors, and support for Mexican irrigation projects, most prominently among them El Palmito.[33] In the meantime, while financing and supplies remained hard to acquire, skilled workers such as machinists and blacksmiths organized workshops to improvise spare parts. They even worked for up to three months at a time without pay by opening stores where they could buy food with vouchers.[34] In this way, despite the hardships, thousands of workers and their families made the Palmito Dam site a lively place to work and a home.

The Palmito Dam "Company Town"

On the day of the dam's dedication in 1946, *El Siglo de Torreón* published an account by a former worker, Enrique Sifuentes Dozal, of a day's work on the dam site. Sifuentes described the mix of hard labor and communal life that enlivened this remote corner of the desert:

> Six in the morning. The sun begins to rise. The bustle of El Palmito inhabitants is already evident. Around the public water troughs, the women go milling around, forming "lines." The little city has awoken!
>
> The nixtamal mills deafen the surroundings, cordially inviting one to leave the riverbed. . . .
>
> The "siren" announces that it's 7:30 am (the end and beginning of the first and second shifts of the day).
>
> An unusual level of activity is noticeable at this hour: power shovels, tractors, trucks, small trucks, pick-ups and other machinery transport the fuel for the eight-hour shift. The starter motors for the power shovels and tractors "fire" up.
>
> Every man is at his post!

On the top of the hill on both sides of the river, the men, resembling "flies," break the rock indefatigably with jackhammers.

I climbed up high to observe at my leisure this compact group of titans (because titans are the men that build this dam, modesty aside).

In the workers' colony, the classrooms empty. In the street corners, myriad groups of workers (drivers, carpenters, mechanics, etc.) cheerfully chat and exchange stories about their day. . . . Families chat happily in the doorways of their homes. In the "collectives" for singles a group of boys sing popular songs, accompanied by guitars. News junkies gather around the radio excitedly to listen to the clear and precise voice of the announcer.[35]

The "little city" to which Sifuentes referred was the campamento built by the CNI—residential quarters to accommodate the técnicos and workers and their families, as well as those providing commercial and other services. At its peak, the campamento housed a population of thirteen thousand (three thousand of whom were the hired workers). After exploring several locations for the campamento, including one that was 2–4 kilometers and another that was 10 kilometers from the dam site, the CNI finally placed it within the reservoir basin to reduce the cost of transporting workers.[36] The campamento consisted of two areas: one was for técnicos and salaried workers, and the other, the *colonia obrera* (workers' quarters) housed the vast majority of seasonal, unskilled workers (see figures 4.2–4.4). Like Boulder City in America, where workers toiling on the mammoth Hoover Dam lived and enjoyed basic comforts at U.S. government expense, the Mexican government initially designated the campamento as a "federal zone," a kind of public company town, with facilities and amenities such as schools, hospitals, electricity, and running water.[37]

In a lengthy report of its work and accomplishments during Cárdenas's term, the CNI described the social mission of the company towns it founded adjacent to dam sites. In fulfilling the "postulate of the Revolution" to spread irrigation throughout the country for "convenient and adequate exploitation of our agricultural resources," campesinos and workers would be imbued with the ideas of "order, *work,* and progress"—a modification of the nineteenth-century positivist slogan of "order and progress."[38] Applying these larger national objectives to its own workers, the CNI highlighted the "internal social construction" that it undertook to amply satisfy its workers' needs by "facilitating those measures for the better accommodation [of the workers] on work sites, in habitation and elements of life and coexistence, and caring for their conditions of health and hygiene."[39] Prior to this mission, the CNI asserted that company

FIG. 4.2 The dam curtain is on the right of the basin, and the colonia obrera (workers' quarters) and campamento are to the left of it. Together the two became a kind of company town of the CNI between 1936 and 1946. *La obra de la Comisión Nacional de Irrigación*, 1940, 195.

FIG. 4.3 (*opposite, top*) The Palmito Dam under construction. *La obra de la Comisión Nacional de Irrigación*, 1940, 48.

FIG. 4.4 (*opposite, bottom*) View of the Palmito campamento. *La obra de la Comisión Nacional de Irrigación*, 1940, 237.

towns established for diverse public works such as railroads, roads, and irrigation were "extremely deficient." This was due in some cases to lack of hygiene and in others to the fleeting nature of campamentos. All of this changed, the CNI proclaimed, with the construction of the flagship dams on the Nazas River, the San Juan River in Tamaulipas (Azúcar), and the Yaqui River (Angostura) in Sonora. The CNI provided the materials and incentives for workers to create comfortable lives for themselves on all of these dam sites. Such projects, moreover, took into account local topographical conditions, the ability of workers to acquire construction materials, and how housing units could be designed to ensure workers did not lack any urban services. Since the accommodations were temporary, the CNI elected to build collective service units.[40]

By July 1937, the CNI announced it had completed construction of the Palmito campamento, prompting local and national newspapers to run numerous glowing accounts, as they had of the dam construction. Taking their cue from the CNI's public relations staff, harmony and cooperation were the papers' preferred themes. For example, one story indicated that, at the suggestion of CNI Director Francisco Vázquez del Mercado, and various employees of El Palmito, the Workers' Union of El Palmito and the CNI cooperated to improve the quality of life in the campamento. The joint effort bore fruit with the creation of two cooperatives. One would provide transportation between the dam site and Bermejillo, the nearest rail depot, and the other would run a cinema. The cinema cooperative started constructing a theater and tried to acquire the most modern equipment for it. It also made plans to organize free events for children of indigent families. Other efforts included purchasing school supplies and hiring a doctor. Various engineers also volunteered to hold educational talks and night classes for workers.[41]

On another occasion, Thorne and his assistant Salas attended a special union meeting. The journalist covering it for *El Siglo de Torreón* described engineers and workers having a "perfect understanding" between them: "workers were able to present various requests for improvements and were immediately attended to." With an enrollment of four hundred students and the campamento's total population increasing to eight thousand, Vázquez del Mercado decreed expansion of the school, construction of more desks, and provision of independent courses for boys and girls (see figure 4.5). He also ordered expansion of the hospital and hiring an additional doctor with an ambulance and a car for house calls. The journalist commented that the hospital did not want for anything, even a dental service, and was as good as any modern hospital in Mexico.

Vázquez del Mercado observed that a "spirit of sacrifice" existed among CNI workers on a number of projects throughout the country. Richer workers

FIG. 4.5 Group picture of Palmito school pupils and teachers. *La obra de la Comisión Nacional de Irrigación*, 1940, 249.

helped poorer ones through loans and cooperative credit arrangements. All twenty-seven thousand CNI workers throughout the country demonstrated "self-abnegation and patriotism" by donating one-day's worth of their monthly wage to repay the national debt Cárdenas incurred when he expropriated foreign oil fields on March 18, 1938. Even Thorne postponed his honorary fees to help repay the debt.[42]

Occasionally, *El Siglo de Torreón* published expressions of tension and dissatisfaction among workers. For instance, in one letter the general secretary of the Workers' Union of the Palmito Dam, Canuto Saucedo, complained about the living conditions in the campamento. He contended that accidents causing injury and even some deaths were frequent and demanded a security commission to address the dangerous work and poor treatment workers faced.[43] Another, anonymous letter accused CNI engineers of going house to house in search of dogs to put down or valuable pigs to round up. But the worst was working twelve hours a day for less than two pesos (which the CNI often paid late). "For all these reasons," said the letter writer, "the workers of this place energetically protest and look to higher authorities to put a stop to these abuses and anomalies taking place in this campamento, of which we are victims."[44] In response, the CNI vehemently denied the accusations and maintained that it had long been observant of norms that Cárdenas's pro-worker administration established. "We have always," the CNI maintained, "cultivated the most cordial relations possible with the workers at our service," and went further by claiming it never made anyone work twelve hours a day, but, in fact, paid double for overtime.[45]

Workers also sometimes appealed directly to the president, as in the case of Luciano Delgado. In July 1940, in a letter to the president accompanied by a photo showing him in the hospital, Delgado wrote that he was working in a tunnel when some of it fell and broke his leg and a few of his ribs: "I have been working three years here, and my minimum salary of $2.15 pesos a day has not been raised. I would like you to have my salary raised given all of the services and favor that I have done for the Nation so that I can support my family since I cannot buy food with what I earn."[46]

In April 1939, on behalf of the El Palmito workers, the national CNI union took out a full-page announcement in a Mexico City newspaper publicizing nine petitions it wanted "resolved in a definitive and immediate manner" after two years of struggle. The demands included raising the minimum wage from 1.68 pesos to 2.4 pesos daily; standardizing salaries across different categories and specialties and linking those salaries to efficiency ("a matter of justice"); hiring a physical education teacher and holding more sporting events; and providing electricity, running water, and sanitary services in the workers' colony to reduce the outbreak of diseases and epidemics and infant mortality. Finally, the union requested that the CNI pay for more construction materials, such as wood and adobe.[47]

In response to these complaints, the CNI conceded in its 1940 report that the existing Statute for Workers at the Service of the State had not been well enforced. To correct this failure, it founded a Department of Social Action in May 1939. The department was to study relations between CNI authorities and its personnel, to "serve as a conduit for better understanding," and to "act as a clearinghouse for the diverse cooperatives which function in a system and orient social action." Among its multiple duties, the CNI asked the department to organize and regularly update a registry of worker qualifications and efficiency; study, investigate, and process all of the union's complaints and petitions; and create and manage a salary and cost-of-living index.[48]

In keeping with its social mission, the CNI tried to address specific labor challenges, but in the case of Palmito there was also a local dispute over the jurisdiction of the campamento. It was initially founded as a federal zone administered by the CNI in 1936, a subagency of the SAF, but the municipality of

Indé, Durango, within which El Palmito was located, began exerting its authority over the campamento in 1941. El Palmito residents did not always appreciate the municipality's efforts, especially when Indé established an office in the town with taxing authority. Nevertheless, in the interest of public health, the CNI still felt obliged to maintain water services, public lighting, and sanitation on its own account.[49] In October 1942, the National Union of Agriculture and Development workers complained to President Ávila Camacho that the campamento was "suffering a situation of disorder, scandal and vice," which was due to "the establishment by permission of the municipality of all classes of prostitution, cantinas, cabarets, gambling halls," and a liquor trade. Upset, the union declared:

> State and Municipality are invading the camp when it should be under federal jurisdiction via the CNI, given that it is temporary, where 95 percent of the population is a floating population. Without trying to undermine the sovereignty of the State of Durango, we are concerned with administrative matters, not political ones; this is because it's precisely from them that all the sins weighing down on our community emanate. [The sins] threaten our morale and public peace. They are a menace to the construction of the Palmito Dam; apart from how much it harms the budget and economy of Durango. The federal status of El Palmito is incompatible with a free village under the control of local and state authorities.[50]

The union demanded compliance with the law by keeping a pretense of morality in the federal zone. In response, Ávila Camacho wrote to the State of Durango's Governor Elpidio Velázquez, admonishing that the campamento "should be a place of high morality." He trusted that Velázquez would bring matters under control with the help of the regional military commander. The governor responded with some action, cracking down on alcohol vendors.[51]

As company towns with a social mission, the CNI's dam sites drew the interest and attention of medical students. To obtain their universities' professional certificates, students had to fulfill a social service requirement for three months every year, and the CNI paid twenty-five students, at least nine of them from the National Autonomous University of Mexico in Mexico City, to live and work at the Palmito campamento.[52] These urban middle-class students produced detailed reports on health and sanitary conditions in the campamento over the course of a decade, revealing information largely omitted from official publications and favorable press accounts. The demographic data that the student Mario Saucedo Galindo obtained in 1942 counted 8,000 inhabitants:

2,500 male workers, 2,000 women, 1,500 children, and 2,000 others (merchants, etc.). Most inhabitants were mestizo from the states of Durango, Coahuila, Zacatecas, and Jalisco.[53] The students reported that the services the CNI provided at Palmito were certainly impressive for the time, citing the campamento's hospital, primary school, individual houses, sports facilities, cinema, and running water and electricity. Not all residents enjoyed these services, however, since the CNI segregated the town into two zones—the colonia obrera and the "main" skilled workers' camp (campamento)—with parallel segregation in housing according to salary level.

The CNI divided housing into three classes, A, B, and C, with the first two belonging to the campamento and the third to the workers' colony or pueblo. Class A had two kinds of housing, both "magnificent" in their hygienic condition: one for superintendents, and the other for resident engineers. Every unit was of masonry construction and contained three bedrooms, a bathroom, a dining room, and full utilities, along with polished wood floors, screened windows, and gardens. Class B houses contained two bedrooms, a dining room, a bathroom, and a kitchen, along with electricity and screened windows. The CNI bought these houses from the Peñoles Mining Company for the use of employees and families who made more than twelve pesos per day. For employees who earned eight pesos or less per day, the CNI provided class C housing, with two well-ventilated rooms but no bathrooms—class C residents had to use public restrooms. Single employees lived in wagons, divided by partitions made of wood or masonry. These included a cleaning service, laundry, and common bathrooms. Guesthouses were clean, and there was one new housing cluster for those who earned more than five pesos.[54]

Workers, peons, and merchants lived in the pueblo. Merchants had adobe houses, most with dirt floors and without utilities. Most workers, according to Saucedo, had adobe houses with dangerous cracks in the walls, full of vermin infestation, and dirt floors, which he described as in "bad hygienic shape." Peons, because of their "low salaries and lack of culture, live in huts built from kindling which are covered and stuck together with mud." Already the peons' huts suffered horrible ventilation, but, in addition, low, thatched roofs of straw or rushes formed into a clump made them dark. In general, the huts lacked windows, save small holes in the walls, which allowed in currents that often carried respiratory diseases. "Their way of living," Saucedo observed disparagingly, "was alarming insofar as morality went; entire families sleep on mats thrown on the floor in the company of animals such as dogs, pigs, cats, etc. Parents execute conjugal acts in front of their little children, gravely harming them, as they are at risk of being burned, for in a corner of the room, [the parents] set their fires to cook their food and leave them ablaze all night during the cold season."[55]

In contrast to such alleged harm at home, there were three schools in the camp for children. Two were made of wood and another, located in the west of the camp near the hospital, was made of cement and offered sports facilities for basketball, volleyball, and baseball, as well as military exercises taught by soldiers. The CNI offered good sanitary facilities at all the schools and in conjunction with the Secretaría de Educación Pública (Ministry of Public Education; SEP) jointly funded the principal school. To Saucedo's chagrin, a ravine separated the pueblo and the camp from the principal school, but nonetheless it had good facilities and supplies; could accommodate fifty to sixty students; and offered ten months of classes, from October to July, five hours per day with one half-hour of recreation. On registration, pupils could get vaccinations from the hospital, and during the year the school offered hygiene courses.[56]

The CNI provided a number of other social services, including child care. The hospital had a maternity ward, attended by one doctor and three assistants. It offered free twenty-four-hour health care for CNI workers and their spouses. Some medical assistants lacked training, however, as Saucedo witnessed one use unsterilized scissors to cut umbilical cords, and many pregnant women employed "uneducated" midwives (there were perhaps five to eight of them). Not only did expectant mothers keep working until they gave birth, but poor nutrition also afflicted the campamento, leading to high infant mortality.

Saucedo concluded that the CNI's company town boasted a variety of modern social services that many cities of the country lacked, such as potable water, chlorination, sewerage, and other comforts, albeit not for everyone. "The campamento is deserving of all praise," he acknowledged but added that even though the CNI had accomplished much, there was always room for improvement. For instance, he had observed elsewhere that the "peons' housing is miserable, but the CNI provided them with materials to build decent habitations; for lack of culture and of civility, they didn't take the opportunity so they continue to live as before. One engineer suggested building different types of houses for workers to rent at reduced prices in accordance with the salary of each, but it wasn't accepted. Hopefully it will be for future projects. Also, a sanitary delegate should be assigned to inspect all sites—hotels, restaurants, etc." These were low priorities for the CNI, however; a much higher priority was completion of the dam, even if it compromised the revolutionary social mission for its flagship company town.[57]

The CNI accelerated dam construction in 1943 after several years of slow progress. In June 1942, following years of battling the cresting flows of the

Nazas River, CNI engineers reported that they had known since 1937 of the risks that técnicos and workers would face in the last year of dam construction. They also knew that river flow could rise to an elevation of 1,580 meters above sea level and discussed moving relatively portable houses located below that level to form a new campamento "of the diversion tunnel" above 1,580 meters—their own houses would be included in the move. The CNI had already constructed thirty-eight new houses at a cost of 700 pesos each for those they would have to remove from the surrounding ranches, ejidos, and settlements of Concepción and San Jerónimo, Rincón de Ramos, and Santa María. The compensation the CNI had to offer for all of these was 300,000 pesos, 50,000 more than the yearly budget for 1942 allocated.[58]

The CNI engineers, however, could not have anticipated the torrential rains that drenched much of Mexico in September 1944. They caused the Nazas to crest at extraordinary elevations just as workers completed the dam curtain. The river had only the three diversion tunnels, each six meters in diameter, through which to pass. At full capacity, the three tunnels could handle a flow of 3,000 cubic meters per second, but the September rains caused the river to flow at double that volume. Unsurprisingly, the unfinished reservoir began to fill rapidly and thereby threaten the remaining housing.[59] In fact, it filled so quickly that not long after the workers had moved into makeshift shelters, rising waters destroyed all of their houses. The CNI then started building new homes and settlements at higher elevations away from the flood-prone areas before the rainy season in 1945. It hired a contractor who carefully surveyed the topographical conditions of the area and paid him 2,400 pesos per housing unit. In effect, the CNI was building a new town by decree of the federal government. The decree ordered that "every worker who lost his house due to the recent flood [would] be provided material from the CNI and given time to proceed with its reconstruction."[60]

The contractor determined that all houses below "curve no. 80," referring to one of the terraced curves on the aerial map of the reservoir vulnerable to flooding, needed to be removed. The new town would consist of three living quarters, where skilled workers and técnicos lived, and the pueblo. The first quarter above curve number 80 had 45 families with 225 people. The second quarter had 108 families with 504 people. In the third quarter, which consisted of shelters, there were 250 families with 1,250 people. The pueblo had 860 families with 4,300 people. Between curves number 74 and 80 there were 300 families (1,500 people) living in the pueblo, 62 families (310 people) living in the first quarter, and 40 families (200 people) of carpenters also living in the first quarter. Two hundred bachelors lived in collectives. Thus, a total of 8,525 people would need new homes, although the CNI estimated the number to be as high as 10,000 because it was not always easy to determine how many people were in each family. This would not, however, change the number of houses it needed to construct. The total estimated cost was 600,000 pesos, but Thorne predicted that would rise to a million pesos. It was a high cost to pay for only two more years of work on the dam, but the CNI deemed it indispensable. Moreover, aware of the jurisdictional complications it might present, engineers recommended that the CNI acquire the land on which the new campamento would be built "to give it all the characteristics of a camp site and avoid as much as possible all those of a pueblo." Nevertheless, local merchants and vendors would still enjoy full concessions, and CNI workers would still enjoy all promised social services.[61]

As the dam construction wound down after nearly ten years—six years behind schedule—and far over budget, the CNI eliminated jobs, and its company town's population declined rapidly, leaving the remaining inhabitants to worry about their fate in the post-dam era. Once the reservoir filled to the higher elevations on which the new campamento rested, they would have to move again. They thus requested that the state and federal governments grant them land to found a new municipality, or a "free zone," so they could maintain their livelihoods and businesses. To help them do so, they organized a Committee of Petitioners for Urban Land to demand land for building houses as compensation for their flooded homes. For two years after the dam was completed, in light of their sacrifices in building one of Mexico's grandest infrastructure projects (see figure 4.6), the remaining workers continued to petition the government for compensation and support for alternative employment. They also complained that medical personnel no longer attended to them; although the need for medical services still existed, the medical personnel felt no incentive to visit the area.[62]

Whether people experienced life and work on the Palmito Dam site as positive or negative, or something in between, depended on their individual circumstances. It is likely that those of higher social and occupational status recalled their experiences more positively than those of lower status. For example, one former resident of the company town, a civil engineer named Joel Rojas Tamez, the son of a mechanic who worked on the dam, wrote a short memoir of his childhood there. El Palmito was like a "family," Rojas recalled, especially while he was a pupil in primary school, where children of all classes would attend and excel. Although there were deficiencies, free primary education for all social classes was one of the "conquests of our social movement of 1910," and Rojas credited that education for sowing the seeds for his successful engineering career.[63]

FIG. 4.6 The completed Lázaro Cárdenas/El Palmito Dam on the Nazas River. Photograph by the author, 2006.

Life and Work in Water-Deprived Ejidos Awaiting Completion of the Dam

Although geographically far from the Laguna's ejidos in the populated areas downriver, the Palmito Dam connected closely to both their present socioeconomic challenges and the prosperous future that Cárdenas promised them on its completion. Beginning in 1937, engineers had begun trucking Laguna ejido leaders to the dam site so they could study the technological wonder and return to inform their companions of the benefits they would gain from it. By order of Carlos Peralta, general director of the Ejido Bank, groups of ejidatarios would visit the dam every Saturday because "the President desires that they notice the large [government] investment in these works so that in approximately three years, all of the ejido communities will be opportunely supplied with the water they need for irrigation, and will thereby secure their harvests." On a visit to an agricultural training school in the former Santa Teresa hacienda, director of federal education José Reyes Pimentel offered to take fifty ejido students to El Palmito for educational purposes.[64]

Since the government and media spread so much propaganda about the dam, many ejidatarios unsurprisingly sought work on its construction, as revealed in archives full of requests from regional ejidos for jobs in El Palmito. Indeed, according to a CNI account, 40 percent of the dam's workforce consisted of regional ejidatarios and small landholders. It was federal policy to hire locally, but relying on such a large percentage of local hands slowed work down considerably. Their availability remained seasonal, and at cotton harvest times, these local workers would return to their ejidos, leaving engineers shorthanded.[65]

The fact that dam construction provided employment for some ejidatarios after the 1936 reparto reflects one of the major paradoxes of ejido life: although ejidatarios received grants of communal land, they could not necessarily work that land. No opinion surveys were ever carried out on ejidatarios' reactions to the reparto; contemporary interviews and subsequent testimonials expressed mixed feelings, reflecting individual circumstances. For instance, in response to the Czech journalist Egon Erwin Kisch's inquiries soon after Cárdenas announced the completion of the reparto de tierras in late 1936, interviewees admitted that life might be the same or worse economically, but "before we lived like beasts. Now at least we are men, and as the harvest grows we earn more."[66] Echoing the sentiment, Simón Quiñones of the ejido San Antonio de los Bravos recalled decades later that "we led a life of slaves; we lived in huts made of mesquite and straw on the roof. We had to get up at four in the morning and work from sunrise to sundown." Manuel Mijares, of the ejido El Vergel, recalled a more mixed picture in the 1980s: "Well, it's true that the bosses were very strict with us at work, but I think one of the things we have to recognize about the hacendados is that they cared, because as peons, we would play some sport, and here the boss don Fernando Rincón had a court built." José Pules García of the ejido Finisterre recalled, "In Tlahualilo, they gave us sandals and shoes, yes sir, indeed, they treated us well." Francisco Santoyo of Matamoros felt differently about his hacienda: "We worked like mere mules; the mules were better fed than us." And in a more elaborated negative critique of the reparto, Francisco Aldaco Jurado of the ejido Luján commented:

> They gave four hectares per ejidatario to campesinos and 150 hectares of the best land to the bosses—or rather, they chose those hectares—and the ejidatarios were left with the poorest quality lands, the most exploited; for that reason they have never had good production and ended up with the lowest quality harvest. The bosses kept the wells, the pumped water and therefore had water all year long. The ejidatario could only wait for river flow when it rained, because before there weren't dams, we didn't have wells, we had nothing. The ejidatario from the beginning needed much, and was turned into a more compromised worker than

ever. The minimum salary disappeared and became a loan with interest and an obligation to pay taxes, turning [the ejidatario] into a total slave. Instead of getting a benefit . . . the campesino has never gotten anything good from this agrarian reform, from then until now.[67]

Multiple factors, of course, accounted for these differing views, but Laguna ejidatarios persistently mentioned access to water, or lack of access, as one of the most important factors that affected the quality of life in their ejidos. In July 1937, less than a year after the reparto, a "strong drought" ruined the ejido cotton crop, especially for those without pump-installed wells. The drought's silver lining, so long as it did not persist much longer, was that pink bollworms could not infest cotton plants because the temperatures were too high.[68] Since little or no river water appeared, ejidos increasingly relied on sinking wells and installing motorized pumps in them. In June 1937, the end of the first agricultural year after the reparto, a cadastral survey of the five major municipalities of the Coahuila portion of the Laguna showed 93,000 hectares of irrigated land using Nazas waters and pumps valued at a mere thirty-eight million pesos.[69] As such, the Ejido Bank supplied credit and helped to raise funds from state and private sources to finance pump-installed wells; in 1939, this amounted to two million pesos for sixty-five agrarian communities.[70] Sinking wells required employing professional "well drillers," a corrupt process that involved kickbacks between favored drillers and the bank.[71] Some drillers were from the United States and supervised groups of Mexican workers from the local Well Drillers' Union. On one occasion in early 1937, the union went on strike against the well driller H. T. Smith and confiscated his equipment before requesting arbitration. The strike came on the heels of another strike that had just ended between the union and the well driller R. R. Midgett.[72]

Given the costs in labor and money, successful installation of one or more new pumps in an ejido was a festive and newsworthy event. For example, at the entrance of the ejido Nazareno, numerous campesinos lined up in formation with government-supplied farming tools in their hands to welcome the representatives of the governor of Durango, the Agrarian Department, the Ejido Bank, and even the government of Nicaragua. All of them were engineers who came to celebrate the new pump-installed wells, which the ejido had christened with names of the president, the CNI director, and the Ejido Bank director, among other politicians and government officials. Each pump had eighty horsepower capable of extracting eight liters of groundwater per second and together, including the labor to dig the well, cost 250,000 pesos. The festivities accompanying the inauguration included a baseball game and other sporting events during the day and a musical at night titled "Tierra y Libertad" (Land and Liberty) featuring ejidatarios in the leading roles.[73] The mass creation of ejidos in Cardenista Mexico intrigued Depression-era American academics, social activists, and artists, including film studios such as Paramount Pictures: it made a film of agricultural life on a successful San Pedro ejido occupying the former Nuevo Texas ranch. The Mexican government hoped the film would "exhibit ejido activities in the Laguna for the entire country, Latin America and various European nations."[74]

As with the Palmito Dam site, the government departments and agencies charged with ejido affairs publicly announced their intention to improve social and cultural life in ejidos. After Cárdenas left office in 1940, this effort not only continued but also, in some cases, intensified. Toward the end of Ávila Cama-cho's term in 1946, for instance, the SEP and ejido organizations, along with the Federal Committee for School Construction, forged an agreement to boost spending on school construction significantly through fifty-fifty cost-sharing arrangements between the government and ejidos. The first stage provided seventy-three ejidos with new schools, which together would constitute 23 percent of the schools in the Laguna. Officials predicted success based on the previous "excellent cooperation" between the 206 collective education centers in ejidos— who enrolled more than eight thousand children—and the national literacy campaign.[75]

In his ethnographic fieldwork in the 1950s and 1960s, the anthropologist Raymond Wilkie noted that the schoolhouse in the ejido of San Miguel, located in Matamoros, was a "point of community pride, as indicated by the fresh paint, the well-watered bushes, flowers, and young piñavete trees, the high, strong, wire fence to protect the children, the elegant outdoor drinking fountain." The pre-1936 hacienda owner was one of a few in the Laguna who had established a school even before the Revolution or the mandate in the 1917 Constitution that employers establish and support elementary schools for the benefit of the community in which they resided. The school, however, had educated the children with only minimal reading and math skills. Shortly after the ejido's creation in 1936, the ejidatarios did not wait for the government to erect a new building. Instead, they obtained a loan and built their own school, "a brightly painted, three-room, U-shaped structure of a style common to other post-1936 schools in the region." Teachers were paid in part by the SEP and in part by the ejido, "whose constitution required the ejidatarios to cultivate a four-hectare plot (*parcela escolar*) collectively for the maintenance of the school." Indeed, Wilkie stressed, "education was clearly valued in the ejido, and the school one of the most important improvements since the ejidatarios took charge" in 1936.[76]

Regarding health care, newspaper reporters found medical authorities in ejidos responding immediately to the outbreak of a typhoid epidemic that allegedly had caused the deaths of several children in 1946. On closer examination, the authorities found that the children died of respiratory ailments but nevertheless accelerated their vaccination efforts in several surrounding ejidos, reaching 84 percent of their populations; only people who could not receive vaccinations, such as pregnant women with complications, infants, and sick children remained unvaccinated. Similar rapid, successful responses had occurred in 1943 and 1944 after smallpox spread from rural areas into San Pedro and Torreón.[77] A campesina interviewed by Kisch during his visit to the Laguna soon after the reparto said "with a cranky tone and gestures" that "our hospital alone makes us feel like people. Before, we could never call the doctor for want of money to pay him. My mother gave birth to me in an open field, out among the plants, and my husband died in the fields vomiting blood. Now, when we are sick we have our hospital."[78]

Wilkie's ethnography of the San Miguel ejido corroborates that before 1936 the hacienda did not offer any health services; nor could the peons afford private doctors. But since then the situation had improved. Once the Ejido Medical Service established a hospital in Torreón, many of San Miguel's ejidatarios used its professional services, with half of their children born there. Much like the CNI's Palmito company town, the medical service provided visiting nurses to teach ejido women the basic principles of infant nutrition and hygiene. Their efforts paid off, for nearly all of the ejido's children were vaccinated against common childhood diseases. Nevertheless, intestinal diseases (which caused the highest infant mortality rate) still afflicted the ejido; the Ejido Medical Service failed to persuade all mothers to boil water for their babies, serve them only well-cooked food, and bathe them regularly.[79]

In contrast to El Palmito, where occupational status according to salary and skill levels explicitly conferred differential access to housing and social services, ejidatarios were in legal principle all equal in their ejidos. Social justice was, after all, the revolutionary ethos of Cardenista agrarian reform. In practice, however, there were differences that made for social inequities in ejidos. In the case of San Miguel, Wilkie identified four "prestige classes," which seemed to be based mostly on "personality characteristics" but also on other indices of status. They included "official positions held in the ejido; effort and skill as a farmer reflected in crop yields; house type; leadership in community activities; and business activities."

Housing in particular indicated status and performance differences. Most houses in the ejido were "unpainted adobe structures of two rooms, with thatched roofs, dirt floor, and adjacent yards enclosed by a high adobe wall, to keep animals in and strangers out." Although each ejidatario had twenty square meters of land for housing, brothers or fathers and sons often combined their grants and lived together. Wilkie noted that all of the houses built after 1936 "were larger and better lighted, ventilated, and furnished than the shacks built by the hacienda owners." Architecturally, however, they were fundamentally the same. Those that stood out for being of superior construction belonged primarily to ejido leaders who typically painted their houses brightly or sometimes made them of brick rather than adobe; they also had tile or brick floors, and some had potable water, metal window screens, and a chimney for the kitchen stove. Unlike at Palmito, where residents of the workers' colony could not afford housing equal to that of the técnicos or skilled workers, superior housing in San Miguel was within the financial means of most ejidatarios. As Wilkie remarked, "Primarily all that was required was a desire and an ability to budget one's income (a trait that unfortunately was not developed in the earlier hacienda period)." Those ejidatarios without a desire and ability were either very old or otherwise not disposed to spend their income on improving their houses; they lived in "dirt-floored hacienda dwellings" that resembled "hovels." The largest of this group were the *libres,* or relatives and employees of ejidatarios who were not themselves ejidatarios and who had no right to work the land and no access to education and health care services without an ejidatario's permission.[80]

Despite impressive efforts to improve housing, health, culture, and education in ejidos, complaints abounded, as they did on the dam site, especially by women. Besides the frequent lack of water and credit, ejido women protested the opening of cantinas in ejidos, which they claimed caused idleness, vice, and wasteful spending among ejido men. Alcoholism was not only a bad influence; it diverted scarce household resources and deprived children of an education. In one notable case, the women of the ejido Sofía requested that the "civil and military authorities" intervene as soon as possible to close the cantina, which they called "a constant threat to the wellbeing, peace, and prosperity of the entire community."[81] As the historian Jocelyn Olcott observes in her study of revolutionary women in the Laguna, the Agrarian Department encouraged rural women to join official Ligas Femeniles (Women's Leagues) to undertake temperance campaigns as part of their "direct role as mother and as an element of social struggle who participates in the acts and assemblies discussing economic and social issues of the ejido." More often than starting petitions to close cantinas and pool halls, to curb gambling, or to add schools, health services, and even water, Olcott found, women often prioritized the purchase of a molino, or corn mill. The molino could save them hours of slave-like labor using the *metate* (a flat stone for grinding) to prepare the corn flour to cook tortillas.[82]

For Cárdenas, however, water, or lack thereof, still defined the viability of ejidos, as revealed in his correspondence with Máximo Álvarez y Álvarez, the vice-consul of Republican Spain in Torreón. Álvarez y Álvarez, who as a farmer was sympathetic to Cárdenas and his agrarian reform, reported to the president what he saw on his tour of various Laguna ejidos in 1937 and 1938. He observed that although campesinos in some ejidos worked productively during normal hours, other campesinos informed him there were poorly organized ejidos in which lack of enthusiasm and labor inefficiency were the norm. He recommended that the president "inject them with a little enthusiasm" to ensure the country's continuing progress. Cárdenas replied that the apathy the vice-consul reported was due "in large part to the lack of sufficient water to irrigate all of the distributed plots [of land]." Cárdenas promised to communicate his reports to the Ejido Bank and the Agrarian Department. Both were in a position to convince ejidatarios that the uncertainty of cotton production would "largely be eliminated by the construction of the dam on the Nazas, which will regulate the distribution of its waters."[83]

When he wrote these words, only a year had elapsed since the agrarian reform decree of October 6, 1936. Despite the numerous economic, political, and envirotechnical challenges técnicos and workers faced, the construction of the Palmito Dam had slowly but surely advanced. As a large social experiment contingent on rapid transformation in land and water distribution, ejidos also faced unavoidable difficulties but in general held their own. Ten years and two presidencies later, authorities finally dedicated the Palmito Dam on behalf of these ejidatarios, many of whom had helped to construct it. Whether their efforts would bear fruit and their expectations would be met had yet to be determined.

5. (Counter)Revolutionary Dam, Pumps, and Pesticides

There has never been a man like Cárdenas, such a good man, because he protected and helped us so much. He gave us land and he gave us [pump-installed] wells, and what's more, Cárdenas ordered the building of a dam that bears his name.

ARTURO RODRÍGUEZ CRUZ, ejidatario of ejido San Felipe of the Laguna

On October 6, 1946, President Manuel Ávila Camacho, former president Lázaro Cárdenas, SAF Secretary Marte R. Gómez, and an entourage of other political dignitaries assembled in El Palmito to dedicate the huge dam that had finally tamed the Nazas River five decades after engineers first proposed it. On this celebratory occasion, they symbolically renamed the dam "Lázaro Cárdenas" in honor of the president who had decreed the historic resolution to subdivide the Laguna's cotton and wheat estates exactly a decade before. In his dedicatory speech, Gómez recalled October 6, 1936, as "the most important agrarian day in the history of the resolution of the land problem in Mexico," to which he added, "The [dam] dedication today [October 6, 1946] which we are attending... may well be called the most important day in the resolution of the irrigation problem in Mexico."[1]

Although the twenty thousand campesinos in attendance, most of whom were beneficiaries of the 1936 agrarian reform, enthusiastically cheered their leaders, the festive occasion could not obscure an undeniable fact: for nearly a decade they anxiously awaited the clean and predictable supply of water that the government promised this mega-engineering project would deliver to their arid lands. For ten years, the reparto de aguas had been integral to the reparto de tierras, yet the envirotechnical challenges posed by the Nazas River regime forced técnicos to design and implement the two separately and distinctly over time and space. Consequently, from 1936 to 1946 técnicos, ejidos, and small landholders became entangled in tense conflicts over both land and water distribution.

On that autumn day, as Ávila Camacho, Cárdenas, and Gómez unveiled the world's hitherto largest earthen embankment dam—300 meters wide at its highest elevation, with a curtain 92 meters high, the entire structure containing more than 200,000 metric tons of cement—the spectators certainly had many reasons to be impressed by and feel proud of the massive logistical, organizational, and technical feat the nation had accomplished. Dozens of Mexican técnicos and thousands of workers under the U.S. engineer Henry Thorne's supervision had toiled for more than a decade to build Cárdenas's flagship dam—the largest of the three in the arid north—and now hoped it would significantly boost agricultural production and ensure the success of Cárdenas's agrarian reform. Fittingly, for the occasion the Comisión Nacional de Irrigación (National Irrigation Commission; CNI) unveiled a giant sculpture of Cárdenas for a site near the dam's hydroelectric plant. Cárdenas, naturally, was at the center, flanked on each side by his workers and técnicos, all of them solemnly looking out at the huge reservoir created by their physical and technical labor (see figure 5.1).

Yet it was the eminently conservative, if not "counterrevolutionary,"[2] Miguel Alemán who would put his stamp on Mexico's quintessential revolutionary dam soon after he assumed the presidency on December 1, 1946. Over his presidency, Alemán vastly expanded and strengthened the CNI, first by transforming it into the Secretaría de Recursos Hidráulicos (Ministry of Hydraulic Resources; SRH), the only government ministry of its kind in the Western Hemisphere, to which he allocated 8–11 percent of the entire annual federal budget.[3] Bearing as it did the name of Lázaro Cárdenas, the dam was originally designed by the CNI técnicos to water revolutionary ejido-based agriculture, but Alemán directed the SRH to relentlessly weaken, socioeconomically and envirotechnically, that previous goal.

Beginning in 1946 and over the next decade, the people and ecosystem of the Laguna, along with much of north-central Mexico and the U.S. West, suffered through one of the most intense and longest-lasting droughts in their recorded history. Known as the "mini–Dust Bowl" in the United States, the late 1940s and 1950s for Mexico were no less devastating than the Dust Bowl of the 1930s had been to the United States. The Dust Bowl occurred when strong winds blew the parched soil of the U.S. Great Plains—the result of indiscriminate plowing of its natural grasslands for decades—into huge dust storms that extended hundreds of miles and darkened the sky during the day in many areas.[4] In response, the federal government under Franklin D. Roosevelt's New

FIG. 5.1 Sculpture of Cárdenas at the dam that bears his name, flanked on each side by his workers and técnicos. Photograph by the author, 2006.

Deal established soil conservation districts throughout the United States, which Cárdenas and Ávila Camacho sought to replicate in Mexico. In 1946, the Mexican Congress under Ávila Camacho passed a landmark soil and water conservation law to prevent soil erosion and flooding. As with its New Deal counterpart, however, the law defined "conservation" of hydraulic resources as damming and diking waterways. In other words, it did not encourage the preservation of free-flowing waterways, which most técnicos deemed unpredictable, destructive, and wasteful—a "defect," they claimed, of nature.[5]

Mike Davis explains that drought is "the recurrent duel between natural rainfall variability and agriculture's hydraulic defenses," and thus "always has a man-made dimension." He distinguishes drought from *hydrological* drought, the latter a phenomenon that "occurs when both natural [streams, lakes, and aquifers] and artificial [reservoirs, wells, and canals] water-storage systems lack accessible supplies to save crops." As a result, he maintains, "Hydrological drought always has a social history."[6] In a detailed analysis of the social and ecological dimensions of the Laguna's agroindustrial economy in the 1980s, the Mexican social scientists Rolando García and Susana Sanz similarly define drought as "a social perception of water deficiency with respect to a socially defined norm on the Nazas-Aguanaval River Basin for agriculture and domestic water needs."[7]

Técnicos and local water users alike formed their social perception of water deficiency by the water level of the Palmito Dam reservoir. By this measure, during the mini–Dust Bowl of the late 1940s and 1950s, as the reservoir plunged to a fraction of full capacity, they judged the Laguna calamitously water deficient. Laguna agriculture thereby became more dependent than ever on groundwater pumping, despite the fact that, beginning in 1948, the SRH's rapidly advanced geohydrological knowledge of Mexico's aquifers had led it to decree a series of *vedas* (prohibitions on pumping). As secretary of the SAF under Ávila Camacho, Gómez had been fully aware of this reality, yet after he left office in 1946 he still energetically worked to form Worthington de México, the Mexican subsidiary of the New York–based multinational Worthington Pump and Machinery. Worthington de México was officially inaugurated with much fanfare in 1951 in Mexico City. As president in the 1950s, Gómez was instrumental in establishing the machinery supply store Equipos Mecánicos de La Laguna (Mechanical Equipment of the Laguna) in 1956, which directly stocked and sold his company's domestically manufactured groundwater pumps.

The Lázaro Cárdenas Dam Turns Alemanista

In its effusive coverage of the dam dedication ceremony, *El Siglo de Torreón* reminded readers that, ever since it began publishing in 1921, the newspaper had always supported the project. Yet it acknowledged that many Laguneros worried whether the completed dam would live up to its promises. The paper remarked the water level was low in the reservoir and the government would need to build another smaller regulatory dam far downriver. As if to confirm suspicions, the CNI had not released water from the reservoir a week after the dedication, and tensions quickly flared among local water users. Various ejidos demanded water to plant their wheat fields, but the manager of the Irrigation District, an engineer auspiciously named Benjamin Franklin, replied that his hands were tied until CNI headquarters in Mexico City issued new, post-dam regulations for water distribution.[8]

Two days later, fearful for their subsistence, the Tlahualilo ejidos demanded that the CNI release water forthwith, but during a tense meeting with the regional ejido association, Franklin reiterated his claim that he still had no instructions from the CNI and thus lacked the authority to open the dam's sluice gates. The following day, ejido association representatives meeting in San Pedro urgently telegrammed the president and the SAF with two demands: immediate release of water and provision of credit to carry out infrastructural repair work in case ejidatarios could not plant due to lack of water. The work included building new canals or repaving old ones to prevent the loss of surface water through filtration underground. For another tense week, ejidos continued to demand water. Finally, on October 22 the CNI authorized opening one sluice gate to deliver a small quantity of water from the reservoir.[9]

For several years, scant precipitation in the Sierra Madre Mountains of Durango meant the reservoir would be constantly slow to fill and lead to scenarios like that in October 1946. Yet the CNI had exacerbated the situation by hastening the dedication of the dam so it would fall precisely on the tenth anniversary of the reparto de tierras, even though técnicos knew the dam would not be fully functional for another few months. This privileging of symbolism over functionality was no surprise to the socialist agronomist Emilio López Zamora and the Spanish engineer Manuel Lorenzo Pardo, both of whom had publicly warned for years about such a risk. In an article published in the Mexico City daily *El Universal* in 1945, López Zamora reiterated the warning he first made in 1940: that the dam could not possibly meet Cárdenas's expectation that it would, along with groundwater pumping, irrigate 300,000 hectares of cropland. At best, López Zamora predicted, total surface water from the reservoir and pumped groundwater together would enable irrigation of 150,000 hectares, an amount equal to what the CNI allocated to the ejido sector alone. Small landholders and others would be left with no water at all if ejidos used all of their tandas (allocated water rounds) to irrigate their lands.[10]

López Zamora was a relative newcomer compared with Pardo, who had staunchly opposed the dam since the 1920s from Spain, where he gained prestige after successfully engineering the Ebro River basin. When the CNI had nearly completed the dam in the summer of 1946, national newspapers published Pardo's harsh critiques of its allegedly flawed technical design for both flood control and irrigation.[11] He warned that two additional diversion tunnels were needed to protect the Laguna against a hypothetical Nazas surge of 8,000 cubic meters per second but omitted the fact that the dam, with only its three existing diversion tunnels, had successfully resisted a surge of 6,000 cubic meters per second in 1944. Caused by the largest Nazas flow since the government began keeping records in 1893, that potentially catastrophic surge might well have severely damaged or even destroyed the Laguna's urban areas and was checked only by the unfinished Palmito Dam. Accordingly, national newspapers and government officials proudly declared that the huge investment in the dam was amply justified.[12]

Pardo appeared wrong about the dam's flood-control capability, but the CNI (SRH after December 1946) engineers remained privately concerned that his irritating critiques—which he kept sending directly to them and the press—could undermine public confidence in the ability of the reservoir to store and deliver water. As the engineers searched for a scapegoat, they deflected blame from the technical design and expected capabilities of the dam and instead pinned responsibility on the water users, especially ejidos, for persisting with what they regarded as traditional and wasteful agricultural practices. For instance, in November 1947, a little more than a year after dedication of the dam, the engineer Pablo Bistráin wrote a confidential memo on the large consumption of reservoir water used to irrigate 67,000 hectares of wheat. One of the foremost reasons for this large consumption, in his opinion, was the "lack of education and adaptation of the user to the new irrigation procedures." He continued, "Most of [the ejidatarios] still have the deep-seated conviction that only the 'aniego' method is the most effective for harvests; as a result we have to struggle against a one hundred-year-old tradition and rapidly and objectively educate the user so that he psychologically evolves and then applies the new irrigation techniques [*procedimientos*] to his plots."

In contrast to the aniego method, Bistráin advocated adoption of the new "semi-aniego," or "embankment irrigation," technique employed by users of the ill-fated Don Martín Dam in northeastern Coahuila and other water projects in the northern zones of Durango and in neighboring Chihuahua.[13] He claimed that the semi-aniego technique used much less water, filling land parcels to a depth of merely 10–20 centimeters, and only as frequently as the crops needed. By contrast, the old technique required indiscriminately filling parcels to a depth of one meter. The new technique also required leveling croplands, which in the water-deprived Laguna, he argued, could save an impressive 10–15 percent of the water currently consumed. The two user groups he identified as being "the most advanced" with regard to the new irrigation techniques were small landholders and a few ejidatarios who had gained experience with the technique in other regions.[14] He implied in his observations that the majority of Laguna ejidatarios defied modernization and stubbornly clung to an outmoded method of irrigation. Yet many merely continued what they had done for decades as hacienda peons prior to the 1936 reparto: practicing what their former bosses—now the small landholders Bistráin lauded—would order them to do. The reality was that, in face of persistent detractors of the dam such as Pardo, eliminating the practice was imperative for the SRH's image.[15]

In a memo a few months later, the engineer Jesús Oropeza, chief of inspection of federal waters, echoed Bistráin, warning the same SRH director that "traditional techniques" had to be changed rapidly through education programs. If not, the manager of the Irrigation District would have to unilaterally reduce water volumes to ejidatarios who persisted in using the old techniques. The problem was one of perception; Oropeza and Bistráin, like most of their colleagues, regarded letting water flood excessively or flow down to the river's terminus as wasteful because if it was saved, that same water could be used more efficiently over larger areas of land. As Oropeza tried to explain the politically volatile situation: "Fortunately, the principal obstacle we would encounter on taking concerted action [to change the old irrigation practices]—which is the systematic opposition of the leaders of the ejidatarios—looks as if it could be removed now and the government would support the new policy, which will achieve a better use of public wealth." His dichotomy between the old, presumably wasteful practices of aniego and the new, more economical and efficient practices of semi-aniego faced another challenge: if semi-aniego failed to conserve reservoir water, Oropeza feared, it would justify Pardo's critique that the dam would never be practical. "But," Oropeza was quick to add, "it could be noted that [these new techniques] owed not to deficiencies in the hydraulic work projects but, rather, to political considerations unrelated to the scientific basis of the dam project."[16]

Oropeza carefully constructed his argument with intriguing logic: if the government removed the political obstacle of ejidos' opposition, the new scientific techniques could take hold, and ejidatarios could presumably use water more efficiently. If they failed to adopt the technique, however, that would be due not to flaws in the hydraulic science behind the dam but, instead, to "unrelated political considerations." In other words, compelling ejidos to adopt the technique was a scientific, not political, matter, but any subsequent failure would be a political, not scientific, problem. By "political," Oropeza was likely referring to resistant ejidatarios who did not regard the new method as more efficient, whereas by "scientific" he likely meant a "correct" method of irrigation compatible with a regulated river. Although Oropeza's use of these terms conveniently conformed to Alemán's technocratic *reforma agrícola* (agricultural reform) designed to emasculate the socially progressive Cardenista agrarian reform,[17] it appears that the terms reflected more of a post-*dam* than a post-Cardenista discourse. After all, like Alemán, Cárdenas had envisioned the dam as synonymous with modernizing the Laguna's irrigation system, but unlike Alemán, he prioritized ejidos in the order of preference for water delivery from its reservoir.

The first year after the dam's completion, environmental conditions initially improved, so SRH engineers did not immediately pressure ejidos to abandon the aniego method. In 1945–46, Laguna farmers irrigated 106,550 hectares, 68 percent from groundwater (averaging 48 hectares per pump-installed well among a total of 1,518 wells in use), and in 1946–47, farmers irrigated 50 percent of nearly 140,000 hectares with surface water.[18] But even during these relatively good years, López Zamora and Pardo's pessimistic forecasts proved optimistic, as, thanks to the mini–Dust Bowl, the region's environmental conditions abruptly deteriorated through the late 1940s and 1950s. In the decades ahead, López Zamora would be instrumental in designing a grand "rehabilitation plan" to save the drought-afflicted and disproportionately affected ejido sector.

As the dam's reservoir level remained extremely low, water evaporated, crops failed, and many Laguneros suffered, the government and media tended to blame ejidos and nature for the disaster (nature being ascribed agency in the drama). Although natural vicissitudes undoubtedly played a large role, it was a constellation of various forces and processes that brought the region to the verge of socioeconomic collapse in the mid-1950s: the state's and private sector's use of ecologically invasive technology in the pursuit of short-term profit; public policies that favored large, resource-intensive, and polluting agroindustry; and the corresponding weakening of and discrimination against the ejido sector. The history of Mexico's groundwater pumping business, personified by Ávila Camacho's SAF secretary, the seasoned técnico and longtime politician Marte R. Gómez, epitomized all of these.

Geohydrological Knowledge versus Pumping Business

In January 1941, soon after Cárdenas left office, the new Ávila Camacho administration ordered Gómez to inspect agricultural conditions in various regions of the country, among which the Laguna was a priority. While he was there, Gómez, despite scathing political criticism from both the left and the right, affirmed Ávila Camacho's support for Cárdenas's agrarian reform.[19] He recognized that irrigation in the region could not rely exclusively on groundwater pumping, but insufficient river flow made it an essential stopgap measure for Laguna farmers until the completion of the Palmito Dam. Although Cárdenas had proclaimed in 1936 that the dam would deliver sufficient water to irrigate as many as 300,000 hectares, one of Gómez's accompanying subordinates, the engineer Donaciano Ojeda O., who was in charge of the agro-economic section, estimated in private field notes that, at a maximum, the Laguna's Irrigation District could yield 160,000 hectares—100,000 hectares from the dam reservoir and 60,000 hectares from wells. He also remarked that the combination of unrestricted well drilling and construction of the dam could disrupt the fragile hydrological cycle between river flow and aquifer recharge that the aniego method had maintained for generations.

Specifically, Ojeda predicted that a more "rational use of water" enabled by the dam would "likely diminish" the volume of groundwater and therefore constrain its use. The deteriorating quality of well water, as "open wells" had demonstrated, was also a "limiting factor" for groundwater use. For instance, groundwater occasionally became so saturated with salt that its use would "not only harm the soil" but could damage the entire regional economy. As a result, much of the land "would have to be abandoned for good." Finally, echoing both Gómez and the Cardenista engineers before him, he reiterated that groundwater pumping could be only a "supplementary," not a principal, source of agricultural water use, and he stressed that no irrigation zone should rely exclusively on groundwater.[20]

A few months later, CNI engineers reported in internal correspondence that the hydraulic works of the Laguna resembled those of the Salt River Project in Arizona. That project "showed that the water available by pump for irrigation is principally the returned water from the excess irrigation water that filters underground and is incorporated into the aquifer. There is a large probability that in the Laguna . . . it is the returned water that actually sustains the wells and will sustain them in the future."[21] In other words, they recognized that by helping recharge the aquifer and making sufficient groundwater available to pump, the aniego method was sustainable, but damming the river would likely disrupt this process.

Yet by 1941, up to a third of Laguna irrigation relied exclusively on groundwater pumping (see figure 5.2). As a result, Gómez called not for pumping restrictions but, instead, for more studies to determine how much water users withdrew and to identify which zones should rely exclusively on surface water and which should rely on a combination of surface and subsurface water. The CNI's top engineers—Antonio Coria and the naturalized Mexican Andrew Weiss—estimated there were as many as 2,500 wells in the Laguna and concluded that "no study has shown the feasibility of using wells. . . . Indicators show it is unfeasible. Some are drawing up salt water." Agustín Zarzosa, owner of the La Granja Ranch near the Noé train station in Gómez Palacio, Durango, and the leader of the association Small Properties of the Laguna, was one small landholder who faced this problem. Even with various pumping plants, "his soil is gradually hardening from using salt water from his wells. This is common and can continue until the soil has to be abandoned. This matter of salt water from water pumps is of prime importance to the life of the land in this region."[22]

FIG. 5.2 An engineer sits on a pipe through which Nazas River water withdrawn by a pump flows into the Guadalupe canal. Two campesinos stand at a little distance to his left. Courtesy of Archivo Histórico del Agua, Mexico City, *Noria extrayendo agua del río Nazas conducida por el canal de Guadalupe,* 1942, San Pedro, Coahuila. CONAGUA-AHA, Fondo Aprovechamientos Superficiales, box 3067, file 42425, 30.

In response to these reports, Ávila Camacho decreed a new regulation in February 1941 on water distribution in the Laguna. As the construction of the Palmito Dam looked to take far longer than its anticipated completion date of 1939, the regulation offered much more precision and clarity than the 1938 provisional regulation.[23] Ávila Camacho gave the CNI the difficult task of demarcating the Laguna's future Irrigation District. To that end, the CNI redivided the district into three units: two within the Nazas basin (above and below the San Fernando Dam) and a third, separate unit consisting of the Aguanaval basin. The unit that comprised the Nazas basin below the San Fernando Dam (the "regulated zone") held by far the most irrigable land, with a maximum capacity of 160,000 hectares. The CNI engineers estimated that the future dam reservoir would supply a little more than half of the needed water, and pumped groundwater would supply the remainder, but they made this estimate without any precise data on the capacity of the region's aquifer. The regulation of 1941 therefore also ordered them to study better ways to extract water from the aquifer, the first explicit inclusion of groundwater in any such regulation.

The regulation ordered furthering of studies already undertaken of the dam's hydroelectric capacity and the feasibility of building a second regulatory dam downriver, near the original site that Francisco I. Madero first proposed in 1907 in the Fernández Canyon. Even as the dam was still under construction, engineers estimated that one major storage dam would be insufficient for regional water needs. The regulation also tried to rectify the problematic distribution of ejidos and small landholders along the canals by authorizing the CNI to charge a uniform fee for water management. The hierarchy of distribution among the various agricultural sectors remained: ejidos and small landholdings that possessed fewer than 20 hectares were exempted from paying the water management fee, whereas properties that possessed more than 20 hectares were required to pay. The regulation mandated that the CNI create a user registry to implement its provisions. While exempting ejidos from any modification of their water rights, the CNI was to redistribute water rights according to an agrological or soil condition survey plan in progress, "on the basis of which property owners with soil of poor quality are compensated with extensions of equal estimated value but which can turn greater profits than at present." Furthermore, the CNI was to study how, on completion of the dam, management of the Irrigation District could be transferred directly to the users themselves in its "economic, technical, and social aspects" or else "to do it with the least intervention of the state" in order to "manage, conserve, and improve" the district.[24]

El Siglo de Torreón published the blunt and bleak assessments of the Laguna's social and environmental realities that some engineers voiced during a National Agricultural Credit Bank conference held in Torreón in August 1941. One was the engineer Pastor García, who made public his analysis of and recommendations for the "problem of water in the Comarca Lagunera in relation to agriculture." He remarked candidly that, according to engineers' observations from the previous two years, the flows of the Nazas and Aguanaval rivers strongly affected the subterranean hydrology of the Laguna, and the hydrostatic level of "nearly the entire region" had fallen so precipitously that wells drilled before the mass creation of ejidos could no longer pump shallow groundwater. Many had to be abandoned. He further warned that some 18,000 ejidatarios would have to find work in other regions because there was insufficient water from surface and subsurface sources to grow crops and repay loans to the Ejido Credit Bank.[25]

The Laguna was only one of several rural and urban regions suffering from groundwater overexploitation in the 1940s. In 1944, William Vogt, an influential American ecologist and ornithologist—then the chief of the Pan American

Union's Conservation Section of the Division of Agricultural Cooperation—submitted a confidential memorandum to the Promotional and Coordinating Commission for Scientific Research in Mexico. In dramatic form, he summarized its conclusions:

> Mexico is a sick country.
>
> It is rapidly losing the soil on which its existence depends.
>
> Its available water, instead of increasing to take care of growing populations and augmented industrial demands, gives every evidence of decreasing.
>
> Its forests, valuable for their products and invaluable as protector of soil and water, are being destroyed far faster than they are being replaced.
>
> Its grasslands, source of forage and likewise protection for soil and water, are so heavily overgrazed that both they and their underlying soil are being destroyed.
>
> Its ecology—the interrelationship of all the environmental factors—has been so thrown out of balance that many important land values are being wasted.
>
> As a result, living standards are constantly being depressed, and disaster lies ahead.

In response to this dire ecological assessment, the report recommended that Mexico "aim at total conservation and not restrict itself to such isolated factors as soil conservation, reforestation, etc. The Mexican environment is the resultant of physiographic, climatic and biotic factors, all of which must be considered at once if the most efficient program is to be developed."[26] In 1945, the government amended Article 27 of the Constitution to place groundwater under federal jurisdiction, and in 1946 Mexico passed the landmark Soil and Water Conservation Law, which stipulated the need for conservation as the basis for agricultural development.[27]

The combination of the 1945 revision and 1946 law had little effect on conservation, however, whether of groundwater or any other natural resource. Simply put, Mexico was rapidly industrializing, for which expansion of commercial agriculture was deemed vital, thus trumping nearly all other considerations. At the same time, the nascent policy of import substitution industrialization (ISI), which Ávila Camacho's successor Miguel Alemán would make into a full-fledged national economic policy, was rife with conflicts of interest and corruption; it made already weak and poorly funded enforcement of laws and regulations even more ineffectual.[28]

Symbolic of this contradiction was Marte R. Gómez himself. Like the industrialist Juan Brittingham, who had lobbied Calles to build the Nazas River Dam in 1925 partly to boost his cement businesses, Gómez was personally invested in promoting pump-installed wells—a likely factor explaining his failure to more forcefully regulate groundwater pumping throughout Mexico. When Ávila Camacho decreed the 1941 regulation for the Laguna, pump sellers were already working to expand their market, as shown by at least two dozen advertisements in *El Siglo de Torreón* for new and used Worthington pumps. There is strong circumstantial evidence that Gómez was involved in this pump business while he served as secretary of the SAF. In September 1945 the organizational umbrella for the Laguna's ejidos, the Collective Ejido Societies, accused Gómez of being an associate of Equipos Mecánicos, the company that allegedly forced ejidos to buy Worthington products. The company, which sold Worthington pumps and engines in Torreón, vehemently denied the charge in a letter to the newspaper. Yet without apparent irony, it also took the opportunity to advertise its products and much lower prices.[29] The Mexican Embassy in Washington, DC, included Equipos Mecánicos in a list of companies it submitted in 1942 to the U.S. secretary of state as equipment suppliers for the Palmito and Azúcar dams in case the U.S. government offered Mexico funds for the projects (which it did a year later).[30]

Gómez was exceptionally well placed to profit from both the environmental conditions drought imposed on the north-central regions of the country and Alemán's ISI policy. Taking advantage of close relationships he cultivated with agro-industrial business interests in both Mexico and the United States during the war as SAF secretary, after leaving the post Gómez established a Mexican subsidiary of the U.S.-based Worthington Pump and Machinery for manufacture of deep well pumps and related products. Gómez had to lobby both Alemán and Worthington to establish a factory in Mexico, but, through considerable cajoling and brinksmanship, in 1949 he succeeded. He had to assure Alemán that the Mexican plant could produce—at cheaper prices, no less—pumps of the same quality and durability as Worthington's plants in the United States. At the same time, he had to convince Worthington of two key matters. First, its investment in a factory would ultimately be more profitable than its longtime reliance on exporting products and selling them through a local Mexican distributor. Second, if Worthington did not establish a factory in Mexico, rising tariffs and import duties as a result of the government's ISI policies would effectively lock the company out of a market virtually guaranteed to surge in coming years. Specifically, the government planned to irrigate 40,000 new hectares of land per year for the decade following 1949 by tapping groundwater, and Gómez anticipated a demand for ten thousand new pumps, or a thousand per year, and perhaps even more as electrification increased and obviated the need for fuel for internal combustion engines. With electrically powered engines, Gómez remarked, one "only has to flip on a switch to activate the pumps." Thus, if Worthington did not actively try to meet this demand, competitors, such as the upstart A. O. Smith (which had expressed interest in a Mexican subsidiary), would happily do so.[31]

Gómez much preferred Worthington to A. O. Smith primarily because of its global name recognition. Worthington was the namesake of the American engineer-inventor Henry R. Worthington, about which one historian of the vertical turbine pump industry wrote, "Certainly if there was one only proper name that meant pumps, it would be Worthington."[32] His invention of the "single direct-acting steam pump" dramatically reduced the manual labor required of steam-powered boats in 1840 and launched his career as a prosperous entrepreneur. For forty years, he improved, expanded, and diversified his inventions and product lines, reaching out to high-volume customers such as the U.S. Navy and municipal waterworks around the country. In 1876, at least eighty major Worthington waterworks pumping engines were installed throughout the United States and Canada, with capacities ranging from a half-million to 15 million gallons daily. In 1883, Worthington began to seek business aggressively outside the United States and Canada, including in Mexico, where it made its first sale in 1886. Less than a decade later, in 1893, Worthington estimated the pumping capacity from its products in use worldwide at nearly three billion gallons in twenty-four hours. By 1940, Worthington was doing business in Europe, Asia, Africa, Oceania, and the Americas—specifically, in nineteen countries of Latin America and the Caribbean. With two—one in Mexico City and the other in Monterrey—Mexico was one of only two Latin American countries (the other, Brazil) with more than one Worthington office.[33]

Worthington's innovation of two types of pumps—the "coniflo" and the "axiflo"—that resolved the challenge of elevating groundwater to the surface, enabled the company to expand into Latin America as the demand for groundwater pumping dramatically increased beginning in the 1920s.[34] These two Worthington pumps were extremely simple yet functioned as powerfully and safely as steam engines, and their repair and maintenance could be entrusted to any competent mechanic without any special knowledge of them.[35] Yet the instruction manual for the pumps forthrightly warned, "The deep well pump must not run without an adequate supply of water."[36]

On May 15, 1951, Miguel Alemán and an entourage of cabinet members and prominent Mexican and American business representatives gathered to inaugurate the newly installed Worthington de México factory in Mexico City. In addition to Gómez, the vice-president of the parent company in New York, Clarence E. Searle, was also present. Both men gave eloquent speeches describing the importance of the occasion and what it promised for Mexico. Searle placed it in the larger context of the Cold War, of "free nations of the world" combating "the forces of totalitarianism," making the "interdependence of our two nations even more significant." In particular, he praised the Mexican government's efforts to augment food production for self-sufficiency. Given that its activities were primarily devoted to the production of turbine pumps for irrigation, Searle announced that Worthington would play a vital role in Mexico's agricultural expansion, but this would be only a beginning; he hoped Worthington would expand to include other types of equipment required for industrial uses.[37]

In his speech, Gómez framed the inauguration of the factory in nationalist terms. Citing a United Nations economic study on the need for Mexico to produce its own capital goods, from tractors to water pumps, he declared founding Worthington de México to be a "matter of economic independence." He noted that its initial paid-up capital of four million pesos was entirely Mexican and eventually would increase to ten million. He did not shy away from announcing the pivotal role the government played in supplying this all-Mexican capital: making use of the Ley de Fomento de Industria de Transformación (Law to Promote Industry), the Treasury Ministry furnished many of the financing and import permits, while the Federal District provided tax exemptions through Title 30 of a 1949 resolution on the subject. In addition, Nacional Financiera, the national development bank, floated "series B bonds" totaling some 25 percent of Worthington de México's total paid-up capital. For his part, Alemán described the process as a "combined effort between Mexican capital and American technical cooperation to satisfy a great need for the country."[38]

According to Gómez, Worthington de México was poised to meet Mexico's need for a major expansion in irrigation capacity. The company would produce and repair seventy to seventy-five "pumps of great power for deep wells" per month of the world-renowned Worthington line. In his inaugural speech, Gómez pointed to the favorable reviews its products had received from the Secretaría de Agricultura y Ganadería (Ministry of Agriculture and Livestock; SAG), formerly the SAF, via the National Agricultural Credit and Ejido Banks, as well as from the SRH; Petróleos Mexicanos (Pemex), the national oil company; and the Federal Electricity Commission (CFE). In other words, as a subsidiary of a U.S. multinational corporation, Worthington de México could already count on a largely protected domestic market, which Gómez tried to guard against domestic and foreign competitors.[39] Anticipating criticism of a sheltered industry, Gómez asserted it was private initiative that had made it possible to bring Worthington to Mexico and import its technical capacity.[40] Speaking directly to Alemán, Gómez nevertheless conceded, "We recognize that without the tutelary existence of the state, without the sympathy and stimulus that it has provided us, Worthington de México might never have been founded."[41]

Numerous Mexican and American companies with branches in Mexico endorsed Worthington de México's successful navigation of ISI policy. National Iron and Steel Works, General Electric, Electric Industries of Mexico, Remington Rand (a maker of office equipment), and Electric Material all filled newspaper pages with their congratulatory messages to Worthington de México after its inauguration.[42] Henry Carney, a New York industrial engineer then residing in Mexico who had planned and directed construction and installation of the Worthington de México pump manufacturing plant, also highly praised Mexican workers, affirming, "Mexican technicians and industrial workers now rank among the best in the world."[43] In the following weeks and months, editorials effusively praised the new and most "modern plant" of its kind in the world. Although the plant was then employing only seventy Mexican workers, Worthington headquarters predicted that it would eventually be able to export machinery to other countries in Latin America.[44]

In spite of the generally euphoric coverage of the plant's inauguration in 1951 and the indispensable role that Gómez played, he was also the target of criticism in some media, to which he replied defensively. In particular, charges arose that he benefited from his favorable connections as Ávila Camacho's SAF secretary to obtain an astounding 60 million peso contract for well drilling. He vehemently denied these charges in a letter he wrote to the newspaper making them. In the letter, which the newspaper published, he replied:

> Agriculture has not given me any contract to drill wells: not for 60 pesos, not for 60 million pesos, but what I have received from the president—and without deserving it, since I didn't lend any service to Alemanismo— are personal considerations, moral and economic support for the organization of the pump factory for which I have dedicated all of my time and energy. From this standpoint, I recognize my indebtedness to President Miguel Alemán; I have said so openly when the occasion has permitted and I don't find it inconvenient to reiterate it in writing.[45]

Although Worthington de México attracted the most media attention, it was not the only company seeking to capitalize on Alemán's ISI push and gain a foothold in the Mexican pump market. A year before the inauguration of Worthington de México, Gómez warned his shareholders that the U.S. companies Fairbanks Morse and Peerless also planned to install factories near, respectively, Mexico City and Guadalajara on the Worthington model.[46] There was also domestic competition such as Talleres Industriales and Fabricación de Máquinas of Monterrey, Bombas Laguna of Torreón, Bombas Nacionales of Puebla, and the Johnston Pump Company de México of San Bartolo Naucalpan. Bombas Peerless Tisa and Talleres Industriales, in particular, made so much progress in their operations that Gómez himself, on a visit to their factories in 1954, suggested that they could even be more advanced than Worthington de México's.[47] By 1954, Worthington de México's profits nevertheless jumped tenfold, from one million to ten million pesos.[48] In that same year, the company obtained a contract to supply twenty-five pumps in Gómez's home state of Tamaulipas, and in the following year, Worthington headquarters in New York lobbied the U.S. government to grant its Mexican subsidiary some $4 million of credit through the U.S. Export-Import Bank.[49] This success prompted Central American diplomats to tour the Worthington de México factory and order a number of products from it, thereby realizing the goal publicly set for it at the inauguration to export "Mexicanized" products in the near future.[50] The growing pump market under ISI would evidently accommodate numerous competitors.

Worthington de México and its competitors could credit much of their success within a short period to two mutually reinforcing processes. The first was the continuance of ISI policies, which they worked together to pressure the government to maintain, especially by cracking down on imported contraband on the border. The second was the non-enforcement of vedas in the face of constantly growing demand for groundwater, a concern that never appeared in Gómez's extensive correspondence and in newspaper articles on his business. For instance, in a trade magazine article entitled "The Man behind the Ideal," the author depicted Gómez as a dedicated public servant who—during his long, distinguished career—came to understand that "the problem of the land is not an individual problem of every farm, ejido or parcel. It is a general national problem—that is, in order to produce one needs water." But, as the author continued, all of the irrigation dams and hydraulic systems Gómez helped install as SAF secretary were insufficient. "We had to find new methods to provide water to a thirsty land," he quoted Gómez as saying. His solution was unsurprisingly "irrigation wells," which could make inhospitable arid lands, especially in the northwest, "vertiginous and prosperous."[51]

Certainly, Gómez's successful groundwater pumping business was critical to providing water to a thirsty land, especially the Laguna, in the postrevolutionary period. As early as 1938, when Cárdenas overhauled the prerevolutionary regulations of 1909 for distribution of the flow of the Nazas River (after domestic uses), ejidos and smallholders possessing fewer than 20 hectares had priority for surface water distribution; next came small landholders who possessed 20 hectares or fewer, followed by those who possessed 20–150 hectares. Then, any water that remained was distributed to landholders who possessed more than 150 hectares. Even after Cárdenas left office in 1940 and during most of the Ávila Camacho presidency, this order of preference endured, although the CNI tried to redistribute irrigated lands more evenly across sectors and geographical locations according to soil quality. The government implemented the 1938 regulations through four river-flow cycles (June to June of every year) until Ávila Camacho's updated regulation in 1941 reserved 800 million cubic meters (out of a median flow of 1.1 billion cubic meters) from the Nazas annually for the exclusive use of ejidos and smallholders possessing fewer than 20 hectares in compliance with Article 75 of the National Property Water Law. However, the Supreme Court struck down the regulation a few years later, deciding that the law's article was unconstitutional and inequitable. Ejidatarios protested, but Alemán, in keeping with his determination to boost commercial agriculture at the expense of ejidos, upheld the court's decision by furnishing ejidos with water for 25 percent of irrigable land and 15 percent for small landholders in the post-dam era. This distribution was a tremendous blow for ejidos as a whole; it effectively reduced irrigable areas for individual ejidatarios from an average of four hectares to one hectare while enabling small landholders an average of 22.5 hectares each of irrigated land—a ratio of 22.5:1 skewed against individual ejidatarios.[52] Even this new, inequitable distribution proved insufficient, however, as drought could be as haphazard as any government policy: ejidatarios and small landholders alike had to drill more wells to install pumps to extract groundwater.

After more than a decade of geohydrological studies clearly indicating that unregulated pumping since the 1920s was causing an alarming depletion and salinization of the aquifer, the government finally acted legislatively: part and parcel of the amendment of Article 27 in 1945 was regulating groundwater alongside surface water. Specifically, the revision stipulated that although landowners might extract and consume groundwater through artificial works, the federal government could regulate this extraction by establishing prohibited areas if "the public interest so requires or others' use is affected."[53] Article 27 in the original 1917 Constitution did not explicitly identify groundwater as national property; rather, it referred only to "water that could be extracted from mines."[54] It did so because of deficient geohydrological knowledge and the scant need for intensive use of groundwater at the time in Mexico.[55]

According to a detailed study of groundwater legislation that the SRH engineer René Carvajal published in the journal *Ingeniería Hidráulica en México* (Hydraulic Engineering in Mexico) in 1967, the only reference to managing groundwater resources before the 1917 Constitution existed in the Civil Code of 1884, which was then fully incorporated into the Civil Code of 1932. Numerous articles of the 1932 code granted individuals the right to drill wells or build diversion dams to capture water as they deemed necessary. However, if water flowed from one property to another, the government could determine it was of "public utility" and, accordingly, subject it to special regulations. In other words, water users could not harm the interests of their neighbors, but they could use their water if they compensated neighbors for it. Although the civil codes did not expressly regulate or restrict groundwater use, they firmly established the principle that the government, as the steward of public waters, could intervene to ensure its availability for all users.[56]

In that vein, the 1934 Federal Water Law distinguished between private and federal waters. It permitted property owners to extract as much water as they needed from their land as long as it did not include rivers or natural deposits that the government designated federal property. If they did take federal waters, the CNI (and later, the SRH) could prevent it or the building of private works to enable it. The law thus granted an absolute individual liberty to extract water on private property if it did not affect federal waters, thereby eliminating the distinction between private and federal waters in certain cases. Although property owners were free to extract water on their lands, if such activity affected the "public interest" or existing uses, the CNI/SRH could regulate use and extraction of groundwater and establish no-use zones as if private water were under federal property.

Consequently, the revision of 1945 and subsequent regulations established a property owner's obligation to inform the CNI/SRH when initiating works to extract groundwater for agricultural but not domestic use. Most important, the new regulations imposed a restriction for the first time that was determined by the geohydrological knowledge from technical studies of a particular zone or region. If the studies determined that technologies to extract groundwater up to its maximum limits were detrimental to the public interest or existing uses, the CNI/SRH could propose a prohibition on groundwater extraction to the president.[57]

The revision went further, authorizing the CNI/SRH to impose penalties for violating the law, including preventing installation of works or technologies that could enable violation of the law and even demolishing such works. Yet for all of the new regulations and restrictions on groundwater use, the revision also charged the CNI/SRH with encouraging groundwater pumping to increase agricultural production rapidly for a growing population. The provisions of the 1945 constitutional revision incorporating groundwater, as in the 1917 original, suffered from an intrinsic tension and worked at cross-purposes.

Despite this tension, the SRH, newly empowered with jurisdiction over groundwater, decreed the first veda in 1948 as part of a broad effort to regulate groundwater pumping nationwide. It was the first of fifty vedas the SRH decreed nationally, primarily in the arid and semi-arid north-central areas of the country (see map 5.1 and table 5.1), from 1948 to 1963—coinciding with the duration of the devastating mini–Dust Bowl.[58]

In March 1949, the SRH decreed the first veda on groundwater pumping in select zones of the Laguna.[59] Yet the lack of reservoir water behind the Lázaro Cárdenas Dam, combined with state agricultural policies that provided incentives for using water-intensive agricultural practices as part of the emergent Green Revolution (discussed later), left private landholders and the few ejidos that could afford the expense little choice but to illegally pump groundwater. In 1951, for instance, the SRH decreed an additional veda in an area of southern Chihuahua bordering the Laguna that shared the region's aquifers. Water users from both the small landholding and ejido sectors, however, pumped in areas outside the prohibited zone or otherwise violated the veda. By January 1952, the drought reached crisis proportions. Seeing that the water table had not stopped falling, in October 1952 the SRH imposed yet another veda in the municipalities of Mapimí and Tlahualilo in the Durango portion of the Laguna. In that month, any hope that the dam reservoir would fill vanished when it failed to snow in the Sierra Madre Mountains for the third year in a row.[60]

In 1953, the U.S. counselor for agricultural affairs reported to the U.S. ambassador that drought was a "serious blow" to Mexico's agriculture, especially in the north. That same year was "the most critical" after eight years of persistent drought had "caused serious economic difficulties because of sharply reduced returns from the sale of agricultural products, the growing unemployment, and non-payment of debts, etc." He even deemed it "the greatest single factor contributing to the increasing exodus of illegal Mexican laborers or 'braceros.'" The numbers proved his point: from January through July 1953, northwestern Mexico received only 65 percent of average rainfall; north-central Mexico received 64 percent; central Mexico received 77 percent; the Gulf North received

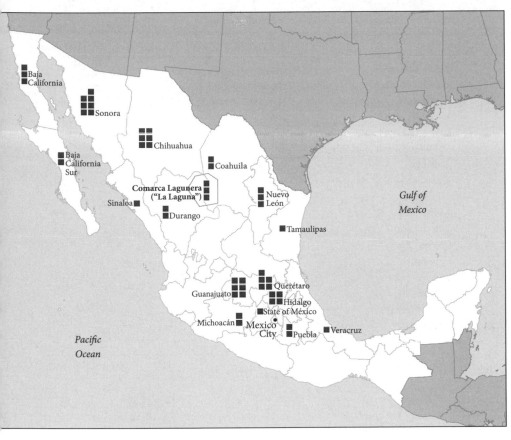

MAP. 5.1 Geographical distribution of prohibitions (*vedas*) on pumping, 1948–63.

61 percent; the Gulf South received 76 percent; and the Pacific South received 95 percent.[61]

The devastation of this prolonged drought in Mexico also garnered headlines in U.S. newspapers, which had been extensively covering its effects all over the United States, including in areas of the generally more humid east. In the pages of the *New York Times,* for instance, the future Pulitzer Prize–winning foreign correspondent, editor, and executive, Sydney Gruson reported the drought had prompted an exodus of an estimated ten thousand rural families from the Laguna whose "land [had] dried to dust." Struggling to escape what Mexico City newspapers described as "imminent starvation," the government had to settle these families in the nearby Cuatro Ciénegas region of Coahuila where test drilling of wells had indicated sufficient groundwater supplies. The drought continued, turning into a catastrophe and compelling farmers to

TABLE 5.1. Vedas (prohibitions) on groundwater use by state, 1948–1963

State	Years of vedas	Total vedas
Baja California	1954, 1955, 1956	3
Baja California Sur	1951, 1954	2
Chihuahua	1951, 1952 (two), 1953, 1954, 1957	6
Coahuila	1951, 1952	2
Comarca Lagunera, Durango, and Coahuila	1949, 1952, 1958	3
Durango	1952, 1956	2
Guanajuato	1948 (two), 1949 (two), 1952, 1957	6
Hidalgo	1954 (two), 1956, 1957	4
Michoacán	1956 (two)	2
Nuevo León	1956 (two), 1958	3
Puebla	1950, 1959	2
Querétaro	1949 (two), 1950, 1951, 1960	5
Sinaloa	1956	1
Sonora	1951, 1954 (two), 1956 (three), 1963	7
State of Mexico	1949	1
Tamaulipas	1955	1
Veracruz	1951	1

SOURCE: René Carvajal Ramírez, "Aspectos legales del agua subterránea en México," *Ingeniería Hidráulica en México* 23, no. 3 (1967): 255.

abandon half of the Laguna's 180,000 hectares of wheat and cotton production as the dam reservoir's level declined to one-tenth of its maximum capacity of three billion cubic meters. The government estimated the resulting crop loss at 200 million pesos, or $23 million—a staggering amount when the total value of national cotton production in 1952 was about 1.4 billion pesos.[62]

In response, Alemán convened a meeting of his secretaries from the SRH and SAG, along with the governors of Durango and Coahuila in January 1952. The government canvassed ejidatarios, directly or via their representatives, and heard consistent complaints that vedas made it impossible for them to compensate for the nearly complete lack of reservoir water. The government responded with an emergency program to combat the situation, but it would prove to be a short-term expedient that exacerbated a long-standing problem. The SRH permitted drilling new wells, promoted mechanization of agriculture to increase yields (which, in turn, would require more water), and pledged funds to recondition and repair canals. The program was inherently contradictory: on the one hand, subsidizing *obras muertas* (dead work) such as cleaning canals and maintaining the hydraulic infrastructure (whether it was needed or not) kept people temporarily employed, whereas on the other hand, mechanization threw people out of work in the long run. The emergency program in 1952 employed thousands of people to work on obras muertas and established an enduring pattern of state-supported drought relief for the region's agroindustrial economy.[63]

This drought-relief strategy bore much resemblance to what Brazilian scholars of drought have termed a "drought industry," which they define as "the misuse of public funds earmarked for drought relief for private gain."[64] In the case of northeastern Brazil, corrupt politicians fueled this industry and built clientelism networks that bound their constituents to them through provision of relief works in exchange for votes. In the Laguna, a similar kind of politics prevailed, as government agencies and ministries averted famine through relief works but allowed widespread hunger and poverty to fester provided conditions did not deteriorate to the point of provoking civil unrest and "disorder," especially armed resistance.[65] The key institution of the Laguna's drought industry was the Ejido Bank, which managed nearly all ejido affairs by providing credit, water, seeds, fertilizers, pesticides, machinery, and other so-called inputs. To obtain them, ejidatarios could plant only what the bank told them to and buy seeds the bank acquired for them, while it sold and marketed the crops, and distributed the profits.

As a result of its overbearing behavior, already apparent soon after the 1936 reparto, the Ejido Bank provoked resistance to its control, notably from Unión Central. Unión Central was a more radical ejido union that sought to launch cooperative health services and food stores, educational and cultural centers, and, more pressingly, gain control of selection, packing, marketing, and processing of ejido crops. The Pedro Rodríguez Triana Ejido Credit Society also separated from the Ejido Bank in 1940, and others left the bank in its wake, obtaining loans from private banks, foundations, state governments, private companies, and local moneylenders. By 1944, nearly a third of ejidos were no longer clients of the Ejido Bank; by 1950, nearly three-quarters were no longer clients.[66]

The remaining quarter or so of ejidos that stayed with the bank suffered corruption and abuse. At election times, bank officials would dispense more credit, machinery, and other inputs to secure the votes for the ruling Institutional Revolutionary Party (PRI) from the ejidatarios under their jurisdiction. Thus, whether it was the organization of production for a "normal" (sufficiently watered) agricultural year or for emergency public works in "abnormal" (insufficiently watered) years, well-connected private companies could feed from the bank trough at ejido (and the general public's) expense through exclusive contracts with the Ejido Bank to furnish supplies, equipment, technology, and technical know-how.[67]

As had been the case since 1936, the most important input for drought-stricken ejidos was groundwater pumps, which required large upfront costs for purchase and installation and skilled technicians for proper maintenance.

Pumping and Spraying for the New White Gold of Dairy

The push to install more and improved groundwater pumps at the national level coincided in the Laguna with the founding of a dairy industry as a key component of a local-state-federal effort to diversify the regional economy. While Gómez was endeavoring to found Worthington de México in 1949 and 1950, the governor of Coahuila worked to secure $4 million in credit to form a union or cooperative of numerous dairy farms to purchase ten thousand calves. These calves would form the basis of a future dairy industry intended to convert the Laguna into the "Wisconsin of Mexico." Equally important was the establishment of a pasteurization plant in Torreón in 1950 to meet new health and hygiene standards for milk production in Mexico.[68] In 1953, the SAG sought to further expand the Laguna's dairy industry by establishing sterilization plants, but the severe and prolonged drought challenged this infant industry in the 1950s.

According to the government of Coahuila, 55,000 cattle perished in 1956, causing enormous losses of approximately $3.75 million statewide. The Laguna was one of the only regions (along with Delicias in Chihuahua) that grew alfalfa for cattle feed. Cattle ranchers desperately needed groundwater to grow their feed, as well as to satisfy the watering needs of cattle, and considering how much they had invested in installing pumping equipment, they worried about their access to groundwater.[69] In 1955, they nevertheless purchased 240 new cattle from Canada at 1,000 pesos per head for stables in Gómez Palacio, Durango, right across the Nazas riverbed from Torreón, which *El Siglo de Torreón* heralded as the beginning of the end of cotton monoculture in the Laguna, and for good reason: unlike the old white gold of cotton, which faced severe competition from foreign producers, synthetics, and other Mexican areas (Mexicali, Lower Río Bravo), there was ever increasing demand for the new dairy products in Mexico's rapidly growing cities. However, like cotton, only far more so, livestock raising for dairy production—from growing cattle feed to the daily drinking needs of dairy cows—was highly water-intensive. In fact, it was far more water-intensive than cotton.[70]

Private farmers were not the only ones interested in partaking of the burgeoning dairy and beef economy. The ejido Emiliano Zapata of Viesca, located a little east of Torreón between the Nazas and Aguanaval rivers, ironically looked to dairy and beef as an economic savior even as over-pumping extinguished its once plentiful springs between 1947 and 1953. Many ejidatarios were often not aware (or even concerned about when they were aware) of the long-term consequences of over-pumping groundwater. The anthropologist Isabel Kelly of the Institute of Inter-American Affairs, the forerunner of the U.S. Agency for International Development, noted the ejidos' myopia in her fieldwork in the ejido of El Cuije near Torreón in 1953:

> In the first place, it may be noted that the Cuije ejidatario tends to see all agricultural problems exclusively in terms of water shortage. That is to say, he is not conscious of deficiencies on other scores. For this reason, El Cuije deliberately has voted a formidable public indebtedness in order to sink new deep wells, secure in the conviction that these will mean the final solution to all its agricultural problems. . . . At the moment, it should be pointed out that even the water problem itself is not viewed by the ejidatario in true perspective. He does not realize that subsurface water is being used at an alarming rate; that every new deep well which is sunk accelerates the consumption of such water and that, if the drought recurs and endures, so that subsurface water is not replenished, the day of reckoning cannot be far removed. Such lack of perspective with respect to local water supply could, in the course of the years, be literally fatal for the whole Laguna. It would seem to apply, incidentally, not to the ejidatario alone, but perhaps in lesser degree, to the private landholder as well.[71]

These ejidatarios, she emphasized, attributed a successful harvest more to luck than to hard work, since they had no control over the supply of water and its distribution, which was in the hands of the SRH's Irrigation District manager. She found this troubling, as it appeared to breed a kind of fatalism into them that devalued any amount of effort and work beyond the minimum needed to produce the yields the Ejido Bank demanded. She perceived this same attitude with regard to other inputs vital for a successful harvest, including use of chemical pesticides and fertilizers; ejidatarios saw no real advantage in employing airplanes to dust cotton crops, even though they acknowledged the utility of pesticides. Rather, they preferred the far more inefficient hand-spraying method, thanks to the apparent failure of plane-dusted pesticides to improve yields significantly the year before.[72]

Although Kelly prominently noted the alarming depletion of the aquifer as being due to unregulated and profligate pumping, she unquestionably presumed pesticides were beneficial. She published her ethnographies in 1954, nearly a decade before Rachel Carson's landmark *Silent Spring* raised awareness of the overlooked and often unperceived dangers of what Carson termed "biocides" for public health and the environment.[73] Carson's powerful narrative of chemical warfare's transformation between the two world wars into civilian weapons against insects in the United States also applied to Mexico in general and to the Laguna in particular. Before 1945, Mexican farmers did not commonly use chemical pesticides, although they had used natural or inorganic pesticides on cotton, including, beginning in 1931, in the Laguna to fight the pink bollworm infestation.[74] After the Second World War, chemical companies introduced organochlorine pesticides, especially DDT (short for dichlorodiphenyltrichloroethane) into the civilian market, and governments employed them worldwide for agriculture and to combat malaria. Between 1948 and 1963, Laguna farmers sprayed their fields with more DDT than any other region of Mexico—by one account 22,000 tons, or 80 percent of national production and 1 percent of world production.[75] Until 1970, Mexico had approximately 60 percent of the installed capacity for the production of DDT in Latin America.[76]

The chemicalization of pesticide and fertilizer use after the Second World War was only one part of what the historian Joseph Cotter termed Mexico's "second" revolution of the twentieth century: the Green Revolution. Retrospectively named in 1968, this revolution, according to Cotter, was ostensibly "apolitical" but nevertheless had "profound social, economic, and political consequences." It had equally profound ecological consequences, as well.[77] Initially sponsored and financed by the Rockefeller Foundation under the auspices of the Mexican and U.S. Agriculture Departments in the early 1940s, the Green Revolution—in its second, more technical and less socially progressive incarnation—was the brainchild of the late Norman Borlaug, a Nobel Prize–winning plant pathologist and geneticist who developed high-yield, disease-resistant wheat varieties in Mexico. In turn, Mexico served as the demonstration site for other developing countries in Latin America, South Asia, and Africa, where the Green Revolution rapidly spread. According to Borlaug, its purposes were purely "humanitarian"—that is, to increase crop yields, productivity, and efficiency, all to feed a rapidly growing global population. Its proponents in the government and private sector fervently believed that this application of science and technology could successfully combat endemic rural and urban poverty, the first by increasing incomes of rural producers and the second by providing affordable basic staples to urban populations.[78]

As a large body of literature has documented, such an outcome did not materialize. The Green Revolution not only failed significantly to reduce urban and rural poverty, it actually accentuated socioeconomic inequities. What is worse, after initially achieving food self-sufficiency in basic grains in the 1960s, Mexico in the 1970s became a net importer of foodstuffs, a situation that has only worsened in the two decades since the implementation of the North American Free Trade Agreement (NAFTA) in 1994.[79] Nevertheless, it is important to note that the Mexican government, particularly under Gómez's tenure as secretary of the SAF, was a willing partner in this massive social and environmental engineering project. In other words, as the historian Tore Olsson shows, neither the U.S. government nor the Rockefeller Foundation imposed the Green Revolution on a reluctant Mexican government. To the contrary, the Mexican government actively solicited, and in time became adept at acquiring, financial and technical support for agricultural development from the U.S. government and private sources.

This active Mexican role was reflected in the Ley de Educación Agrícola (Agricultural Education Law), for example, which mandated technical training and "practical" agricultural education at all levels of government (federal, state, municipal, district, and territories), including funding for study at foreign universities. The law's authors paid due respect to both Article 27 of the 1917 Constitution and the 1946 Law on Soil and Water Conservation by incorporating their contradictory conservationist provisions into article 14 of the law. This article specified that the law's intention was to realize "agricultural improvement and rational utilization of natural resources in the zones of influence of the practical schools of agriculture" while "training the adult campesino population for the better exploitation *and* conservation of natural resources by collaborating in realizing the *spirit* of agrarian reform" through extension services. Accordingly, on the Mexican government's request, the Rockefeller Foundation helped fund dozens of fellowships for Bank of Mexico employees to acquire technical training in various fields. Among them were "definite subjects of obvious national interest," including "subterranean hydrology," in which two bank employees enrolled for study at the California Institute of Technology.[80]

Similarly, the foundation helped fund and facilitate operation of the Mexican-American Agricultural Commission with a budget of nearly a half-million dollars by the end of 1946. The commission was composed of high-level technical personnel from each country who would meet regularly without diplomatic formalities to discuss bilateral agricultural problems, among them plant industry, animal industry, agricultural economics, conservation of natural resources, rural sociology, and exchange of scientific information and personnel. Although they were ostensibly equals, it was implicit that Mexico was the little brother to its northern big brother; the Mexican section sent eight technical advisers, while the U.S. section sent twelve; and in virtually every area

U.S. advisers predominated. The commission's "cooperative" ventures included spray applications of DDT on a "large scale" using airplanes in parts of Matamoros, Tamaulipas, and the Laguna "in an effort to find better control measures for the 'pink worm' and other cotton pests."[81]

In 1946, *El Siglo de Torreón* reported on the collaborative experiments between entomologists of the U.S. Department of Agriculture and Guillermo Torres Cordera, the regional phytosanitary engineer of the Laguna. At the time, no truly effective chemical agent existed to control the pink bollworm, so Torres led a team applying DDT and other pesticides. *El Siglo de Torreón* provided detailed information on the collaboration, including how the severity of damage to cotton (4–20 percent of the crop) determined site selection, and implored that selected "small landholders and ejidatarios must have discipline and determination to cooperate for the experimentation's success" and "comply with the instructions that the U.S. Commission considers pertinent to provide as it begins collecting harvest [samples]."[82]

Beginning in 1948, as experiments indicated success in significantly reducing pestilence, Laguna farmers sprayed massive amounts of pesticides on their land. While these synthetic toxins seeped into the groundwater and contaminated it, farmers drilled their pump-installed wells more deeply into the aquifers to levels that contained naturally occurring arsenic and other toxic substances. Despite the imposition of three vedas from 1948 to 1952, and their renewal by 1956, when drought returned after a brief hiatus, the local groundwater pumping business boomed, encouraged by opening of a local distribution store, Equipos Mécanicos, which carried Worthington de México's products. In addition to Gómez, representatives of various government ministries and local and national banks attended.[83] The store also stocked tractors, truck parts, windmills, pesticides, and fertilizers from companies such as International Harvester, Hudson, and McCormick, along with Worthington de México.[84]

In the meantime, the severe drought persisted and Laguna ejidatarios in particular continued to struggle as water, credit, and agricultural markets literally and figuratively dried up, compelling the federal government to rehabilitate the Laguna envirotechnically by reengineering its land and water regimes.

6. Rehabilitating El Agua de la Revolución

There's nothing intrinsically evil about mining groundwater, as long as everyone understands just what he's doing. The alternative is to leave it underground and simply enjoy knowing that it's there.

STEVE REYNOLDS, New Mexico state engineer, about depleting the Ogallala aquifer

In 1956, ten years after the dedication of the Palmito Dam and twenty years after the reparto, Laguna farmers faced a stark reality of crippling drought and desperate need for water in an economically and demographically growing region and nation. As we saw, the prevailing envirotechnical paradigms of invasive hydraulic infrastructure building and agricultural chemicalization encouraged by Green Revolution policies provided short-term relief, even as they worsened conditions in the medium and long run. The benefits of this relief were not equitably distributed, however, especially between ejidos and engineers-cum-politicians-cum-businessmen such as Marte R. Gómez, who was well aware of the social and environmental consequences of using groundwater pumps that he manufactured and sold. It was understandable, though not justifiable, that Gómez would use the political connections and expertise he acquired as a former secretary of the Ministry of Agriculture and Development to profit as a private citizen, given the endemic corruption under President Miguel Alemán in the late 1940s and 1950s, but the same could not be said about técnicos who continued to serve in the government.

One such técnico was Emilio López Zamora, a member of the League of Socialist Agronomists who, in 1940, co-wrote the league's influential and constructive critique of the Cardenista reparto. By the late 1960s he was a leading architect of a decade-long government "rehabilitation plan" for the Laguna.

Calling it the Laguna's "second agrarian reform," López Zamora stated that the plan's objective was to fix the errors of earlier, "irresponsible técnicos" who had not respected "nature's limits" when they carried out the poorly coordinated reparto de tierras and reparto de aguas of the 1930s and 1940s.[1] López Zamora insightfully diagnosed a persistent affliction in the Laguna, yet the plan's cure of deploying more invasive hydraulic technology to increase Laguna agricultural efficiency, productivity, and crop diversity was worse than the disease. By 1972, he had overseen a complete overhaul of the region's irrigation network but one that exacerbated aquifer depletion and sowed the seeds for an even greater environmental crisis. Ejidos enjoyed a short-lived period of prosperity, but in the long run, the crisis only further weakened the ejido sector while facilitating the rise of an "acuifundio" based on water-intensive dairy production.

López Zamora sought to rehabilitate El agua de la Revolución, by deploying hydraulic technology to make water use fulfill the promises of Article 27 of the 1917 Constitution for more equitable distribution of natural resources and to conserve them. Toward that end, the architects of the plan simultaneously incorporated advancing geohydrological understanding of Mexico's water resources, on one hand, and, on the other, an unbridled faith in transforming water use through ever more invasive hydraulic technology—even when deployment of that technology had already proved ecologically unsustainable.[2]

Defiant Pumping

In the late 1950s, severe drought persisted in the Laguna and much of northern Mexico, disproportionately affecting ejidos because of inequities primarily in access to water, but also other associated inputs such as credit, machinery, fertilizers, and pesticides. Where direct governmental assistance failed, ejidatarios found other ways to cope and survive, such as obtaining credit from informal moneylenders. Yet in general their subordinate and dependent status compelled them to plead for policies that exacerbated their socioeconomic and environmental deterioration—namely, subsidized employment through unnecessary public works, loans for drilling more wells (undermining the vedas), and increased application of chemical fertilizers and pesticides.

As a reflection of the gendered dimension of Mexican agrarian life, presidential archives contain numerous letters sent by Laguna women throughout the 1950s and 1960s pleading for help on behalf of husbands and sons ostensibly too proud to ask. In January 1959, President Adolfo López Mateos (1958–64) received an alarming telegram claiming that twenty-five thousand landless and hungry campesinos and campesinas were begging the government to "occupy us cleaning canals." In a letter from February 1959, an affiliate of the Democratic Union of Mexican Women of the Comarca Lagunera wrote to López Mateos that "our husbands, sons and other family members do not have work to secure a salary which can allow them to give us what is most indispensable to maintain our homes." They noted that the private sector's technology meant that farm labor was now done "according to agricultural modernization that does not permit employing large numbers of workers who do not have land." The union claimed that even the federal government, through the Irrigation District and the Ejido Bank, employs "machinery that deprives rural workers of the only opportunity they have to participate in such works and as a result misery increases in every Laguna rural worker's home." Months later, the union sent López Mateos another letter informing him that on December 27, 1959, campesinas and urban women members took part in a "grand rally" alongside campesinos against unemployment in both the country and the city "for our men."[3]

Sympathetic to such popular protests, López Zamora criticized Alemán and his successors' drought-alleviation strategies (or the "drought industry" discussed in chapter 5) as wasteful and unproductive, especially the envirotechnical mismanagement of the dam reservoir: "The simple fact that the dam systematically empties out every year means in practice that it has ceased to exist for the one function it was designed for: to store the hydraulic reserves in abundant years to satisfy the demand for irrigation in drought years. The responsibility for this situation cannot be attributed to Laguna campesinos, and much less to nature."[4]

Yet government representatives and journalists often blamed campesinos and nature for the deteriorating social and ecological conditions in the region. Although anthropologists commissioned by the Mexican and U.S. governments such as Isabel Kelly reported a lack of concern for the long-term consequences of profligate groundwater pumping in the ejidos in which they did their ethnographic fieldwork, groundwater access was in fact highly inequitable in the Laguna, to the clear disadvantage of ejidos in the 1950s and 1960s. This trend, already in place by 1936, appears in the anthropologist Raymond Wilkie's ethnography of the San Miguel ejido in the Laguna:

> Since the 1930s the wells have furnished one third of the region's irrigation water in normal years, and as much as two-thirds in periods of drought. The water table is dropping, however, and there is a danger that wells may be of little use in a decade or two. The situation was already critical in the 1950s; many wells were dry, and the government had forbidden the

construction of new ones except in case of extreme emergency. Moreover, much of the well water is bad. For agricultural use it has been classified this way: bad, definitely should not be used, 26 percent; doubtful, probably should not be used, 20 percent; saline but can be used, 43 percent; good, not saline, 11 percent. Use of the two worst classes as the lone source of irrigation water would ruin the land in less than ten years. However, since irrigation is done with well water alone in drought years only, the situation is somewhat better than it might seem.[5]

In 1958, Eduardo Chávez, secretary of the Secretaría de Recursos Hidráulicos (Ministry of Hydraulic Resources; SRH), took the unusual step of announcing in national papers an "exclusive warning" about the Laguna's aquifer, declaring that the region could face "disappearance" within fifteen years if no "favorable factors" were generated and "if immoderate pace of exploitation of subterranean water" persisted.[6] In addition to the three vedas in the Laguna, by 1958 the SRH had decreed fifty others throughout the country since 1948. That same year, it classified its vedas into three kinds: prohibited zones where it is not possible to increase extraction without dangerously depleting water tables, zones where the capacity of aquifers can only permit extraction for domestic use, and zones where the capacity permits limited extraction for domestic, industrial, irrigation, and other uses.[7]

As elsewhere in Mexico, the SRH rarely enforced its vedas in the Laguna. There were several reasons for this. First, the SRH claimed it could not monitor groundwater withdrawal from individual wells, for it was a difficult task that only grew harder as wells increased in number to more than three thousand by 1958. Moreover, as indicated in table 6.1, there was a discernible disparity in the environmental impact of ejidos and small landholders' pumping. Although both sectors pumped water from prohibited zones, small landholders, who were fewer in number, did so far more disproportionately than ejidatarios. Indeed, ejidos possessed twice as many pumps in the non-prohibited zones as small landholders. Estimates from total users and agricultural productivity point to the conclusion that though ejidos possessed more pumps overall, their per capita water use was likely far lower than small landholders. For instance, in 1957–58, there were 34,081 individuals farming 185,784 hectares of irrigated land in the Laguna. Ejidos constituted 32,483 people, or 95 percent, farming 109,782 hectares, or 59 percent, of the land. The remaining 5 percent, or 1,643 private landholders, farmed 76,002 hectares, or 41 percent, of the land. This translated into 3.4 hectares per individual among ejidos and 21.6 per individual among private landholders.[8] No matter who owned the land, the aggregate

TABLE 6.1. Distribution and type of 3,087 wells in Laguna:
Prohibited and non-prohibited zones between ejidos and small landholders, 1958

Well numbers and zoning	Durango	Coahuila	Totals
Prohibited zone, small landholders	472	618	1,090
Prohibited zone, ejidos	310	625	935
Non-prohibited zone, small landholders	158	187	345
Non-prohibited zone, ejidos	552	165	717
Motor pump-powered wells	402	665	1,067
Electric pump-powered wells	1,092	930	2,022
Pump totals of small landholders	630	805	1,435
Pump totals of ejidos	862	790	1,652
State totals	1,492	1,595	3,087

SOURCE: "Las norias en operación en esta comarca," *El Siglo de Torreón*, August 4, 1958.

effect of pumping by all was environmentally devastating: the water table declined precipitously along with water quality, for the farther one drilled, the more likely noxious and poisonous substances such as salt and arsenic leeched into the groundwater (see table 6.2).

Second, farmers reacted differently to the SRH's vedas. Some, like the conservation group Amigos del Suelo (Friends of the Soil) and the Agricultural Association of Durango, petitioned vigorously for enforcement. The association blamed lack of knowledge of the law, economic conditions, and negligence among its members for noncompliance with vedas.[9] Although this association's primary concern was economic, Amigos del Suelo articulated an explicitly ecological concern regarding the Laguna's alarming groundwater situation. It anticipated the concept of sustainable development made popular worldwide by the United Nations' Brundtland Report of 1987. Inspired by the 1946 law on soil and water conservation and founded in 1949, by 1957 Amigos del Suelo had taken to releasing pleas in the local press for respect for government vedas: "It's an elemental principal [*sic*] of our Association to be vigilant so that future generations receive the lands, waters, fauna and flora and all the natural resources in a satisfactory state of conservation, without present generations using them exclusively." Yet they expressed concern that "at present natural resources are being exploited, without regard for the future, to the detriment of present and future generations."[10]

Other agricultural associations, including many ejidos, petitioned for temporary or complete lifting of vedas, or that they not be expanded without more careful studies.[11] These differing reactions appeared to stem from the level

TABLE 6.2. Estimate of wells drilled and in use in Laguna, 1920–1980

Year	Wells drilled	Wells in use
1920	12	12
1926	114	114
1932	365	365
1938	996	996
1944	1,546	1,546
1950	2,014	2,014
1956	2,704	2,704
1962	2,947	2,748
1968	3,035	2,554
1974	3,088	2,367
1980	3,334	2,467

SOURCE: Rolando Víctor García and Susana Sanz, *Deterioro ambiental y pobreza en la abundancia productiva: El caso de la Comarca Lagunera* (Mexico City: Centro de Investigación y de Estudios Avanzados, Instituto Politécnico Nacional, 1988), 74.

of confidence in the SRH's technical studies, the economic impact of drought conditions, and geographical location within the region. For many, concerns for conservation were few or nonexistent because drilling wells was often a matter of survival.

In the late 1950s and 1960s, Worthington de México and other pump manufacturers continued to capitalize on the severe environmental conditions that drove the mushrooming demand for pumps throughout the arid and semi-arid areas of Mexico. In 1957, eighty of Worthington de México's pumps extracted 60,000 gallons of freshwater per minute in Mexico City, and the company had plans to expand to Puebla, Acapulco, and Matamoros. By 1965, the company manufactured more than a hundred models of pumps for both industrial and agricultural use, and its net worth had grown threefold, to 30 million pesos (which made the company's president, Marte R. Gómez, a very wealthy man).[12] This defiance of natural limits extended to Worthington de México's advertisements in local newspapers, which depicted pumps as the savior of the hardy Mexican farmer, able to tap into and secure a seemingly endless source of water. In one noteworthy instance, Worthington de México placed an advertisement in *El Siglo de Torreón* entitled "An Inexhaustible Torrent of Water for Sowing Your Fields with Worthington Pumps." It featured an illustration of a farmer standing beside his motorized pump pouring a torrent of water like a giant spigot into his field (see figure 6.1). It promised, "Rain or no rain, farmer friend, your crops are safe with a proper Worthington pump."

FIG. 6.1 The headline of the advertisement reads, "An inexhaustible torrent of water for your crops with Worthington pumps," as a farmer stands next to his pump with water gushing forth. *El Siglo de Torreón,* June 19, 1961.

Defiant Pesticide Use

Whereas Worthington de México and its competitors defiantly peddled their pumps, implicitly encouraging their consumers to disregard government vedas and pump illegally, there was no legal prohibition whatever on profligate chemical pesticide usage. As Alan E. Hool, the economic assistant to the U.S. ambassador to Mexico, noted in 1950 in a report on the pesticide market in Mexico, besides the requirement that all organic pest control products be registered with the Secretaría de Agricultura y Ganadería (Ministry of Agriculture and Livestock; SAG) before commercial sale in Mexico, "There are no other regulations affecting production, labor conditions, consumption, etc." He further observed that "firms dealing in agricultural insecticides are engaging increasingly in advertising campaigns that directly contact the farmer. Agents located in agricultural districts distribute pamphlets to the farmers which advertise the relative merits of the products handled. Ad space is also purchased in the local newspapers while a common form of publicity consists of slide and spot advertising in the rural motion picture establishments." He commented that in Torreón, insecticide producers advertised on radio "with a view to reaching the many well-to-do cotton farmers in that district." Hool believed this direct "educational advertising" was one of three principal factors influencing the fiftyfold growth in the Mexican pesticide market during the previous five years. The other two were "the ever growing acreage being planted in cotton as a result of high world prices and the U.S. cotton purchasing policy" and the "work of the U.S. Department of Agriculture in Mexico in teaching and demonstrating new methods of insect control and crop improvement."[13]

The reality, however, was that insects developed immunity and pesticides ceased to be effective after short-term use, producing a perpetual cycle of applying newer and stronger pesticides even though insects and worms continuously found ways to resist their eradication. In July 1953, the counselor for agricultural affairs for the U.S. ambassador to Mexico reported on a joint meeting held in July 1953 in Mexico City between U.S. and Mexican entomologists and other technicians working to eradicate the pink bollworm. The director of Defensa Agrícola (Agricultural Defense), the engineer Esteban Uranga, headed Mexico's team of entomologists, cotton association representatives, growers, ginners, and buyers. Officials of both Anderson Clayton and the Mexican National Confederation of Cotton Producers "took an active part in arranging and supporting the meeting." Uranga reviewed the accomplishments of joint cooperation between U.S. and Mexican técnicos since their first meeting in 1939 and "pledged continued wholehearted support."[14]

TABLE 6.3. Percentage of cotton crop infested with pink bollworm and larvae per boll in the Laguna, 1942–1959

Year	Infestation (%)	Larvae per boll
1942	NA	6.4
1943	72	NA
1944	69	NA
1945	67	NA
1946	65	NA
1947	47	NA
1948	30	0.7
1949	17	0.3
1950	16	0.2
1951	7.8	0.13
1952	16.8	0.2
1953	5.9	0.06
1954	12	0.2
1955	16.9	0.3
1956	10.7	NA
1957	12.3	NA
1958	21.1	0.6
1959	23.9	0.4

SOURCE: *El Siglo de Torreón*, December 10, 1959.

Yet six years later in 1959, the Mexican agronomist A. Porfirio Hernández observed that the pink bollworm seemed to be resurgent after a decade of significant reduction, despite heavy doses of DDT sprayed through 1959 (see table 6.3). Emphasizing various "principal" causes for the resurgence—from improper use to poor-quality products and the easing of drought from 1957, which returned more larvae-friendly moisture to the region—Hernández ever so cautiously pointed to another "potential" cause he wished was not so: "the resistance in greater or lesser degree of the pink bollworm to its greatest enemy, DDT."[15] In spite of his excessive caution, he forthrightly reported that DDT concentrations in applied pesticides had increased 10–20 percent and between 3,307 and 8,818 pounds (1,500 and 4,000 kilos) per application during the same period.

Hernández cautiously hoped application of the new "sevin" formula combined with DDT would reverse the resurgence. But his hope was dashed when a joint Mexican and U.S. team of entomologists determined the product had failed to achieve the desired results during the 1960–61 agricultural year.[16]

At the time, the public health effects of massive DDT spraying rarely garnered attention or concern, in part because they took years to manifest. In one brief column titled "Salud es Vida" (Health Is Life), Dr. Herman N. Bundesen, president of the Chicago Health Council, dismissed any claims that DDT posed a health hazard. He cited a 1958 study, endorsed by the American Medical Association, of Dr. Orteles of Savannah, Georgia, who determined, after examining forty individuals with high exposure to DDT for six-and-a-half years, that there was no relation whatever between any abnormalities and contact with the toxin, save for minor irritations on the skin and eyes.[17] As Angus Wright has shown, Mexican public health officials largely looked to U.S. authorities for guidance on such matters. But while publication of Rachel Carson's *Silent Spring* and other exposés prompted a public outcry so strong that the U.S. government finally banned DDT's agricultural use in 1972, it took another two decades for Mexico to follow suit. Even then, enforcement and compliance left much to be desired.[18]

As the ticking public-health time bomb of pesticides continued unseen or discounted, growing pest resistance became undeniable in the following years. Unfortunately, alternatives such as biological controls, whether natural (as in predators introduced from elsewhere) or artificial (as in predators bred in laboratories), proved no more effective than chemical pesticides. Although they flourished in tropical or subtropical climates, neither natural nor artificial predators could adapt to the Laguna's arid climate and its dramatic temperature fluctuations of up to 61 degrees Fahrenheit (16 degrees centigrade) from day to night.[19]

Unaware that pests were building immunity to pesticides, many ejidatarios who still obtained credit from the Ejido Bank blamed it for selling them weak or ineffective products which they were obliged to buy. Mexican journalists, in turn, tended to blame ejidos for their travails as the drought industry persisted through the late 1950s and 1960s. In February 1963, for instance, the reporter Alardo Prats of the national Mexico City–based *Excélsior* newspaper traveled to the Laguna to investigate conditions in ejidos. He filed several reports during the few days he spent there. In the first report he remarked, "The appearance of a small white cloud in the clearness of the atmosphere is an infrequent phenomenon." He interviewed a delegate of the ejido Perú, near Torreón, who told him, "When it rains, the little children get scared and cry. They're so little accustomed to see and hear it rain." Despite the testimony, Prats remained positive: "The situation is grave, but not desperate." He noted that the government lifted the ban on drilling wells for ejidos and every well with a pump could irrigate 30 hectares. Moreover, the government had begun construction of a new canal, on which 7,300 campesinos were working in rotations. "The canal is being built Chinese-style, with stick and hoe at double the price it would cost using machines," he added.[20] A report prepared for the U.S. Embassy in Mexico by the counselor for agricultural affairs in 1955 similarly noted that

> relatively little machinery and equipment are used by most Mexican farmers. . . . Mexico has an abundance of cheap labor; capital is scarce and interest rates are high; hence most farmers are unable to buy expensive equipment. The average inventory value of machinery and equipment on Ejido farms in 1950 was only equivalent to $22.50, or $3.00 an acre of crop land. On the larger private farms (data for the small private farms are not available) the machinery inventory was $231, or $8.20 a crop acre compared with an average investment in the United States of $2,520 per farm, or $32 per acre of cropland in 1950. Only three-quarters of ejido farms had their own plows and only a little over one-half of these were modern moldboard plows. Only one in about 500 ejido farmers had a tractor or truck.[21]

Prats reported that, in the case of cotton production, the Laguna's 357 ejidos epitomized such general inefficiencies. In most other cotton areas (Matamoros, Mexicali, Sinaloa, Sonora, Chihuahua, and others), he noted, an investment of 2,500 pesos per hectare would suffice, while, in the Laguna, 5,000 pesos per hectare were needed because ejidos had to use more fertilizers and pesticides to increase yields to a comparable level. This inefficiency was a significant change from 1948–52, during which time the U.S. counselor for agricultural affairs observed that Mexico out-produced the United States in cotton by 305 pounds to 283 pounds per harvested acre (although it lagged far behind in corn and wheat production and somewhat behind in bean production).[22] The continued demographic explosion in the region, he added, had increased the ranks of landless ejidatarios, or "libres," to fifty-five thousand. As Kelly described them, "Untrained, the libres are unskilled agricultural workers, who are essentially the hangers-on in the ejido. When work is scarce, the ejidatario is given preference, so that the libre cannot always count on manual labor to maintain himself and his family."[23] Indeed, landlessness within ejidos was already identified as a major problem soon after the 1936 reparto, for President Lázaro Cárdenas's técnicos had not planned ahead for the offspring of nearly forty thousand beneficiaries of the reform who were not allowed to inherit ejido land—land that was effectively leased state property. This glaring oversight compelled libres to join informal rural labor markets. With its high costs of production, no land to offer, and few jobs available, the Laguna could not accommodate them, but no matter how much the land appeared to scorn them, libres remained attached to it.

In the ejido Ana, for example, Prats found that only 20 percent of the descendants of the original ejidatarios were prepared to leave the region, even if the government granted them land in another area of the country—a sentiment that Kelly had also detected in the Cuije ejido a decade earlier. Cuije ejidatarios showed little enthusiasm to move to the Papaloapan area of southeastern Mexico in Oaxaca and Veracruz, where the government sought to relocate a total of forty thousand to fifty thousand farmers from drought-prone areas.[24] The Ana ejido was once the most "prosperous" ejido of the Laguna, Prats observed, but it had fallen into a sorry state. He then offered a culturally normative explanation for the change in fortune: "In times of bonanza, they happily squandered away their earnings; in times of extreme penury, like the present, they entrust the help of the government to find the immediate solution to their problems, be it in the form of additional credit beyond what they normally receive or in emergency assistance services. In general, their future is bleak and their reaction in the face of these economic problems, which are the logical consequence of their lack of foresight, is to play 'victim' [*es la del damnificado*]."

More frustrating to him was to find that the ejido Ana, as with so many others in the Laguna, did not produce for subsistence: "Not one single hectare is dedicated to the cultivation of maize, beans or garden vegetables . . . this is absurd. A campesino in this environment and anywhere in the world, should live primordially from the fruits of the land, at least from that minimum part which is required to feed his family." It was not all the ejidatarios' fault, he conceded, since the Ejido Bank would only provide credit for cotton, wheat, grapes, alfalfa, and other forage—the most commercially viable.[25] Here was the crux of the ejido's—and, by extension, the Laguna's—problem: subsistence agriculture was not profitable, yet it required less water and fewer pesticides, and made more economic sense. In 1964, a newspaper cartoonist took note of the Laguna's situation and duly mocked the phenomenon (see figure 6.2). Founded upon the erroneous hope that an envirotechnical solution could solve the Laguna's problems, the government's grand solution only exacerbated such deteriorating social and ecological conditions.

From Reform to Rehabilitation

The Laguna's constant crises arose from a combination of social, economic, and natural forces—sometimes deliberately shaped by and at other times escaping the control of the state. Against this backdrop, in 1963 the López Mateos administration (1958–64) unveiled the first incarnation of the Plan de Rehabilitación (Rehabilitation Plan) as a permanent solution to the region's problems.

FIG. 6.2 Newspaper cartoon of the Laguna Crisis of 1964. In it are depicted "insecticides," "plagues," "ignorant farmers," and "irresponsible people" attacking cotton bolls. Biblioteca Lerdo de Tejada.

The primary purpose was to "rationalize" water use by making the canals between the dam and the Laguna's fields more efficient. As if on cue, that year the reservoir nearly dried up completely. Although their declarations in newspapers and private correspondence demonstrate that the principal representatives of the Laguna's rural sector broadly supported López Mateos's ambitious plan, they still engaged in a war of words over the origins of the crisis.

In 1960, an anonymous letter to López Mateos purporting to represent ejidos' interests entitled "What is the cause of this grave situation?" accused "enemies of the agrarian reform" of spreading lies that ejidatarios were in a bad condition "due to ignorance and unemployment." Rather, they insisted that "this bad situation is a result of ejidatarios having been deprived in large part of the product of their labor." This deprivation came in different forms. One was from unscrupulous individuals who had enriched themselves by exploiting campesinos. Foremost in the author's mind was the "insulting" grand fortunes of Anderson Clayton and former functionaries of ejidos and other campesino leaders who colluded with the "rural bourgeoisie." But the greatest outrage, according to the letter, was the reduction in crop yields because of the Ejido Bank's ineffective and costly fertilizers. The bank was more interested in ensuring the profits of fertilizer retailers than ensuring the well-being of ejidatarios. Further proof of the bank's intentions was the even more serious problem of pesticides: they had not succeeded in preventing infestations but had done much to increase debt. The letter writer claimed that the bank had even publicly recognized the inefficacy of these pesticides, which in 1959 had allegedly cost 30 million pesos, a catastrophic amount for ejidos. They charged that much the same had occurred with the sale of chemicals to destroy an infestation of mice. Ejidatarios were left feeling betrayed by bank agents, who deceived those who "had placed their faith in the knowledge of scientists and técnicos . . . incapable of analyzing a chemical formula in order to test its effectiveness."[26]

By contrast, the Cotton Association of the Laguna, whose slogan was "augmenting Mexico's economic potential by consuming more cotton," primarily blamed ejidos and uncontrolled natural forces. Composed of small landholders forming part of the National Cotton Associations of Mexico, the association absolved itself of any responsibility for the crisis. In a letter to López Mateos dated December 1960 the association wrote, "The soil is increasingly impoverished, for lack of adequate attention to the use of chemical and green fertilizers, improvers, and a rational rotation of crops." Sounding much like the ejido representatives, they claimed that the last of these was due to the bank's lending practices, which prioritized cotton and wheat, but they also recognized that excessive groundwater pumping and scant recuperation of the aquifer from deficient rainfall had caused the water table to fall precipitously. As a result, "Every day the wells must be drilled deeper, automatically requiring the use of more powerful, and thus more expensive, equipment." Unable to upgrade their pumping equipment to increase efficiency, or to offset rises in energy costs, farmers did not "know how to secure their crops." Faced with this situation, the association emphasized the importance of "property guarantees . . . to prevent the exploitation of land without fulfilling the solemn obligation of conserving soil"—that is, conservation through increased use of chemical fertilizers and pesticides, since unlike many ejidatarios, small landholders were not as constrained by bank lending conditions and free to purchase higher-quality products.[27]

With regard to water, the association alleged *it* was the victim, not the ejidos. The association pointed to several factors that it claimed disadvantaged it: the high cost of wells; evaporation; the permeability of earthen (as opposed to concrete-lined) canals and acequias, which led to the loss of much water conveyed from the dam reservoir; and maldistribution of water. Even when the reservoir partially filled, the association still perceived "waste of reservoir water by ejidos." It proposed lowering energy prices, revising the water regulations, and paving over canals and acequias.

Other problems the association identified included inadequate yields and impoverished soil, fungi that killed up to 60 percent of plants in certain areas, lack of fertilizers and other soil improvers, and profits so small that it could not reinvest in sufficient cultivation. As with Prats but for different reasons, the most serious problem private landholders identified was low cotton prices, for which they proposed crop diversification. Although they criticized ejidos for their allegedly wasteful practices, these private landholders felt that the government should facilitate this diversification by subsidizing pesticides, fertilizers, and machinery. They wanted industrialization of agricultural products such as alfalfa and tomatoes, promotion of a cattle industry, and creation of stables and dairy farms. The agricultural chambers of Durango and the cities of Torreón, San Pedro, and Mapimí all weighed in, calling for subsidies and guaranteed prices to alleviate the crisis.[28]

The López Mateos administration largely adopted the recommendations and guidelines of the local cotton association but did so in the name of an amorphous, undifferentiated class of campesinos, which the regional branch of the Confederación Nacional Campesina (National Confederation of Campesinos; CNC) endorsed. Seeing through the subterfuge, scores of Laguna campesinos and campesinas continued to protest in the following months, as they had done for years, to urge the president to fulfill his promise to "save the [Laguna] zone from chaos." Two hundred women and four male "assistants" (accompanying them for safety) set off from San Pedro to Saltillo (about a two hundred-mile trek through barren desert) and planned to continue on to Mexico City to deliver a petition personally to the president. In the petition, they demanded that the government create industries in San Pedro, provide work to unemployed campesinos, morally reprimand ejido leaders, replace bureaucrats from the Secretaría de Agricultura y Ganadería (Ministry of Agriculture and Livestock; SAG), and pay campesino salaries in cash. Indeed, the protesters' ultimate goal was to strengthen ejidos' autonomy by revitalizing the regional economy.[29]

Although differing in their analyses of the origins of the crisis and the social and political activism it helped to trigger, nearly all of the representatives of the various Laguna stakeholders actively lobbied the government to deploy new technology to save the agroindustrial economy. The national newspaper *El Universal* also editorialized on the demise of the "romantic or lyrical stage" of the Laguna's agrarian reform:

> Now it is time to seriously apply ourselves to make the land produce according to modern techniques and exigencies of our era. We should transform the old methods of agricultural exploitation and frame the agrarian reform in economic terms. We have to radically and implacably purify systems and men. What we have to do today is to produce, produce and produce. . . . The crisis in the Laguna has sounded an alarm. If the debacle of the campesinos of the Laguna is consummated, it will undoubtedly become a national debacle.[30]

As the SRH saw it, overhauling the Laguna's irrigation network was vital to this "purifying transformation": it would require lining hundreds of miles of earthen canals with concrete; leveling and compacting soil for more efficient water use; training campesinos in new agricultural techniques to conserve the newly compacted soil; and building a long-planned, second, smaller dam on the Nazas to complement the Cárdenas Dam. With the possible exception of ejidos' complaints about unscrupulous and greedy individuals, a compromised "revolutionary" government, water deprivation, and ineffective chemical agents, there was little opposition to the generalized call for radically refurbishing canals and other irrigation works. Rather, the CNC, speaking for ejidos, agreed with private-sector actors that this "advanced revolutionary technique in water, soil and crop management for obtaining larger and better harvests" was indispensable for regional agriculture.[31]

The project to build a second dam on the Nazas River was named the Lomas Coloradas or "Las Tórtolas," after an area on the river near the Fernández Canyon some fifty miles upstream from Torreón. The project resembled Francisco I. Madero's original conception of where he believed the first dam should be built when he advocated it in 1907. For its proponents, the second dam offered two principal benefits: first, it augmented the capacity of the Cárdenas Dam by enabling additional control of river flows and would allow the dam to generate hydropower (as initially designed); and second, it enhanced flood control.[32] In the 1950s, however, when severe drought was the major concern, flood control and hydropower generation seemed remote and problems the Cárdenas Dam reservoir was unlikely to alleviate. Envisioning a panacea for ills the first dam was unable to remedy, promoters of a second dam argued it would help regenerate the Laguna's overexploited aquifers at a time that uncontrolled well drilling continued unabated. In their parched desperation, Laguneros seemed to pay little attention to the frequently changing claims—or, if they did pay attention, they did not publicly contest them.[33]

As they did in the 1920s and 1930s for the first dam, técnicos candidly made their assessments in their internal correspondence of the likely ecological impact of this second dam. In September 1954, for instance, the chief of technical consulting for the SRH, the engineer Antonio Coria, commented on the proposal for the Lomas Coloradas Dam:

> It is not evident in what form the dam could contribute to the recuperation of the underground aquifers, as is indicated in the initiative here analyzed. If it is due to filtration through the reservoir, the filtrated volume of water will do no more than be transformed from water exploitable by gravity to water that will have to be extracted by means of wells, with a probable large reduction in its volume. In other words, this supply to the aquifer would be harmful rather than beneficial. In this reservoir, like in all those for capturing water, inevitable losses from evaporation in the basin will have to be expected.[34]

Apparently, few regional actors with the power to seriously question and delay the project paid much heed to such warnings. Unlike the first dam in the 1920s and 1930s, there was—to judge from extensive research in national archives and local and national newspapers—no detectable opposition to the second. This indifference was probably a consequence of the far less polarized sociopolitical landscape of the 1960s, compared with the 1920s and 1930s. In the earlier era, the central government was too weak to control radical unions and agraristas, on one hand, while, on the other, large landowners still exerted considerable political influence before their expropriation in 1936. In the 1960s, the ruling PRI largely co-opted campesinos, but should they become too independent, or in any way challenge PRI hegemony, it could respond with harsh repression. Moreover, national agricultural policies since Alemán had favored (and continued to favor) large-scale commercial agriculture at the expense of ejidos, and the ejidos found they could not compete on an uneven playing field even when they grew commercially viable crops. There was thus none of the earlier era's fear among elites that the deployment of hydraulic technology would potentially radicalize agrarian workers.

More than a generation later, the only partial exception to this apathy in the archived correspondence to López Mateos was from a former Laguna peon. In an anonymous letter, he added his two cents "in service to my country by making a suggestion in order to resolve the case of the Laguna":

I was familiar with this privileged region at the end of the decade of the 1920s working as a peon in the cotton fields. I was just a young worker of fifteen who moved around the Comarca throughout the different haciendas, and although now I am fifty and reside in my home state of Durango, I have not lost touch with the Laguna. So I am authorized to offer my opinion.

Little by little the Laguna can once again regain its lost prosperity by doing one thing: flooding the land to the brim of the embankments as it was done before the river current was captured in [the] Palmito [Dam reservoir]. Nowadays the water comes to the land clean—that is, without natural fertilizers. Add the monoculture to this, and the result is impoverished soil. When the river current would flood all that is possible, the water would filter back underground and make the aquifer levels rise with the following result: water to pump.

This former peon believed the Palmito/Cárdenas Dam was compatible with the old aniego technique. As he explained, "With one large release of water from the reservoir, enough for the entire network of canals before the natural fertilizers settle in the reservoir, abundant harvests of wheat, maize, beans, melons, watermelons, etc., were achievable leaving enough groundwater to pump for cotton. . . . I am convinced that this a good remedy that could cure the ill that will not disappear by throwing at it millions and millions [of pesos]." He concluded his letter with a casual, "Think about it."[35]

The former peon, however, was incorrect to assume that aniego was compatible with the dammed Nazas. Aniego in the Laguna was an envirotechnical adaptation to the unique Nazas River regime, which would deliver sediment-rich nutrients to fertile lands. Although highly irregular, the uncontrolled Nazas flow was the aquifer's best source of recharge. Yet returning to aniego as farmers practiced it before the 1940s was not something the SRH ever seriously considered, especially amid persistent drought spells. To fully revive aniego throughout the Laguna would have required decommissioning the Cárdenas Dam, an inconceivable prospect in the 1950s and 1960s (and today to a large extent). The former peon did not realize that if the dam stored water as it was designed to, natural fertilizing sediments would settle in the reservoir basin and could not flow out with released water—and yet engineers had long acknowledged his point regarding aquifer recharge, at least in internal correspondence.[36]

In the early 1960s, building dams and eliminating aniego were taken for granted, and not at all debatable, to the detriment of the diminishing aquifer.

Instead, the debate over the region's future centered on what further steps were needed to make an increasingly dysfunctional canal system—one designed for aniego—compatible with a fully regulated river, or how to eliminate this old irrigation method entirely. In spite of their frank assessments of what the dam and profligate well drilling did to the aquifers, técnicos believed that constructing new canals and lining them with concrete would augment efficiency, since water flowing through them could not seep underground as easily. Lining canals with concrete would also reduce the evaporation of water flowing from the reservoir through the canals to the fields. With unpaved earthen canals, the only way to compensate for this "loss by conduction" was to release more water from the reservoir, so, theoretically, paving the canals made sense: less water flowing more quickly through seep-proof canals lined with concrete would help diminish the reliance on the huge numbers of wells that drained the aquifer.

Focusing primarily on the water situation, López Mateos ordered the SRH and SAG in 1963 to devise a plan to revamp the irrigation network. Through their efforts, the government obtained a loan from the World Bank, a leading bankroller of the Green Revolution, for 29 percent of the cost.[37] The first stage consisted of constructing a new network of concrete-lined canals branching out from the old Sacramento Canal, which served the Tlahualilo area. The goal was to establish a compacted irrigated area of 5,700 hectares to which the Tlahualilo ejidos would be moved from their original locations (see figure 6.3).

Abelardo Amaya Brondo, an agricultural engineer and general director of the SRH's Irrigation Districts nationwide, explained in a detailed article that the Tlahualilo ejido lands were widely dispersed across 22,000 hectares but able to irrigate a mere 1,200 hectares with water diverted from the Nazas River through the forty-mile Sacramento Canal. With so little water and so much land, ejidatarios believed it was beneficial to plant in a different area every year and thereby let the land rest. This meant that small irrigation works had to be moved yearly and was the primary reason, Amaya pointed out, that leveling croplands had never been cost-effective.[38] The SRH's compacting effort amounted to a major social and environmental engineering project that faced numerous challenges during its first five years.

The Laguna's Second Agrarian Reform

At a seminar sponsored by the SRH in Torreón in 1968, López Zamora, the leading architect of its second stage from 1966, assessed the progress of the first stage of the rehabilitation plan in its fifth year and remarked that things had

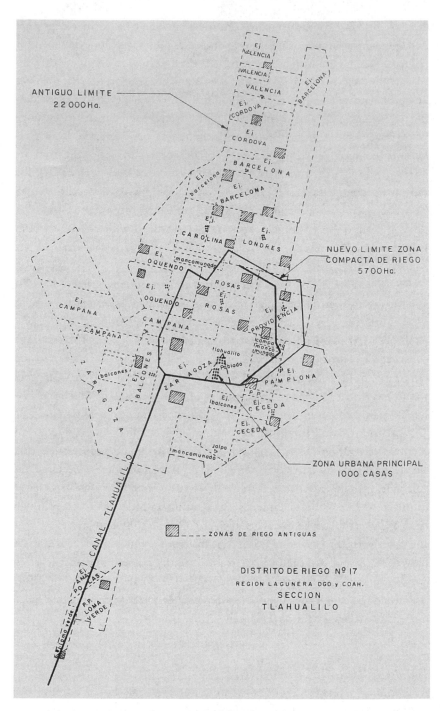

FIG. 6.3 These are the seventeen Tlahualilo ejidos before their lands were reduced from 22,000 hectares to 5,700 hectares through compaction to raise the efficiency of water use. Abelardo Amaya Brondo, "Plan de rehabilitación del Distrito de Riego Núm. 17 Comarca Lagunera, Coahuila y Durango," *Ingeniería Hidráulica en México* 24, no. 1 (1970): 70.

not worked out as planned regarding compacting ejido lands. Rather, after lining canals with concrete, ejidatarios adamantly refused to move, despite promises of new houses, electricity, running water, and more schools. Given the harsh conditions of life for ejidos in the region, this perplexed government officials and engineers. Moreover, before López Mateos launched the plan in 1963, the government had reached an agreement with ejido representatives and regional campesino committees of the CNC to transfer ejidatarios from their original ejidos to the new, compacted irrigated zone.[39] Ejidos held an understandable sentimental attachment to their land, but another important reason that they—unlike their often corrupt and out-of-touch representatives—refused to move was straightforward and principled: the government did not hold any general assemblies in the ejidos, which were required, by law, to obtain approval of all ejidatarios before relocating them. In 1966, the administration of President Gustavo Díaz Ordaz, who had succeeded López Mateos in 1964, acknowledged its mistake and established an inter-ministerial commission expressly to tackle the relocation problem of the Tlahualilo ejidos. It deemed gaining these ejidos' consent indispensable to resolving the general relocation problem in the entire region.[40]

The sub-secretaries of the SRH, SAG, and Department of Agrarian and Colonization Affairs made up the commission. All three carefully studied the Tlahualilo case and then, in view of the region's severe unemployment, recommended that the plan be expanded beyond rehabilitating the irrigation network to rehabilitating the regional economy. In response, nearly thirty years after Cárdenas decreed the expropriation of the Laguna's large landholdings of more than 150 hectares, Díaz Ordaz promulgated a decree of his own, promising it would benefit all of the Laguna Irrigation District's farmers. (For the distribution of land in 1968, see table 6.4.) The SRH was responsible for supervising the plan; the SAG, for diversifying crop production to employ campesinos permanently; and the Department of Agrarian and Colonization Affairs, for relocating irrigated ejido lands to new compacted areas. The decree stipulated that the government would inform ejidatarios of its relocation plans beforehand so they could "express their points of view" on the matter.[41]

Charged with implementing the fourth item of the decree, López Zamora called the new rehabilitation plan the "second agrarian reform." As important as the first reform, which had "liquidated the latifundista regime and distributed the land," the second reform, López Zamora declared, was now achieving the actual objective of the first: "raising the economic and social level of the campesino family." Convincing ejidatarios that this was the intended objective of the plan, however, proved to be a formidable challenge.

TABLE 6.4. Classification of agricultural property of small landholders and ejidatarios of the Laguna region as of July 30, 1968

| Group of users | Number of users | Surface area in hectares | | | |
		Irrigable (1)	Nonirrigable (2)	Additional nonarable land (3)	Sum of 1–3
Parcel sizes of small landholders (hectares)					
0–5	727	1,205	6	109	1,320
5.1–10	674	5,419	9	1,257	6,685
10.1–20	533	9,259	12	1,476	10,747
20.1–30	119	3,271	–	2,740	6,011
30.1–40	135	4,937	35	4,277	9,249
40.1–50	201	9,812	–	1,374	11,186
50.1–100	247	18,634	–	3,380	22,023
100+	79	10,279	365	9,312	19,956
Totals	2,715	62,825	427	23,925	87,177
Of individual ejidatarios					
0–5	41,623	152,675	13,997	443,891	610,563
5.1–10	842	5,247	2,495	8,975	16,717
10.1–20	–	–	–	–	–
20+	7	300	–	–	300
Totals	42,472	158,222	16,492	452,866	627,580
Grand total	45,187	221,047	16,919	476,791	714,757

SOURCE: Abelardo Amaya Brondo, "Plan de rehabilitación del Distrito de Riego Núm. 17 Comarca Lagunera, Coahuila y Durango," *Ingeniería Hidráulica en México* 24, no. 1 (1970): 64.

As it was his responsibility, López Zamora described in detail his experiences trying to convince ejidatarios to accept the plan. In a patronizing tone, he depicted the ejidatarios alternately as distrustful, inflexible, and accommodating. For instance, in one meeting, a campesino insisted that the SRH was trying to take away the land that Cárdenas had granted ejidatarios in 1936: "We're fed up with promises; we want canals, and we get goats. But know that we are prepared to defend our lands even with weapons in our hands." Another spoke emphatically that "although we are illiterate, we know that in order to improve our yields we need to rotate the soil; this business of lining canals and compacting land has just destroyed our parcels." By contrast, an ejidatario from the long recalcitrant Tlahualilo zone who was already resettled in another ejido, conceded, "Things haven't been bad, but not good, either, and we're already compacted." In the Ceceda ejido, a campesino affirmed, "Lázaro Cárdenas is not dead, and he will help us so that the reactionaries do not take away our lands," adding that he had decided not to give one square meter of land for compacting. "Those of us who don't know the laws, well, we suffer, but they who do know them, they manage things like this, like a key chain [simulating a finger spinning the chain around it]" In other words, he felt that the new law to rehabilitate the Laguna would reverse the 1936 reparto, leaving ejidatarios spinning helplessly around someone else's controlling finger.[42]

Other campesinos echoed similar fears that the hallowed decree of 1936 would be overturned and that the new federal program would take advantage of their ignorance of laws and new agricultural techniques, as well as divisions within ejidos. Slowly but surely, however, the government managed to win over a majority of ejidos through a combination of *pan y palo* (carrots and sticks). As of January 1969, six years into the plan, the SRH reported that 81.7 percent of ejidos had accepted it and 18 percent had not:

> We have spoken with 100 [percent] of Laguna ejidos. The coordinator and Office of Relocation were informed that it would be convenient to visit anew 37 of the 53 ejidos that have not accepted the Rehabilitation Plan, since these 37 ejidos will not cede land or move. Objective is that by end of February a special visit will be made in order to have a last talk with the resistant ejidos and from there decide the next step, which could consist of a decree obliging the minority of ejidos to accept the plan.[43]

After two years of working on the plan, López Zamora could point to its success in having raised the region's efficiency in water use, agricultural productivity, and ejido income. For instance, before the 1936 reparto, the Tlahualilo Company had produced an average of 487 kilograms of cotton per hectare. Later, with the consolidation of the ejido regime, productivity had increased to 888 kilograms of cotton per hectare. By 1958–59, during a reprieve of the severe drought, it increased again, to 1,200 kilograms per hectare, thanks to improvements in agricultural techniques. But with the installation of the new canal network in 1963, and increased use of more potent fertilizers and pesticides (evidently capable of overcoming pests' resistance, as detected by Hernández), the average output of cotton reached 3,364 kilograms per hectare during the 1966–67 agricultural cycle. López Zamora also cited statistics on ejidos' income showing that they posted a profit of 12 million pesos because of this rapid increase in productivity. López Zamora declared the plan not only an unqualified success, but also a demonstration of "the honorability of the campesinos and their capacity to assimilate and apply the most advanced agricultural techniques."[44]

In the 1960s, however, despite the rapid increases in productivity, cotton was fast losing its status as principal crop. In addition, other regions were overtaking the Laguna in production; by 1948, Matamoros was producing double the hectareage of the Laguna (80,000 hectares versus 160,000 hectares), and just two years later, it produced three times as much (100,000 hectares versus 300,000 hectares), while Mexicali slightly overtook it (100,000 hectares versus 107,000) hectares.[45] Meanwhile, a new, and more profitable, commodity emerged: dairy. In 1948, 4,000 head of cattle were producing 33,000 liters of milk per day, and in 1962, 18,000 head were producing 175,000 liters per day (see appendix 3). Under the Programa Nacional de Ganadería (National Livestock Program), the government had made the burgeoning dairy and beef industries integral to its 1966 rehabilitation plan, and many ejidatarios joined small, private cotton producers to request inclusion. They informed the government that they needed 500–800 cattle head per ejido to ensure profitability, given the high operating costs and low official prices, and not the mere 100 the government was then currently offering. As a result, cotton cultivation watered by the Nazas declined to 50 percent of all (primarily ejido-based) agriculture in the Laguna, while groundwater used to grow cattle feed expanded— although that, too, reached a limit as it competed with less groundwater-intensive fruit production in the late 1960s and 1970s.[46]

As the second, smaller Tórtolas Dam came on line in 1968, precipitation levels rose, and the Palmito reservoir filled to historic levels. Water released from the two reservoirs now flowed faster through more and more concrete-lined canals delivered to increasingly compacted lands, and commodity prices rebounded due to a combination of more favorable market conditions and government price supports in the 1970s. In this confluence of events, Laguneros enjoyed a newfound sense of prosperity. Judith Adler Hellman describes the peculiar kind of redistribution the prosperity enabled: "Throughout the region, peasant leaders, both official and independent, began to speak with optimism of 'una Laguna nueva,' and ordinary peasants started to appear on the streets of Torreón in the shirts, felt hats, cowboy boots, and wristwatches that ten years earlier had been the exclusive sartorial prerogative of corrupt ejidal officers."[47]

Overall, on completion of its various stages in 1972, the rehabilitation plan-cum-second agrarian reform was undeniably a grand envirotechnical success: its técnicos had applied cutting-edge agronomic and hydraulic science and engineering to greatly improve economic conditions in the region. The national

El Sol de México expressed this widespread sentiment in an editorial as early as 1968:

> With this program a whole cycle of errors and demagogies has closed, so to speak, with regard to the situation and necessities of the Laguna. With technical and not exclusively political criteria, viable formulas were found to overcome the risks of monoculture in the face of international market fluctuations, inadequate management of irrigation canals, decline of cultivable land, and dispersion of campesino groups. The Laguna has stopped being a cauldron of passions and resentments, a field of charlatans and adventurers, and has reconstituted itself once more into the hope of Mexico and symbol of the entrepreneurial genius and capacity to work of our people.[48]

Ecologically, however, the story was very different. Through detailed diagrams of the changing morphology of the aquifer as the plan was implemented, engineers pointed out in their internal assessments the tragic irony of their projects' outcome. For instance, in a lengthy report produced by the SRH's Department of Subterranean Hydrology for arid areas in 1978, they considered the state of the region's aquifers "seriously threatened" without strict regulation of groundwater pumping. They noted that natural recharge of the aquifer before the development of agriculture and intensive irrigation was approximately 100 million cubic meters annually. With agricultural development and intensive use of river water for aniego, recharge increased to 400 million–500 million cubic meters annually, making more water available for pumping. If water users had struck a proper balance between artificial flood recharge and pumping, therefore, they could have devised a relatively sustainable new regional hydrology. But beginning in 1940, an imbalance emerged, and by 1958 users were pumping a massive 15 billion cubic meters of water via 2,400 wells. As a dramatic illustration of the impact of this imbalance on the water table, a potential well could be drilled less than 10 meters deep to extract groundwater with a pump in the 1930s, but by 1978, the engineers calculated, the same well had to be 40–90 meters deep.[49]

As alarming as these numbers must have appeared to local and federal officials, the report's most critical assessment forthrightly stated:

> The rehabilitation of the district, realized during the period 1963–72, came to newly modify the geohydrological conditions in the plain, but now in a form that is totally adverse for the aquifer. In effect, with the paving over of more than 1,000 kilometers of canals, the concentrations

of cultivable land and the mechanization of irrigation, the losses from conduction and the recycling from irrigation have been reduced to a minimum. The consequence: from 1972 the aquifer recharge remained at a reduced 200 million cubic meters annually, a volume principally constituted by subterranean flow from fluvial valleys and from surrounding plains.[50]

The engineers' verdict was that nature still managed to recharge only a fraction of the aquifer Laguneros demanded of it.

The SRH engineers had more unwelcome news to report. Another "unfavorable characteristic" they detected in the subterranean water supply was the "content of arsenic far higher than the corresponding norm." At first, engineers thought the sources of this arsenic were artificial, yet all available information at their disposal suggested that the principal source was naturally occurring— that is, the arsenic was coming from its "own geological formations." Although its presence in the water and in the soil is relatively common, arsenic had never previously posed a public health problem. But as farmers pumped water ever more deeply and as naturally occurring particulates became more concentrated, this geologically poisonous brew grew into a disaster. For instance, according to medical studies of the National Institute of Nutrition, 30–60 percent of the local population suffered diverse somatic traumas caused by chronic arsenic intoxication.[51] Other studies have revealed the presence of arsenic in crops, milk, and meat from the Laguna, including one that found concentrations of pesticides ranging from 1.21 parts per million to 35 times that, depending on the substance, and well above limits established by the World Health Organization.[52] The current of undeniable envirotechnical success met a horrific toxic countercurrent.

Predicting that users would have to drill wells as deep as 130 meters to extract water in a few years' time, the SRH report declared, "The reduction of pumping is, obviously, the only effective method to put a brake on the descent of water levels. The speed of depletion will decrease approximately in proportion to the reduction in extraction." It cited other possible extraction methods, such as tapping clay rock aquifers, but the SRH engineers did not judge them to be effective. As with previous reports going back decades, they emphasized that vedas and other groundwater regulations should consider the larger Nazas and Aguanaval river valleys, as well as the farmlands of the Irrigation District, given the "hydrological interconnection" between them.[53] That interconnection was apparent to local water users, who bore the brunt of the consequences of the plan's envirotechnical success.

In one representative instance, in June 1968, during the rehabilitation plan's second stage, Josefina Ríos de Mendoza, a small landowner from San Pedro who owned 60 hectares distributed between two properties, wrote to the SRH's general director of hydraulic concessions. She submitted documentation from 1948 showing she held original water rights to the Rubio-Bilbao and Guadalupe canals, from which she used to take water and demanded that they be restored to her. She explained that for the previous twenty years she had irrigated with water pumped from her well, but because of a large concentration of salt, the water had become noxious to her crops, and fertility at one of her properties had declined shockingly. This was not the case at her other property, however, because she had no well and had continued to irrigate with Nazas water, which had been "kept free of this contamination." She thus wanted the rights to one canal transferred to her other uncontaminated property, but the Irrigation District refused her request. She considered the refusal "completely unfounded" and contrary to the Federal Water Law of 1951.[54]

For técnicos such as López Zamora, however, rehabilitating the Laguna by lining canals with concrete and compacting land by pressuring thousands of ejidatarios to relocate made conduction of water more efficient. Along with continued use of increasingly powerful chemical pesticides and fertilizers, rehabilitation significantly boosted agricultural productivity. Indeed, López Zamora was a firm believer in positive state action to improve socioeconomic conditions for the rural poor.[55] Yet the plan for which he took credit severely disrupted the regional hydrological cycle in two ways. First, it impeded released reservoir water—already at a greatly diminished volume from what the free-flowing, sediment-rich Nazas current would irregularly deliver—from filtering underground into the aquifer.[56] And second, it accelerated the rise of a new industry dominated by dairy and cattle interests, which coalesced in the late 1970s into the La Laguna (LALA) agroindustrial group.

One of Mexico's largest dairy companies today, LALA was formed from various smaller enterprises that had grown exponentially since the 1940s. By 1978, they produced a million liters of milk daily.[57] Consequently, Laguna farmers gradually converted land used for cotton and wheat to alfalfa and other fodder for cattle. The conversion created a "neo-latifundio" that concentrated scarce groundwater supplies to produce the new white gold of the region. At the same time, the ejido sector deteriorated overall as reduced credit, diminishing water supplies, demographic growth, poor governance, and sociopolitical and economic forces impelled by industrialization and urbanization squeezed them relentlessly after the short-lived prosperity of the 1970s. One local landowner called the rise of LALA the beginning of a new "acuifundio"—large water monopolizer—that intensified the Laguna water table's relentless decline.[58] Meanwhile, in 1981 the government imposed its fifth veda since 1949, which it did not enforce and with which users seldom complied.

López Zamora astutely remarked in the late 1960s that "the drama of the Laguna should be a lesson for our politicians. They have learned in the process that the welfare of Mexico demands that our irrigation and colonization policies must be adjusted in the future within the limits that nature imposes, and that those limits cannot be breached with impunity."[59] To be sure, López Zamora's proposed cure in the form of a rehabilitation plan appeared to belie such words, especially as técnicos forthrightly reported on its ecological consequences. Nevertheless, his diagnosis of the region prefigured what more environmentally minded, if not environmentalist, researchers working with the United Nations Research Institute for Social Development concluded in the 1980s. With the benefit of hindsight, they critiqued the rehabilitation plan as a politically palatable and economically successful short-term solution with major medium- and long-term social and environmental costs. They embraced the socially equitable outcomes that Cárdenas initially envisioned for his agrarian reform but advocated a fundamental shift away from the unsustainable use of natural resources to achieve them. They termed the Laguna's predicament a paradox of "productive abundance" amid environmental deterioration and widespread poverty.[60] This predicament, although common to many other countries and areas of the world, was the historical outcome of inherently contradictory national and regional dynamics—ones that must be painstakingly researched case by case.

Epilogue The Legacies of Water Use
and Abuse in Neoliberal Mexico

Today water shouts at us and demands from us that we manage it in a way that is completely unexpected. Water, as the ultimate representative of nature, domesticates and civilizes us.

VÍCTOR M. TOLEDO, "Mexican@s, al grito del agua"

In the past fifteen years, three Mexican presidents—Vicente Fox, Felipe Calderón, and Enrique Peña Nieto—have successively declared protecting water a "matter of national security."[1] Their terminology invokes the drug war, reflecting the gravity of Mexico's current water crisis as borne out by (conservative) government statistics: groundwater alone accounted for 38 percent of all water use in 2013, and 106 of the country's 653 aquifers—totaling 60 percent of the nation's groundwater—were severely overexploited and contaminated. Due to rapid demographic growth during much of the twentieth century, water availability declined from 18,053 cubic meters per capita in 1950 to 3,982 in 2013.[2] Massive hydraulic infrastructure building, including high dams, canals lined with concrete, and motorized groundwater pumps, made formerly unavailable water supplies more accessible yet also dangerously vulnerable. In the past couple of decades, the greater prevalence and duration of severe droughts exacerbated or induced by anthropogenic climate change has rendered Mexico's reliance on invasive hydraulic technology even more unsustainable.

Through an envirotech history of the emblematic central-northern arid Laguna region, this book shows how and why Mexico's postrevolutionary governments, like so many others around the globe in the twentieth century (and to this day), continued to deploy invasive hydraulic technologies for state development *even though* they knew it was unsustainable. It highlights the role of engineers, or técnicos, as formative actors who implemented the indispensable "hydraulic complement" of the reparto de tierras (distribution of the land): a revolutionary dam to facilitate the reparto de aguas (distribution of the water). Progeny of Article 27 of the revolutionary 1917 Constitution, the two repartos were conjoined twins that had to act in unison, despite confusing and contradictory directions; together they had to insure access to land and water as a state-granted social right and yet also conserve natural resources from granted lands and waters as both a state and societal duty. This conservationist provision made manifest the tension latent in the sentiments and ambitions of revolutionaries who wanted resource-intensive agriculture and yet also understood the need to conserve scarce and fragile water resources. Técnicos encountered this tension as they sought to deploy technology for revolutionary social and political purposes. Mediating the human demands of nature against its boundaries was just one aspect of their role as mediators of envirotechnical knowledge between state and society, particularly politicians, landowners, and campesinos.

Informal and partial, Mexican técnicos were hardly exemplars of social and environmental responsibility based on sound science. Yet despite their limitations, they repeatedly warned of the dangers of profligate water use, particularly aquifer depletion, which they began detecting as early as 1930. It took fifteen years, but in 1945 the state finally incorporated their warnings by amending Article 27 to subject groundwater pumping to federal jurisdiction. Empowered by the amendment, the government began imposing increasingly restrictive regulations on pumping in 1948, yet seldom enforced them; unsurprisingly, water users seldom complied with them. Three corrosive factors accounted for the lax enforcement and compliance, which continue to the present: conflicts of interest between some técnicos and their business investments in pump manufacturing, insatiable demand for water driven by resource-intensive agribusinesses, and general disregard for the long-term consequences of short-term extractive activities.[3]

Although the negative consequences of lax enforcement and compliance disproportionately affected poorer farmers, principally ejidatarios, who remained more strictly regulated in their water use and consequently had less access to water, *all* those involved in agriculture contributed to depletion and contamination of the Laguna's scarce water resources.[4] Though fully imbued with a late nineteenth-century and early twentieth-century mind-set that damming rivers to create reservoirs for human use signified "conservation," several prominent técnicos nevertheless questioned the wisdom of building the Nazas River dam. They were concerned that the dam might obstruct the river's natural fertilizing function through the aniego (flood) method of irrigation, however irregular and indifferent to property and water rights that inundating flow could be. Soil fertility was not the only concern among técnicos; some presciently worried that damming the river would prevent natural recharging of the aquifer when groundwater pumping burgeoned in the 1930s and 1940s. They were not alone. For decades, the majority of Laguna landowners shared these técnicos' concerns about the impact of damming the Nazas on aniego (while at the same time enthusiastically embracing groundwater pumping).

These findings demonstrate two critical processes that scholars of Mexican postrevolutionary state formation, environmental history and history of technology in Latin America, and global development studies have largely overlooked: globally prevalent utilitarian conservationism, which has garnered so much historical attention, was only a distant influence on Lázaro Cárdenas's unbridled confidence in dams to solve the nation's water woes. Of more immediate import was the simple fact that many Mexicans, including campesinos, *wanted* dams and carried out lobbying campaigns at the local, regional, and national levels and succeeded in placing them on the nation's developmental agenda—most notably, the Six-Year Plan of 1934. The plan, which served as a guide for Cárdenas's presidency (1934–40), focused national attention on specific dam projects such as the Nazas, which was itself the successful culmination of a decades-long local and national lobbying campaign launched by Francisco I. Madero in 1906—years before the Revolution made agrarian reform and conservation national priorities through the 1917 Constitution. After Madero's political revolution unleashed the "tiger" (to use the deposed Porfirio Díaz's alleged term) of social revolution that he could not control, the Nazas dam campaign grew and merged with the far larger mass mobilization and union organizing of Laguna campesinos and workers to demand better wages and working conditions on haciendas, and eventually, land and water of their own in the 1920s and 1930s. Campesino unions generally supported the Nazas Dam project not only because its construction would create jobs, but also because they were persuaded that it would regulate unpredictable agricultural cycles that caused unemployment and hardship in the region. From this perspective, it is not surprising that Cárdenas invested considerable state economic, social, and political capital in the Nazas and other dams.

The story of the Nazas Dam as told in this book also reveals the interdependence of environmental and technological history exemplified by the envirotech approach. Indeed, the story of how people interacted with the Nazas River is, at its core, a story of the deployment of ever more sophisticated and invasive hydraulic technology, but one that increasingly blurred the boundaries between human ingenuity and nature. And like so much envirotech history, the story begins with ideas—namely, people had to imagine the Nazas dam before they could build it. The dam was thus a nodal site around which a wide range of historical actors envisioned the sociopolitical and envirotechnical components of agrarian reform converging in the future. Yet once completed in 1946, the dam as really existing technology remained more imagined than substantive, for the country had dramatically changed since 1936 when Cárdenas broke ground on it. His successors, especially Miguel Alemán, were so far to the right of him that even if the dam had fulfilled its envirotechnical expectations, it is highly unlikely that ejidos would have been its principal beneficiaries, as Cárdenas had intended in 1936. Whereas Cárdenas wanted the dam to principally serve ejidos through preferential access to its reservoir water, Alemán wanted it mainly to help private landowners at the expense of ejidos. Although they were ideological opposites within the emergent postrevolutionary one-party state, both the left-of-center, downwardly redistributionist (rich-to-poor) Cárdenas and the right-of-center, upwardly redistributionist (poor-to-rich) Alemán shared a technological optimism in dams and other hydraulic infrastructure as politically "neutral" facilitators of their developmentalist programs.[5]

Agrarian Reform Has Ended: Long Live Its Hydraulic Complement!

The technological optimism common to the ideological opposites Cárdenas and Alemán mirrored the transcendent geopolitical appeal that large-scale hydraulic infrastructure held globally in the U.S.-led state capitalist, Soviet-led state socialist, and nonaligned blocs.[6] As the high social and environmental costs of deploying grand hydraulic (and other) infrastructure became more and more apparent worldwide during the late twentieth century, public, but not necessarily state, confidence in the technology generally declined. Mexico was no exception, for the state's confidence remained high despite heavy social and ecological costs that the public was less willing to bear.

Epitomizing this process was Carlos Salinas de Gortari, who in February 1992, four years into his presidency, congratulated the Mexican Congress for passing a revision of Article 27 that he had forged and energetically championed. With no apparent sense of irony, Salinas invoked the legacy of Emiliano Zapata to legitimate the revision even though it effectively terminated seventy-five years of constitutionally mandated agrarian reform for which Zapata had fought and died during the Revolution. He explained that although the agrarian reform accomplished many of its goals, Zapata's "Agrarian Law"— or the 1911 Plan of Ayala and Article 27 of the 1917 Constitution that incorporated it—had, as he perceived it, outlived its utility as a "world example of justice" in a country that was now primarily urban and had no more cultivable land to distribute. This transformation was apparent by the 1970s, he claimed, when food production could no longer keep pace with population growth. The result was a *rezago agrario* (agrarian backlog) in granting titles for new ejidos, expansion of existing parcels, and other elements central to the continued viability of the agrarian reform. Moreover, in addition to land distribution, the massive resources that the government had invested in subsidies, price controls, and technical training proved incapable of halting, let alone slowing, agriculture's precipitous decades-long economic decline; by 1990, the agricultural sector contained 30 percent of the population but accounted for only 7 percent of Mexico's gross domestic product.[7]

To be sure, Salinas deftly formed an impressive coalition to craft a much needed and overdue revision of Article 27.[8] Powerful rural organizations and unions, the majority of the ruling PRI (Partido Revolucionario Institucional/Institutional Revolutionary Party), the right-wing opposition Partido Acción Nacional (National Action Party; PAN), and renowned scholars of agrarian reform such as Arturo Warman all supported the revision. Despite this rich variety of viewpoints he could have referenced, even while ignoring the left-wing opposition PRD (Partido de la Revolución Democrática/Revolutionary Democratic Party), he omitted a number of important explanatory factors for Mexico's agricultural decline, especially within the ejido sector, in his analysis. First, GDP calculations did not account for rural subsistence production and domestic female labor;[9] second, the Alemanista constitutional amendments of the 1940s and 1950s had already largely achieved Salinas's goal by emasculating much of the Cardenista agrarian reform of the 1930s; and third, Mexico's agricultural modernization, which included adoption of the water and chemical-intensive Green Revolution, resulted in a sharp upward distribution of social, economic, and natural resources to the disproportionate detriment of ejidos and Mexico's food self-sufficiency in basic staples by the 1970s.

Although he was apparently oblivious to how more subtle, interconnected influences could have enormous impacts, Salinas, like every one of his predecessors, was in awe of grand hydraulic technology. The one critical component of the government's massive decades-long investment in the rural sector and agrarian reform that he felt had borne fruit was, indeed, Mexico's advanced capabilities in, and deployment of, hydraulic technology that had enabled it to rank seventh globally in irrigated land area.[10] Mexico had nearly five thousand dams, but Salinas proudly attributed this envirotechnical success to the construction of five hundred high dams (15 meters or higher) that together impounded 143 billion cubic meters of water and thirty thousand miles of canals, as well as to the installation of sixty thousand motorized pumps that drew up a third of the country's groundwater.[11] At the same time, he was the first president to fully embrace the global discourse of environmentalism that had emerged in the 1970s and 1980s by incorporating ecological concerns in state developmental planning, especially deforestation and urban air pollution.

Like his predecessors, however, his solution to the dwindling supply and degradation of surface and subsurface waters was to further *expand* grand hydraulic infrastructure. While he congratulated himself on a number of provisions in the 1992 revision of the agrarian reform that protected the natural environment of ejidos via more sustainable land use and forestry practices, when it came to water, Salinas overlooked the dangerous consequences of Mexico's envirotechnical successes in historical dam and canal building and groundwater pumping.[12] Even at the cusp of the twenty-first century, the former president could not conceive that free-flowing rivers were a form of conserving water resources, a fact that reflects the long-standing conflation between conservation of native forests (and other land-based ecosystems) and reservoirs created from dammed rivers.[13] Notably, in this historical context, the very terms *ecología* and *medio-ambiente* (environment)—as opposed to the long-prevailing terms *naturaleza* and *conservación,* which Mexican técnicos predominantly employed through the 1960s—did not consistently appear in documents and public discourse before the 1970s. Beginning in the 1970s, the emergence of an international environmental movement influenced Mexican institutions and political discourse, helping raise the profile of the small, long-standing domestic conservationist movement and moving it, gradually, into the "mainstream."[14] This mainstreaming culminated in the founding of a Secretaría de Medio Ambiente, Recursos Naturales y Pesca (Ministry of the Environment, Natural Resources, and Fisheries; SEMARNAP, later changed to SEMARNAT) under Salinas in 1994 in the wake of the 1992 United Nations Conference on the Environment in Rio de Janeiro, which popularized the concept of "sustainable development," a term coined in 1987 by the United Nations Brundtland Commission. Significantly, with respect to water, Salinas reformed the Ministry of Hydraulic Resources and Agriculture (the two had merged in 1976) into the Comisión Nacional del Agua (National Water Commission; CNA) in 1989, which subsequently became part of the SEMARNAT in 1994.[15] Commanding an impressive 75 percent of the ministry's budget in 2008, the semiautonomous CNA is the most powerful of federal bureaucracies within the SEMARNAT. Although the CNA sounds like a concerned environmental organization and furnishes much useful data on its website and other media on Mexico's water resources, it persists in promoting ecologically invasive hydraulic infrastructure projects, not unlike its less high-minded National Irrigation Commission (CNI) and Ministry of Hydraulic Resources (SRH) predecessors.[16]

Like the Cardenista agrarian reform in the 1930s, the Salinista termination of it in 1992 also made the Laguna its template. None other than Raúl Salinas, the president's brother, co-wrote an important, detailed survey in 1994 of Laguna ejidatarios to assess how aware they were of government agrarian policies and whether their awareness influenced their plans to sell or keep their lands.[17] The survey concluded that most respondents supported the government's "reforming the agrarian reform." Yet the availability of water was the central issue that ejidatarios wanted resolved before the government implemented any changes. The two authors put numbers to the public's concern over the "lack of water," explaining that it "was cited by 71% of the producers as the cause for the non-utilization of arable lands, while 25% and 21% of them cite the cause as poor rains and the lack of credit, respectively."[18]

Ironically, the survey also concluded that there was "a marked lack of concern on the part of the campesinos for the preservation of the environment and the rational use of natural resources" and that "their productive decisions (crop changes for example) are not influenced, at least not explicitly, by the lack of water in a region where the scarcity of water resources and the irrational use of water has threatened the region's very existence." This finding pointed "to the need for permanent consciousness-raising campaigns among the rural population around the environment, natural resources and their conservation."[19] Yet nowhere in the study did Raúl Salinas mention the relationship between campesinos' lack of concern or consciousness and the government's construction of vast hydraulic works, which for decades had promised to "conserve" those resources on their behalf.

Furthermore, they shouldered an oversize portion of the blame, for ejidatarios were not the only Lagueros lacking awareness or education on these vital issues. At a public roundtable held in Torreón in 1990, for instance, three members of the Laguna elite—the hydraulic engineer Francisco Castro Bernal; Braulio Fernández Aguirre, the former mayor of Torreón and governor of Coahuila; and the landowner Enrique Vázquez Ávila—convened to discuss the severe drought of the 1950s and 1960s that devastated the region. Although the federal government's massive Rehabilitation Plan helped to overcome the drought-induced crisis of the 1950s and 1960s by diversifying the regional economy, the discussants acknowledged that water resources had actually worsened a great deal since then. The Nazas and Aguanaval rivers, and the underground aquifers they once recharged, the three acknowledged, were severely overexploited. This overexploitation was primarily due to an agricultural sector that consumed more than 90 percent of their water while accounting for only 30 percent of the regional economy. As the region's lifeblood, the embattled Nazas stood at the center of every discussion that day. Castro launched the public roundtable by speaking of three "epochs" in the river's history:

> One . . . ended in 1946; until then the river would flow uncontrollably; farmers would irrigate when it flowed down. On June 21, 1946, the Lázaro Cárdenas Dam began to store water [in its reservoir] and from that moment the second stage began, in 1968, when [the reservoir] filled for the first time. During this time [1946 to 1968], there were many problems; there wasn't water to irrigate every year; there were years when small property owners would cede their water allocations to ejidos. With regard to the wells there wasn't a problem. If there was a crisis, it was because the water from the dam did not reach the ejidos.[20]

Castro's narrative perfectly articulated his technologically determinist view of history. First, all pertinent history regarding the river and its role in the crisis began for him in 1946, when the first major dam was completed and the river ceased to "flow uncontrollably." Second, he summarily dismissed the history of groundwater over-drafting with the phrase "there wasn't a problem." One audience member, the physician and environmentalist Luis Maeda, challenged Castro's narrative, countering that Laguneros had faced a two-pronged assault on their public health: below ground, over-pumping enabled naturally occurring arsenic to leech into the aquifer, and above ground, Laguna farmers' application of DDT—the most intensive anywhere in Mexico—contaminated the food supply, especially dairy. Rounding out the panel's discussion, Vázquez, by contrast, briefly discussed the reparto de tierras that created the ejidos in 1936 and the fact that, due to rapid demographic growth, ejidos had long lacked water for their insufficient 4 hectare plots.

Each panelist offered fragments of a larger and deeper history, yet neither they nor any audience member explicitly connected the three factors largely responsible for the crisis they gathered to publicly discuss: the planning and building of the El Palmito/Lázaro Cárdenas Dam from 1906 to 1946; the mass creation of the water-deficient ejidos in 1936 for which the dam was expressly built; and how over-pumping, a serious problem since 1930, rapidly depleted and contaminated the principal aquifer, which before 1946 was recharged by the uncontrolled Nazas. Indeed, these elite Laguneros—all of whom had lived through, participated in, or studied the historical events of the 1950s and 1960s they discussed—appeared as equally ignorant of the key factors in the region's environmental and agricultural crisis as the ejidatarios whom Raúl Salinas surveyed. Here again, the Laguna was a microcosm of the nation. The public roundtable garnered a number of local newspaper headlines and television sound bites, and a local journal subsequently published and archived its transcript, but to no avail. Two years later, in 1992, the government officially terminated the Laguna's largely forgotten reparto de tierras *and* reparto de aguas of the late 1930s.

In the following decade, fortunately, nongovernmental organizations and local environmental activists raised public awareness of the high social and ecological costs of grand hydraulic infrastructure building. In 2003, the CNA's plan to dam the Aguanaval River provoked controversy of a kind remarkably similar to that which Nazas River dam proponents had from 1906 to 1936. Despite being separated by nearly three-quarters of a century, public debate over a dam's merits and demerits once again cut across socioeconomic class, rural sector, and ideology. Since the CNA proposed building two kinds of dams simultaneously—a storage dam and a smaller regulatory dam (the latter designed exclusively to mitigate flooding)—the Aguanaval case was initially more complicated than the Nazas case. Some groups favored one dam or the other, whereas others were opposed to any and all dams on the Aguanaval. Among those in favor were ejidatarios in the upriver area who allied with agribusiness interests seeking to regulate costly flooding. Other ejidatarios, especially those who continued to employ the aniego method of irrigation in the lower river area, opposed the project. Fearing that damming the river would harm the aquifer, the ecological reserve in the lower-river Jimulco Canyon area, and the protected Cuatro Ciénegas biosphere nearby to the north, the municipalities of Torreón, Matamoros, and Viesca; the Agricultural and Livestock Chamber of Torreón; industry groups; and local environmentalist groups joined these ejidatarios in opposition. All of them appealed to history by accurately pointing out that the two Nazas dams had adversely affected the aquifer.

Yet unlike in the 1920s, the putatively environmentalist CNA announced its plan to dam the Aguanaval in 2003 without prior local consultation. It then became secretive, guarding its plans closely. Unlike in the 1920s, when government and nongovernment lobbyists for the Nazas dam had to work hard to reassure skeptical local residents that it would not adversely affect them socially, economically, or ecologically, in the 1990s the CNA was legally required to conduct an environmental impact assessment but did not do so until local civic groups brought pressure.[21] Two generations before, in 1936, Nazas River dam opponents ultimately had no choice but to accept Cárdenas's decision to build the dam, but in the 2000s a more liberal democratic government under the opposition PAN had to be more calculating. Unable to simply mandate it, as Cárdenas had done, the government successfully employed a strategy of ob-fuscation, high-handedness, and divide-and-rule to push the Aguanaval Dam project through. In 2007, the Aguanaval met the same fate as its big sister, the Nazas: both a storage dam and small regulatory dam now control the Aguanaval's torrential flows and, in the process, have largely suppressed the last vestiges of the centuries-long method of more ecologically sustainable aniego irrigation.[22]

In 2006, long after environmentalism had become mainstream in Mexico, President Vicente Fox appointed a former chief executive of LALA, Mexico's largest dairy producer and groundwater consumer in the Laguna, to direct the CNA.[23] The CNA's five-year plan for 2007–2012, publicly released that same year, promised "adequate management and preservation of water, given its im-portance for social welfare, economic development, and the preservation of the ecological wealth of the country."[24] While in spirit the CNA's language re-flects modern environmentalist sensibilities, in practice the wording in the CNA's plan closely resembled the revisions of Article 27 passed by Congress in 1945 and 1992. Both revisions pursued two important objectives—development and conservation—but, notably, without stipulating how they would make these two, otherwise contradictory objectives complementary. Thus far, the CNA has mostly followed in its predecessors' footsteps in the Laguna. Beginning in 2003, it not only dammed the Aguanaval; it has also allowed slow desicca-tion of the nearby crystal blue ponds in the Cuatro Ciénegas biosphere reserve by failing to regulate over-pumping by local alfalfa growers. All the while, as the CNA continues to advance the interests of large-scale agricultural producers, it has ignored domestic and foreign biologists, environmental groups, and gov-ernment agencies, including the U.S. National Aeronautics and Space Admin-istration, which has even stated that the Cuatro Ciénegas's unique ecosystem provides clues to discovering life on Mars. The situation is a classic case of "reg-ulatory capture," or a government agency in effect run by the very interest groups it is supposed to regulate (the proverbial fox guarding the henhouse).[25]

In the same year, the National Institute of Ecology (INE), an autonomous research institute within the SEMARNAT that receives a tiny percentage of the CNA's budget, warned that the Laguna's weather will get progressively hotter and drier as climate change accelerates. Yet in contrast to the bleak picture of regulatory capture deterring environmental progress, the INE highlighted a "positive aspect" about the Laguna: "There are social, educational and entre-preneurial organizations that have developed more consciousness about the environment than in other parts of the country."[26] With agrarian reform jettisoned for nearly a generation, whether such organizations can reverse the regulatory capture of the CNA and other government agencies by private industry so that they will consistently act in the public interest—and therefore fulfill the promises of the Mexican Revolution for complementary development and conservation of water and other natural resources—remains to be seen.

Volume of Nazas River Flow and Harvested Area of Cotton in the Laguna, 1852-1965.

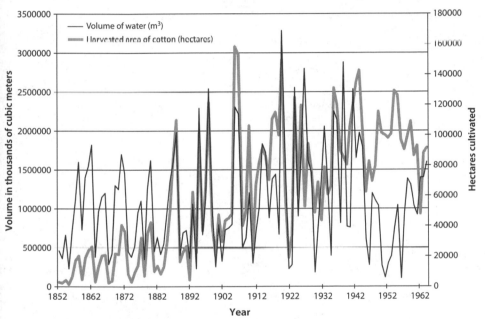

Source: Quixote Irrititla, "400 años de historia del Río Nazas, 1594-1994."

Cotton Production in Mexico 1897–1989

Year	Area harvested in hectares	Average yield kg per hectare	Production		Average rural price		Value of production in thousands of pesos
			Tons	Bales	$/ton	$/bale (230 kg)	
1897	124,247	265	32,915	143,109	389	89	12,804
1898	166,132	275	45,643	198,448	151	35	6,881
1899	74,171	306	22,708	98,730	207	48	4,698
1900	89,546	249	22,280	96,870	277	64	6,181
1901	89,272	265	23,656	102,852	275	63	6,515
1902	98,609	242	23,818	103,557	379	87	9,027
1903	131,453	279	36,642	159,313	216	50	7,912
1904	196,316	282	55,299	240,430	288	66	15,955
1905	515,857	288	148,574	645,973	226	52	33,658
1906	202,476	249	58,517	254,422	321	74	18,819
1907	135,076	265	33,659	146,343	327	75	11,010
1908	93,253	270	24,712	107,443	263	60	6,488
1909	103,704	290	28,000	121,739	396	91	11,094
1910	104,114	378	30,193	131,274	520	120	15,700
1911*	115,082	378	43,462	188,973	507	117	22,015
	(94,304)		35,647	154,986	507		18,056
1912	83,162	418	34,752	151,102	376	87	13,070
	(132,452)	239	31,656	137,639	376		11,906
1913	180,918	280	50,657	220,246	428	98	21,676
1914	127,852	290	37,077	161,206	456	105	16,911
1915	70,604	270	19,063	82,882	317	73	6,034
	(64,826)		17,503	76,098			5,540

(continued)

Cotton Production in Mexico 1897–1989

Year	Area harvested in hectares	Average yield kg per hectare	Production Tons	Bales	Average rural price $/ton	$/bale (230 kg)	Value of production in thousands of pesos
1916	112,418	280	31,477	136,856	412	95	12,974
1917	134,296	274	36,797	159,988	665	153	24,471
	(125,682)		34,437	149,726			22,901
1918	132,700	270	35,829	155,780	1,021	235	36,577
	(126,444)	270	34,140	148,434			34,853
	(172,335)	272	46,830	203,608			47,807
1919	108,883	332	36,149	157,170	1,057	243	38,200
	(101,383)	332	33,659	146,343			35,569
	(137,447)	333	45,770	199,000			48,367
1920	96,782	330	31,938	138,866	1,333	307	42,562
1921	97,486	327	31,878	138,606	601	138	19,155
1922	138,723	315	43,698	189.999	644	148	28,129
1923	118,089	322	38,025	165,333	907	209	34,472
1924	210,243	307	64,609	280,920	1,065	245	68,825
1925	171,929	253	43,467	188,986	1,019	234	44,278
1926	248,184	314	78,016	339,200	782	180	61,045
1927	132,041	294	38,862	168,965	1,051	242	40,838
1928	203,243	297	60,376	262,504	1,017	234	61,430
1929	198,938	268	53,344	231,930	782	180	41,701
1930	157,944	244	38,487	667,335	604	139	23,250
1931	129,114	353	45,581	198,178	479	110	21,848
1932	77,854	283	22,015	95,717	627	144	13,807
1933	171,696	329	56,465	245,500	802	184	45,269
1934	169,123	286	48,345	210,196	927	213	44,806
1935	266,062	257	68,256	236,170	811	186	55,339
1936	342,967	251	86,127	372,648	936	215	80,629
1937	335,991	219	73,591	320,552	957	219	70,397
1938	259,782	256	66,494	288,413	991	228	65,874
1939	262,308	258	67,645	292,343	1,048	241	70,860
1940	253,657	258	65,495	284,761	988	227	64,693
1941	316,097	257	81,209	353,083	1,176	270	95,486
1942	362,216	284	102,952	447,617	1,603	387	165**
1943	408,893	283	115,873	503,795	1,866	429	216.2
1944	389,614	272	106,120	461,391	1,908	439	202.5
1945	365,816	267	97,586	224,287	1,947	448	190.0

Cotton Production in Mexico 1897–1989

Year	Area harvested in hectares	Average yield kg per hectare	Production		Average rural price		Value of production in thousands of pesos
			Tons	Bales	$/ton	$/bale (230 kg)	
1946	327,443	278	91,137	396,248	2,496	574	227.5
1947	332,832	288	95,297	417,074	2,694	620	258.5
1948	404,678	296	119,668	520,295	3,238	745	387.5
1949	548,786	378	207,690	903,000	3,970	913	824.6
1950	760,534	342	260,019	1,030,517	6,019	1,384	1,565
1951	883,504	326	287,612	1,250,486	5,217	1,200	1,500.6
1952	784,304	337	264,542	1,150,182	5,241	1,206	1,386.6
1953	753,484	363	273,699	1,189,995	5,205	1,197	1,424.6
1954	922,135	424	390,941	1,699,743	6,624	1,524	2,589.7
1955	1,058,990	480	508,473	2,210,752	6,466	1,488	3,288
1956	873,469	487	425,747	1,851,073	6,385	1,469	2,718.6
1957	915,645	522	477,648	2,076,730	6,355	1,462	3,035.6
1958	1,027,803	512	526,208	2,287,860	6,049	1,391	3,183.2
1959	751,159	506	380,429	1,654,039	5,997	1,379	2,281.4
1960	899,122	523	470,347	2,044,986	6,056	1,393	2,848.3
1961	793,964	566	449,730	1,955,347	6,434	1,440	2,893.5
1962	787,025	617	485,785	2,112,608	6,272	1,443	3,046.9
1963	846,580	632	535,340	2,327,565	6,310	1,451	3,378
1964	808,690	699	565,349	2,458,039	6,363	1,463	3,597.2
1965	813,318	710	577,342	2,510,182	6,399	1,472	3,694.5
1966	695,379	750	521,270	2,266,391	6,403	1,473	3,337.7
1967	662,018	747	494,541	2,150,178	6,378	1,467	3,153.9
1968	705,335	839	591,961	2,573,743	6,382	1,468	3,777.6
1969	513,224	774	397,056	1,726,330	6,287	1,446	2,496.2
1970	411,172	812	333,688	1,450,838	6,579	1,513	2,195.5
1971	457,799	866	396,657	1,724,594	7,541	1,734	2,991.2
1972	523,426	796	416,512	1,810,922	8,358	1,923	3,481.2
1973	425,134	922	392,161	1,705,048	13,929	3,204	5,462.4
1974	578,322	887	512,758	2,229,382	11,267	2,593	5,777
1975	226,783	907	205,796	894,765	12,065	2,777	2,483
1976	234,981	953	223,963	234,981	27,116	6,238	6,072.5
1977	419,630	997	418,428	419,630	27,610	6,350	11,553
1978	349,767	1,048	366,343	349,767	30,434	7,000	11,152
1979	374,878	935	349,152	374,878	31,113	7,156	10,863.3

(continued)

Cotton Production in Mexico 1897–1989

Year	Area harvested in hectares	Average yield kg per hectare	Production		Average rural price		Value of production in thousands of pesos
			Tons	Bales	$/ton	$/bale (230 kg)	
1980	355,330	1,050	372,934	355,330	38,737	8,909	14,446.3
1981	354,977	943	334,745	354,977	28,190	6,480	9,435.9
1982	185,647	895	166,177	185,647	95,000	2,189	15,786.8
1983	232,000	984	229,000	232,000	47,741	4,798	47,741
1984	316,000	916	290,000	316,000	n.a.	n.a.	n.a.
1985	197,000	1,628	317,000	197,000	15,134	1,098	15,174
1986	157,000	913	144,000	157,000	38,360	6,127	38,360
1987	222,000	943	220,000	222,000	n.a.	n.a.	n.a.
1988	362,000	646	490,000	362,000	n.a.	n.a.	n.a.
1989	191,000	640	256,000	191,000	n.a.	n.a.	n.a.

Notes: * Statistics varied during the Mexican Revolution due to the difficulty of collecting data.
** From 1942, figures are in millions of pesos.
Source: Sistema para la consulta de las Estadísticas Históricas de México, Instituto Nacional de Geografía y Estadística http://dgcnesyp.inegi.org.mx/cgi-win/ehm2014.exe/CI090090030 (accessed June 25, 2015).

Milk, Cattle, and Cotton Production in Laguna, 1948–2004

Year	Liters per day	Heads of cattle	Area of cotton in hectares
1948	33,000	4,000	80,100
1962	175,000	18,000	90,443
1967	220,000	35,000	84,217
1970	450,000	45,000	81,084
1977	1,087,671	90,000	72,236
1980	1,150,684	73,421	65,886
1988	1,290,410	109,000	66,490
1990	1,475,674	200,584	52,281
2000	4,461,281	415,596	8,284
2004	4,850,000	470,000	15,860

SOURCE: "El manejo del agua en la Laguna, México," Elías García, Instituto de Desarrollo del Campo http://www.bancomundial.org/cuartoforo/text/D-CASO-RecursosNaturales.pdf.

INTRODUCTION

Epigraphs: Cosío Villegas, "La crisis de México," 39; Rulfo, *The Burning Plain and Other Stories*, 11–12.

1. Kourí, "Claroscuros de la reforma agraria mexicana," *Nexos en línea*, http://www.nexos .com.mx/?p=14062, accessed February 22, 2016.

2. For a detailed history of the company and its operations, see Cerutti and Rivas Sada, "El Grupo Industrial LALA."

3. Brunk, *Emiliano Zapata*, 43–44.

4. Clipping of Marshall Hail, "Cárdenas Hailed by Crowds as Messiah for Land Reforms," *Washington Times*, November 21, 1936, Archivo General de la Nación (AGN), Ramo Presidenciales (RP), Lázaro Cárdenas (LC), 404.1/706, 922.

5. Enrique Vázquez Ávila, Laguna farmer and engineer, interview by the author, Torreón, Coahuila, April 25, 2006.

6. As the general map at the front of this book shows, the Aguanaval River also waters the Laguna; hence, the region is located in the Nazas-Aguanaval river basin (see map FM.1). The flow of the Aguanaval River, however, is a fraction of that of the Nazas and will thus be mentioned only occasionally throughout this book. For a map of Mexico's thirty-seven river basins, see Comisión Nacional del Agua, *Estadísticas del agua en México*, 19.

7. I define environmental history as the study of the relationship between people—their society, culture, and politics—and the environment, broadly defined, over time, and the history of technology as the study of how people have made and done things using different kinds of techniques, objects, and materials that interact with society, culture, politics and the environment over time.

8. Reuss and Cutcliffe, eds., *The Illusory Boundary*, vii, 1; Jørgensen, Jørgensen, and Pritchard, eds., *New Natures*.

9. Mitchell, *Rule of Experts*, 34–35. For an explicitly envirotech history of the Rhône during the late twentieth century, see Pritchard, *Confluence*.

10. Medina, da Costa Marques, and Holmes, eds., *Beyond Imported Magic*.

11. Latin American environmental historiography is now large and growing rapidly. For an overview, see Carey, "Commodities, Colonial Science, and Environmental Change in Latin

American History." For environmental histories of water in Mexico, see Tortolero, ed., *Tierra, agua y bosques;* Loreto López, ed., *Agua, poder urbano y metabolismo social;* Evans, "Water and Environmental Change in the U.S.-Mexico Borderlands"; and Boyer, ed., *A Land between Waters,* among others. Boyer's volume includes chapters on various natural resources published by Mexican and U.S. environmental historians together for the first time. Likewise, the historiography of technology in Latin America is large and growing. For an overview, see Beatty, Pineda, and Sáiz, "Technology in Latin America's Past and Present." For book-length studies, see, among many others, Beatty, *Technology and the Search for Progress in Modern Mexico*; Domínguez Martínez, *La ingeniería civil en México;* and Medina, da Costa Marques, and Holmes et al., *Beyond Imported Magic;* Safford, *The Ideal of the Practical.* Medina and colleagues' volume is also part of the large literature on history of science in Latin America that often overlaps with the history of technology but less regularly with that of environmental history. For overviews of history of science in Latin America, see Glick, "Science and Independence in Latin America"; Saldaña, *Science in Latin America*; and Fishburn and Ortiz, eds., *Science and the Creative Imagination in Latin America.* For a notable exception that integrates environmental history with the history of science and technology in colonial Mexico City, see Candiani, *Dreaming of Dry Land.*

12. There is no comprehensive study of engineers and engineering throughout Mexican history, but there are several useful studies of engineering education and particular kinds of engineers and engineering during specific periods: Candiani, *Dreaming of Dry Land,* 171–75; Ramos Lara and Sánchez Estrada, "Antecedentes históricos del Colegio de Ingenieros"; Ervin, "The Art of the Possible"; Lucena, "De Criollos a Mexicanos"; Gortari Rabiela, "Educación y conciencia nacional"; Ayala, Herrera, and Pons, ed., *Ingenieros en la Independencia y la Revolución;* Chávez, *Ingeniería y humanismo;* Moles Batllevell, *La enseñanza de la ingeniería mexicana, 1792–1990;* Domínguez Martínez, *La ingeniería civil en México, 1900–1940.*

13. Jiménez, "La contribución de la Comisión Nacional de Irrigación en adelanto de la ingeniería en México."

14. Smith and Marx, eds., *Does Technology Drive History?,* xii.

15. Scott, *Seeing Like a State.* See also Josephson, *Industrialized Nature* and Josephson, *Resources under Regimes.* For examinations of China, Cuba, and Germany that implicitly and explicitly adopt Scott's model of high modernity, see, respectively, Shapiro, *Mao's War against Nature;* Díaz-Briquets and Pérez-López, *Conquering Nature;* and Blackbourn, *The Conquest of Nature.* For a trenchant critique of Scott, see Coronil, "Smelling Like a Market." For more nuanced critiques, see, respectively, Jess Gilbert, "Low Modernism and the Agrarian New Deal"; Mathews, *Instituting Nature.*

16. Joseph and Nugent, eds., *Everyday Forms of State Formation,* x.

17. Mitchell, *Rule of Experts,* 15, 51; the italics are mine. Mitchell differentiates himself from Scott in this way by focusing on the social and political practices that simultaneously produce the powers of modern states and science—as opposed to (primarily authoritarian socialist) states' abusing science and imposing it on civil societies unable to resist. While I embrace this difference, I would also add that the powers of any state (liberal democratic, state capitalist, rightist, and fascist, as well as socialist) and science are not only mutually constitutive; they also synergistically produce knowledge and awareness of natural

resource scarcity and the corresponding need for conservation, a point on which I elaborate later. For additional definitions of technopolitics complementary to, but slightly modified from, Mitchell, see Hecht, *Entangled Geographies: Empire and Technopolitics in the Global Cold War*, 3.

18. On plant scientists in the Caribbean, see McCook, *States of Nature*. On Mexican agronomists, see Ervin, "The 1930 Agrarian Census in Mexico." On urban environmental planners and engineers working on the desagüe of Mexico City, see Vitz, " 'The Lands with Which We Shall Struggle' " and Candiani, *Dreaming of Dry Land*. On Mexican and Chilean foresters, see, respectively, Boyer, *Political Landscapes* and Klubock, *La Frontera*.

19. Carey, *In the Shadow of Melting Glaciers*, 6. On the similar role that "political engineering" played in Francoist Spain, see Camprubí, *Engineers and the Making of the Francoist Regime*. On the role that the "technological imaginary" or "imagineering" played in wartime Japan, see Moore, *Constructing East Asia*.

20. Latour, *Reassembling the Social*, 39.

21. White, *The Organic Machine*.

22. I do not hereby suggest that developed countries have solved their environmental problems or that their politicians do not make the same arguments about the burdensome economic "cost" of environmental protection (without, of course, accounting for the far costlier "externalities" of development). The difference is that having already achieved "developed" status, they speak not of catching up developmentally but instead of maintaining global competitiveness. For a critical global history of development, see Rist, *The History of Development*.

23. Gifford Pinchot popularized the concept of wise use as one that made no distinction between development and the conservation of natural resources. As he wrote, "The first principle of conservation is development, the use of the natural resources now existing on this continent for the benefit of the people who live here now." Statements such as these, taken out of context, inspired the conservative anti-environmentalist (virtually synonymous with anti-regulatory) wise-use movement in the western United States in the late 1980s and 1990s, recently revived in the mid-2010s. Pinchot made it clear that he envisioned a strong federal role in conservation to prevent unnecessary "waste" of resources. This included a redistributive regulatory agenda of preserving natural resources "for the benefit of the many, and not merely for the profit of a few." Pinchot, *The Fight for Conservation*, chap. 4. For how this conception of wise use in Mexico applied to conservation of oil resources in Mexico, see Santiago, *The Ecology of Oil*.

24. Boyer and Wakild, "Social Landscaping in the Forests of Mexico." See also Wakild, *Revolutionary Parks: Conservation, Social Justice, and Mexico's National Parks, 1910–1940*; Boyer, *Political Landscapes*.

25. Worster, *Rivers of Empire*, 154–55. For Mexican perspectives and attitudes on water control in the late nineteenth century and early twentieth century, see Gayol, *Dos problemas de vital importancia para México*, Herrera y Lasso, *Apuntes sobre irrigación*, and Molina Enríquez, *Los grandes problemas nacionales*. For Worsterian but revisionist studies of European and North American rivers, see Mauch and Zeller, eds., *Rivers in History*. Peter Perdue points out a similar change in Chinese attitudes toward free-flowing rivers between Confucianists and Daoists. The former advocated water conservancy by controlling river flow whereas the

latter advised letting water flow freely and resettling people accordingly. Perdue, "A Chinese View of Technology and Nature?," 107.

26. It should be noted that in the United States there was a difference between "conservationists" and "preservationists" that was not as marked in Mexico. U.S. conservationists believed a balance between the utilization and the protection of natural resources could be struck while preservationists felt forests should remain basically intact. Worster, *Nature's Economy*, 258–90. The U.S. preservationist John Muir also opposed large dam projects to preserve river basins on aesthetic grounds, such as the Hetch Hetchy in Yosemite, a bitter battle which he lost.

27. Boyer, "Revolución y paternalismo ecológico." Like in Europe, however, applying scientific forestry for "maximum sustained yield" logging, which also included creating monocrop tree plantations in place of old-growth forests, could be considered "conservation" in Mexico: Boyer, *Political Landscapes*, 8. For Chilean foresters, too, conservation from the late nineteenth century came to signify replacing old- and second-growth forest, or lands deforested of them, with tree plantations, especially in the south. They generally advocated conserving old and second-growth forest primarily within national parks and preserves that—unlike Mexico in this case—excluded campesinos and indigenous communities: Thomas Klubock, *La Frontera: Forests and Ecological Conflict in Chile's Frontier Territory*. Neither Boyer nor Klubock, however, explicitly explore the role that technology played in fostering changing notions of forest conservation in Mexico and Chile, respectively.

28. De Quevedo, *Relato de mi vida*, 39–40. The government of Benito Juárez had in fact established a federal forestry statute in 1861, decades before the United States did in 1894. Simonian, *Defending the Land of the Jaguar*, 54.

29. De Quevedo, *Relato de mi vida*, 39–40.

30. In his survey of Latin American liberalism and its role in promoting social rights globally, the historian Greg Grandin described Mexico's 1917 Constitution as the "world's first fully conceived social-democratic charter, enshrining the right to organize unions, the right to work, a minimum wage, equal pay for men and women, welfare, education, and healthcare." Grandin, "The Liberal Traditions in the Americas," 74–75. But the Constitution's key social right was agrarian reform in a predominantly rural country where the majority lacked land and therefore an opportunity for a decent livelihood. My use of "environmental" is admittedly anachronistic in a pre-environmentalist (pre-1980s) historical context. To be sure, the terms *ambiente* and *medio-ambiente* for the natural environment were not in common use in Mexico before the 1970s, as attested by keyword searches in Mexican digital newspaper archives covering the years 1910–70. By using the English word, I am referring to rights to *access* and *use* natural resources, not to protect or venerate them as if they had intrinsic value. People at the time may or may not have felt they had intrinsic value, depending on their particular sociocultural experiences with, and attitudes toward, nonhuman nature.

31. For excerpts translated into English, see Joseph and Henderson, eds., *The Mexico Reader*, 400. For the full text of Article 27 in the original Spanish, see http://www.juridicas .unam.mx/infjur/leg/conshist/pdf/1917.pdf, 13–14, accessed February 22, 2016.

32. For discussion of early water law in the context of property after independence, see Núñez Luna, "Water Law and the Making of the Mexican State, 1875–1917," PhD diss., Har-

vard University, Cambridge, MA, 2011, 45–52. Although Article 27's objective was *not* sustainable resource management of the kind advocated from the late twentieth century, it nevertheless "established a juridical framework that is notably similar to the thesis of the new environmental philosophy of the past decades," according to the Mexican ecologist Víctor Toledo in the 1990s. Toledo, "The Ecological Consequences of the 1992 Agrarian Law of Mexico," 254.

33. It would take nearly thirty years for groundwater to be placed under federal jurisdiction and nearly fifty years before it was unequivocally defined as national property. For details, see chap. 5 in this volume.

34. Aboites, *El agua de la nación*, 107–12.

35. Aboites, *El agua de la nación*, 16. In many ways, the work was a synthetic successor to his previous case study, *La irrigación revolucionaria*, discussed in chap. 2 and Kroeber's *Man, Land, and Water*, a tome surveying various water projects throughout Mexico and their intellectual and policy genealogies during the late Porfiriato. Kroeber showed that by the time of the Revolution, an incipient national irrigation policy was in formation on which revolutionary leaders would greatly expand.

36. The agrarian historiography of Mexico, especially on agrarian reform since the Revolution, is enormous. A few prominent examples include Simpson, *The Ejido;* Silva Herzog, ed., *El agrarismo mexicano y la reforma agraria;* Eckstein, *El ejido colectivo en México;* Hamilton, *The Limits of State Autonomy;* Sanderson, *Land Reform in Mexico, 1910–1980; Historia de la cuestión agraria mexicana* (9 volumes); Gledhill, *Casi Nada;* Randall, ed., *Reforming Mexico's Agrarian Reform;* Fallaw, *Cárdenas Compromised;* Morett Sánchez, *Reforma Agraria*; and Dwyer, *The Agrarian Dispute.* For selected works on the Laguna, which has generated an impressive subfield of "Lagunology" due to its emblematic agrarian reform, see, among others: Senior, *Democracy Comes to a Cotton Kingdom;* Mendizábal, "El problema agrario de la Laguna"; Restrepo and Eckstein, *La agricultura colectiva en México;* Carr, "The Mexican Communist Party and Agrarian Mobilization in the Laguna, 1920–1940"; Olcott, *Revolutionary Women in Postrevolutionary Mexico*, chap. 4; and Rivas Sada, "Cambio tecnológico, dinámica regional y reconversión productiva en el norte de México. La Comarca Lagunera, 1925–1974."

37. In addition to many dozens of articles published regularly in the quarterly *Boletín del Archivo Histórico del Agua* since 1994, these include, among many others, Castañeda González, *Irrigación y reforma agraria*, Suárez Cortez and Gardida, *Dos estudios sobre usos del agua en México (siglos XIX y XX)*, Suárez Cortez, *Historia de los usos del agua en México*, Aboites, ed., *Fuentes para la historia de los usos del agua en México (1710–1951)*, Aboites, *Demografía histórica y conflictos por el agua*, Aboites and Estrada, eds., *Del agua municipal al agua nacional*, Camacho Altamirano, *Empresarios e ingenieros en la ciudad de San Luis Potosí*, Escobar Ohmstede and Rojas Rabiela, eds., *Estructuras y formas agrarias en México*, Durán, Sánchez, and Escobar Ohmstede, eds., *El agua en la historia de México*, Escobar, Sánchez, and Gutiérrez, eds., *Agua y tierra en México, siglos XIX y XX,* and Escobar and Butler, eds., *Mexico in Transition.* The last four edited volumes have advanced the field considerably through their diversity, breadth, and depth of case studies and are prompting broad revision of fundamental tenets of Mexican agrarian history, particularly land disentailment (or privatization) before the Revolution; agrarian reform after it; and the transformation in natural resource

use, management, and jurisdiction surrounding them, with an emphasis on water as integral to land.

38. Aboites, *El agua de la nación*, 92.

39. Lanz Cárdenas, *Legislación de aguas en México*, 425–27.

40. Joseph and Henderson, *The Mexico Reader*, 398–99; italics added.

41. There is much debate in the historiography of the Mexican Revolution as to what kind of revolution it was, and how popular it was, on a continuum from elite-led and mass-manipulated at one end to radically democratic and participatory at the other. Wherever along the definitional continuum one pinpoints the Revolution, one thing is clear: agrarian reform was the central revolutionary demand in an agrarian country beset with highly unequal land distribution. It is in this sense that I subscribe to Alan Knight's view that the Mexican Revolution was "a popular, agrarian movement—the precursor, the necessary precursor, of the *étatiste* 'revolution' of post-1920." Knight, *The Mexican Revolution*, vol. 1, xi.

42. There is a large body of literature on the Nazas question, primarily for the Porfiriato: see Núñez Luna, "Water Law and the Making of the Mexican State"; Meyers, *Forge of Progress, Crucible of Revolt;* Plana, *El reino del algodón en México;* Kroeber, "La cuestión del Nazas hasta 1913"; Villa Guerrero, "Una mina de oro blanco." For a study incorporating this discussion that goes beyond the Porfiriato through the twentieth century, see Wolfe, "El Agua de la Revolución."

43. Not one técnico I quote in this book directly referenced the conservationist provision of Article 27, though he (all were men) was concerned with conserving water.

44. Mathews, *Instituting Nature*, 40, points out that environmental scientists currently believe the theory "is only partially correct."

45. Fradkin, *A River No More.*

46. Moreno Vázquez, *Por abajo del agua*, 55.

CHAPTER 1. RIVER OF REVOLUTION

Epigraph: Othón, *Obras de Manuel José Othón,* vol. 1, 238. I am grateful to Ana Minian and Lisa Surwillo for their assistance in translating this poem.

1. Madero, *Estudio sobre la conveniencia de la construcción de una presa*, 53–55.

2. Madero, *Estudio sobre la conveniencia de la construcción de una presa*, 27.

3. As early as 1895, after reconnoitering the Nazas and Aguanaval rivers, commission engineers and a geologist from the National Geological Institute concluded that "it was apparent there would be silting problems and possible detriment to fertilizing lands." They anticipated the arguments against the project that Madero would try to counter by referencing subsequent studies, about which more below. See "Remitiendo informe general de los trabajos relativos a la presa el cañón de Fernández," 1904 (AHA), Aguas Superficiales (AS), box 4350, file 577731; Riemann, *Memoria del Distrito de Riego de la Región Lagunera, Coahuila y Durango,* 7.

4. In the colonial documentation, the now so-called Comarca Lagunera refers more to a "region in which there are lakes" than a "region where there is a lake," the latter lake denoting the "Laguna de Mayrán": Corona Páez, *El País de La Laguna*, 21n2.

5. Irrititla, *400 años de historia del Río Nazas*, 6. Of the twelve rivers (Fuerte, Sinaloa, Mocorito, Pericos, Culiacán, San Lorenzo, Elota, Piaxtla, Quelite, Presidio, Baluarte, Nazas) that

originate in the Sierra Madre Occidental in Durango and Sinaloa, the Nazas is the only one to drain inland and eastward rather than westward into the Pacific.

6. Irrititla, *400 años de historia del Río Nazas*, 3–4, 6.

7. This fluvial boundary was the subject of dispute and recrimination between the two states for much of the nineteenth century: see Román Jáquez, *Del Aguanaval a Sierra Mojada*.

8. There has been a considerable change in the regional climate over the centuries due to natural causes, human transformations in local land and water use, industrialization and urbanization, demographic increases, deforestation in the mountains, and, in the past several decades, global climate change. The extent to which recent advances in scientific understanding of, and increasing certainty about, anthropogenic climate change on a global scale can account for regional historical climatic variations and just how far back in time is the subject of ongoing research. For a recent overview, see Carey, "Climate and History."

9. Irrititla, *400 años de historia del Río Nazas*, 4.

10. Mapimí is located in the northeastern portion of Durango and was an important regional mining town for much of the colonial period.

11. Among these endemic creatures are the crayfish and one species of aquatic herpetofauna (the salamander *Pseudoeurycea galeanae*): Abell, *Freshwater Ecoregions of North America*, 191.

12. Wolaver, Sharp, Rodríguez, and Flores, "Delineation of Regional Arid Karstic Aquifers," 407, 411. Two centuries ago, Humboldt remarked similarly, "The lakes with which Mexico abounds, the greater part of which appear annually on the decline, are merely the remains of immense basins of water, which appear to have formerly existed on the high and extensive plains of the Cordillera . . . the lakes of Mextitlan and Parras in New Biscay": Humboldt and Taylor, *Selections from the works of the Baron de Humboldt, relating to the climate, inhabitants, productions, and mines of Mexico*, 16.

13. Corona Páez, *El País de La Laguna*, 25. One older work, citing a historical geography of Coahuila from 1897, states that "the waters of the Nazas *also* extended to the north or until the Bolsón of Tlahualilo during a period which seems to have ended in 1829": Martínez del Río, *La Comarca Lagunera a fines del siglo XVI y principios del XVII según las fuentes escritas*, 18; italics added. It adds that Mexico's most renowned nineteenth-century geographer, Manuel Orozco y Berra, confused the various intermittent lakes of Tlahualilo (Caimán), Mayrán, and Parras (Viesca) in his *Atlas y catecismo de geografía y estadística de la República Mexicana*. Indeed, Matías Romero, Porfirio Díaz's three-time treasury secretary and minister to the United States, repeated this error, as did Meyers and Plana nearly a century later: see Romero, *Geographical and Statistical Notes on Mexico*, 68; Meyers, *Forge of Progress, Crucible of Revolt: Origins of the Mexican Revolution in La Comarca Lagunera, 1880–1911*, 22; Plana, *El reino del algodón en México: La estructura agraria de La Laguna, 1855–1910*, 116n.46. Vargas-Lobsinger, *La hacienda de "La Concha,"* 14, however, states that the river flow alternated between north and east. It is more likely that the river flowed intermittently in both directions until sometime between 1829 and 1845, then flowing only east.

14. Annotated text from the 1787 map (figure 1.1).

15. According to Humboldt, the United States produced 3,000 bales, or 681,000 kilograms, of cotton in 1790, and exported 229 bales in 1791, compared with 1,374 exported by New Spain: von Humboldt, *Political Essay on the Kingdom of New Spain*, 19. In 1810, the

United States produced 178,000 bales of cotton and exported 124,600. By 1840, it produced 1,346,000 bales, or 60 percent of world production, and exported a little more than a million of that, while Mexico was a net importer of cotton from the United States: Smith and Cothren, eds., *Cotton*, 435–36.

16. Smith and Cothren, eds., *Cotton*, viii.

17. Humboldt, *Political Essay on the Kingdom of New Spain*, 19.

18. Humboldt, *Political Essay on the Kingdom of New Spain*, 21.

19. Smith and Cothren, *Cotton*, 1–2.

20. For a recent global history of cotton, see Beckert, *Empire of Cotton*.

21. Wendel and Grover, "Taxonomy and Evolution of the Cotton Genus," in *Cotton*, ed. Fang and Percy, *Agronomy Monograph* 57, 4.

22. Smith and Cothren, *Cotton*, 4, 12.

23. Smith and Cothren, *Cotton*, 10, 13, 22. The authors state that "anecdotal evidence suggests that seed of this cotton type were smuggled into Mississippi from Mexico City as stuffing in a number of dolls."

24. Brown, *Cotton*, 1–2; Davis, *Late Victorian Holocausts*, 296.

25. Stark, Heller, and Ohnersorgen, "People with Cloth," 9.

26. Brown, *Cotton*, 18.

27. Berdan, "Cotton in Aztec Mexico," 237.

28. Berdan notes that the raw material of cotton "was moved about extensively by field owners, by purchasers, and by professional long-distance merchants of the *oztomeca* variety, who also dealt with similarly bulky cacao": Berdan, "Cotton in Aztec Mexico," 247. Jonathan Sauer also comments that cotton "cultivation spread among maize growing peoples northwest through Mexico into what is now the southwestern United States in prehistoric times. Annual forms were selected that are able to flower outside the tropics in long summer days. The trade in cotton cordage and textiles and perhaps also in cotton fiber extended beyond the range of the crop": Sauer, *Historical Geography of Crop Plants*, 104. Coahuilan Indians, who settled within the modern Laguna region, also cultivated cotton to make fabric and thread to wear as headdresses: Valdés, *La gente del mezquite,* 91.

29. Smith and Cothren, *Cotton*, vii.

30. The following paragraphs are primarily drawn from older works, Brown and Ware (1927 and 1958 editions), cross-checked with Smith and Cothren (1999) for more recent findings on cotton morphology and physiology.

31. Smith and Cothren, *Cotton*, vii.

32. Brown and Ware, *Cotton*, 96.

33. The Spanish commander of the western internal provinces, Bernando Bonavía y Zapata, released a communiqué in 1813 calling for the production of raw cotton in light of the disorders caused by the war of independence during the preceding three years. Fittingly, he sent his document to all of the principal pueblos of the Laguna region of the time, including Cuencamé, Cinco Señores (Nazas), Mapimí, San Pedro del Gallo, San Juan de Casta (León Guzmán, Durango), Álamo de Parras (Viesca, Coahila), and Parras. They were all part of the "país de la Laguna" in the colonial documentation, long predating the railroad hub, Torreón-centered Laguna of the 1880s: Corona Páez, *El País de La Laguna*, 51–52. Another indication that significant cotton production existed in the Laguna prior to the 1880s is that the pueblo

of Nazas, located in the upriver region, produced one-quarter of Mexico's national production in 1867 (7,500 of 31,000 bales), second only to the vastly larger Veracruz coast (10,000 bales). The historian Francisco R. Calderón commented, "Already in this period [1867] the lands of the Laguna and the eastern part of Durango were the most appropriate for the cultivation of cotton; it was assured that 'every drop of the Nazas would produce a bud.' The lack of cheap and convenient communications impeded the expansion of the harvested area, yet that area nevertheless yielded 1,362,000 kilograms of ginned cotton annually": Calderón, "La República Restaurada," 44.

34. Saravia, "Minucias de historia de Durango," 75, 273.

35. For a preliminary history of cotton growing during this period in the Laguna using a variety of sources, see Corona Páez, "Producción de algodón en la Comarca Lagunera a fines de la era virreinal y primera mitad del siglo XIX," 13. One such source for the midcentury is the memoir of a German medic who accompanied an advance column of the U.S. Army during the Mexican-American War. In May 1847, a year before Leonardo Zuloaga's Torreón ranch—the namesake of the modern city—was founded, he noted, "The Nasas [sic] is the Nile of the Bolsón de Mapimí; the wide and level country along the river is yearly inundated by its risings, and owes to that circumstance its great fertility. Besides wheat and corn, they raise a good deal of cotton in the valley of the river, and wine has been tried, too, with success. The climate, I understood, is so mild, that the root of the cotton shrub is seldom destroyed in the winter, and continues to thrive for many years": Wislizenus, *Memoir of a Tour to Northern Mexico*, 69.

36. Vargas-Lobsinger, *La hacienda de "La Concha,"* 34.

37. Gutiérrez, *El algodonero*, 10–12.

38. Gutiérrez, *El algodonero*, 12–13.

39. Gutiérrez's normative depiction of these mestizo laborers differs from colonial and early national accounts of their Tlaxcalan forebears. Those accounts described them as "active, energetic, intellectual, entrepreneurial, loyal, generous, docile, understanding," among many other positive adjectives: see Corona Páez, *El País de La Laguna*, 62–63.

40. Gutiérrez, *El algodonero*, 13. This description anticipates a federal engineering commission's observations in the late 1920s that cotton farmers finished most planting and sowing before pink bollworm infestations could devastate the cotton crop from the 1910s in the upper river area of Durango, as I discuss in chap. 2 of this volume.

41. Archivo Municipal de Torreón (AMT), Fondo Tlahualilo (FT), box 12, file 7, 67. The author of this report, the engineer Manuel Marroquín y Rivera, noted that two American varieties were imported into Mexico. One was from Louisiana, which was annual, and the other was from Texas, which in the Laguna's climate would last years. Both appeared to need a lot of water, however.

42. Rafael Arocena was a Spanish immigrant originally from Arrancudiaga in Vizcaya who became one of the most prosperous farmers in the Laguna. He arrived in the Laguna from Mexico City in the mid-1870s and became a small merchant, rented land from the Spanish *hacendado* Santiago Lavín in the San Antonio *rancho*, and successfully planted this American cottonseed. He imported the seed by ox cart from Matamoros, Tamaulipas, on the Texas border and then sold it to other Laguna farmers. Four years later, in 1897, he bought the Santa Teresa hacienda along with another Spanish tenant, Leandro Urrutia, and took full

possession in 1906: Vargas-Lobsinger, *La Comarca Lagunera*, 103–4; Vargas-Lobsinger, *La hacienda de "La Concha,"* 34.

43. There is a large body of literature on this question. See Román Jáquez, *Del Aguanaval a Sierra Mojada*; Meyers, "Politics, Vested Rights, and Economic Growth in Porfirian Mexico," 425–54; Kroeber, "La cuestión del Nazas hasta 1913," 428–56; Núñez Luna, "Water Law and the Making of the Mexican State, 1875–1917," PhD diss., Harvard University. For contemporary partisan accounts, see Ortiz, "Juicio arbitral"; Mallet Prevost, *The Tlahualilo Company vs. The Government of Mexico*; Bulnes, *La cuestión del Tlahualilo confidencial*; Francisco Viesca, ed., *Refutación a la demanda de la Compañía Agrícola Industrial Colonizadora del Tlahualilo*.

44. Pavel Kraus, *Irrigation Ecology*, 19. For a detailed description of similar methods historically employed in the Lerma-Chapala region of Mexico, see also Sánchez Rodríguez, "Mexico's Breadbasket: Agriculture and Environment in the Bajío," 50–72.

45. Cháirez Araiza, "El impacto de la regulación de los ríos en la recarga a los acuíferos," 38. He understates the degree to which farmers were at the whim of the fickle Nazas flow and the adverse social and economic consequences this caused before the advent of motorized pumps. Deep wells and other means of tapping aquifers were long prevalent in the Laguna and Mexico as a whole before the advent of motorized pumps, which drastically transformed regional water use and hydrology from the 1920s. For a general national overview, see Arreguín Mañón, *Aportes a la historia de la geohidrología en México*, 40–41. In the Laguna specifically, archaeologists and anthropologists have uncovered the remains of colonial-era hybrid Mesoamerican-Hispanic subterranean filtration galleries installed by Jesuit and Tlaxcalan Indian colonists in nearby Parras. According to Frank Wislizenus, by the 1840s there were also "large and deep" wells drawn by mules, where "good water is got everywhere in this valley by digging to a certain depth." Moreover, he observed in 1847, "San Lorenzo is a town of about 1,000 population, and lies on the right bank of the Nasas; but the waters of the river had here so far disappeared that only some pools were left, and in the dry sandy bed of the river some wells had been dug. In these wells, from 10 to 20 feet deep, I saw below the sand a layer of clay; artesian wells might therefore succeed here": Wislizenus, *Memoir of a Tour to Northern Mexico*, 68–70. A few years later, John Bartlett, exploring the region as the first international boundary commissioner for the United States after the Mexican-American War, remarked, "Every house [in Parras] of any extent has its own well": Bartlett, *Personal Narrative of Explorations*, 482.

46. These are the same kinds of fish and fowl that the Spanish colonizers observed in the Laguna's naturally occurring lakes in the early seventeenth century. In his study of similar processes in the late nineteenth-century and early twentieth-century Snake River Valley of Idaho, Mark Fiege has termed such landscapes "hybrid," where nonhuman nature adapts to human artifice interactively to form new hybrid ecologies: see Fiege, *Irrigated Eden*. I use the terms "irrigation ecology" and "irrigated landscapes" to describe this similar phenomenon in the Laguna.

47. Cháirez Araiza, "El impacto de la regulación de los ríos en la recarga a los acuíferos," 60. Such a description is based on interviews he conducted in 2002 with the few remaining farmers still using these methods, which have been transmitted generationally.

48. October 24, 1892, AMT, FT, box 12, file 7, 1–2.

49. March 12, 1893, AMT, FT, box 12, file 7, 26–29.

50. March 12, 1893, AMT, FT, box 12, file 7, 59. In the 1920s, the extent to which the Nazas was a source of natural fertilizers became contentious among técnicos and landowners for and against building a high dam on the river, as I describe in chap. 2 of this volume. This "extraordinary" yield of approximately 2,000 kilograms per hectare appears erroneous. The annual average yield per hectare in all of Mexico from 1897 to 1909 never exceeded 300 kilograms. Indeed, the highest annual yield through 1989 was 1,628 kilograms, achieved in 1985: http://dgcnesyp.inegi.org.mx/cgi-win/ehm2014.exe/CI090090030.

51. Ornelas, "La Comarca Lagunera." Like the engineers of the Nazas Inspection Committee, Ornelas asserted that the upriver diversion dams were unworthy of the name. Those dams diverted water only to flood the land excessively and inadvertently destroyed their own works. In the lower river area, by contrast, dams were mobile and much more resistant to flooding. This greater technological sophistication and efficiency helped downriver areas offset the 2:1 ratio in distribution of the Nazas flow in favor of upriver users.

52. March 12, 1893, AMT, FT, box 12, file 7, 61–64.

53. March 12, 1893, AMT, FT, box 12, file 7, 63–65.

54. On the pacification and development of the northern frontier, see Coatsworth, *Growth against Development*, and Katz, *The Life and Times of Pancho Villa*, chap. 1. For the transnational dimensions of "barbarous" Indian border wars, see DeLay, *War of a Thousand Deserts*. For the colonial period in Nueva Vizcaya, which encompassed the modern Laguna, see Ortelli, *Trama de una guerra conveniente*.

55. March 12, 1893, AMT, FT, box 12, file 7, 30.

56. Lanz Cárdenas, *Legislación de aguas en México*, 359–60.

57. Díaz y Díaz, "El litigio del Tlahualilo," 133. For a detailed legal analysis of the evolution of late nineteenth-century and early twentieth-century Mexican water law and this litigation, see also Núñez Luna, "Water Law and the Making of the Mexican State."

58. Quoted in Cháirez Araiza, "El impacto de la regulación de los ríos en la recarga a los acuíferos," 65. The engineer Quixote Irrititla, however, in his unpublished history of the Río Nazas of 1994, provides precise measurements from 1852, but without explaining how and where he derived his data. See Appendix 1 for an adaptation of his data in graph form.

59. The attorney for the Tlahualilo Company, Sergio Mallet Prevost, in his complaint against new government regulations favoring downriver users in 1909 likened land without water to "flesh without blood." Mallet Prevost, *The Tlahualilo Company versus the Government of Mexico*, 45.

60. For the social and cultural history of Parras and its viticulture, see Corona Páez, *El País de La Laguna*; Martínez Serna, "Vineyards in the Desert"; and Churruca Peláez, Willeford, and Kelley, *Before the Thundering Hordes*. For the ingenious methods of groundwater extraction via mineshafts jointly developed by the Tlaxcalans and Jesuits, see Eling and Martínez García, "Cambios, innovaciones y discontinuidades en los sistemas de riego por galería filtrante en Parras de la Fuente, Coahuila, México."

61. Unless indicated otherwise, the following three paragraphs draw primarily from Meyers, *Forge of Progress, Crucible of Revolt*; Plana, *El reino del algodón en México*.

62. See map FM.1 for the parcelization of Matamoros and San Pedro in 1914.

63. Plana, *El reino del algodón*, 211–18. As impressive as these numbers are, Plana does not include figures for Mapimí, Durango, which had a population of about 62,000; and Nazas, Durango (the leading Laguna cotton producer until at least 1867), with 14,000 in 1907. "Anuario estadístico del Estado de Durango," 7.

64. Corona Páez, "El Valle de Parras en el siglo XX," 14–15.

65. Villa Guerrero, "Una mina de oro blanco," 113.

66. Díaz y Díaz, "El litigio del Tlahualilo," 155. Among the colonization schemes that the Tlahualilo Company promoted according to the 1888 contract that allowed it to use up to 25 percent foreign colonists for labor was one that brought seven hundred U.S. blacks, primarily from Alabama, to the Laguna in 1895. They met a tragic fate: never adjusting to the climate and culture, especially during a severe drought, and not receiving the housing and land that was promised to them, some became ill, fled, and died in the desert, while the majority petitioned the U.S. consul for funds to return to the United States via Texas. Tlahualilo had to pay their transportation costs and blamed the failure on the alleged deficiencies of the colonists. Although a small contingent of several dozen remained, from then on the company abandoned all efforts at colonization by foreigners and hired two thousand local agricultural workers at low wages for their labor needs: Meyers, *Forge of Progress, Crucible of Revolt*, 128; Plana, *El reino del algodón*, 185–87.

67. Villa Guerrero, "Una mina de oro blanco," 111–16. The impetus for the law also appeared to be nepotistic, as the third-largest shareholder was José de Teresa y Miranda, Díaz's brother-in-law: see Núñez Luna, "Water Law and the Making of the Mexican State," 193–94.

68. Meyers, "Politics, Vested Rights, and Economic Growth in Porfirian Mexico," 11.

69. Villa Guerrero, "Una mina de oro blanco," 116. Díaz y Díaz comments that "it is important to recall that, according to the 1852 agreement forged in Lerdo, the excess water from the San Fernando diversion dam was not the property of Señor Flores but rather of the owner of the Santa Rosa dam; through this agreement, Señor Flores was transmitting water use rights to Tlahualilo which did not in fact belong to it": Díaz y Díaz, "El litigio del Tlahualilo," 148–49.

70. Díaz y Díaz, "El litigio del Tlahualilo," 143.

71. Meyers, *Forge of Progress, Crucible of Revolt*, 159. Mallet Prevost employed another interesting metaphor in his complaint on behalf of Tlahualilo, saying, "When I, as the owner of a house, keep it closed, I do not use it, but I am nevertheless in possession. . . . When I, as the owner of a definite quantity of water, allow this to flow by, it means that I do not use the water, but it does not mean that I thereby cease to possess it": Mallet Prevost, *The Tlahualilo Company versus the Government of Mexico*, 40. Flowing water, on which people's livelihoods and even survival depend, however, is not quite like a house (i.e., "immovable property"), on which no neighboring homeowner's livelihood, much less survival, necessarily depends.

72. Lanz Cárdenas, *Legislación de aguas en México*, 548–49.

73. Meyers, *Forge of Progress, Crucible of Revolt*, 48, 51, 159; Meyers, "Politics, Vested Rights, and Economic Growth in Porfirian Mexico," 434–39. During this time, there were also many other disputes, including ones over wages, carteling among agroindustrial firms producing cotton byproducts, and local and state elections and appointments as Díaz tried to maintain stability for his continued decades-long rule. There was also a boom in guayule, a natural

rubber-producing plant that grew in the downriver region and required irrigation. The Madero family was heavily invested in guayule, which from 1904 to 1911 rivaled cotton in profits and attracted the interest of U.S. rubber producers in fierce competition with the family.

74. Mallet Prevost requested that this information about British water rights in Egypt and other colonies not be publicized in Mexico: Meyers, "Politics, Vested Rights, and Economic Growth in Porfirian Mexico," 26. It was no great secret, however. Mexican engineers had been publicizing the irrigation systems and water laws of other countries for years for possible adoption in Mexico as Díaz sought to increase agricultural production. For contemporary examples, see Gayol, *Dos problemas de vital importancia para México;* Palacios, *El problema de la irrigación.* For British water works in Egypt, see Mikhail, *Nature and Empire in Ottoman Egypt.*

75. His call was not heeded, however. It should be noted that Cobián and many others had Spanish citizenship or were dual nationals: Feliciano Cobián to Don Gilberto Lavín, May 31, 1902, Archivo Agustín de Espinosa de la Universidad Iberoamericana 11–0301.

76. "Se quejan de los peligros de las inundaciones en que se encuentra esa población y Gómez Palacio en las grandes avenidas del río," AHA, AS, box 576, file 8361, 1–15; "Abuso cometido por compuertas Tlahualilo que abrió sin autorización," February 28–June 11, 1898, AHA, AS, Box 269, File 2587, 1–14.

77. "Colonos de Tlahualilo piden agua del río para riego de terrenos," November 23, 1898, AHA, AS, box 269, file 2585, 12.

78. Meyers, *Forge of Progress, Crucible of Revolt,* 170–71.

79. Vargas-Lobsinger, *La hacienda de "La Concha,"* 92. From 1910 to 1912, during the first two years of the Revolution, cotton cultivation declined to a much lower yearly average of about 80,000 bales.

80. Madero, *Estudio sobre la conveniencia de la construcción de una presa,* 2. Of course, the autocratic Díaz did not necessarily *need* that support.

81. Madero changed the estimated cost several times. For example, in a caption for a photo of the proposed dam site, he cited a figure of 5.6 million pesos; on the first page of the first introductory chapter, he wrote "around six million pesos"; and in a chapter titled "financial section," he cited ten million pesos. The last figure is the one he used to calculate the annual repayment amount of 900,000 pesos.

82. Madero, *Estudio sobre la conveniencia de la construcción de una presa,* 1, 19, 36, 49.

83. Madero, *Estudio sobre la conveniencia de la construcción de una presa,* 44. The debate over natural versus chemical fertilizers surrounding construction of the dam would reemerge in the late 1920s and 1930s.

84. Madero, *Estudio sobre la conveniencia de la construcción de una presa,* 16, 46. For detailed descriptions of migrant laborers and their social conditions, see also Meyers, *Forge of Progress, Crucible of Revolt,* chap. 5.

85. Madero, *Estudio sobre la conveniencia de la construcción de una presa,* 19, 27; Vargas-Lobsinger, *La hacienda de "La Concha,"* 92. This extraordinary figure was surpassed only once (in 1930, by just 22,000 bales) through 1949, around the time pesticides and chemical fertilizers came into widespread use in the Laguna and nationally. For national cotton statistics, see appendix 2. The Mexican American Juan F. Brittingham, owner of the Jabonera Soap

Factory in Gómez Palacio, Durango, which controlled nearly all cottonseed grown in the country, was, however, "in a better position to make an estimate of cotton production than any other observer." His estimates were "regarded as the most reliable obtainable on the cotton crop in Mexico," according to the U.S. Department of Commerce and Labor. Brittingham estimated 81,000 bales for 1905 and 162,000 for 1906, showing that the Mexican "government estimate is very erroneous and probably mixes seed cotton with lint": Clark, *Cotton Goods in Latin America, Part I*, 28.

86. Clark, *Cotton Goods in Latin America, Part I*, 29. Based on the British Foreign Office records that Meyers consulted, Díaz "attempted to placate the British further [regarding the Tlahualilo dispute] by telling them privately that the British firm of S. Pearson and Son would receive the half-million pesos contract for surveying and planning the proposed Río Nazas Dam. The president also implied that if matters went well the same firm would be granted the entire construction contract of more than thirty million pesos": Meyers, *Forge of Progress, Crucible of Revolt*, 166. S. Pearson and Son and Tlahualilo were different companies, of course. Given that they were both British, however, it is possible that Díaz thought (wrongly, as it turned out) that he could informally "compensate" the British government for the Tlahualilo water dispute by granting another British company a lucrative contract. In any event, the only contract S. Pearson and Son officially signed and completed work for was to survey and plan the dam, not to construct it.

87. "Actitud de la Co. Tlahualilo en la junta de ribereños," March 24, 1909, Archivo Municipal de Torreón (AMT), box 29, file 1. According to Kroeber, the Tlahualilo Company argued against building the dam, but he does not give a reason: Kroeber, *Man, Land, and Water*, 210. The company likely considered it detrimental to its uncompromising position that the government must return to the regulation of 1891, which had benefited it on the basis of faulty river flow measurements. In the 1920s, the company helped lead the campaign against revival of the project, as I discuss in chap. 2.

88. In a review of these studies in 1940, the CNI stated that the drillings S. Pearson and Son made "indicated that at a depth of 41 meters there was no rock that could cement the curtain": Riemann, *Memoria del Distrito de Riego de la Región Lagunera, Coahuila y Durango*, 7.

89. S. Pearson and Son, *Informe presentado por los señores Pearson and Son*, 47.

90. Kroeber surmises that these three "of the most outstanding hydraulic experts in Mexico" may not have accepted S. Pearson and Son's findings because of missing field notes that could not prove whether rock formations at El Palmito were impermeable according to the drillings the company allegedly had made: Kroeber, *Man, Land, and Water*, 159–60. Other possibilities were that some hostile landowners opposed to the construction of a high dam obstructed the fieldwork; that another project involving diversion via tunnel of the waters of Lake Guatimapé in Durango to the Nazas looked more promising (although this was also shelved); that the government lacked specific experience in planning or building a huge dam in Mexico; or that personality conflicts and national pride interfered. Kroeber nevertheless emphasizes the missing field notes as the probable reason the experts laid "aside this fine project."

91. Among the uses prioritized for water concessions, *entarquinamiento de terrenos* (*aniego*), or storage of floodwaters in embanked lots, as was practiced in the Laguna, was listed last, after domestic uses for population clusters, public services, irrigation, production of en-

ergy, and other industrial services, in that order. For the full text of the law and its six chapters, see Lanz Cárdenas, *Legislación de aguas*, 425–27. Yet aniego *was* the Laguna's (and other regions') irrigation method. It is thus possible that makers of water law were either ignorant of the method or expected it to be eliminated through modernization. Elimination of aniego through modernization would in fact occur decades later in the Laguna, as the following chapters will show.

92. For this clarification of the Tlahualilo case, based on painstaking analysis of the actual legal contents of the massive documentation that it produced, see Núñez Luna, "Water Law and the Making of the Mexican State," 254.

93. Notably, he organized his vaunted División del Norte in Lerdo, Durango, on the left bank of the Nazas, which two prominent anti–Huerta Lagunero revolutionaries who had been fighting since 1911, Calixto Contreras and Orestes Pereyra, then joined: Vargas-Lobsinger, *La Comarca Lagunera*, 29. For an eyewitness account of Villa in the Laguna, see Reed, *Insurgent Mexico*.

94. Tortolero Villaseñor, "Water and Revolution in Morelos, 1850–1915," 129–30, 144. As he explains, "The state's continued development depended on landowners' ability to expand irrigation networks and, crucially, to gain access to enough water for their thirsty crops." By 1910, "Morelos had some of the most intensively irrigated land in the country . . . because sugar planters had built numerous irrigation projects to take advantage of all this water [from two major watersheds that lay within its borders]." Moreover, although "90 percent of sugar haciendas' property was used for rain-fed agriculture (*temporal*) or was held in reserve or was forested, mountainous, or otherwise unusable for agriculture . . . cane was the crop most sensitive to water, which could be delivered only through irrigation in the dry season."

95. Katz, *The Life and Times of Pancho Villa*, 436–37. Katz characterizes Zapata as "regional" because of his far more limited military capability (consisting of an army primarily of peasants clad in white cotton shirts and *huarache* sandals and brandishing a motley assortment of rifles and guns) but with a more "national" social reform agenda. By contrast, he characterizes Villa as "national" because of his much greater military capability (consisting of a more professionalized army with U.S.-supplied khaki uniforms and arms) but with a more "regional" social reform agenda. Alan Knight similarly comments, "While in Morelos *agrarismo* dictated the character of the civil war, in the north the civil war dictated the character of *agrarismo*": Knight, *The Mexican Revolution*, vol. 2, 186. The process of semiofficial postrevolutionary mythmaking exalted Zapata as the agrarian symbol and standard-bearer of the Revolution while Villa was marginalized in official discourse until his rehabilitation in the late 1960s and 1970s. For an illuminating study of this process, see Brunk, *The Posthumous Career of Emiliano Zapata*.

96. Vargas-Lobsinger, *La Comarca Lagunera*, 35–37.

97. Knight, *The Mexican Revolution*, vol. 1, 287.

98. Plana, "La cuestión agraria en La Laguna durante la Revolución," 61.

99. Meyers, "Seasons of Rebellion," 63–94. I would not go so far as Meyers to argue that river flow, and the climate and weather that underlay it, "determined" the patterns of rebellion. Rather, I would argue that they *influenced* them. On the relationship between agricultural cycles and revolutionary activity, see also Knight, *The Mexican Revolution*, vol. 1, 277; Fernández de Castro Martínez, "Agrarian Reform from Below."

100. The Carrancista conception of ejido signified communal farmland, while the Plan of Ayala differentiated between farmland (*campo de labranza*) and ejido. The ejido primarily designated non-farming land uses (trash deposit, hunting, wood collection, and so on). By contrast, the Villista Law did not mention ejidos per se; it made just a vague reference in its fourth article to "surrounding lands of indigenous pueblos": see José Rivera Castro and Palomo, eds., *El agrarismo mexicano*, 78. For a historical overview of the redesignation of ejido land use during the late nineteenth century, see Wolfe, "The Sociolegal Redesignation of Ejido Land Use."

101. Rivera Castro and Hernández Palomo, *El agrarismo mexicano*, 78. For the differences among Carranza, Villa, and Zapata regarding agrarian reform, see Katz, *The Life and Times of Pancho Villa*, 476–77. It should be noted that in October 1915, Villa and Zapata jointly decreed the Ley Agraria de la Soberana Convención Revolucionaria (Agrarian Law of the Sovereign Revolutionary Convention), which combined elements of both revolutionaries' agrarian plans while omitting others. For instance, it kept the distinction between pueblos and ejidos as per the Zapatista conception but eliminated Villa's inclusion of specific stipulations on assessing agronomic and soil conditions in each area, including water use, except when delimiting parcel sizes with respect to irrigable lands in particular climates: see Córdova, *La ideología de la Revolución Mexicana*, 471–77.

102. Vargas-Lobsinger, *La Comarca Lagunera*, 43–46. In August 1917, eight months after the promulgation of the 1917 Constitution and Article 27, the U.S. Consulate in Durango commented, "The season has not been a good one in the Laguna. There has been no rain and as the rains are late up in Durango and have not yet been heavy enough to bring down the Nazas River, there has been much loss and even the cotton crop has suffered. There has been no rain in the Laguna since September 1916": Telegram from American Consulate in Durango to U.S. Secretary of State, August 14, 1917, National Archives and Records Administration (NARA), Records of the U.S. State Department Relating to Internal Affairs of Mexico, 1910–1929. Central File: Decimal File 812.00, Internal Affairs of States, Mexico, Political Affairs, June 9, 1917–September 25, 1917.

103. The only reference to groundwater in the article was indirectly to "waters extracted from mines."

104. "Provisional Government of the Revolution. United Mexican States. Department of Agriculture. Decree No. 1. Storing of Water and Works of Irrigation," February 19, 1913, Records of the U.S. State Department Relating to Internal Affairs of Mexico, 1910–1929, Central File: Decimal File 812.00, Internal Affairs of States, Mexico, Political Affairs, February 3, 1913–March 7, 1913, NARA, 1331.

CHAPTER 2. THE DEBATE OVER DAMMING

Epigraph: "Creo y sostengo que el fraccionamiento sin el riego es absurdo, inconveniente y torpe": Pastor Rouaix, quoted in Silva Herzog, ed., *El agrarismo mexicano y la reforma agraria*, 165.

1. See http://www.memoriapoliticademexico.org/Textos/6Revolucion/1933PSE.html; emphasis added.

2. This is not to deny that there was a significant change in public attitudes toward dams over the course of the twentieth century from cautiously positive to increasingly negative as

more and more riverine communities experienced their adverse impacts throughout the world. For a recent Mexican case, see Hindley, "Indigenous Mobilization, Development, and Democratization in Guerrero"; and "Mexico: Chiapas Indigenous Protest Dams, Electric Rates," http://ww4report.com/node/10891. For cases throughout the world, including other references to Mexico, see Josephson, *Industrialized Nature;* Khagram, *Dams and Development;* McCully, *Silenced Rivers;* Pearce, *When the Rivers Run Dry;* Woelfle-Erskine, Cole, and Allen, eds., *Dam Nation.*

3. Vargas-Lobsinger, *La Comarca Lagunera*, 8.

4. Vargas-Lobsinger, *La Comarca Lagunera*, 51. Unfortunately, only issues from 1917 to 1920 and 1927 are still extant, although the publication continued until the 1930s.

5. *Boletín de la Cámara Agrícola Nacional de la Comarca Lagunera*, February 1920. For more detailed information on land tenure, see tables 2.1–3 below.

6. *Boletín de la Cámara Agrícola Nacional de la Comarca Lagunera*, September 1920. The editors used *plaga* in the metaphorical sense of a biblical plague or scourge afflicting the region; hence, it is in the sense that I use the Spanish term to describe pest infestations, as well as the scourges, from their perspective, of volatile cotton prices, drought, unpredictable river flow, unions, and so forth.

7. Smith and Cothren, *Cotton*, 499.

8. Hunter and Pierce, *Mexican Cotton-Boll Weevil*, 15.

9. Hunter and Pierce, *Mexican Cotton-Boll Weevil*, 16. On the U.S. side, it had spread to half a dozen counties in the Brownsville region of Texas. According to the state Division of Entomology, the weevil was designated an enemy of cotton in 1894. The division's recommendation to stymie its spread by establishing a belt along the Río Grande, however, was not heeded, and subsequent events vindicated the warning. The entomologist C. H. T. Townsend was subsequently stationed in Mexico to find a parasite or disease that harmed the weevil, but none was found.

10. Hunter and Pierce, *Mexican Cotton-Boll Weevil*, 18. One other source, published in 1907, corroborates this account. "So far the [cotton] crops have been fortunately free from boll-weevils or other insect pests": Martin, *Mexico of the Twentieth Century*, 27. Another source, however, claims that weevil destruction was blamed for the poor harvests of 1904 and that in 1907 government inspectors "checked every pound of seed going into the Laguna, burning all which contained the trace of a weevil. The inspectors announced they had controlled the pest, but foreign observers in 1909 reported that Mexican cotton was severely affected by insect damage." Keremitsis, *The Cotton Textile Industry in Porfiriato, Mexico, 1870–1910*, 170–71. Still another source, in 1910, claimed that until some means were found to combat the boll weevil, "Mexico cannot arise over 200,000 bales" of cotton: Clark, *Cotton Goods in Latin America, Part I*, 29.

11. Naranjo, Butler, and Henneberry, "A Bibliography of the Pink Bollworm, *Pectinophora gossypiella* (Saunders)"; "La lucha por la extinción de las plagas," *El Siglo de Torreón*, September 20, 1922; "Biología del gusano rosado," *El Siglo de Torreón*, September 24, 1922, 26.

12. For cotton prices on the national level, see appendix 2.

13. See appendix 1; Vargas-Lobsinger, *La Comarca Lagunera*, 53. Government cotton production statistics during the Porfiriato were likely inaccurate. Because of widespread flooding, the figure of 225,000 bales was considerably smaller than it could have been, given that

roughly one million cubic meters of water yielded 100,000 bales. The variable quantity and quality of human labor and pink bollworm infestations, in addition to many other socio-ecological factors, made it difficult for such a precise ratio of water to bales to prevail consistently.

14. "Como 3255 obreros sin trabajo en la Laguna serán transportados a sus hogares por el gobierno," *El Porvenir—El Diario de la Frontera*, November 29, 1923.

15. For detailed discussion of the influence of Magonismo in the Laguna before the Revolution, see Meyers, *Forge of Progress, Crucible of Revolt*, 7–8, 187–88. On Villismo during the Revolution, see Vargas-Lobsinger, *La Comarca Lagunera*, 35–42.

16. Vargas-Lobsinger, *La Comarca Lagunera*, 56–57. For more general treatment of labor, unions, and the impact of the Russian Revolution on Mexico, see Carr, *Marxism and Communism in Twentieth-Century Mexico;* Middlebrook, *The Paradox of Revolution;* Spenser, *The Impossible Triangle*.

17. Carr, *Marxism and Communism in Twentieth-Century Mexico*, 89.

18. For the Porfirian background to the semi-proletarianization of the rural workforce, see Meyers, *Forge of Progress, Crucible of Revolt*, chap. 5.

19. Rivera Castro and Hernández Palomo, eds., *El agrarismo mexicano*, 101–2.

20. Carr, *Marxism and Communism in Twentieth-Century Mexico,* 89; Liga de Agrónomos Socialistas, *El colectivismo agrario en México,* 36. Pancho Villa was also given land to form the Canutillo hacienda in Durango in 1920, where he took up residence along with an armed escort of fifty men. Laguna landowners united to donate 29,000 pesos to acquire the machinery for the new hacienda: Vargas-Lobsinger, *La Comarca Lagunera,* 57.

21. There could, of course, be conflict between rural and urban workers or among unions within each sector for ideological or other reasons. As Carr comments, there was no "unified stratum of rural proletarians. While many hacienda peons formed combative unions, other resident wage workers on Laguna haciendas were attacked by agrarista peasants for their policies of collaboration with their employers, a familiar complaint in other regions of Mexico": Carr, *Marxism and Communism in Twentieth-Century Mexico*, 90.

22. Joseph and Henderson, eds., *The Mexico Reader: History, Culture, Politics,* 399.

23. Vargas-Lobsinger, *La Comarca Lagunera,* 59–61.

24. Herzog, ed., *El agrarismo mexicano y la reforma agraria,* 283; Simpson, *The Ejido,* 84; Vargas-Lobsinger, *La Comarca Lagunera,* 59–61.

25. For accounts of Obregón's agrarian decrees and laws, which changed quickly and confusingly, see Hall, "Álvaro Obregón and the Politics of Mexican Land Reform, 1920–1924"; Simpson, *The Ejido,* 78–88; Silva Herzog, ed., *El agrarismo mexicano y la reforma agraria,* chap. 8.

26. Simpson, *The Ejido,* 86, 722.

27. Vargas-Lobsinger, *La Comarca Lagunera,* 69. See chaps. 5 and 6 of this volume for more discussion of obras muertas in the context of a "drought industry."

28. "Memorial que el presidente de la Cámara Agrícola Nacional de la Comarca Lagunera, agricultores, propietarios y socios de dicha cámara, elevan al C. Presidente de la República, general Álvaro Obregón," April 1924, Archivo Agustín Espinoza de la Universidad Iberoamericana (AAE), Fondo Vargas-Lobsinger (FVL).

29. AAE, Fondo Arocena (FA), 35, 1.

30. Secretary-General to Obregón, September 28, 1923, Archivo Histórico del Agua (AHA), Aguas Nacionales (AN), box 266, file 2555, bundle 1/8, 2.

31. Virtually any reference to the origins of the Laguna's regional development in the post-revolutionary period was to the first small diversion dams and canals that several "pioneers" built on the Nazas in the mid-nineteenth century. Despite the historical revisionism of the past two decades of prominent Laguna historians such as Sergio Corona-Páez, who draw on incontrovertible documentary evidence of nearly three centuries of Hispano-Tlaxcalan irrigated viticulture in the colonial "país de la Laguna" centered on Parras and its offshoots of Viesca and San Pedro in the heart of the modern Laguna, this foundational narrative persists in popular local and national discourse.

32. Despite this landowner appeal, informed by the hegemonic mythical foundational narrative of the Laguna effacing its colonial history, Calles accepted the applicability of agrarian reform laws to colonial pueblos first colonized by Tlaxcalans and other settled Indians from Parras (likely unbeknownst to him) in the 1730s and 1740s: Mayrán, Las Habas and San Nicolás, and San Pedro, all bordering the terminus of the Nazas. In 1925, Calles granted them a fraction (2,418 hectares) of their original concession of thirty-two sitios de ganado mayor, or 60,000 hectares, from 1740 to form ejidos. Viesca, the more substantial Tlaxcalan offshoot of Parras founded in 1731, was granted 4,570 hectares, of which 424 were arable, to form ejidos in 1927. On the concessions, see Vargas-Lobsinger, *La Comarca Lagunera*, 210. For the history of these pueblos' Tlaxcalan heritage, see Corona Páez, *El País de La Laguna*.

33. Núñez Luna nevertheless points out that Huerta's reinstatement of Tlahualilo's water concession in the April 1913 contract renewal, which ignored the Supreme Court rulings against it in 1911 and 1912, granted the company even broader rights than it had initially acquired in 1888 under Díaz: "Water Law and the Making of the Mexican State, 1875–1917," 313.

34. James E. Kitchin, representative of Tlahualilo Company, to SAF, November 6, 1916, AHA, Aprovechamientos Superficiales (AS), box 4367, file 57879, 5–10. Rouaix subsequently politely rejected the complaint because it merely expressed its disagreement without requesting any specific legal action or application of any particular law in favor of Tlahualilo.

35. Romero Navarrete, "El reparto ejidal a la ciudad de Lerdo, Durango, 1917–1924," 48; Contreras Cantú and Castellanos Hernández, *El registro público de la propiedad social en México*, 41.

36. James E. Kitchin to T. M. Fairburn, December 13, 1922, James E. Kitchin to T. M. Fairburn, January 24, 1923, Archivo Municipal de Torreón (AMT), Fondo Tlahualilo (FT), box 59, files 2–3. Fortunately for them, 1923 was a year of plentiful river flow that produced a bumper crop. In 1926, although the company complained that it was deprived of 17.7 million cubic meters of water or one-third of its San Fernando water allocation for diversion to the Lerdo ejido, it still kept operating at least through October 1935, or just a year prior to full expropriation: T. M. Fairburn to John Murray, October 19, 1935, AMT, FT, box 76, file 11.

37. Vargas-Lobsinger, *La Comarca Lagunera*, 81–82.

38. T. M. Fairburn to H. A. Vernet (London), January 17, February 26, Fairburn to James E. Kitchin (Mexico City), March 17, 1925, AMT, FT, box 51, file 5. He also noted that Britain's non-recognition of Mexico made it difficult for British nationals to express their grievances to the Mexican president. This was in contrast to the United States, which had reached an

agreement with Mexico (the Bucareli Accords in 1923) over questions of land and natural resource ownership, especially oil, to restore diplomatic relations.

39. "El almacenamiento de las aguas del Nazas," *El Siglo de Torreón*, December 22, 1922, 3.

40. "Proyecto de almacenamiento de las aguas del río nazas en el sitio denominado 'el Palmito,'" AHA, Consultivo Técnico (CT), box 142, file 1129, 5–7; italics added. The file is undated, but 1923 was penciled in. The use of "guaranteed" is noteworthy, as it shows how far trust in a largely untested technology had taken hold.

41. Gumaro García de la Cadena to Luis Arturo Romo, November 10, 1925, Archivo Calles-Torreblanca (ACT), file 36, inventory 5096.

42. Vargas-Lobsinger, *La Comarca Lagunera*, 73. The advent of motorized pumps is discussed in more detail later.

43. Nájera, López Portillo, and Peña, *Informe general de la Comisión de Estudios de la Comarca Lagunera*, 149–50.

44. Gumaro García de la Cadena to Luis Arturo Romo, November 10, 1925, Archivo Calles-Torreblanca (ACT), file 36, inventory 5096. The Sinaloan Gonzalo Escobar was not actually Spanish, of course. Arturo Romo used the term disparagingly, reflecting the long-standing anti-Spanish (*gachupín*) sentiment in the region. Gonzalo Escobar was the chief of military operations in the Laguna and rebelled against the central government in March 1929 as head of the "Renovation Movement" in opposition to the newly founded Partido Nacional Revolucionario, which he deemed tyrannical. He fought federal forces in Torreón for seventy-five days, involving thirty thousand men on both sides; it ended with the defeat of his rebellion, two thousand dead, and execution of the rebels. It was also the first time in Mexico that aerial bombardment was used on a dense urban area: see Vargas-Lobsinger, *La Comarca Lagunera*, 121–22. For graphic accounts of the bombings, see the March 1929 issues of *El Siglo de Torreón*.

45. Aboites, *El agua de la nación*, 107–12.

46. On Calles's influences and thinking on agriculture, see Aboites, *La irrigación revolucionaria*. For his political background in Sonora, see Buchenau, *Plutarco Elías Calles and the Mexican Revolution*, chaps. 2–3. For California water history, see Hundley, *The Great Thirst*.

47. Herrera y Lasso, *Apuntes sobre irrigación*, ix–x. He adopted U.S. white racist discourse on Native Americans, although as a revolutionary técnico he was likely sympathetic to Mexican indigenismo.

48. T. M. Fairburn to James E. Kitchin, July 6, 1925, AMT, FT, box 63, file 1.

49. Copiadores de cartas, vol. 71, August 1925, AAE, Fondo Juan Brittingham. On Brittingham's various business interests, see Juan Barragán, *Juan F. Brittingham y la industria en México, 1859–1940*, 111–57.

50. "La erección de la presa en el Nazas," *El Siglo de Torreón*, February 3, 1926. At this engineers' convention, Javier Sánchez Mejorada, one of the CNI's first directors, proclaimed: "It is needless to speak of the need for irrigation in a country like ours with so little precipitation in several of its regions, irregularity in others, and with a hydrographic system so poor in its majority. The northern frontier states and several in the center form an extensive arid zone with scarce agricultural production and desert fields": quoted in Aboites, *El agua de la nación*, 107–8.

51. "Folleto de la Asociación para el Fomento de la Presa sobre el río Nazas," February 15, 1926, AHA, CT, box 160, file 1915, 1–59. In this transcription of the meeting reproduced as a pamphlet (p. 40), Salvador Valencia in particular made these arguments by presenting what he called "very realistic" statistical data.

52. Vargas-Lobsinger, *La Comarca Lagunera*, 77–78. Domestic textile producers were joined by the CROM in their call for lowering import tariffs on cotton to protect the jobs of some 40,000 textile workers. Obregón sided with Laguna cotton farmers, however, since he wanted the hard currency from export revenues for national reconstruction.

53. "Folleto de la Asociación para el Fomento de la Presa sobre el río Nazas," February 15, 1926, AHA, CT, box 160, file 1915, 2, 34.

54. *El Siglo de Torreón*, February 15, 1926.

55. F. F. Smith, "Estudio sobre el Río Nazas," *Irrigación en México* 5, nos. 2–6 (1932).

56. For a brief biography, see "Manuel Lorenzo Pardo (1881–1963)," http://mcnbiografias .com/appbio/do/show?key=lorenzo-pardo-manuel (accessed June 8, 2013).

57. For one of Pardo's many critiques, see AHA, CT, box 148, file 1139, 1–37. For one of many CNI refutations of those critiques, see AHA, CT, box 136, file 1121, 340–52. Mexican engineers regularly called him "Pardo" so I will do so as well throughout this book.

58. Smith to Weiss, September 14, 1936, Archivo General de la Nación (AGN), Ramos Presidenciales (RP), Lázaro Cárdenas (LC), 508/6, vol. 579, referring to a previous letter of June 27, 1933; italics added.

59. As far as I have been able to discern from extensive review of archival, newspaper, and journal sources, these data were made "public" at an engineering convention in 1938, two years after ground was broken on the dam. After the Río Grande/Bravo, which was the subject of heated dispute between the United States and Mexico for decades, and the Río Lerma, which supplied water to Mexico's two largest cities (Mexico City and Guadalajara), as well as for much agricultural land in central Mexico, the Nazas garnered the most attention from engineers, judging from the number of entries (more than three thousand) in the Historical Water Archive database.

60. Benassini, F. F. Smith, and Allen to CNI, undated but probably 1935, AHA, AS, box 2537, file 35382, 18; italics added.

61. Pardo to Allen, March 28, 1936, AHA, CT, box 142, file 1129, 307–8. For the late 1940s, see also chap. 5.

62. De Quevedo, "La necesaria protección forestal de las cuencas receptoras de los principales ríos de la república y especialmente del Río Nazas," 20–22. It should be noted that, in general, environmental scientists consider classic desiccation theory as espoused by the French-trained De Quevedo only "partially correct," for around the world there are "heated controversies" over its scientific validity: Matthews, *Instituting Nature*, 40.

63. A mining engineer agreed with Quevedo's opposition to the dam in 1925 and extolled the potential of groundwater pumps for solving the Laguna's water woes: Villarello, "Algunos datos acerca de las aguas subterráneas de la Comarca Lagunera de Torreón, Coahuila."

64. "Elementos generales para riego por medio del bombeo en La Laguna," *El Siglo de Torreón*, August 11, 1922.

65. "El agua de bombeo," *El Siglo de Torreón*, August 2, 1923.

66. "El agua de bombeo," *El Siglo de Torreón*, August 2, 1923.

67. Villarello, "Algunos datos acerca de las aguas subterráneas de la Comarca Lagunera de Torreón, Coahuila," 752.

68. Nájera et al., *Informe general de la comisión de estudios de la Comarca Lagunera*, 195–96.

69. Nájera et al., *Informe general de la comisión de estudios de la Comarca Lagunera*, 196–97; Vargas-Lobsinger, *La Comarca Lagunera*, 73.

70. Nájera et al., *Informe general de la comisión de estudios de la Comarca Lagunera*, 197.

71. Nájera et al., *Informe general de la comisión de estudios de la Comarca Lagunera*, 194–95.

72. García and Sanz, *Deterioro ambiental y pobreza en la abundancia productiva*, 74.

73. A. R. V. Arellano, "Memorial to Paul Waitz (1876–1961)," 74.

74. Arreguín Mañón, *Aportes a la historia de la geohidrología en México, 1890–1995*, 21, 25.

75. Waitz, "Algunos datos sobre el agua subterránea y su aprovechamiento," 31.

76. Vivar, "Recursos de agua de la hacienda de Hornos, municipio de Viesca, estado de Coahuila," 224.

77. "La Gran Bomba para La Laguna," *El Siglo de Torreón*, classified section, October 23, 1934. There were also advertisements on September 27 and October 5 of that year.

78. He was also a distributor for other companies, including Bombas Compresoras, Nartillos, Medidores de Agua, A. D. Cook, Bombas Verticales, Koerting Motores, and Siemens-Mexico, but apparently not Layne and Bowler.

79. AHA, CT, box 148, file 1139, 87–96. In his doctoral thesis of 2005, on which I partially draw in chap. 1 to describe aniego, the engineer Carlos Cháirez Araiza shows that it is precisely the opposite of what happened and was predictable at the time. He argues that the dam reservoirs have prevented the recharging of the Laguna's diminishing aquifers, while unregulated use of pumps is currently one of the most pressing problems in the region. Nearly all of the estimated three thousand pump-installed wells are contaminated with arsenic and other poisonous substances. However, Cháirez Araiza was not aware of how much well drilling had already adversely affected regional hydrology in the 1930s.

80. *La Opinión*, March 7 and March 10, 1926. There is some irony in this prediction: Alfalfa would later become a leading crop of the Laguna from the 1970s as the region converted to cattle and dairy production for which alfalfa was vital as forage. The assistant general manager of the Tlahualilo Company, which was a member of the chamber and also opposed the dam, wrote to his superior: "People in favor of the Nazas Dam are at least getting on the front page of the local papers. I have an idea that those opposed to the project are just a little afraid of making any big propaganda for fear they may get in wrong with the Fed govt. but we'll see." T. M. Fairburn to J. E. Kitchin, February 18, 1926, Archivo Municipal de Torreón (AMT), Copiadores de Cartas, 1. Two years later, he claimed that 80 percent of farmers opposed the dam and were "acting in unison" against it: February 11, 1928, AMT, Copiadores de Cartas, 9.

81. *El Siglo de Torreón*, December 16, 1929.

82. Nájera et al., *Informe general de la comisión de estudios de la Comarca Lagunera*, 340.

83. Nájera et al., *Informe general de la comisión de estudios de la Comarca Lagunera*, 8.

84. Nájera et al., *Informe general de la comisión de estudios de la Comarca Lagunera*, 185.

85. AAE, FA, file 35, Box 1. Although undated, his unpublished memoirs appear to have been written in 1929. His claims had a basis in fact: Juan Brittingham, as we saw, was a Mexi-

can American entrepreneur heavily invested in the cement business, with close ties to the Terrazas-Creel family of Chihuahua, and Aymes was a Franco-Mexican downriver landowner and attorney who later got caught up in corruption scandals that garnered numerous headlines in Torreón newspapers of the late 1920s and 1930s.

86. José Bonilla, "Los sedimentos del Nazas," July 31, 1931, AHA, CT, box 136, file 1121, 1–19; Narro, "El proceso de desintegración de la arena de los limos del Río Nazas, estudiado en su forma y su tiempo," November 1931, AHA, CT, box 136, file 1121, 25, 37.

87. *El Siglo de Torreón*, November 29, 1929; italics added.

88. Simpson, *The Ejido*, 110–11.

89. Buchenau, *Plutarco Elías Calles and the Mexican Revolution*, xxv.

90. Specifically, the Tlahualilo manager remarked that the president asked the chamber "not to pay any attention to the steps being taken by the Pro-Presa [pro-dam] group, and also to the statements made by engineer De la Fuente and Mr. García de la Cadena. He further stated that the Contra-Presa [anti-dam] group should not worry, as there was nothing to this question": AMT, Copiadores de Cartas, 8, January 23, 1928.

91. Aboites, *El agua de la nación*, 108.

92. Simpson, *The Ejido*, 92.

93. In May 1930, an agreement (*convenio*) was reached between the chamber and the SAF. It exempted the Laguna from large-scale agrarian reform by declaring the region an "agricultural district" in which "there is no place for ejidos" except for ejido land already granted to about three thousand people. In exchange, the chamber agreed to conduct a cadastral survey to determine what extensions of unused lands in Lerdo, Matamoros, San Pedro, and Viesca could be granted to new ejidos. If no land could be found, the secretary would locate other hacienda land to distribute, the cost of which would be covered by prorating among all of the Laguna landowners according to their cadastral land values. President Abelardo Rodríguez then traveled to the Laguna in March 1934 to negotiate another agreement to provide marginal lands from the Hornos hacienda in the downriver zone of Coahuila for 2,300 ejidatarios: Vargas-Lobsinger, *La Comarca Lagunera*, 125, 139–41.

94. Simpson, *The Ejido*, 111–20. Simpson comments that Calles's "purported new views on the agrarian problem were promptly denied and others considerably softened as soon as he returned to Mexico." Nevertheless, opponents of agrarian reform persisted in regarding the New York interview as a victory for their cause.

95. Ervin, "The Art of the Possible," 257. Ortiz Rubio, who was an engineer, appointed the hydraulic engineer and agronomist Marte R. Gómez secretary of the SAF. Gómez supported the agronomists' mobilization to reverse the slowing and eventual termination of agrarian reform.

96. There was in fact much buying and selling during this time. For example, the Lavín perimeter within the Gómez Palacio municipality was sold off piece by piece to the French company Société Française pour l'Industrie au Méxique: Vargas-Lobsinger, *La Comarca Lagunera*, 128–30.

97. Plácido Vargas to Calles, February 18, 1933, ACT, File 27, Inventory 5795. Calles replied that he received the message.

98. Governor of Durango to Calles, April 7, 1933, ACT, File 81, Inventory 4766, Bundle 2/4, 72–76.

99. *El Siglo de Torreón*, August 4, 1933. The capital letters are in the original. De la Fuente appears to have changed his position on the declaration of Nazas waters in 1929 for public utility ex post facto, for in a 1927 telegram to Calles he asked that it not be declared as such.

100. Vargas-Lobsinger, *La Comarca Lagunera*, 134–35.

101. "El Plan Sexenal," *El Siglo de Torreón*, December 8, 1933. See also "La presa del Nazas y el Plan Sexenal," *El Siglo de Torreón*, December 8, 1933.

102. AAE, FVL, copy of AGN document 205-G-54.

103. "Opina acerca de la presa en el Nazas," *El Sigo de Torreón*, December 18, 1929.

104. "El problema de la presa," *El Siglo de Torreón*, February 18, 1932. "Obrera del Municipio de Torreón" likely refers to the Casa del Obrero, the headquarters of the Socialist League of Torreón founded in 1929. González de Montemayor, ed., *Efemérides del Municipio de Torreón*, 19.

105. "Otra opinión a propósito de la presa," *El Siglo de Torreón*, February 23, 1933.

CHAPTER 3. DISTRIBUTING EL AGUA

Epigraph: Liga de Agrónomos Socialistas (League of Socialist Agronomists), cited in Vargas-Lobsinger, *La Comarca Lagunera*, 198.

1. Landeros, "Llevarán a cabo actividades cívicas," *El Siglo de Torreón*, October 6, 2012, reports on the ejido "6 de Octubre" in Gómez Palacio, Durango, celebrating the seventy-sixth anniversary of the reparto, including placement of an offering and an honor guard in front of a monument of Cárdenas. For reports of other Laguna ejidos in Francisco I. Madero and San Pedro, Coahuila, doing much the same, see Fraire, "El campo 'sí tiene que celebrar,'" *El Siglo de Torreón,* October 6, 2012.

2. Vargas-Lobsinger, *La Comarca Lagunera*, 172. Other prominent regions were Yucatán, Lombardía, and Nueva Italia in Michoacán; El Valle del Yaqui en Sonora; and Los Mochis in northern Sinaloa. Not all were profitable at the time Cárdenas subdivided them: Eckstein, *El ejido colectivo en México*, 58.

3. An American delegation investigating cooperative agriculture in Mexico in the early 1950s noted that the term "collective" was inaccurate. It misleadingly evoked the image of Soviet state farms operating within an entirely command economy, which Mexico's state capitalist economy was not. In the midst of the Cold War, it was "causing embarrassment to the government so they're trying to drop it in favor of cooperative." As the delegation understood it, a collective ejido practiced cooperative as opposed to individual farming to a more comprehensive degree, but that "there is no sharp division in practice is suggested by the fact that some of the ejidos contain elements of both types and are classified, therefore, as mixed": Infield and Freier, *People in Ejidos*, 18–19. For further analyses of what constituted a collective ejido in practice and theory, see Eckstein, *El ejido colectivo en México;* Restrepo and Eckstein, *La agricultura colectiva en México.*

4. From 1917 to 1934, the year Cárdenas assumed power, dozens of decrees, resolutions, laws, regulations, and reforms, many of them contradictory or replacing and nullifying previous ones, were passed pertaining to land and water use and rights. Their swift passage made the already confusing legacy of the Spanish colonial period and nineteenth century even more complex. For partial listings of them, see Silva Herzog, ed., *El agrarismo mexicano y la reforma agraria,* 365; Simpson, *The Ejido,* 7, 19–55.

5. "Se decretó el reparto en esta comarca," *El Siglo de Torreón*, October 8, 1936; Vargas-Lobsinger, *La Comarca Lagunera*, 174–75.

6. According to one controversial source, an estimated 30–35 percent of eligible agrarian reform beneficiaries resisted joining ejidos, especially those who had worked on the more prosperous estates: Hernández, *¿La explotación colectiva en la Comarca Lagunera es un fracaso?*, 8–9.

7. "Se decretó el reparto en esta comarca"; Vargas-Lobsinger, *La Comarca Lagunera*, 180–81.

8. November 16, 1936, Archivo General de la Nación (AGN), Ramos Presidenciales (RP), Lázaro Cárdenas (LC), 404.1/706, 966–67. Four days earlier, he gave a similar speech in a local theater to a skeptical crowd of Tlahualilo workers trying to convince them of the advantages of forming state-supported ejidos. Vargas-Lobsinger, *La Comarca Lagunera*, 183.

9. The three presidents were not puppets as each tried to pursue his own agenda, especially when Calles was abroad or ill. Calles unduly influenced only Ortiz Rubio, while Abelardo Rodríguez succeeded in acting quite independently of the Jefe Máximo: Buchenau, *Plutarco Elías Calles and the Mexican Revolution*, 169–72.

10. For various accounts of his presidency, see Aguilar Camín and Meyer, *In the Shadow of the Mexican Revolution*, esp. chap. 4; Gilly, *El cardenismo, una utopía mexicana;* Knight, "Cardenismo: Juggernaut or Jalopy?" For "regimented empowerment," see Boyer, *Becoming Campesinos*, 226.

11. Carr, "The Mexican Communist Party and Agrarian Mobilization in the Laguna, 1920–1940," 397; Vargas-Lobsinger, *La Comarca Lagunera*, 151–53.

12. Interview with his daughter, the historian María Vargas-Lobsinger, December 9, 2005.

13. "Banco Algodonero Refaccionario," March 3, 1935, Archivo Calles-Torreblanca (ACT), file 24, inventory 475, 49–70.

14. Carr, "The Mexican Communist Party and Agrarian Mobilization in the Laguna," 371.

15. Vargas-Lobsinger, *La Comarca Lagunera*, 153–57; Barry Carr, *Marxism and Communism in Twentieth-Century Mexico*, 94–97.

16. A. Balderrama to T. M. Fairburn, September 13, 1935, AMT, FT, box 76, file 11.

17. A. Balderrama to T. M. Fairburn, December 7, 1935, AMT, FT, box 76, file 11.

18. July 28–29, 1936, AGN, RP, LC, 404.1/706, 765–69. Cárdenas optimistically anticipated that the reservoir would contain enough water to both expand irrigation using surface water and produce energy for existing pump-powered wells to extract groundwater for supplementary irrigation.

19. Ashby, *Organized Labor and the Mexican Revolution under Lázaro Cárdenas*, 159.

20. Mariano Padilla to Lázaro Cárdenas, September 22, 1936, AGN, RP, LC, 404.1/706, 241.

21. Benigno Martínez to Lázaro Cárdenas, September 7, 1936, AGN, RP, LC, 404.1/706, 245.

22. Pedro Suinaga Luján to Lázaro Cárdenas, September 23, 1936, AGN, RP, LC, 404.1/706, 258.

23. Chief of Agrarian Department (name cut off) to Lázaro Cárdenas, August 29, 1936, AGN, RP, LC, 404.1/706, 304.

24. J. Isabel García to Lázaro Cárdenas, September 19, 1936, AGN, RP, LC, 404.1/706, 273.

25. E. Rojas Miranda to Lázaro Cárdenas, September 23, 1936, AGN, RP, LC, 404.1/706, 282.

26. Enrique Calderón R. to Lázaro Cárdenas, September 30, 1936, AGN, RP, LC, 404.1/706, 248.

27. Pedro V. Rodríguez Triana to Lázaro Cárdenas, September 23, 1936, AGN, RP, LC, 404.1/706, 182. He also reported in a separate telegram the same day that urban labor unions operating in the region were sowing dissension among campesinos and that the proper authorities should intervene to "prevent clashes" between campesinos.

28. Vicente Lombardo Toledano to Lázaro Cárdenas, September 21, 1936, AGN, RP, LC, 404.1/706. He also wrote that they were waiting for a technical commission to begin land subdivisions, although engineers were already in the region surveying land.

29. Carr, *Marxism and Communism in Twentieth-Century Mexico*, 100–101; Vargas-Lobsinger, *La Comarca Lagunera*, 166: Ashby, *Organized Labor and the Mexican Revolution under Lázaro Cárdenas*, 159–60.

30. For an in-depth examination of Gómez Morín's ideas on agriculture, and agricultural credit in particular, see Nicole Mottier, "Ejidal Credit and Debt in 20th Century Mexico," PhD diss., University of Chicago, 2013, chap. 1.

31. Vargas-Lobsinger, *La Comarca Lagunera*, 169–70. The Nazas flow, pink bollworm infestations, and volatility in cotton prices were three of the same "plagas" that had framed the agricultural chamber's views in its 1920 newsletter of the Laguna's emerging postrevolutionary envirotechnical landscape described in chap. 2. Thirty years later, in 1966, Gómez Morín retrospectively critiqued the Cardenista reparto in an "I told you so" fashion, claiming that the experiment had been a political, not a technical, one, and therefore largely a failure: Wilkie and Wilkie, *México visto en el siglo XX*, 148–49.

32. Vargas-Lobsinger, *La Comarca Lagunera*, 182; Eckstein, *El ejido colectivo en México*, 135. Ashby cites somewhat differing statistics: nearly thirty-four thousand heads of families received land in ejidos: Ashby, *Organized Labor and the Mexican Revolution under Lázaro Cárdenas*, 165.

33. Marshal Hail, "Cárdenas Hailed by Crowds as Messiah for Land Reforms," *Washington Times*, November 21, 1936, clipping, AGN, RP, LC, 404.1/706, 922. The Spanish Republicans had partially modeled their 1931 draft constitution after Mexico's 1917 Constitution and their agrarian reform law of 1932 after its Article 27. Mexican newspapers regularly printed news stories about events in Spain, so their readers were well informed about the parallels between the two. For example, an article headlined "Reparto agrario a 30,000 familias en España" (Land Distributed to 30,000 Families in Spain), published in *El Siglo de Torreón* on March 24, 1936, just a few months before the Laguna's general strike and reparto, reported that rural families throughout the country had converged on Madrid in "hunger marches" for financial assistance to cultivate the land parcels they had received. At the same time, landowners complained to the leftist government of inadequate compensation for land cessions. For a general history of the agrarian reform during the Spanish Civil War, see Javier Tébar Hurtado, *Reforma, revolución y contrarrevolución agrarias: Conflicto social y lucha política en el campo (1931–1939)*.

34. Marshal Hail, "Some Peons Laud Land Program, but Others Fear New Cares," *Washington Times*, November 25, 1936, clipping, AGN, RP, LC, 404.1/706, 925.

35. AMT, FT, box 89, file 1.

36. Marshal Hail, "Anglo-American Lands Fall Afoul of Mexican Collectivism," *Washington Times,* November 24, 1936, clipping, AGN, RP, LC, 404.1/706, 924.

37. Hellman, "Capitalist Agriculture and Rural Protest." See also López Zamora, *El agua, la tierra,* 170, about which there is more discussion in chaps. 5 and 6. It was argued in the 1930s that for the hacendados to comply with the labor code by providing permanent work with Sunday pay, as well as giving the semiproletarianized campesinos all the advantages to which they would have a right under the code, would very quickly bring about "the complete ruin of the hacendados" of the Laguna. There would be no lasting benefit for the workers. Cárdenas saw the ejido as a solution to this because the labor code could be applied while its collective exploitation was capable of the industrialized production of the hacienda it replaced. Individual ejidatarios, however, would be too poor to be able to produce on the same scale: Ashby, *Organized Labor and the Mexican Revolution under Lázaro Cárdenas,* 149, 158.

38. Ornelas, "La Comarca Lagunera," 345.

39. Whether Ornelas actually conceived of the system himself seems questionable, given his bias. However, it was certainly of German origin, as the German immigrant engineer Federico Wulff designed the Trasquila. Moreover, he made them mobile, like many downriver dams, and thus more resistant to damage from flooding. Wulff also planned much of Torreón's urban grid in the late nineteenth century and produced an impressively detailed map of the Laguna region, published in 1914, on which the general map at the front of this book is based.

40. For a detailed account of the founding of the PNR, see Buchenau, *Plutarco Elías Calles and the Mexican Revolution,* 145–53.

41. Eduardo Kern Andere and Galdino P. Palafox, "Informe de los trabajos llevados a cabo por la Comisión Mixta de Aguas de la Comarca Lagunera creada por acuerdo presidencial de 6 de octubre 1936," to Lázaro Cárdenas, January 22, 1937, AHA, AS, box 347, file 7226, 3–8.

42. Aboites, *El agua de la nación,* 115–16.

43. "Informe de los trabajos llevados a cabo por la Comisión Mixta de Aguas de la Comarca Lagunera creada por acuerdo presidencial de 6 de octubre 1936."

44. "Informe de los trabajos llevados a cabo por la Comisión Mixta de Aguas de la Comarca Lagunera creada por acuerdo presidencial de 6 de octubre 1936"; capital letters are in original. As Gil Ornelas described the Nazas River Inspection Commission's work in 1919, "The work of this corps of engineers is hard and protracted, especially during periods of river cresting, since every diversion dam is attended to by one of these engineers during these periods with his corps of gatekeepers and peons who help him with river flow measurements. It is an operation that is practiced three times a day and generates a corresponding statistic of water used in order to increase, diminish or suspend a distribution, per the instructions received from the central office where the data are sent however many times measurements are taken": Ornelas, "La Comarca Lagunera," 344.

45. "Informe de los trabajos llevados a cabo por la Comisión Mixta de Aguas de la Comarca Lagunera creada por acuerdo presidencial de 6 de octubre 1936," 6–8.

46. "Ley de Aguas de Propiedad Nacional de 1934," *Diario Oficial de la Federación,* August 31, 1943. The article also stipulated that if users presented no complaints within two years, they would be considered in agreement with a new regulation or modification thereof.

47. "Reglamentación actual de los Ríos Nazas y Aguanaval y necesidad de modificarla," January 13, 1937, AHA, AS, box 347, file 7226, 45. The best data on land area, location of irrigated terrains, and property boundaries came from the Callista engineers' commission study of 1928, and those were only estimates.

48. The modifications between the 1895 and 1909 regulations consisted of adjustments in volume of water allocated to certain dams and canals, lowering volumes primarily for upriver ones, and adding municipal usage for the growing cities of Torreón, Lerdo, Gómez Palacio, and San Pedro. Urban water use, however, accounted on average for less than a tenth of agricultural use: "Reglamentación actual de los Ríos Nazas y Aguanaval y necesidad de modificarla," 45–46.

49. "Reglamentación actual de los Ríos Nazas y Aguanaval y necesidad de modificarla," 47, 58–59. It should be noted that there is a large discrepancy between the 90 percent figure of the CNI engineers and the 67 percent figure cited by the League of Socialist Agronomists; the latter seems more accurate. Perhaps the CNI was anticipating an eventual, not the actual, percentage of ejidos that would collectively own irrigable land.

50. "Reglamentación actual de los Ríos Nazas y Aguanaval y necesidad de modificarla," 62–65.

51. Allen to José G. Parres, June 14, 1938, AHA, AS, box 347, file 7226, 155.

52. "Reglamentación actual de los Ríos Nazas y Aguanaval y necesidad de modificarla," 59.

53. Comisión Mixta de Aguas to Lázaro Cárdenas, November 16, 1936, AHA, AS, box 347, file 7226, 14.

54. "Corte informe preliminar sobre las perforaciones y estaciones de bombeo de la Comarca Lagunera de Torreón," April 12, 1937, AHA, box 136, file 1121, 73–74.

55. "Corte informe preliminar sobre las perforaciones y estaciones de bombeo de la Comarca Lagunera de Torreón," 75. For a detailed study of the energy required for groundwater pumping in the Laguna, including the role of the CFE, founded in 1937, see Rivas Sada, "Cambio tecnológico, dinámica regional y reconversión productiva en el norte de México. La Comarca Lagunera, 1925–1974," 179–80. She points out that the CFE was inadequately equipped and prepared to expand the electricity network in the face of burgeoning demand, providing only 36 percent of the supply compared with 36 percent from internal combustion engines and 28 percent from thermoelectric plants. Nevertheless, the CFE could sell energy at far lower cost.

56. "Corte informe preliminar sobre las perforaciones y estaciones de bombeo de la Comarca Lagunera de Torreón," 76.

57. Allen to Parres, June 14, 1938, AHA, AS, box 347, file 7226, 159.

58. "Futura reglamentación para el uso y aprovechamiento de las aguas del río Nazas," September 9, 1938, AHA, AS, box 347, file 7226, 190–91. Lerdo residents were forced to rely on prohibitively expensive imported water, about which they vociferously protested to the president, the governor of Durango, and local officials, which none of the older residents could ever before recall having occurred: "El problema del agua en Lerdo origina protestas enérgicas de los vecinos," *El Siglo de Torreón*, June 11, 1938.

59. Vargas-Lobsinger, *La Comarca Lagunera,* 174.

60. "Aviso importante a los Señores Hacendados de esta Comarca," *El Siglo de Torreón*, January 5, 1937.

61. PPACL to José G. Parres, July 6, 1938, AHA, AS, Box 347, File 7226, 168–69.

62. "La distribución del agua tratada por agricultores de vital importancia para la C. Lagunera," *El Siglo de Torreón*, June 15, 1938.

63. "La distribución del agua tratada por agricultores de vital importancia para la C. Lagunera." In a memo, Serrano commented that the PPACL's request contravened the agrarian legislation's clear prioritization of ejidos over small properties in times of water scarcity: "Proposiciones para la reglamentación del uso de las aguas de los Ríos Aguanaval y Nazas, Dgo-Coah," April 27, 1939, AHA, AS, box 347, file 7226, 251–55.

64. "La distribución del agua tratada por agricultores de vital importancia para la C. Lagunera." In a memo analyzing ejidos in Coahuila, the Mixed Regulatory Commission cited 2,113 campesinos "libres," or those who were not ejidatarios working for either small landholders or ejidos. Their unaffiliated status, the commission warned, made their situation "truly precarious." It was therefore urgent to resolve their economic, social, and legal situation, "since for obvious reasons the existence of these irregular workers is what generates the formation of discontented and even antagonistic groups to the collective-ejidal regime": "Comarca Lagunera Coahuila," March 22, 1938, AHA, AS, box 347, file 7226, 93–94.

65. Liga de Agrónomos Socialistas, *El colectivismo agrario en México, La Comarca Lagunera*, 145–47.

66. Liga de Agrónomos Socialistas, *El colectivismo agrario en México*, 145–47.

67. "Comarca Lagunera Coahuila," 96.

68. "Completa miseria en el ejido Águila," *El Siglo de Torreón*, February 10, 1938.

69. Ejido E. Viñedo de Durango to Cárdenas, March 16, 1939, AHA, AS, box 347, file 7226, 203–4. They wrote the letter in poor Spanish. Implementation of the new water regulation would also victimize some small landholders.

70. PPACL to Cárdenas, March 30, 1939, AHA, AS, Box 347, File 7226, 208–11.

71. "Comarca Lagunera Coahuila," 93–94. Those "refined methods" (*métodos depurados*) dated back to colonial times. In other reports, engineers were far more critical of the agricultural practices of ejidos, believing them to be backward and an impediment to modernization of the irrigation system.

72. Ashby, *Organized Labor and the Mexican Revolution under Lázaro Cárdenas*, 148, citing Cárdenas's speech of November 30, 1936. He also repeated this verbatim in an interview in Michoacán after he left the presidency and was working on the Tennessee Valley Authority–inspired Tepalcatepec Commission to bring regional development through irrigation to that river basin in the late 1940s and 1950s: Infield and Freier, *People in Ejidos*, 127. See also Pérez Prado, "Visiones sobre la construcción del sistema de riego Cupatitzio-Cajones y la política de la memoria," 191–92.

73. Walsh, *Building the Borderlands*, 117–23, based on research in the CONDUMEX archive. Walsh remarks that "while both Cárdenas and Clayton benefited from their business relationship, neither was entirely comfortable with it, and both took pains to hide their dealings from public scrutiny" (122). Indeed, according to Walsh, no reference to these dealings appears in Cárdenas's published reports on his policies or in his presidential archive.

74. "A los señores agricultores: Acabamos de recibir la siguiente carta del Sr. J. Paul King representante de los señores Anderson Clayton en la C. de México," *El Siglo de Torreón*, February 22, 1925.

75. "Declaróse el boicot a la paca cilíndrica," *El Siglo de Torreón*, August 6, 1928; "Anderson y Clayton contestaron ayer a la Cámara Agrícola," *El Siglo de Torreón,* August 10, 1928; "El boicot contra la Casa ACCO," *El Siglo de Torreón,* August 13, 1928.

76. "Ventajas de la paca cilíndrica: Aclaraciones al margen de una campaña," *El Siglo de Torreón*, September 10, 1928; capital letters in the original.

77. "La paca cilíndrica representa un progreso," *El Siglo de Torreón*, September 16, 1928.

78. "El conflicto algodonero," *El Siglo de Torreón*, October 5, 1929.

79. "Los arreglos con Anderson Clayton," *El Siglo de Torreón*, February 9, 1930.

80. "Los industriales gestionan la libre entrada de algodón," *El Siglo de Torreón*, May 30, 1932.

81. "La primera refacción a los agricultores del sistema no. 5," *El Siglo de Torreón*, June 14, 1936.

82. "Algodón vendido por $140,000," *El Siglo de Torreón*, January 20, 1937.

83. "La compra de 85,000 pacas," *El Siglo de Torreón*, February 18, 1938.

84. "Remitido," *El Siglo de Torreón*, March 18, 1937.

85. "Se perforan norias en cinco ejidos," *El Siglo de Torreón*, November 11, 1939.

86. Vargas-Lobsinger, *La Comarca Lagunera*, 184.

87. Mayor Alfredo Paz Gutiérrez to Parres, June 14, 1938, AHA, AS, Box 347, File 7226, 630; Serrano to Chief of Office, March 4, 1939, AHA, AS, Box 347, File 7226, 632–36.

88. Paz Gutiérrez to Parres, September 26, 1939, AHA, AS, box 347, file 7226, 626.

89. Serrano to Chief of Office, March 4, 1939, AHA, AS, Box 347, File 7226, 634.

90. Serrano to Chief of Office, March 4, 1939, AHA, AS, Box 347, File 7226, 635–36. Romero Navarrete points out that the new April 1938 regulation effectively abrogated water rights recognized under the 1909 regulations and therefore exclusive use of water removals from the river by previous orders: Romero Navarrete, "El reparto agrario y la redistribución del agua en La Laguna," 25. A few months after the government promulgated the regulation, the PPACL urged its members in a newspaper announcement to provide it with exemption certificates if they had owned less than 100 hectares prior to the reparto. The Agrarian Department could thereby recognize the new owners, and the CNI would count them as users with rights to federal waters: "Aviso importante," *El Siglo de Torreón*, September 10, 1938.

91. Weckmann to Parres, October 25, 1939, AHA, AS, box 347, file 7226, 703–4.

92. Tavares to Cárdenas, December 29, 1939, AHA, AS, box 347, file 7226, 719.

93. Serrano to Chief of Office, AHA, AS, box 347, file 7226, January 23, 1940, 723–26; July 11, 1940, AHA, AS, box 347, file 7226, 750.

94. Orive Alba, *La irrigación en México*, 178–79.

95. Romero Navarrete, "El reparto agrario y la redistribución del agua en La Laguna," 24–25. For an in-depth institutional analysis of the reparto de aguas, see also Romero Navarrete, *El río Nazas y los derechos de agua en México*.

96. Serrano to Chief of Office, July 11, 1940, AHA, AS, Box 347, File 7226, 750–52.

97. Díaz Covarrubias, August 22, 1940, AHA, AS, box 347, file 7226, 767.

98. Parres to General Manager of Laguna Irrigation District, undated but probably July 1941, AHA, AS, box 347, file 7226, 787.

99. Grupo de Pequeños Fraccionistas del Perímetro del Tlahualilo to Ávila Camacho, January 27, 1941, AHA, AS, box 347, file 7226, 806–7.

100. Negrete to José G. Parres, March 24, 1941, AHA, AS, box 347, file 7226, 811.

CHAPTER 4. LIFE AND WORK ON THE DAM SITE

Epigraph: Diego Rivera, http://www.milenio.com/cdb/doc/impreso/9028315. Although Rivera is speaking about the water works built to divert part of the Lerma River to Mexico City, which he painted in a mural, he could easily have spoken of similar works constructed throughout Mexico, including in the Laguna. (For a photograph of the mural, see figure Intro.3.)

1. Orive Alba, *La irrigación en México,* 82–83.

2. Eduardo Suárez and Ricardo J. Zevada, "Requisitos y bases para el Concurso 1936," December 20, 1935, Archivo Histórico del Agua (AHA), Consultivo Técnico (CT), box 153, file 1147, 3. Newspaper accounts in 1936 emphasized Mexico's good international credit standing for obtaining loans internationally for its hydraulic works. Suárez in particular claimed North American banks were ready to finance them. Of the 66 million pesos (about $16.5 million) budgeted for this trio of dams, 19 million pesos (about $6 million) was to go "preferentially" to El Palmito over the others, including 3.5 million pesos (about $1 million) worth of machinery purchases in the United States, such as for cranes and trucks: "Mexico Building Three Dams to Irrigate Wide Areas," *New York Times,* January 14, 1936; "19 millones destinados para construir 3 presas," *El Nacional,* November 23, 1936; "Se comenzarán las obras de las presas del 'Palmito,' 'Angostura,' y del 'Azúcar,'" untitled newspaper, November 27, 1936, in Fondo "Laguna," Archivo Económico, Biblioteca Lerdo de Tejada.

3. "El Padre Nazas vertió sus dones magníficos sobre la C. Lagunera," *El Siglo de Torreón,* August 23, 1923.

4. "La primera avenida del Nilo lagunero," *El Siglo de Torreón,* July 13, 1929, 3.

5. Correspondence between SAF irrigation engineers and between engineers and water meter readers, April 1921–September 1934, AHA, CT, box 2578, file 36079. The next three paragraphs are drawn from this source.

6. The engineer Enrique Nájera, from Calles's Engineering Commission and who was sent to the Laguna in 1926, indicated that far more gauging stations had been installed than in this report. "Since 1926 the service was organized in a more efficient way, extending the network of the states of Zacatecas, Durango and Coahuila to the Nazas-Aguanaval basin; although it still does not produce a perfect statistic, hopefully they'll be more complete from now on in the Laguna. Stations in Durango installed: Lerdo, Tlahualilo, Durango, El Ojo, San Juan de Guadalupe, Santa Lucía, Tapona, El Salto, Santiaguillo, Santiago Papasquiaro, Nazas, Peñón Blanco, El Oro, Guanaceví, Tepehuanes, El Rodeo, La Concepción y Pedriceña. In Coahuila, La Flor de Jimulco, Matamoros, Sierra Mojada, Concordia y El Burro. Lerdo was the headquarters for meteorological stations": Enrique Nájera, Manuel López Portillo, and Estanislao Peña, *Informe general de la Comisión de Estudios de la Comarca Lagunera, designada por el secretario de Agricultura y Fomento,* 22. By contrast, a CNI report on the dam from 1940, cited at length later, listed these hydrometric stations in operation: San Fernando, Municipio, Santa Rosa, Sacramento, San Ramón, La Concha, El Cuije, Tlahualilo, San Antonio, Santa Cruz Relámpago, Torreón, El Coyote. As for the Rincón de Ramos station at El Palmito, the

one that so troubled engineers, the report claimed that its measurements were "doubtful" from 1925 to 1929 but "sure" from January 1929. Notably, only in December 1929 did the federal government declare the Nazas of "public utility" and, thus, subject to damming.

7. In 1930, an expert did not hesitate to affirm, "Our current knowledge of hydrologic phenomena is very limited and incomplete, despite the gigantic advances in the other natural sciences over the last two centuries." He pointed out that the U.S. Weather Bureau, founded in 1891, had five thousand meteorological stations, and these were insufficient. Thirty years later, Mexico had only five hundred stations, mostly in state capitals and a few other important cities. Flow data for more than twenty years, considered the minimum necessary for long-term predictions, existed for only three rivers. Aboites, *El agua de la nación*, 123. The Nazas was one of them, but even its flow data were not necessarily reliable. Nevertheless, Calles ordered the CNI to forge ahead with dam building and other hydraulic works in the late 1920s, despite woefully inadequate data.

8. Paul Waitz to Alfredo Becerril Colín, April 8, 1934, AHA, CT, box 142, file 1129, 79–87.

9. Unnamed engineer to Becerril Colín, April 17, 1934, AHA, CT, box 142, file 1129, 74–76.

10. Jorge Blake to CNI Accounting Department, March 19, 1935, AHA, CT, box 142, file 1129, 137.

11. Jorge Blake to Paul Waitz, July 27, 1935, AHA, CT, box 142, file 1129, 149–50.

12. Paul Waitz to Jorge Blake, August 2, 1935, AHA, CT, box 142, file 1129, 148.

13. Jorge Blake to Francisco Vázquez del Mercado, August 25, 1935, AHA, CT, box 142, file 1129, 99.

14. Jorge Blake to Francisco Vázquez del Mercado, September 18, 1935, AHA, CT, box 142, file 1129, 97–98. Unfortunately, the file ends before revealing whether Blake was able to leave, but he ultimately did, since he reappears in subsequent documents in different contexts.

15. Riemann, *Memoria del Distrito de Riego de la Región Lagunera, Coahuila y Durango*, 61–66.

16. Wolfe, "Bringing the Revolution to the Dam Site," 9.

17. "Una semblanza del Ing. Thorne constructor de la presa de Palmito," *El Siglo de Torreón*, October 6, 1946, 1.

18. "La inspección a las obras de El Palmito," *El Siglo de Torreón*, March 13, 1938.

19. Riemann, *Memoria del Distrito de Riego de la Región Lagunera, Coahuila y Durango*, 13–14.

20. Riemann, *Memoria del Distrito de Riego de la Región Lagunera, Coahuila y Durango*, 24–27.

21. Riemann, *Memoria del Distrito de Riego de la Región Lagunera, Coahuila y Durango*, 28–30.

22. Riemann, *Memoria del Distrito de Riego de la Región Lagunera, Coahuila y Durango*, 40.

23. Riemann, *Memoria del Distrito de Riego de la Región Lagunera, Coahuila y Durango*, 61–67.

24. Riemann, *Memoria del Distrito de Riego de la Región Lagunera, Coahuila y Durango*, 68–85.

25. Riemann, *Memoria del Distrito de Riego de la Región Lagunera, Coahuila y Durango*, 132. One U.S. dollar was worth 5.4 Mexican pesos in 1940. Estimates of total cost when national newspapers covered its announced groundbreaking in 1936 varied from 15 million to 19 million pesos. On how the costs of thousands of dam projects globally usually exceeded projections, often by a large margin, throughout the twentieth century, see World Commission on Dams, *Dams and Development*.

26. Schuler, *Mexico between Hitler and Roosevelt*, 101.

27. Henry Van Rosenthal Thorne to Vázquez del Mercado, September 17, 1938, AHA, CT, box 148, file 1139, 179–81; Henry Van Rosenthal Thorne to Andrew Weiss, September 25, 1938, AHA, CT, box 148, file 1139, 167–70.

28. "Memo sobre la terminación y financiación de las obras del Palmito presentado por la compañía constructora mexicana, SA," undated but probably 1939, Archivo General de la Nación (AGN), Ramos Presidenciales (RP), Lázaro Cárdenas (LC), 508/6.

29. Andrew Weiss to M. Levitt, March 1939, AHA, CT, box 148, file 1139, 200–3.

30. Henry Van Rosenthal Thorne to CNI, June 25, 1941, AHA, CT, box 137, file 1122, 375.

31. Orive Alba, memoranda, April 18, 1942, April 25, 1942, AHA, CT, box 141, file 1128, 167.

32. "48-Year Low Seen in Cotton Acreage," *New York Times*, July 5, 1943.

33. Niblo, *War, Diplomacy, and Development*, 93.

34. Rojas, "Cuéntame un siglo," 26–27.

35. "Un día en el Palmito, Dgo.," *El Siglo de Torreón*, October 6, 1946. This is an excerpt from a much longer account.

36. "Antecedentes sobre la localización del campamento de construcción para la presa 'El Palmito,'" Durango Dirección de Construcción, AHA, CT, box 138, file 1123, 549–50.

37. Dunar and McBride, *Building Hoover Dam*.

38. Comisión Nacional de Irrigación, *La obra de la Comisión Nacional de Irrigación*, 12–13; italics added.

39. Comisión Nacional de Irrigación, *La obra de la Comisión Nacional de Irrigación*, 240.

40. Comisión Nacional de Irrigación, *La obra de la Comisión Nacional de Irrigación*, 238–40.

41. "Dos cooperativas en 'El Palmito,'" *El Siglo de Torreón*, February 28, 1938.

42. "El reajuste en El Palmito, Dgo.," *El Siglo de Torreón*, August 14, 1938.

43. "Lo que el público reclama," *El Siglo de Torreón*, June 4, 1937.

44. "Lo que el público reclama," *El Siglo de Torreón*, August 14, 1937.

45. "Lo que el público reclama," *El Siglo de Torreón*, August 25, 1937. The complaints persisted, however, with workers charging that merchants and food cooperatives were gouging prices: "Lo que sufren en El Palmito," *El Siglo de Torreón*, October 5, 1939. For the response denying the charges, see "Aclaración de lo que pasa en El Palmito," *El Siglo de Torreón*, October 17, 1939.

46. Luciano Delgado to Lázaro Cárdenas, July 31, 1940, AGN, RP LC, 601.1/451. There was no individualized reply to Delgado, but Cárdenas did take such complaints from workers seriously.

47. Full-page, untitled newspaper advertisement, April 26, 1939, AGN, RP LC, 601.1/451.

48. Comisión Nacional de Irrigación, *La obra de la Comisión Nacional de Irrigación*, 241.

49. "Antecedentes sobre la localización del campamento de construcción para la presa 'El Palmito,'" 550.

50. Sindicato Nacional de Trabajadores de Agricultura y Fomento to Manuel Ávila Camacho, October 6, 1942, AGN, RP, Ávila Camacho (AC), 553/19.

51. Manuel Ávila Camacho to Elpidio Velázquez, October 20, 1942, November 14, 1942, AGN, RP, AC, 553/19.

52. Comisión Nacional de Irrigación, *La obra de la Comisión Nacional de Irrigación*, 240.

53. Saucedo Galindo, "Informe y estudio médico social de campamento y pueblo de El Palmito, Dgo.," 13. The following section is drawn from this source. Nearly all of the nine thesis writers corroborated this version, primarily changing statistics only according to the year during which they completed their study. Medical students studied the campamentos of other dams throughout the country, and their theses are available at the Universidad Nacional Autónoma de México Thesis Department and the University of Texas, Austin, library. For more on the education of these medical students, see Soto Laveaga, "Bringing the Revolution to Medical Schools."

54. Saucedo Galindo, "Informe y estudio médico social de campamento y pueblo de El Palmito, Dgo.," 28–29.

55. Saucedo Galindo, "Informe y estudio médico social de campamento y pueblo de El Palmito, Dgo.," 29–30. For works that examine the secular missionary zeal of Cardenismo that these students demonstrated with their culturally normative observations of the poor of El Palmito, see Adrian A. Bantjes, *As If Jesus Walked on Earth: Cardenismo, Sonora, and the Mexican Revolution;* Becker, *Setting the Virgin on Fire;* Vaughan, *Cultural Politics in Revolution.*

56. Saucedo Galindo, "Informe y estudio médico social de campamento y pueblo de El Palmito, Dgo.," 31–33.

57. Saucedo Galindo, "Informe y estudio médico social de campamento y pueblo de El Palmito, Dgo.," 51–52.

58. AGN, RP LC, 601.1/336, "Campamento," June 13, 1942.

59. Rojas, "Cuéntame un siglo," 27.

60. "Información compendiada relativa a la visita que practicaron los señores Weiss, King, Bustamante y el suscrito a las obras de El Palmito, Las Lajas, El Azúcar, Purificación, Las Adjuntas y Xicoténcatl, durante los días 4 al 12 de octubre de 1944," AHA, CT, box 138, file 1123, 254–57.

61. "Información compendiada relativa a la visita que practicaron los señores Weiss, King, Bustamante y el suscrito a las obras de El Palmito, Las Lajas, El Azúcar, Purificación, Las Adjuntas y Xicoténcatl, durante los días 4 al 12 de octubre de 1944," 254–57.

62. AHA, CT, box 138, file 1123, "Comité Pro-Nuevo Palmito," Jan. 29, 1946, 345.

63. Rojas, "Cuéntame un siglo," 27.

64. "Visita a las obras de 'El Palmito,'" *El Siglo de Torreón*, July 25, 1937; "Gira de escolares a 'El Palmito,'" *El Siglo de Torreón*, June 11, 1938.

65. Arturo Sandoval to Lázaro Cárdenas, February 28, 1938, AGN, RP LC, 702.2/9126; José Escobar to Lázaro Cárdenas, April 7, 1938, AGN, RP LC, 702.2/9126.

66. Cited in Joseph and Henderson, eds., *The Mexico Reader*, 448.

67. Dirección General de Culturas Populares, *Los primordiales del 36*, 28, 33–34, 41, 61.

68. "La sequía causa perjuicios a ejidos," *El Siglo de Torreón*, June 21, 1937, 1.

69. "El catastro de los ejidos," *El Siglo de Torreón*, June 18, 1937, 4.

70. "Proyectan perforar norias en ejidos," *El Siglo de Torreón*, December 9, 1939, 1.

71. Mottier, "Ejidal Credit and Debt in 20th Century Mexico," PhD diss., University of Chicago, 2013, 162. She documents how the Ejido Bank took bribes from favored drillers in exchange for exclusive contracts, which ejidatarios were compelled to accept lest they were denied credit. One well driller in particular, Rogelio Braña, allegedly had connections to Ávila Camacho's SAF Secretary Marte R. Gómez, according to the agronomist Emilio López Zamora. Gómez, however, charged López Zamora with profiting from his own pump business in the following decades. Both Gómez and López Zamora were politically well-connected técnicos and businessmen who likely engaged in corrupt practices. Mottier argues that there was not always a neat correlation between water access and credit by showing that ejidos who already had pump-installed wells, usually from the expropriated haciendas they took over, were in a better position to obtain credit than those who were not so fortunate. Their advantage, however, was contingent on toeing the political line of the ruling party through obeisance to the Ejido Bank. As a result, many ejidos broke relations with the bank, as reported in numerous newspaper articles. For how private moneylenders offered an alternative to the bank, see Mottier, "Ejidal Credit and Debt in 20th Century Mexico," chap. 5.

72. "Las dificultades de los perforadores," *El Siglo de Torreón*, June 11, 1937, 7.

73. "Inauguración de 10 norias," *El Siglo de Torreón*, March 29, 1937, 1.

74. "Una película de los ejidos," *El Siglo de Torreón*, February 5, 1937, 1.

75. "En los ejidos se construirán otras 13 escuelas," *El Siglo de Torreón*, November 1, 1945, 1.

76. Wilkie, *San Miguel*, 27, 99–100.

77. "Las epidemias en los ejidos," *El Siglo de Torreón*, December 22, 1946, 1.

78. Quoted in Joseph and Henderson, *The Mexico Reader*, 449.

79. Wilkie, *San Miguel*, 35.

80. Wilkie, *San Miguel*, 31–32, 90.

81. "Las mujeres del ejido Sofía denuncian cantina," *El Siglo de Torreón*, June 13, 1944, 1.

82. Olcott, *Revolutionary Women in Postrevolutionary Mexico*, 138, 148.

83. Álvarez y Álvarez to Cárdenas, October 20, 1937, AGN, LC RP, 404.1/706, 2774; Cárdenas to Álvarez y Álvarez, October 28, 1937, 2769; Álvarez y Álvarez to Cárdenas, May 2, 1938, 2735. It appears that the vice-consul also had a self-interest in keeping Cárdenas abreast of events in the Laguna: he requested the president's intervention to obtain a bank loan to sink a well in his vineyards. The president forwarded the request to the relevant bank, which then rejected it.

CHAPTER 5. DAM, PUMPS, AND PESTICIDES

Epigraph: Arturo Rodríguez Cruz, quoted in Dirección General de Culturas Populares, *Los primordiales del 36*, 62.

1. "Gran jornada de la irrigación en México," *El Siglo de Torreón*, October 7, 1946.

2. Niblo, *War, Diplomacy, and Development*, 183.

3. Wilkie, *The Mexican Revolution*, 134–35.

4. See, among many others, Lookingbill, *Dust Bowl, USA;* Worster, *Dust Bowl: The Southern Plains in the 1930s.*

5. Simonian, *Defending the Land of the Jaguar*, 114. For discussion of various meanings of conservation when applied to surface and subsurface water, see the introduction in this volume.

6. Davis, *Late Victorian Holocausts*, 18–19. In a more technical study, the U.S. National Drought Mitigation Center found more than 150 known definitions of drought reflecting global geographic and climatic diversity on a continuum between very arid and very humid. They synthesized and grouped the definitions into four broad types: meteorological, agricultural, hydrological, and socioeconomic drought. Although these types can overlap, each represents a progressively greater degree of water deficiency, in the order seen here, as meteorological drought persists with correspondingly more severe effects on people, plants, and animals: U.S. National Drought Mitigation Center, http://drought.unl.edu/DroughtBasics/TypesofDrought.aspx.

7. García and Sanz, *Deterioro ambiental y pobreza en la abundancia productiva*, 20–21.

8. *El Siglo de Torreón*, October 12, 1946.

9. *El Siglo de Torreón*, October 14, 1946, October 23, 1946.

10. *El Universal*, November 17, 1945.

11. Pardo barely mentioned the dam's hydroelectric component, which also failed to live up to expectations: it could not generate electricity with such a low reservoir level, whose entire water amount was allocated to irrigation. For detailed discussion of the energy dimension of the Laguna's water management, see Eva Luisa Rivas Sada, "Cambio tecnológico, dinámica regional y reconversión productiva en el norte de México, La Comarca Lagunera, 1925–1974," PhD diss., Universidad Complutense de Madrid, 2010, 196–218.

12. *Novedades*, August 2, 1946. The flooding in 1944 was nationwide.

13. Ironically, the Don Martín Dam was one of the CNI's true white elephants, a poorly designed project whose reservoir filled only once during its first decade of operation, in 1936. As the Rockefeller Foundation described it in 1941, "A series of dry years followed, and the project is dotted now with abandoned adobe houses and irrigation ditches. . . . Irrigation was attempted on only about one-quarter of the project this year": "Agricultural Conditions and Problems in Mexico: Report of the Survey Commission of the Rockefeller Foundation," 1941, Rockefeller Foundation Archive, 323 Agriculture.

14. Bistraín to SRH Director, November 14, 1947, Archivo Histórico del Agua (AHA), Aprovechamientos Superficiales (AS), box 2539, file 35408, 4–5.

15. This contrasts with engineers who had a very positive assessment of aniego shortly after the reparto of 1936 described in chap. 3.

16. Jesús Oropeza to SRH Director, January 17, 1948, AHA, AS, box 2539, file 35408, 87–88.

17. Niblo, *Mexico in the 1940s*, 185. See also Kourí, "Lo agrario y lo agrícola."

18. Mario Veytia Barba, "Informe relativo al estudio geohidrológico de la región lagunera en los estados de Coahuila y Durango," April 1948, AHA, Consultivo Técnico (CT), box 43, file 7218, 6.

19. Marte R. Gómez to Antonio Luna Arroyo, August 22, 1962, Archivo Marte R. Gómez (AMRG), 1960 L-M. For background on Gómez, see Ervin, "Marte R. Gómez of Tamaulipas."

20. Donaciano Ojeda O., "Notas sobre los acuerdos tomados por el Señor Ingeniero Marte R. Gómez durante su visita al Distrito de Riego de la Región Lagunera," January 31, 1941, AHA, AS, box 2541, file 35437, 23–24.

21. Andrew Weiss and Antonio Coria to CNI Director, "Informe sobre las observaciones efectuadas en el Distrito de Riego de la Región Lagunera," April 12, 1941, AHA, AS, box 3067, file 42425, 38.

22. Weiss and Coria to CNI Director, "Informe sobre las observaciones efectuadas en el Distrito de Riego de la Región Lagunera," 38.

23. Ávila Camacho and Gómez, "Acuerdo Presidencial sobre el distrito de riego de la Region Lagunera," February 12, 1941, AHA, CT, box 137, file 1122, 214.

24. Ávila Camacho and Gómez, "Acuerdo Presidencial sobre el distrito de riego de la Region Lagunera," 214–24. Although never carried out at the time, this stated objective of transferring water management from the federal to state and local levels anticipated the policy of "decentralization" that took hold in the 1980s and 1990s: see Valencia, Díaz, and Ibarrola, "La gestión integrada de los recursos hídricos en México," http://www2.inecc.gob .mx/publicaciones/libros/452/valencia.html.

25. *El Siglo de Torreón*, August 30, 1941, 7. Although some ejidatarios did move, the majority stayed, as they remained attached to their land grants and apparently hoped that construction of a dam on the Nazas and access to groundwater pumps would provide more water. Many worked for small landholders, worked part time on the Palmito Dam and other public works projects, or found work in the cities or the United States via the Bracero Program or as undocumented migrants.

26. Vogt, "Confidential Memorandum Submitted to the Comisión Impulsora y Coordinadora de la Investigación Científica de México," U.S. National Archives and Records Administration (NARA), 812.611/12 1544, November 1944; underlining in original.

27. Specifically, "The present law's objective is to promote, protect and regulate the conservation of soil and water resources basic for national agriculture": "Se publicó Ley de Conservación de Agua y Suelo," *El Siglo de Torreón*, June 24, 1946, 5. I was unable to ascertain whether drafters of the law were aware of Vogt's report, but it is likely that they were given the influence of the Pan American Union, the precursor to the Organization of American States, on Mexico and the fact that it was submitted to a commission for scientific research in Mexico.

28. For a comprehensive study of the regionally based nature of the political economy of postrevolutionary Mexican industrial development, see Gauss, *Made in Mexico*. For an account of the corruption of the period, see Niblo, *Mexico in the 1940s*, chap. 5. For an overview of some of the severe environmental impacts of postwar Mexican industrialization, see Simonian, *Defending the Land of the Jaguar*, chap. 6.

29. "Importante aclaración a los ejidatarios," *El Siglo de Torreón*, July 7, 1945, 9. Five years later, and four years after Gómez left office, however, his private activities made such charges appear to have some grounds. In a letter to Miguel Alemán in June 1950, Gómez called Equipos Mecánicos "our [Worthington de México's] distributors": Gómez to Alemán, June 3, 1950, AMRG, 1950 H-M.

30. Embassy of Mexico in Washington, DC, to U.S. Secretary of State, "Confidential Memorandum prepared by SAF," May 6, 1942, NARA 812.61/138.

31. Gómez to Alemán, September 12, 1949, Archivo General de la Nación (AGN), Miguel Alemán Valdés (MAV), 508.1/614, 1–2; Sepúlveda to Gómez and Gómez to Sepúlveda, January 11, 1949, January 21, 1949, February 8, 1949, March 15, 1949, May 18, 1949, AMRG, I-Z, 1949.

32. Everett Lundy, "History of the Vertical Turbine Pump Industry," ms., in my possession.

33. Worthington Pump and Machinery Corporation, *100 Years, 1840–1940, Worthington*, 8, 14, 71, 75. Worthington was also a major supplier to the U.S. oil companies in Mexico, to which Pemex turned for supplies, as well, after Cárdenas's nationalization of foreign oil companies in 1938. Worthington reluctantly refused because of the boycott imposed by the U.S. oil industry on Mexico in retaliation for the nationalization. As a newspaper report explained, "Recently a Mexican purchasing agent asked the Worthington Pump Company to sell $40,000 worth of spare parts for oil refining machinery, offering to pay cash. Worthington refused, explained it did $900,000 annual business with Standard and Sinclair (whose properties have been seized by Mexico) and that these companies might boycott Worthington if it sold to the Mexican government. So Mexico bought from Germany": "The Washington Merry-Go-Round," *Spokane Daily Chronicle*, January 17, 1939.

34. "Desarrollo de los sistemas de riego," *El Siglo de Torreón*, August 2, 1929.

35. Advertisement, *El Siglo de Torreón*, September 8, 1925, 12.

36. "Instruction Book and List of Parts for Axiflo and Coniflo Deep Well Pumps," Worthington Pump and Machinery, Bulletin D-312, August 1925, American Historical Museum Archive, Worthington Corporation Records, 1859–1960, 19 (uncatalogued).

37. *Novedades*, May 15, 1951, AMRG, Worthington Clippings Volume.

38. In a private letter to Alemán, Gómez thanked the president for Nacional Financiera's purchase of 1 million pesos worth of preferential stock in exchange for 3 million pesos of common stock "in our possession": Marte R. Gómez to Miguel Alemán, January 13, 1950, AMRG, 1950 H-M.

39. For evidence that Gómez sought to keep competitors out see Niblo, *Mexico in the 1940s*, 190.

40. Cotter also notes that Gómez became the *prestanombre*, or name lender, for Worthington in Mexico to circumvent laws requiring 51 percent Mexican ownership of companies: Cotter, *Troubled Harvest*, 242.

41. *Novedades*, May 15, 1951, AMRG, Worthington Clippings Volume.

42. *Novedades*, May 16, 1951, AMRG, Worthington Clippings Volume.

43. *The News*, May 16, 1951, AMRG, Worthington Clippings Volume.

44. *Jornadas Nacionales*, n.d., AMRG, Worthington Clippings Volume.

45. *Zócalo*, October 9, 1950, AMRG, Worthington Clippings Volume. This accusation arose in the context of Gómez being a suspected "Henriquista," or a supporter of Miguel Henríquez Guzmán, a Cardenista who would break with the PRI to run an independent campaign against it in 1952.

46. Specifically, Gómez wrote to Alemán that he was seriously worried about the attitude various foreign factories, especially Fairbanks Morse, took by offering up to 15 million pesos in credit to a number of Mexican agricultural credit banks to purchase just the kind of pumps from abroad that he planned to manufacture. He appealed to Alemán, as well as to the

government ministries and banks in question, not to accept such offers until he could make Worthington's case—namely, that it would help spur Mexican industrialization and be able to manufacture the same goods at better prices: Gómez to Alemán, January 13, 1950, June 3, 1950.

47. *El Porvenir—El Periodico de la Frontera*, April 8, 1954, AMRG, Worthington Clippings Volume.

48. *El hombre tras el ideal*, Mexico City, August 21, 1955, AMRG, Worthington Clippings Volume.

49. "Notable aumento hubo en la producción industrial," *La Prensa*, January 28, 1955, AMRG, Worthington Clippings Volume.

50. "México vende maquinaria a varios paises del sur," *El Universal*, July 25, 1956, AMRG, Worthington Clippings Volume.

51. *El hombre tras el ideal*, Mexico City, August 21, 1955, AMRG, Worthington Clippings Volume.

52. López Zamora, *El agua, la tierra*, 179.

53. Instituto de Investigaciones Jurídicas, Universidad Nacional Autónoma de México, http://info4.juridicas.unam.mx/ijure/fed/9/28.htm?s=.

54. See http://www.100constitucion.unam.mx/constitucion-online, 15.

55. Carvajal Ramírez, "Aspectos legales del agua subterránea en México," 253–55. For the longer historical background to the evolution of medieval Spanish and colonial Mexican groundwater law that independent Mexico inherited in the nineteenth century, see Meyer, "The Living Legacy of Hispanic Groundwater Law in the Contemporary Southwest." He comments on this inheritance at the time of the Mexican American War: "The distinct ownership pattern between surface and subsurface water can be explained on several grounds. At the time Spanish water law evolved, the science of hydrology was still in its infancy and knowledge of aquifers was quite rudimentary. This law took little or no cognizance of the percolation process by which underground water could pass from one property to another nor did it distinguish between confined (artesian) and unconfined aquifers. The source of underground water was unknown and the supply certainly seemed limitless. Moreover, there was no appreciation of the fact that aquifers could be hydraulically connected to form a groundwater basin and that depleting an underground reserve on a given piece of property could have a direct impact on the supply of a non-adjacent neighbor or even on the flow of a perennial stream. In any event the technology for the pumping of groundwater was so primitive that depletion of the aquifer was never an issue to be addressed" (295–96).

56. Carvajal Ramírez, "Aspectos legales del agua subterránea en México," 253–55. Article 969 of the Civil Codes of the Federal District and Baja California of 1884 states, "If one drills a well on his property, and although the water diminishes on another's property as a result, he is not obliged to compensate." The Mining Code of 1884 similarly states, "The following are the exclusive property of the owner of the soil, who can exploit and use them without special notification or adjudication: the salts which exist aboveground, the pure and salty waters, superficial or subterranean, the oil and the gaseous springs or the thermal and medicinal waters." See Lanz Cárdenas, *Legislación de aguas en México*, 345, 351–52.

57. Carvajal Ramírez, "Aspectos legales del agua subterránea en México," 253–55.

58. From 1948 to 2007, the SRH and its successor agencies imposed a total of 148 vedas: Comisión Nacional del Agua, *Atlas del agua en México,* 8.

59. Irrititla, *400 años de historia del Río Nazas, 1594–1994,* 53.

60. According to the Palmer Drought Severity Index, the 1950s drought was more severe than the 1940 drought, considered the worst until the recent one, insofar as multiyear duration is concerned. See http://webmap.ornl.gov/wcsdown/dataset.jsp?ds_id =10019.

61. Paul G. Minneman, Counselor for Agricultural Affairs, to Ambassador, "Drought a Serious Blow to Mexico's Agriculture in 1953," September 4, 1953, NARA, 812.23/9–453 XR 812.49. Braceros were not in fact illegal; they were legalized guest workers from 1942 to 1966. Many more laborers, however, were undocumented.

62. Gruson, "Exodus Starts in Mexican Region as Drought Threatens Famine," *New York Times,* January 28, 1952.

63. Gruson, "Exodus Starts in Mexican Region as Drought Threatens Famine."

64. Lemos and Oliveira, "Can Water Reform Survive Politics? Institutional Change and River Basin Management in Ceará, Northeast Brazil." For the longer historical genesis of these policies, see also Buckley, "Drought and Development," PhD diss., University of Pennsylvania, 2006.

65. For an example of how persistent repression and unfulfilled promises toward poor and hungry campesinos became the casus belli of the Jaramillo insurgency in Morelos, named after a Zapatista veteran who led it from the 1940s to the 1960s, see Padilla, *Rural Resistance in the Land of Zapata.* The PRI's short-term public works in the Laguna placed a floor on hunger and poverty that may successfully have preempted a Jaramillista-style insurgency.

66. Mottier, "Ejidal Credit and Debt in 20th Century Mexico," PhD diss., University of Chicago, 2013, 165, 185.

67. Rello notes that, thanks to its power of the purse, the bank was more powerful than the Confederación Nacional de Campesinos (National Confederation of Peasants; CNC), which was the official political representative of ejidos and somewhat more responsive to their concerns. The CNC was nevertheless consistently marginalized due to the scant influence it had on the bank's operations: Rello, *State and Peasantry in Mexico.*

68. "Un proyecto de granjas lecheras en esta región: Crédito de 4 millones de dólares para establecerlas," *El Siglo de Torreón,* September 1, 1949.

69. Rivas Sada, "Cambio tecnológico, dinámica regional y reconversión productiva en el norte de México," 347, 350.

70. "Adquisición de 240 vacas lecheras: Fin al monocultivo del algodón en Región Lagunera de Durango," *El Siglo de Torreón,* December 8, 1955. It is not clear whether these dairy cattle perished along with tens of thousands of others the following year. Given that the dairy industry grew exponentially, it is likely that they survived and constituted the core of a new generation of cattle. Today it is estimated that two thousand gallons of water are required to produce one gallon of milk from dairy cows: Fred Pierce, "Earth: The Parched Planet," *New Scientist,* February 25, 2006. http://www.newscientist.com/article /mg18925401.500. In 1919, two agricultural extension agents in Iowa concluded in a study of several dairy cows that they needed a total of 550 pounds of freshwater to produce 100 pounds of milk during the summer months: A. C. McLandish and W. G. Gaessler, "Water

Requirements for Milk Production," *Journal of Dairy Science*, vol. 2, no. 1, January 4–8, 1919, http://www.journalofdairyscience.org. In 1959, dairy cows in the United States required 151 liters a day each just for drinking: "Requieren agua abundante las vacas lecheras," *El Siglo de Torreón*, July 26, 1959.

71. Kelly, *Notes on the Culture of the Laguna Zone*, 10–11. According to a survey carried out by Raúl Salinas forty years later in 1994, Laguna ejidatarios had scarcely changed their attitudes toward water and environmental management. For more discussion of this continuity, see the epilogue in this volume.

72. Kelly, *Notes on the Culture of the Laguna Zone*, 12.

73. Carson, *Silent Spring*, 8.

74. In the 1930s, *El Siglo de Torreón* reported glowingly on new machines for spraying fungicides and pesticides, though it did not appear they were in widespread use yet, especially after the reparto of 1936. See, e.g., "Cómo combatir las plagas en la Comarca Lagunera," *El Siglo de Torreón,* July 18, 1937, touting the "Shunk" spray apparatus of the Allis Chalmers Agency.

75. This is the physician and environmentalist Dr. Luis Maeda's figure, as transcribed at an oral history roundtable in Torreón held in 1990: see Castro, Fernández, Vázquez, and Jaime, "La crisis de los 50 y 60," 44. Two sources do not specify tonnage but corroborate the percentages: Albert, "Persistent Pesticides in Mexico," 6; North American Commission on Environmental Cooperation, "History of DDT in North America to 1997," http://www3.cec .org/islandora/en/item/1620-history-ddt-in-north-america-1997-and-1996-presentation -mexican-ministry-en.pdf. For an overview of the historical relationship between chemical warfare and pesticides focused primarily on the United States, see Russell, *War and Nature*.

76. Albert, "Persistent Pesticides in Mexico," 4–6.

77. Cotter, *Troubled Harvest*, 1.

78. There are numerous studies of the Green Revolution in Mexico, among them Cotter, *Troubled Harvest;* Hewitt de Alcántara, *Modernizing Mexican Agriculture;* Lewontin, "The Green Revolution and the Politics of Agricultural Development," PhD diss., University of Chicago, 1983; Wright, *The Death of Ramón González*. See also Olsson, *Agrarian Crossings*, for a recent revisionist account of the Green Revolution's origins in Mexico and its relationship to the New Deal in the U.S. South.

79. Browning, "Corn, Tomatoes, and a Dead Dog."

80. "Diario Oficial: Ley de Educación Agrícola," March 26, 1946, Rockefeller Foundation Archive (RFC), Mexico Agriculture collection, record group 1.1, series 323, box 35, folder 395, and "Report on the Fellowships of the Industrial Bank of Mexico, S.A." October 19, 1946, RFC, Mexico Agriculture collection, record group 1.1, series 323, box 35, folder 1; italics added.

81. RFC, Mexican-United States Agricultural Commission, 1944–1946, record group 6.13, series 1.1, box 35, folder 395. The Patronato para la Investigación, Fomento y Defensa Agrícola de la Comarca Lagunera (Board for Agricultural Research, Promotion, and Defense in the Laguna) also wrote to the foundation on May 20, 1952, to request technical collaboration with Paul C. Duffield to resolve "the complicated problems which challenge our agriculture": RFC, Mexican-United States Agricultural Commission, 1952–1956, record group 5.13, series 1.1, box 49, folder 557.

82. "Los experimentos con DDT en contra de las plagas del algodonero," *El Siglo de Torreón*, July 10, 1946, 8.

83. "Prominentes asistentes," *El Siglo de Torreón*, September 15, 1956, 2. It is unclear whether the store was reopened or opened as a new store, given that one with the same name had already existed since at least the mid-1940s. Indeed, in 1953 it was reported that "la empresa de Equipos Mecánicos, S.A." accepted a loan guarantee from the Ejido Bank to drill and equip twenty-five wells on request of ejidos in Durango at a cost of 150,000 pesos per equipped unit with Worthington pumps: "Agradecen ejidatarios atención del gobierno," *El Siglo de Torreón*, March 15, 1953.

84. "Equipos Mécanicos de La Laguna para servicio del agricultor," *El Siglo de Torreón*, September 15, 1956, 2. The article described the store building's architecture as "beautiful" and "elegant," of which Torreón "can feel proud" to have the "best building" of its type in the country.

CHAPTER 6. REHABILITATING EL AGUA

Epigraph: Reynolds, quoted in Ashworth, *Ogallala Blue*, 11.

1. López Zamora, *El agua, la tierra*, 168–69.

2. For instance, in the late 1940s and 1950s engineers estimated that Mexico's aquifers contained between 185,000 and 350,000 cubic megameters of water, the total varying according to the method and instruments they employed: Moreno Vázquez, *Por abajo del agua*, 55. It took until the 1980s before engineers could make far more precise estimates using superior technology.

3. Telegram, anonymous, January 20, 1959, María López to López Mateos, February 12, 1959, telegram, anonymous, October 15, 1959, Unión Democrática de Mujeres Mexicanas de la Laguna to López Mateos, December 27, 1959, all in Archivo General de la Nación (AGN), Ramos Presidenciales (RP), López Mateos (LM), 565.4/7.

4. López Zamora, *El agua, la tierra*, 170.

5. Wilkie, *San Miguel*, 5. Given that drought years would continue to recur in the Laguna, the situation was perhaps not quite as sanguine as Raymond perceived when his book was published in 1971.

6. *Excélsior*, February 26, 1958.

7. Comisión Nacional del Agua, *Atlas del agua en México*, 80. For maps and tables for vedas from 1948 to 1963, see chap. 5 in this volume.

8. Eckstein, *El ejido colectivo en México*, 149.

9. "Se previenen infracciones a la veda," *El Siglo de Torreón*, May 16, 1951; "Deben respetar la zona de veda, piden agricultores," *El Siglo de Torreón*, July 27, 1957.

10. "Los Amigos del Suelo contestan a Robles S.," *El Siglo de Torreón*, January 17, 1957.

11. "Daño por veda en Ceballos: Los agricultores no creen que se justifique esa drástica medida," *El Siglo de Torreón*, January 16, 1953; "Pide la 40–55 que no amplíen la veda para norias," *El Siglo de Torreón*, June 18, 1955.

12. Untitled newspaper article, January 29, 1965, Archivo Marte R. Gómez (AMRG), Worthington Clippings Volume.

13. Hool to U.S. Ambassador in Mexico, "Market for New Organic Pest Control Products-Mexico," May 19, 1950, U.S. National Archives and Records Administration (NARA), 812.22/5–1950.

14. Minneman to U.S. Ambassador in Mexico, "Mexican-U.S. Technicians Meet re: Cotton Pink Bollworm Control," August 4, 1953, NARA, 812.22/8–353. Minneman attached to his memo "ten resolutions approved at the closing session of the Mexican-American Convention on the Pink Bollworm," which included expanding the campaign among more stakeholders, launching educational campaigns, expanding inspections, and exchanging studies and findings in both countries more frequently.

15. Hernández, "¿El rosado ha adquirido resistencia al DDT?" *El Siglo de Torreón*, December 10, 1959, 4.

16. "Conclusiones sobre las pruebas de insecticidas contra gusano rosado," *El Siglo de Torreón*, November 5, 1961, 5.

17. "Salud es Vida," *El Siglo de Torreón*, April 4, 1960.

18. Wright, *The Death of Ramón González*.

19. "El control biológico de las plagas de algodón no produce buenos resultados," *El Siglo de Torreón*, May 31, 1964.

20. *El Excélsior*, February 5–7, 1963.

21. Minneman to Chargé d'Affaires ad interim via Foreign Service Despatch, American Embassy in Mexico, "Mexico's Agricultural Policy and Programs," November 30, 1954 (rev. May 17, 1955), NARA, 812.20/11–3054, 22.

22. Minneman to Chargé d'Affaires ad interim via Foreign Service Despatch, 9.

23. Isabel Tuesdell Kelly, *Notes on the Culture of the Laguna Zone*, 8. In 1963, the Laguna had a population of 608,000, or 2.5 times higher than in 1936. The regional population boom reflected national trends from the 1940s, as a decline in infant mortality, greater access to medical care, and a pro-natalist government policy raised the rate of annual population growth to 3.2 percent: see Cabrera, "Demographic Dynamics and Development," 20.

24. Minneman to Chargé d'Affaires ad interim via Foreign Service Despatch, 16. Not all ejidatarios and libres felt the same way throughout the Laguna, for as we saw in chap. 5, in the early 1950s ten thousand of them agreed to be settled in the Cuatro Ciénegas area a little farther north of the Laguna to escape hunger and drought. The proximity of Cuatro Ciénegas was likely more appealing than moving to the distant and culturally distinct southeast.

25. *Excélsior*, February 5–7, 1963.

26. Unsigned letter to López Mateos, January 7, 1960, AGN, RP, LM, 565.4/7. They were evidently unaware or ignored reports that pests were building immunity to chemical pesticides, although the alleged poor quality of those pesticides certainly could have further reduced their effectiveness. In the late 1920s and 1930s, a major issue in the heated debate over the wisdom of building a major storage dam on the Nazas was its potential impact on the natural fertilizing function of the river. The engineer José Bonilla of the CNI questioned whether the Nazas even delivered such nutrients to Laguna lands. He was later thoroughly refuted by the agronomist Rafael B. Narro, whose warnings were prescient. He wrote, "The [fertilizing] mud of the Nazas is irreplaceable . . . The possibility of obtaining the natural conditions of soil fertility through artificial chemical procedures is very improbable": "El proceso de desintegración de la arena de los limos del Río Nazas, estudiado en su forma y en el tiempo," November 1931, Archivo Histórico del Agua (AHA), Consultivo Técnico (CT), box 136, file 1121, 25.

27. Asociación Algodonera de la Laguna to López Mateos, December 31, 1960, AGN, RP, LM, 565.4/7.

28. Cámara Agrícola y Ganadera de Torreón et al. to López Mateos, October 29, 1962, AGN, RP, LM, 565.4/7. A dairy industry was already well established and growing by this time, so it is unclear whether the association was feigning ignorance of this or wishing to be included in the industry.

29. "'Marcha de Hambre' de campesinos laguneros: Pedirán la intervención de ALM para salvar del caos a la zona," *Excélsior*, May 22, 1963. The political scientist Judith Adler Hellman also noted in her detailed studies of peasant politics in the region that the Communist-affiliated Central Union leadership "possessed the organizational capabilities to mount regular mass demonstrations in Torreón, send a steady stream of delegates to Mexico City, and, every so often, to carry off a full-scale hunger march to the capital involving the transportation and housing of hundreds of peasant men, women, and children accompanied by representatives of numerous solidary organizations": Hellman, "The Role of Ideology in Peasant Politics," 17.

30. Editorial, *El Universal*, February 28, 1963.

31. CNC to López Mateos, May 11, 1962, AGN, RP, LM, 565.4/7. Soon after, the Confederación Revolucionaria de Obreros y Campesinos de la Región Lagunera (Revolutionary Confederation of Workers and Campesinos of the Laguna Region; CROC) requested that the government employ ejidos to reforest desert areas of the Laguna with the goal "to make the region the richest in the country": CROC to López Mateos, October 22, 1962, AGN, RP, LM, 565.4/7. As Miguel Ángel de Quevedo argued—according to what was then the prevalent (and only partially correct) desiccation theory, which informed the 1946 law on soil and water conservation—deforestation adversely affected agricultural performance by reducing water supplies and eroding soil. Yet reengineering of the irrigation network that técnicos simultaneously advocated would do far more harm to regional hydrology than any kind of reforestation could offset.

32. For a comprehensive examination of the Laguna's energy regime as it related to water management, and groundwater pumping in particular, see Rivas Sada, "Cambio tecnológico, dinámica regional y reconversión productiva en el norte de México."

33. For a positive view of these arguments, see Irrititla, "*400 años de historia del Río Nazas, 1594–1994*," 56.

34. Coria to Chief Engineer of Irrigation and River Control, September 28, 1954, AHA, Aprovechamientos Superficiales (AS), box 136, file 1121, 503.

35. Unsigned letter to López, Mateos, March 16, 1963, AGN, RP, LM 565.4/7. Although the regularized river made it more difficult to use aniego, according to SRH engineers in the late 1970s, the river was still able to partially recharge the aquifer through its reservoir-released flows until 1960 or so.

36. For numerous examples, see AHA, AS, box 136, file 1121, 1–345.

37. Amaya Brondo, "Plan de rehabilitación del Distrito de Riego Núm. 17 Comarca Lagunera, Coahuila y Durango," 68.

38. Amaya Brondo, "Plan de rehabilitación del Distrito de Riego Núm. 17 Comarca Lagunera, Coahuila y Durango," 64.

39. Hellman states that the plan "represented the state's response to the struggles initiated and led by the [non-PRI] Central Union in the 1950s and 1960s": Hellman "The Role of Ideology in Peasant Politics," 24–25.

40. López Zamora, *El agua, la tierra*, 180–81.

41. López Zamora, *El agua, la tierra*, 181.

42. López Zamora, *El agua, la tierra*, 183–84.

43. "Informe de la visita a la Comarca Lagunera efectuada durante los días 18 al 23 de enero de 1969," n.d., AHA, AS, box 136, file 1121, 601–2.

44. López Zamora, *El agua, la tierra*, 186–87. His claims seem to fly in the face of the earlier analyses by Mexican and U.S. observers in the 1950s that Laguna ejidos lacked basic machinery and thus were far more backward than ejidos in other areas and, especially, U.S. farmers. Although Laguna ejidos may well have increased their efficiency and productivity over the decades even without much machinery, they still lagged far behind others in the 1960s.

45. "Mexican Overtures for a 100 Million Dollar Credit for Irrigation Purposes," February 3, 1950, NARA, 812.211/2–350.

46. Rivas Sada, "Cambio tecnológico, dinámica regional y reconversión productiva en el norte de México," 350.

47. Hellman, "The Role of Ideology in Peasant Politics," 22.

48. "La rehabilitación de la Laguna," *El Sol de México*, March 15, 1968.

49. "Nota informativa de las condiciones geohidrológicas de la Comarca Lagunera, Coah.-Dgo.," August 31, 1978, AHA, CT, box 24, file 1081, 3.

50. "Nota informativa de las condiciones geohidrológicas de la Comarca Lagunera, Coah.-Dgo.," August 25, 1978, 7.

51. "Nota informativa de las condiciones geohidrológicas de la Comarca Lagunera, Coah.-Dgo.," August 25, 1978, 7.

52. Albert, "Organochlorine Pesticide Residues in Human Milk Samples from Comarca Lagunera, Mexico, 1976," 135–38.

53. "Nota informativa de las condiciones geohidrológicas de la Comarca Lagunera, Coah.-Dgo.," August 25, 1978, 8.

54. Mendoza to SRH, June 4, 1968, AHA, AS, box 464, file 7864, 459.

55. According to Marte R. Gómez's autobiography, the socialist López Zamora also, like him, "became a capitalist, selling motors and drilling machines": quoted in Joseph Cotter, *Troubled Harvest,* 242. Though not an implausible claim, it needs independent confirmation especially because Gómez and López Zamora were rival agronomists.

56. For investigation of similar kinds of water projects in the United States, see Glennon, *Water Follies.*

57. Cerutti and Rivas, "El Grupo Industrial LALA," 249.

58. Interview with Enrique Vázquez Ávila, Laguna landowner, April 25, 2006.

59. López Zamora, *El agua, la tierra*, 170.

60. García and Sanz, *Deterioro ambiental y pobreza en la abundancia productiva.*

EPILOGUE

Epigraph: "Hoy el agua nos grita y nos exige una modalidad de gestión completamente inédita. El agua, como máxima representante de la naturaleza, nos domestica y nos civiliza": Víctor M. Toledo, "Mexican@s, al grito del agua," March 31, 2015, http://www.jornada.unam.mx/2015/03/31/opinion/016a2pol.

1. "El agua es un asunto de seguridad nacional: Presidente Vicente Fox," March 22, 2004, http://fox.presidencia.gob.mx/actividades/comunicados/?contenido=7773; "Cuidar el agua es asunto de seguridad nacional: Calderón," March 25, 2008, http://www.adnradio.cl /noticias/cuidar-el-agua-es-asunto-de-seguridad-nacional-calderon/20080325/nota/567313 .aspx; "Cuidar el agua es asunto de seguridad nacional: Peña Nieto," March 23, 2013, http:// www.oem.com.mx/eloccidental/notas/n2924035.htm.

2. Comisión Nacional del Agua, "Programa Nacional Hídrico," 23–30, http://www .conagua.gob.mx/Contenido.aspx?n1=1&n2=28&n3=28. By comparison, Saudi Arabia's per capital water availability is as low as 85 cubic meters, and Canada's is as high as 84,483 cubic meters. There were no reliable measurements of total groundwater supply in Mexico before 1950.

3. Moreno Vázquez has termed the phenomenon "agricultural mining" or "conquest" in the closely analogous case of Sonora: Moreno Vázquez, *Por abajo del agua*, 22.

4. On its surface, the case may bear resemblance to the ecologist Garrett Hardin's influential 1968 thesis of the "tragedy of the commons," although it is in fact its opposite. According to the 1945 revision of Article 27 of the 1917 Constitution, groundwater was regarded as a common resource only when individual taking of it adversely affected a third party, at which point the government was empowered to regulate the resource to ensure equal access for all. The Water Law of 1972 explicitly nationalized groundwater, but the government never properly regulated it in a water-intensive, agroindustrial economy that incentivized maximal use of the resource and disincentivized conservation. For discussion of the similar inapplicability of Hardin's thesis to Mexican forestry, see Boyer, *Political Landscapes*, 246–47.

5. For how this "optimism" extended as far back as Humboldt (circa 1800), see Luis Aboites, "Notas sobre el optimismo mexicano y los vínculos entre geografía, ingeniería hidráulica y política (1926–1976)." As William Summerhill explains, infrastructure that "facilitates the production and exchange of private goods occupies a strategic position in the capital stock of modern economies." Various factors, however, complicate this position—in particular "political factors," which "reigned supreme in the processes of infrastructure concession, subsidy, and regulation": Summerhill, "The Development of Infrastructure," 294.

6. For examples, see, among many others, Hecht, ed., *Entangled Geographies;* Josephson, *Resources under Regime;* Mitchell, *Rule of Experts;* Scott, *Seeing Like a State.*

7. Salinas de Gortari, *México*, 673–74, 676.

8. Among the principal complaints of ejidatarios was the inability to rent or sell their land legally and thereby acquire clear and recognized titles to their parcels, along with greater autonomy from the stifling bureaucracy that managed ejido affairs. For a wide-ranging discussion of these matters and of the complexity of the revision of Article 27 that enabled ejidatarios to legally sell and lease their individual parcels but only after obtaining a majority vote to do so in ejido assemblies, see Randall, ed., *Reforming Mexico's Agrarian Reform.* Some historians of Mexico oversimplify the revision, incorrectly claiming that it "dismantled" the ejido by mandating its privatization.

9. For an incisive discussion of the post-Cardenista transformation of GDP accounting under U.S. pressure, see Niblo, *Mexico in the 1940s*, 15–29.

10. Salinas de Gortari, *México*, 676.

11. Salinas de Gortari, *México*, 402. In 2010, the CNA counted a total of 4,462 dams in Mexico, of which it defined 667 as "large," impounding 153 billion cubic meters of water: Comisión Nacional del Agua, *Estadísticas del agua en México*, 78. In 1910, when the Mexican Revolution began, Mexico had less than one billion cubic meters of reservoir capacity and negligible groundwater extraction: Aboites, *La decadencia del agua de la nación*, 25.

12. Salinas de Gortari, *México*, 698, 710. Although Salinas boasted of having completed thirty-two dams that increased national reservoir capacity by 10 percent during his presidency, he nevertheless proudly singled out one as proof of his environmentalism: the cancellation of a large hydroelectric dam on the southern Usumacinta River that saved Mayan archaeological sites and large areas of rainforest: Salinas de Gortari, *México*, 397, 402. He did not explain the discrepancy between supporting thirty-two dams and canceling just one. Perhaps the Usumacinta project had a higher profile because it would disproportionately affect the State of Chiapas, where the neo-Zapatista rebellion of 1994 became a huge thorn in the side of his neoliberal modernization project. Among many grievances, the neo-Zapatistas protested that the majority, and disproportionately indigenous, poor of Chiapas had not reaped the benefits of massive federal hydroelectric projects completed there from the 1960s to the 1980s: Simon, *Endangered Mexico*, chap. 4.

13. See the introduction in this book for further discussion of this concept of conservation. Luis Aboites usefully terms the neoliberal turn in the 1980s and 1990s led by Salinas with respect to water policy *el agua mercantil-ambiental* (mercantilist-environmental water), or the simultaneous (re)commodification and decentralized management of water resources as an explicitly environmental policy in Mexico: Aboites, *La decadencia del agua de la nación*.

14. Simonian, *Defending the Land of the Jaguar*, chap. 6. Mexican conservationists contributed much to the international environmental movement of course.

15. See http://www.semarnat.gob.mx/conocenos/antecedentes.

16. The SEMARNAT budget in 2008 was nearly 40 billion pesos, of which nearly 30 billion pesos were allocated to the CNA: http://www.apartados.hacienda.gob.mx/presupuesto/temas/pef/2008/temas/tomos/16/r16_apurog.pdf.

17. Salinas de Gortari and Solís González, *Rural Reform in Mexico*, 41.

18. Salinas de Gortari and Solís González, *Rural Reform in Mexico*, 12.

19. Salinas de Gortari and Solís González, *Rural Reform in Mexico*, 41. This attitude was virtually identical to what the anthropologist Isabel Kelly observed in 1953 among Laguna ejidatarios, as noted in chap. 5.

20. Castro Bernal et al., "La crisis de los 50 y 60," 45.

21. The Secretaría de Agricultura y Fomento (Ministry of Agriculture and Development; SAF) did, however, invoke Article 27 in the 1920s to demand that timber companies file environmental impact studies of the land they planned to log, although few did so: Boyer, *Political Landscapes*, 79.

22. For detailed discussion of the Aguanaval damming controversy, see Cháirez Araiza and Palerm Viqueira, "Importancia del Río Aguanaval en la recarga al acuífero principal de la región lagunera de Coahuila y Durango"; Romero Navarrete, "Gestión hidráulica y concertación social."

23. See http://fox.presidencia.gob.mx/gabinete/?contenido=15031.

24. "Plan Nacional Hídrico," http://www.cna.gob.mx.

25. "Captura regulatoria trágica, Comisión Nacional del Agua," http://www.gabrielquadri .blogspot.com/2011_10_01_archive.html. It should be noted that the author of this blog, the Mexican civil engineer and environmentalist critic Gabriel Quadri, is a partisan source, having run for president as a third-party candidate. Regulatory capture in Mexico, of course, is not unique. Virtually every government in the world experiences some degree of regulatory capture.

26. "Empeora clima en la region," http://www.elsiglodetorreon.com.mx/noticia/680861 .empeora-clima-en-la-region.html.

ARCHIVES
American Historical Museum Archive
    Worthington Corporation Records, 1859–1960
Archivo Agustín Espinoza de la Universidad Iberoamericana (AAE)
    Fondo Arocena (FA)
    Fondo Juan Brittingham (FJB)
    Fondo Vargas-Lobsinger (FVL)
Archivo Calles-Torreblanca (ACT)
Archivo Económico, Biblioteca Lerdo de Tejada
    Fondo "Laguna"
Archivo General de la Nación (AGN)
    Ramos Presidenciales (RP)
        Lázaro Cárdenas (LC)
        Manuel Ávila Camacho (AC)
        Miguel Alemán Valdés (MAV)
        Adolfo López Mateos (LM)
Archivo Histórico del Agua (AHA)
    Aguas Nacionales (AN)
    Aprovechamientos Superficiales (AS)
    Consultivo Técnico (CT)
Archivo Marte R. Gómez (AMRG)
    Worthington Clippings Volume
Archivo Municipal de Torreón (AMT)
    Fondo Tlahualilo (FT)
Rockefeller Foundation Archive (RFC)
U.S. National Archives and Records Administration (NARA)

NEWSPAPERS AND JOURNALS
Boletín de la Cámara Agrícola Nacional de la Comarca Lagunera
Diario Oficial de la Federación

Excélsior
Ingeniería Hidráulica
Irrigación en México
El Nacional
New York Times
Novedades
La Opinión de Torreón
El Porvenir—El Diario de la Frontera
Revista de Ingeniería y Arquitectura
El Siglo de Torreón
El Sol de México
Spokane Daily Chronicle
El Universal

PUBLISHED PRIMARY AND SECONDARY SOURCES

Abell, Robin A. *Freshwater Ecoregions of North America: A Conservation Assessment.* Washington, DC: Island, 1999.

Aboites, Luis. *El agua de la nación: Una historia política de México (1888–1946).* Mexico City: Centro de Investigaciones y Estudios Superiores en Antropología Social, 1998.

———. *La decadencia del agua de la nación: Estudio sobre desigualdad social y cambio político en México (segunda mitad del siglo XX).* Mexico City: El Colegio de México, 2009.

———. *Demografía histórica y conflictos por el agua: Dos estudios sobre 40 kilómetros de historia del río San Pedro, Chihuahua.* Mexico City: Centro de Investigaciones y Estudios Superiores en Antropología Social, 2000.

———, ed. *Fuentes para la historia de los usos del agua en México (1710–1951).* Hidalgo: Centro de Investigaciones y Estudios Superiores en Antropología Social y Comisión Nacional del Agua, 2000.

———. *La irrigación revolucionaria: Historia del Sistema Nacional de Riego del Río Conchos, Chihuahua, 1927–1938.* Mexico City: Secretaría de Educación Pública and Centro de Investigaciones y Estudios Superiores en Antropología Social, 1988.

———. "Notas sobre el optimismo mexicano y los vínculos entre geografía, ingeniería hidráulica y política (1926–1976)." In *XX Coloquio de Antropología e Historia Regionales: Agua, medio ambiente y desarrollo en México*, ed. Patricia Ávila García, 158–67. Zamora, Mich.: El Colegio de Michoacán, 1998.

———. *Pablo Bistráin, ingeniero mexicano.* Tlalpan, Mexico: Centro de Investigaciones y Estudios Superiores en Antropología Social and Instituto Mexicano de Tecnología del Agua, 1997.

Aboites, Luis, and Valeria Estrada Tena, eds. *Del agua municipal al agua nacional: Materiales para una historia de los municipios en México 1901–1945.* Mexico City: Centro de Investigaciones y Estudios Superiores en Antropología Social, Archivo Histórico del Agua, Comisión Nacional del Agua, and El Colegio de México, 2004.

Aguilar Camín, Héctor, and Lorenzo Meyer. *In the Shadow of the Mexican Revolution: Contemporary Mexican History, 1910–1989.* Austin: University of Texas Press, 1993.

Albert, Lilia A. "Organochlorine Pesticide Residues in Human Milk Samples from Comarca Lagunera, Mexico, 1976." *Pesticides Monitoring Journal* 15, no. 3 (1981): 135–38.

———. "Persistent Pesticides in Mexico." *Reviews of Environmental Contamination and Toxicology* 147 (1996): 1–44.

Amaya Brondo, Abelardo. "Plan de rehabilitación del Distrito de Riego Núm. 17 Comarca Lagunera, Coahuila y Durango." *Ingeniería Hidráulica en México* 24, no. 1 (1970): 59 82.

Arellano, A.R.V. "Memorial to Paul Waitz (1876–1961)." *Geological Society of America Bulletin* 74 (July 1963): 107–12.

Arreguín Mañón, José P. *Aportes a la historia de la geohidrología en México, 1890–1995.* Mexico City: Centro de Investigaciones y Estudios Superiores en Antropología Social and Asociación Geohidrológica Mexicana, 1998.

Ashby, Joe C. *Organized Labor and the Mexican Revolution under Lázaro Cárdenas.* Chapel Hill: University of North Carolina Press, 1967.

Ashworth, William. *Ogallala Blue: Water and Life on the High Plains.* Woodstock, VT: Countryman, 2007.

Ayala, Beatriz, Graciela Herrera, and Nuria Pons. *Ingenieros en la Independencia y la Revolución.* Mexico City: Universidad Naciona:l Autónoma de México, Instituto de Investigaciones Históricas, Sociedad de Exalumnos de la Facultad de Ingeniería, 1987.

Bantjes, Adrian A. *As If Jesus Walked on Earth: Cardenismo, Sonora, and the Mexican Revolution.* Lanham, MD: Scholarly Resources, 1998.

Barragán, Juan. *Juan F. Brittingham y la industria en México, 1859–1940.* Monterrey, Mexico: Urbis Internacional, 1993.

Bartlett, John Russell. *Personal Narrative of Explorations and Incidents in Texas, New Mexico, California, Sonora, and Chihuahua, Connected with the United States and Mexican Boundary Commission during the Years 1850, '51, '52, and '53.* Chicago: Rio Grande, 1965.

Beatty, Edward. *Technology and the Search for Progress in Modern Mexico.* Oakland: University of California Press, 2015.

Beatty, Edward, Yovanna Pineda, and Patricio Sáiz, "Technology in Latin America's Past and Present: New Evidence from the Patent Records." *Latin American Research Review* Vol. 52, no. 1 (March 2017).

Becker, Marjorie. *Setting the Virgin on Fire: Lázaro Cárdenas, Michoacán Peasants, and the Redemption of the Mexican Revolution.* Oakland: University of California Press, 1996.

Beckert, Sven. *Empire of Cotton: A Global History.* New York: Vintage, 2014.

Berdan, Frances F. "Cotton in Aztec Mexico: Production, Distribution and Uses." *Mexican Studies/Estudios Mexicanos* 3, no. 2 (1987): 235–62.

Blackbourn, David. *The Conquest of Nature: Water, Landscape and the Making of Modern Germany.* London: Jonathan Cape, 2006.

Boyer, Christopher R., ed. *A Land between Waters: Environmental Histories of Modern Mexico.* Tucson: University of Arizona Press, 2012.

———. *Becoming Campesinos: Politics, Identity, and Agrarian Struggle in Postrevolutionary Michoacán, 1920–1935.* Stanford, CA: Stanford University Press, 2003.

———. *Political Landscapes: Forests, Conservation, and Community in Mexico.* Durham, NC: Duke University Press, 2015.

———. "Revolución y paternalismo ecológico: Miguel Ángel de Quevedo y la política forestal en México, 1926–1940." *Historia Mexicana* 57, no. 1 (2007): 91–138.

Boyer, Christopher R., and Emily Wakild. "Social Landscaping in the Forests of Mexico: An Environmental Interpretation of Cardenismo, 1934–1940." *Hispanic American Historical Review* 92, no. 1 (2012): 73–106.

Brown, Harry Bates. *Cotton: History, Species, Varieties, Morphology, Breeding, Culture, Diseases, Marketing, and Uses.* New York: McGraw-Hill, 1927.

Brown, Harry Bates, and J. O. Ware. *Cotton*, 3d ed. New York: McGraw-Hill, 1958.

Browning, Anjali. "Corn, Tomatoes, and a Dead Dog: Mexican Agricultural Restructuring after NAFTA and Rural Responses to Declining Maize Production in Oaxaca, Mexico." *Mexican Studies/Estudios Mexicanos* 29, no. 1 (Winter 2013): 85–119.

Brunk, Samuel. *Emiliano Zapata: Revolution and Betrayal in Mexico.* Albuquerque: University of New Mexico Press, 1995.

———. *The Posthumous Career of Emiliano Zapata: Myth, Memory, and Mexico's Twentieth Century.* Austin: University of Texas Press, 2008.

Buchenau, Jürgen. *Plutarco Elías Calles and the Mexican Revolution.* Lanham, MD: Rowman and Littlefield, 2007.

Buckley, Eve E. "Drought and Development: Technocrats and the Politics of Modernization in Brazil's Semi-arid Northeast, 1877–1964." Ph.D. diss., University of Pennsylvania, Philadelphia, 2006.

Bulnes, Francisco. *La cuestión del Tlahualilo confidencial.* Mexico City: Ministro de Fomento, 1909.

Cabrera, Gustavo. "Demographic Dynamics and Development: The Role of Population Policy in Mexico." *Population and Development Review* 20 (1994): 105–20.

Calderón, Francisco R. *La Républica Restaurada: Vida económica.* Vol. 2 of Daniel Cosío Villegas, *La Historia Moderna de México.* Mexico City: Editorial Hermes, 1971.

Camacho Altamirano, Hortensia. *Empresarios e ingenieros en la ciudad de San Luis Potosí: La construcción de la presa de San José, 1869–1903.* San Luis Potosí, Mexico: Instituto de Cultura de San Luis Potosí, 2001.

Camprubí, Lino. *Engineers and the Making of the Francoist Regime.* Cambridge, MA: MIT Press, 2014.

Candiani, Vera. *Dreaming of Dry Land: Environmental Transformation in Colonial Mexico City.* Stanford, CA: Stanford University Press, 2014.

Contreras Cantú, Joaquín, and Eduardo Castellanos Hernández. *El registro público de la propiedad social en México.* Mexico City: Centro de Investigaciones y Estudios Superiores en Antropología Social, 2000.

Carey, Mark. "Commodities, Colonial Science, and Environmental Change in Latin American History." *Radical History Review* 107 (2010): 185–94.

———. *In the Shadow of Melting Glaciers: Climate Change and Andean Society.* New York: Oxford University Press, 2010.

Carr, Barry. *Marxism and Communism in Twentieth-Century Mexico.* Lincoln: University of Nebraska Press, 1992.

————. "The Mexican Communist Party and Agrarian Mobilization in the Laguna, 1920–1940: A Worker-Peasant Alliance?" *Hispanic American Historical Review* 67, no. 3 (1987): 371–404.

Carson, Rachel. *Silent Spring*, 40th anniversary ed. Boston: Houghton Mifflin, 2002.

Carvajal Ramírez, René. "Aspectos legales del agua subterránea en México." *Ingeniería Hidráulica en México* 23, no. 3 (1967): 249–58.

Castañeda González, Rocío. *Irrigación y reforma agraria: Las comunidades de riego del valle de Santa Rosalía, Chihuahua, 1920–1950.* Mexico City: Comisión Nacional del Agua and Centro de Investigaciones y Estudios Superiores en Antropología Social, 1995.

Castañón Cuadros, Carlos. "Una perspectiva hidráulica de la historia regional: Economía y revolución en el agua de La Laguna." *Buenaval*, no. 3 (Winter 2006): 7–30.

Castro Bernal, Francisco, Braulio Fernández Aguirre, Enrique Vázquez Ávila, and Francisco Jaime Acosta. "La Crisis de los 50 y 60." *El Puente* (July-August 1990): 37–44.

Cerutti, Mario, and Eva Rivas Sada. "El Grupo Industrial LALA: Orígenes, transformación y expansión (1950–2005)." In *De la colonia a la globalización: Empresarios cántabros en México,* ed. Mario Cerutti and Rafael Domínguez Martín, 231–60. Santander, Mexico: Servicio de Publicaciones de la Universidad de Cantabria, 2006.

Cháirez Araiza, Carlos. "El impacto de la regulación de los ríos en la recarga a los acuíferos: El caso del acuífero principal de la Comarca de la Laguna." Ph.D. diss., Colegio de Postgraduados en Ciencias Agrícolas, Montecillo, Texcoco, Estado de México, 2005.

Cháirez Araiza, Carlos, and Jacinta Palerm Viqueira. "Importancia del Río Aguanaval en la recarga al acuífero principal de la región lagunera de Coahuila y Durango." *Boletín Archivo Histórico del Agua* 10, no. 29 (2005): 5–20.

Chávez, Eduardo. *Ingeniería y humanismo.* Villahermosa, Mexico: Gobierno del Estado de Tabasco, 1988.

Churruca Peláez, Agustín, Glenn P. Willeford, and Ellen A. Kelley. *Before the Thundering Hordes: Historia Antigua de Parras.* Alpine, TX: Center for Big Bend Studies, Sul Ross State University, 2000.

Clark Graham, W. A. *Cotton Goods in Latin America, Part I: Cuba, Mexico, and Central America.* Washington, DC: U.S. Government Printing Office, 1909.

Coatsworth, John H. *Growth against Development: The Economic Impact of Railroads in Porfirian Mexico.* DeKalb: Northern Illinois University Press, 1981.

Comisión Nacional del Agua. *Atlas del agua en México.* Mexico City: Secretaría de Medio Ambiente y Recursos Naturales, 2009.

————. *Estadísticas del agua en México.* Mexico City: Secretaría de Medio Ambiente y Recursos Naturales, 2010.

Comisión Nacional de Irrigación. *La obra de la Comisión Nacional de Irrigación.* Mexico City: Comisión Nacional de Irrigación, 1940.

Contreras Cantú, Joaquín, and Eduardo de Jesús Castellanos Hernández. *El registro público de la propiedad social en México.* Mexico City: Registro Agrario Nacional, Centro de Investigaciones y Estudios Superiores en Antropología Social, and Consejo Nacional de Ciencia y Tecnología, Secretaría de Educación Pública, 2000.

Córdova, Arnaldo. *La ideología de la Revolución Mexicana: La formación del nuevo régimen* (1973), 1st edition. Mexico City: Ediciones Era, 2006.

Corona Páez, Sergio Antonio. *El país de La Laguna: Impacto hispano-tlaxcalteca en la forja de la Comarca Lagunera*. Torreón, Mexico: Universidad Iberoamericana, 2011.

———. "Producción de algodón en la Comarca Lagunera a fines de la era virreinal y primera mitad del siglo XIX." *Estudios Trasandinos* 13 (2006): 55–85.

———. "El Valle de Parras en el siglo XX. Génesis y apogeo de su industria vitivinícola." In *Coahuila (1910–2010): Economía, historia económica y empresa*, vol. 2, ed. Mario Cerutti and Javier Villarreal Lozano. Saltillo, Mexico: Gobierno del Estado de Coahuila y la Universidad Autónoma de Coahuila, 2012.

Coronil, Fernando. "Smelling like a Market." *American Historical Review* 106, no. 1 (2001): 119–29.

Cosío Villegas, Daniel, "La crisis de México." *Cuadernos Americanos* 32 (March–April 1947): 29–51.

Cotter, Joseph. *Troubled Harvest: Agronomy and Revolution in Mexico, 1880–2002*. Westport, CT: Praeger, 2003.

Davis, Mike. *Late Victorian Holocausts: El Niño Famines and the Making of the Third World*. London: Verso, 2001.

DeLay, Brian. *War of a Thousand Deserts: Indian Raids and the U.S.-Mexican War*. New Haven, CT: Yale University Press, 2008.

Díaz-Briquets, Sergio, and Jorge F. Pérez-López. *Conquering Nature: The Environmental Legacy of Socialism in Cuba*. Pittsburgh: University of Pittsburgh Press, 2000.

Díaz y Díaz, Martín. "El litigio del Tlahualilo: Presagio de un derecho de propiedad sin arrogancia." *Revista de Investigaciones Jurídicas* 14, no. 14 (1990): 129–94.

Dirección General de Culturas Populares. *Los primordiales del 36: Testimonios de los protagonistas del reparto agrario en La Laguna*. Durango, Mexico: Secretaría de Educación Pública, Dirección General de Culturas Populares, Unidad Regional Norte-La Laguna, 1994.

Domínguez Martínez, Raúl. *La ingeniería civil en México, 1900–1940: Análisis histórico de los factores de su desarrollo*. Mexico City: Instituto de Investigaciones sobre la Universidad y la Educación, Universidad Nacional Autónoma de México, 2013.

Dunar, Andrew J., and Dennis McBride. *Building Hoover Dam: An Oral History of the Great Depression*. New York: Twayne, 1993.

Durán, Juan Manuel, Martín Sánchez, and Antonio Escobar Ohmstede, eds. *El agua en la historia de México: Balance y perspectiva*. Guadalajara, Mexico: Universidad de Guadalajara, 2005.

Durango State Statistical Bureau. *Anuario estadístico del Estado de Durango*. Durango: Impresora del Gobierno, 1907.

Dwyer, John Joseph. *The Agrarian Dispute: The Expropriation of American-owned Rural Land in Postrevolutionary Mexico*. Durham: Duke University Press, 2008.

Eckstein, Salomón. *El ejido colectivo en México*. Mexico City: Fondo de Cultura Económica, 1966.

Eling, Herbert J., and Cristina Martínez García. "Cambios, innovaciones y discontinuidades en los sistemas de riego por galería filtrante en Parras de la Fuente, Coahuila, México." In

Agua y tierra en México, siglos XIX y XX, ed. Antonio Escobar Ohmstede, Martín Sánchez Rodríguez, and Ana María Gutiérrez Rivas, 125–50. Zamora, Mich.: El Colegio de Michoacán and El Colegio de San Luis, 2008.

Ervin, Michael. "The Art of the Possible: Agronomists, Agrarian Reform, and the Middle Politics of the Mexican Revolution, 1908–34." Ph.D. diss., University of Pittsburgh, 2002.

———. "Marte R. Gómez of Tamaulipas: Governing Agrarian Revolution." In *State Governors in the Mexican Revolution, 1910–1952: Portraits in Conflict, Courage, and Corruption,* ed. Jürgen Buchenau and William H. Beezley. Lanham, MD: Rowman and Littlefield, 2009.

———. "The 1930 Agrarian Census in Mexico: Agronomists, Middle Politics, and the Negotiation of Data Collection." *Hispanic American Historical Review* 87, no. 3 (August 2007): 537–70.

Escobar Ohmstede, Antonio, and Matthew Butler, eds. *Mexico in Transition: New Perspectives on Mexican Agrarian History, Nineteenth and Twentieth Centuries.* Austin: Lozano Long Institute of Latin American Studies, University of Texas, Austin, and Centro de Investigaciones y Estudios Superiores en Antropologia Social, 2013.

Escobar Ohmstede, Antonio, and Teresa Rojas Rabiela, eds. *Estructuras y formas agrarias en México: Del pasado y del presente.* Mexico City: Registro Agrario Nacional Archivo General Agrario and Centro de Investigaciones y Estudios Superiores en Antropología Social, 2001.

Escobar Ohmstede, Antonio, Martín Sánchez, and Ana María Graciela Gutiérrez Rivas, eds. *Agua y tierra en México, siglos XIX y XX,* 2 vols. Zamora, Mexico: El Colegio de Michoacán and El Colegio de San Luis, 2008.

Evans, Sterling. "Water and Environmental Change in the U.S.–Mexico Borderlands," in *Latin American History Oxford Research Encyclopedia,* May 2016; http://latinamericanhistory .oxfordre.com/view/10.1093/acrefore/9780199366439.001.0001/acrefore-97801993 66439-e-58?rskey=hyDT67&result=16.

Fallaw, Ben. *Cárdenas Compromised: The Failure of Reform in Postrevolutionary Yucatán.* Durham, NC: Duke University Press, 2001.

Fernández de Castro Martínez, Patricia Eugenia. "Agrarian Reform from Below: The Mexican Revolution in Durango, 1910–1915." Ph.D. diss., University of Chicago, August 2008.

Fiege, Mark. *Irrigated Eden: The Making of an Agricultural Landscape in the American West.* Seattle: University of Washington Press, 1999.

Fishburn, Evelyn, and Eduardo L. Ortiz, eds. *Science and the Creative Imagination in Latin America.* London: Institute for the Study of the Americas, 2005.

Fradkin, Philip L. *A River No More: The Colorado River and the West.* Berkeley: University of California Press, 1996.

García, Rolando Víctor, and Susana Sanz. *Deterioro ambiental y pobreza en la abundancia productiva: El caso de la Comarca Lagunera.* Mexico City: Federación Internacional de Institutos de Estudios Avanzados, 1987.

Gauss, Susan M. *Made in Mexico: Regions, Nation, and the State in the Rise of Mexican Industrialism, 1920s–1940s.* University Park: Pennsylvania State University Press, 2010.

Gayol, Roberto. *Dos problemas de vital importancia para México: La colonización y el desarrollo de la irrigación.* Tlalpan Jiutepec, Mexico: Centro de Investigaciones y Estudios Superiores en Antropología Social and Instituto Mexicano de Tecnología del Agua, 1994.

Gilbert, Jess. "Low Modernism and the Agrarian New Deal: A Different Kind of State." In *Fighting for the Farm: Rural America Transformed*, ed. Jane Adams, 129–46. Philadelphia: University of Pennsylvania Press, 2002.

Gilly, Adolfo. *El cardenismo, una utopía mexicana.* Mexico City: Cal y Arena, 1994.

Gledhill, John. *Casi Nada: A Study of Agrarian Reform in the Homeland of Cardenismo.* Austin: University of Texas Press, 1991.

Glennon, Robert Jerome. *Water Follies: Groundwater Pumping and the Fate of America's Fresh Waters.* Washington, DC: Island, 2002.

Glick, Thomas. "Science and Independence in Latin America." *Hispanic American Historical Review* 71 (1991): 307–34.

González de Montemayor, Beatriz, ed. *Efemérides del Municipio de Torreón, Coah.* Torreón, Mexico: Patronato del Archivo Municipal y Centro Histórico "Eduardo Guerra," 1999.

Gortari Rabiela, Rebeca de. "Educación y conciencia nacional: Los ingenieros después de la revolución mexicana." *Revista Mexicana de Sociología* 49, no. 3 (July–September 1987): 123–41.

Grandin, Greg. "The Liberal Traditions in the Americas: Rights, Sovereignty, and the Origins of Liberal Multilateralism." *American Historical Review* 1, no. 117 (February 2012): 68–91.

Gutiérrez, Donato. *El algodonero. Memoria, escrita.* Mexico City: Oficina tipográfia de la Secretaría de Fomento, 1885.

Hall, Linda B. "Álvaro Obregón and the Politics of Mexican Land Reform, 1920–1924." *Hispanic American Historical Review* 60, no. 2 (May 1980): 213–38.

Hamilton, Nora. *The Limits of State Autonomy: Post-Revolutionary Mexico.* Princeton, NJ: Princeton University Press, 1982.

Hecht, Gabrielle, ed. *Entangled Geographies: Empire and Technopolitics in the Global Cold War.* Cambridge, MA: MIT Press, 2011.

Hellman, Judith Adler. "Capitalist Agriculture and Rural Protest: The Case of the Laguna Region, Mexico." *Labour, Capital and Society* 14, no. 2 (November 1981): 30–46.

———. "The Role of Ideology in Peasant Politics: Peasant Mobilization and Demobilization in the Laguna Region." *Journal of Interamerican Studies and World Affairs* 25, no. 1 (February 1983): 3–29.

Hernández, Alfonso Porfirio. *¿La explotación colectiva en la Comarca Lagunera es un fracaso?* Mexico City: B. Costa-Amic, 1975.

Herrera y Lasso, José. *Apuntes sobre irrigación: Notas sobre su organización económica en el extranjero y en el país.* Mexico City: Instituto Mexicano de Tecnología del Agua and Centro de Investigaciones y Estudios Superiores en Antropología Social, 1994.

Hewitt de Alcántara, Cynthia. *Modernizing Mexican Agriculture: Socioeconomic Implications of Technological Change, 1940–1970.* Geneva: United Nations Research Institute for Social Development, 1976.

Hindley, Jane. "Indigenous Mobilization, Development, and Democratization in Guerrero: The Nahua People versus the Tetelcingo Dam." In *Subnational Politics and Democratization in Mexico*, ed. Todd Eisenstadt, Wayne A. Cornelius, and Jane Hindley, 207–38. La Jolla: Center for U.S.-Mexican Studies, University of California, San Diego, 1999.

Historia de la cuestión agraria mexicana, 9 vols. Mexico City: Siglo Veintiuno Editores and Centro de Estudios Históricos del Agrarismo en México, 1988.

Humboldt, Alexander von. *Political Essay on the Kingdom of New Spain.* London: Longman, Hurst, Rees, Orme, and Brown, 1822.

Humboldt, Alexander von, and John Taylor. *Selections from the Works of the Baron de Humboldt, Relating to the Climate, Inhabitants, Productions, and Mines of Mexico: with Notes by John Taylor.* London: Longman Hurst Rees Orme Brown and Green, 1824.

Hundley, Norris. *The Great Thirst: Californians and Water, 1770s–1990s.* Berkeley: University of California Press, 1992.

Hunter, W. D., and W. Dwight Pierce. *Mexican Cotton-Boll Weevil: Message from the President of the United States, Transmitting a Communication from the Secretary of Agriculture Submitting a Report on the Mexican Cotton-Boll Weevil.* Washington, DC: U.S. Government Printing Office, 1912.

Infield, Henrik F., and Koka Freier. *People in Ejidos: A Visit to the Cooperative Farms of Mexico.* New York: Praeger, 1954.

Irrititla, Quixote. *400 años de historia del Río Nazas, 1594–1994.* Mexico City: Comisión Nacional del Agua and Centro de Investigaciones y Estudios Superiores en Antropología Social, 1994.

Jiménez, César. "La contribución de la Comisión Nacional de Irrigación en adelanto de la ingeniería en México." *Irrigación en México* 17, no. 1 (1938): 3–8.

Jørgensen, Dolly, Finn Arne Jørgensen, and Sarah B. Pritchard, eds. *New Natures: Joining Environmental History with Science and Technology Studies.* Pittsburgh: University of Pittsburgh Press, 2013.

Joseph, G. M., and Timothy J. Henderson, eds. *The Mexico Reader: History, Culture, Politics.* Durham, NC: Duke University Press, 2002.

Joseph, G. M., and Daniel Nugent, eds. *Everyday Forms of State Formation: Revolution and the Negotiation of Rule in Modern Mexico.* Durham, NC: Duke University Press, 1994.

Josephson, Paul R. *Industrialized Nature: Brute Force Technology and the Transformation of the Natural World.* Washington, DC: Island, 2002.

———. *Resources under Regimes: Technology, Environment, and the State.* Cambridge, MA: Harvard University Press, 2004.

Katz, Friedrich. *The Life and Times of Pancho Villa.* Stanford, CA: Stanford University Press, 1998.

Kelly, Isabel Truesdell. *Notes on the Culture of the Laguna Zone: Population and Sustenance.* Mexico City: Institute of Inter-American Affairs, 1954.

Keremitsis, Dawn. *The Cotton Textile Industry in Porfiriato, Mexico, 1870–1910.* New York: Garland, 1987.

Khagram, Sanjeev. *Dams and Development: Transnational Struggles for Water and Power.* Ithaca, NY: Cornell University Press, 2004.

Klubock, Thomas. *La Frontera: Forests and Ecological Conflict in Chile's Frontier Territory.* Durham, NC: Duke University Press, 2014.

Knight, Alan. "Cardenismo: Juggernaut or Jalopy?" *Journal of Latin American Studies* 26, no. 1 (1994): 73–107.

———. *The Mexican Revolution: Counterrevolution and Reconstruction*, vol. 2. Lincoln: University of Nebraska Press, 1990.

———. *The Mexican Revolution: Porfirians, Liberals and Peasants*, vol. 1. Lincoln: University of Nebraska Press, 1990.

Kourí, Emilio. "Claroscuros de la Reforma Agraria Mexicana." *Nexos en línea* (December 1, 2010). http://www.nexos.com.mx/?p=14062, accessed February 22, 2016.

Kraus, Pavel. *Irrigation Ecology.* Zurich: Verlag der Fachvereine Zèurich, Geographisches Institut, Eidgenèossische Technische Hochschule Zèurich, 1992.

Kroeber, Clifton B. "La cuestión del Nazas hasta 1913." *Historia Mexicana* 79 (January–March 1971): 428–56.

———. *Man, Land, and Water: Mexico's Farmlands Irrigation Policies, 1885–1911.* Berkeley: University of California Press, 1983.

Lanz Cárdenas, José Trinidad. *Legislación de aguas en México: Estudio histórico*, vol. 1. Mexico: Consejo Editorial del Gobierno del Estado de Tabasco, 1982.

Latour, Bruno. *Reassembling the Social: An Introduction to Actor-Network-Theory.* Oxford: Oxford University Press, 2005.

Lemos, M. C., and J. L. F. Oliveira. "Can Water Reform Survive Politics? Institutional Change and River Basin Management in Ceará, Northeast Brazil." *World Development* 32, no. 12 (2004): 2121–37.

Lewontin, Stephen. "The Green Revolution and the Politics of Agricultural Development." Ph.D. diss., University of Chicago, 1983.

Liga de Agrónomos Socialistas. *El colectivismo agrario en México, La Comarca Lagunera.* Talleres de Industrial Gráfica, S.A., Mexico City, 1940.

Lookingbill, Brad D. *Dust Bowl, USA: Depression America and the Ecological Imagination, 1929–1941.* Athens: Ohio University Press, 2001.

López Zamora, Emilio. *El agua, la tierra: Los hombres de México.* Mexico City: Fondo de Cultura Económica, 1977.

Loreto López, Rosalva. *Agua, poder urbano y metabolismo social.* Puebla, Mexico: Benemérita Universidad Autónoma de Puebla, Instituto de Ciencias Sociales y Humanidades "Alfonso Vélez Pliego," 2009.

Lucena, Juan C. "De Criollos a Mexicanos: Engineers' Identity and the Construction of Mexico." *History and Technology* 23, no. 3 (September 2007): 275–88.

Madero, Francisco I. *Estudio sobre la conveniencia de la construcción de una presa.* San Pedro, Coahuila [Mexico]: Impreso en los Talleres de Tipografía Benito Juárez, 1907.

Mallet Prevost, Sergio. *The Tlahualilo Company versus the Government of Mexico: Memorandum in re Water Rights under Mexican Law*, ed. General Counsel for the Tlahualilo Company. New York: Tlahualilo Company, 1909.

Martin, Percy F. *Mexico of the Twentieth Century*. London: E. Arnold, 1907.

Martínez del Río, Pablo. *La Comarca Lagunera a fines del siglo XVI y principios del XVII según las fuentes escritas*. Mexico City: Universidad Nacional Autónoma de México Instituto de Historia, 1954.

Martínez Serna, José Gabriel. "Vineyards in the Desert: The Jesuits and the Rise and Decline of an Indian Town in New Spain's Northeastern Borderlands." Ph.D. diss., Southern Methodist University, Dallas, TX, 2009.

Matthews, Andrew S. *Instituting Nature: Authority, Expertise, and Power in Mexican Forests*. Cambridge, MA: MIT Press, 2011.

Mauch, Christof, and Thomas Zeller, eds. *Rivers in History: Perspectives on Waterways in Europe and North America*. Pittsburgh: University of Pittsburgh Press, 2008.

McCook, Stuart George. *States of Nature: Science, Agriculture, and Environment in the Spanish Caribbean, 1760–1940*. Austin: University of Texas Press, 2002.

McCully, Patrick. *Silenced Rivers: The Ecology and Politics of Large Dams*. London: Zed, 2001.

Medina, Eden, Ivan da Costa Marques, and Christina Holmes, eds. *Beyond Imported Magic: Essays on Science, Technology, and Society in Latin America*. Cambridge, MA: MIT Press, 2014.

Mendizábal, Miguel Othón de. "El problema agrario de la Laguna." In *Obras Completas*, vol. 4, 225–70. Mexico City: Cooperativa de trabajadores de los talleres gráficos de la nación, 1946–47.

Meyer, Michael. "The Living Legacy of Hispanic Groundwater Law in the Contemporary Southwest." *Journal of the Southwest* 31, no. 3 (Autumn 1989): 287–99.

Meyers, William K. *Forge of Progress, Crucible of Revolt: Origins of the Mexican Revolution in La Comarca Lagunera, 1880–1911*. Albuquerque: University of New Mexico Press, 1994.

———. "Politics, Vested Rights, and Economic Growth in Porfirian Mexico: The Company Tlahualilo in the Comarca Lagunera, 1885–1911." *Hispanic American Historical Review* 57, no. 3 (August 1977): 425–54.

———. "Seasons of Rebellion: Nature, Cotton Production and the Dynamics of Revolution in La Laguna, Mexico, 1910–1916." *Journal of Latin American Studies* 30, no. 1 (1998): 63–94.

Middlebrook, Kevin J. *The Paradox of Revolution: Labor, the State, and Authoritarianism in Mexico*. Baltimore: Johns Hopkins University Press, 1995.

Mikhail, Alan. *Nature and Empire in Ottoman Egypt: An Environmental History*. Cambridge: Cambridge University Press, 2011.

Mitchell, Timothy. *Rule of Experts: Egypt, Techno-politics, Modernity*. Berkeley: University of California Press, 2002.

Moles Batllevell, Alberto. *La enseñanza de la ingeniería mexicana, 1792–1990*. Mexico City: Sociedad de Exalumnos de la Facultad de Ingeniería de la Universidad Nacional Autónoma de México, 1991.

Molina Enríquez, Andrés. *Los grandes problemas nacionales*. Mexico City: Ediciones Era, 1978.

Moore, Aaron Stephen. *Constructing East Asia: Technology, Ideology, and Empire in Japan's Wartime Era, 1931–1945*. Stanford, CA: Stanford University Press, 2013.

Morett Sánchez, Jesús Carlos. *Reforma agraria: Del latifundio al neoliberalismo.* Mexico City: Plaza y Valdés and Universidad Autónoma Chapingo, Departamento de Sociología Rural, 2003.

Moreno Vázquez, José Luis. *Por abajo del agua: Sobre explotación y agotamiento del acuífero de la Costa de Hermosillo, 1945–2005.* Hermosillo, Mexico: El Colegio de Sonora, 2006.

Mottier, Nicole. "Ejidal Credit and Debt in 20th Century Mexico." Ph.D. diss., University of Chicago, 2013.

Nájera, Enrique, Manuel López Portillo, and Estanislao Peña. *Informe general de la comisión de estudios de la Comarca Lagunera, designada por el secretario de Agricultura y Fomento.* Mexico City: Editorial Cultura, 1930.

Naranjo, Steven E., George D. Butler Jr., and Thomas J. Henneberry, "A Bibliography of the Pink Bollworm, *Pectinophora gossypiella* (Saunders)." U.S. Department of Agriculture, Agricultural Research Service, Bibliographies and Literature of Agriculture no. 136, http://www.ars.usda.gov/is/np/pinkbollworm/pinkbollworm.pdf.

Niblo, Stephen R. *Mexico in the 1940s: Modernity, Politics, and Corruption.* Wilmington, DE: Scholarly Resources, 1999.

———. *War, Diplomacy, and Development: The United States and Mexico, 1938–1954.* Wilmington, DE: Scholarly Resources, 1995.

North American Commission on Environmental Cooperation. "History of DDT in North America to 1997." http://www3.cec.org/islandora/en/item/1620-history-ddt-in-north-america-1997-and-1996-presentation-mexican-ministry-en.pdf.

Núñez Luna, Alejandra. "Water Law and the Making of the Mexican State, 1875–1917." Ph.D. diss., Harvard University, Cambridge, MA, 2011.

Olcott, Jocelyn. *Revolutionary Women in Postrevolutionary Mexico.* Durham, NC: Duke University Press, 2005.

Olsson, Tore C. *Agrarian Crossings: Reformers and the Remaking of the US and Mexican Countryside.* Princeton, NJ: Princeton University Press, 2017.

Orive Alba, Adolfo. *La irrigación en México.* Mexico City: Grijalbo, 1970.

Ornelas, Gil. "La Comarca Lagunera." *Boletín de la Sociedad Mexicana de Geografía y Estadística*, vol. 9, no. 2 (July-August 1919): 339–50.

Orozco y Berra, Manuel. *Atlas y catecismo de geografía y estadística de la República Mexicana.* Mexico City: Imprenta de Flores y Monsalve, 1874.

Ortelli, Sara. *Trama de una guerra conveniente: Nueva Vizcaya y la sombra de los apaches (1748–1790).* Mexico City: Centro de Estudios Históricos El Colegio de México, 2007.

Ortiz, Carlos, plaintiff. *Juicio arbitral: Don Carlos Ortiz contra la Compania del Tlahualilo.* Tipografía Económica, Mexico, 1901.

Othón, Manuel José. *Obras de Manuel José Othón,* vol. 1. Mexico City: Secretaría de Educación Pública, 1928.

Padilla, Tanalis. *Rural Resistance in the Land of Zapata: The Jaramillista Movement and the Myth of the Pax Prísta, 1940–1962.* Durham, NC: Duke University Press, 2008.

Palacios, Leopoldo. *El problema de la irrigación.* Mexico City: Centro de Investigaciones y Estudios Superiores en Antropología Social and Instituto Mexicano de Tecnología del Agua, 1994.

Pearce, Fred. *When the Rivers Run Dry: Water, the Defining Crisis of the Twenty-First Century.* Boston: Beacon, 2007.

Perdue, Peter. "A Chinese View of Technology and Nature?" In *The Illusory Boundary: Environment and Technology in History,* ed. Martin Reuss and Stephen H. Cutcliffe, 101–19. Charlottesville: University of Virginia Press, 2012.

Pérez Prado, Luz Nereida. "Visiones sobre la construcción del sistema de riego Cupatitzio-Cajones y la política de la memoria." In *Entre campos de esmeralda: la agricultura de riego en Michoacán,* ed. Martín Sánchez, 167–98. Zamora, Michoacán [Mexico]: El Colegio de Michoacán and Gobierno del Estado de Michoacán, 2002.

Pinchot, Gifford. *The Fight for Conservation.* New York: Doubleday, Page, 1910.

Plana, Manuel. "La cuestión agraria en La Laguna durante la Revolución." *Historia Mexicana* 50, no. 1 (2000): 57–90.

———. *El reino del algodón en México: La estructura agraria de La Laguna, 1855–1910.* Monterrey, Mexico: Universidad Autónoma de Nuevo León, 1984.

Pritchard, Sara B. *Confluence: The Nature of Technology and the Remaking of the Rhône.* Cambridge, MA: Harvard University Press, 2011.

Quevedo, Miguel Ángel de. "La necesaria protección forestal de las cuencas receptoras de los principales ríos de la república y especialmente del Río Nazas: Trabajo presentado a la IV Convención de Ingenieros, celebrada en Torreón durante los días 11 a 20 de septiembre de 1925." *Revista Mexicana de Ingeniería y Arqitectura* 4, no. 1 (January 15, 1925): 14–24.

———. *Relato de mi vida.* Mexico City: n.p., 1943.

Ramos Lara, María de la Paz, and Alejandra Sánchez Estrada, "Antecedentes históricos del Colegio de Ingenieros." *México en el Tiempo* (May–June 1999): 24–29.

Randall, Laura, ed. *Reforming Mexico's Agrarian Reform.* Armonk, NY: Sharpe, 1996.

Reed, John. *Insurgent Mexico.* Harmondsworth, U.K.: Penguin, 1983.

Rello, Fernando. *State and Peasantry in Mexico: A Case Study of Rural Credit in La Laguna.* Geneva: United Nations Research Institute for Social Development, 1987.

Restrepo, Iván, and Salomón Eckstein. *La agricultura colectiva en México: La experiencia de La Laguna.* Mexico City: Siglo Veintiuno Editores, 1975.

Reuss, Martin, and Stephen H. Cutcliffe, eds. *The Illusory Boundary: Environment and Technology in History.* Charlottesville: University of Virginia Press, 2010.

Riemann, Armando. *Memoria del Distrito de Riego de la Región Lagunera, Coahuila y Durango.* Mexico City: Comisión Nacional de Irrigación, 1940.

Rist, Gilbert. *The History of Development: From Western Origins to Global Faith.* London and New York: Zed Books, 2014.

Rivas Sada, Eva Luisa. "Cambio tecnológico, dinámica regional y reconversión productiva en el norte de México. La Comarca Lagunera, 1925–1974." Ph.D. diss., Universidad Complutense de Madrid, Instituto Universitario de Investigación Ortega y Gasset, Madrid, 2010.

Rivera Castro, José, and José Jesús Hernández Palomo, eds. *El agrarismo mexicano: Textos y documentos, 1908–1984.* Sevilla: Escuela de Estudios Hispano-Americanos, Consejo Superior de Investigaciones Científicas, 1991.

Rojas Tamez, Joel. "Cuéntame un siglo: La presa El Palmito, en Durango: Ámbito de trabajo de una familia numerosa." *Vertientes* 8, no. 75 (February 2002): 26–28.

Román Jáquez, Juana Gabriela. *Del Aguanaval a Sierra Mojada: El conflicto de límites entre Durango y Coahuila, 1845–1900.* Saltillo, Mexico: Ceshac, 2001.

Romero, Matías. *Geographical and Statistical Notes on Mexico.* New York: Putnam, 1898.

Romero Navarrete, Lourdes. "Gestión hidráulica y concertación social: Las presas en el río Aguanaval." *Enlace* 4, no. 4 (2006).

———. "El reparto agrario y la redistribución del agua en La Laguna." *Boletín del Archivo Histórico del Agua*, no. 24 (May–August 2003): 21–26.

———. "El reparto ejidal a la ciudad de Lerdo, Durango, 1917–1924." *Boletín del Archivo General Agrario*, no. 15 (2001): 46–53.

———. *El río Nazas y los derechos de agua en México: El conflicto y negociación en torno a la democracia, 1878–1939.* Mexico City: Centro de Investigaciones y Estudios Superiores en Antropología Social, 2007.

Rulfo, Juan. *The Burning Plain and Other Stories.* Austin: University of Texas Press, 1971.

Russell, Edmund. *War and Nature: Fighting Humans and Insects with Chemicals from World War I to Silent Spring.* Cambridge: Cambridge University Press, 2001.

S. Pearson and Son. *Informe presentado por los señores Pearson and Son, Sucesores S.A. al Sr. Ministro de Fomento sobre el proyecto de captación de las aguas del Río Nazas.* Mexico City: Secretaría de Fomento, 1909.

Safford, Frank. *The Ideal of the Practical: Colombia's Struggle to Form a Technical Elite.* Austin: University of Texas Press, 1976.

Saldaña, Juan José. *Science in Latin America: A History.* Austin: University of Texas Press, 2006.

Salinas de Gortari, Carlos. *México: Un paso difícil a la modernidad.* Barcelona: Plaza y Janés Editores, 2000.

Salinas de Gortari, Raúl, and José Luis Solís González. *Rural Reform in Mexico: The View from the Comarca Lagunera in 1993.* Transformation of Rural Mexico, no. 4. San Diego: Ejido Reform Research Project Center for U.S.-Mexican Studies, University of California, San Diego, 1994.

Sanderson, Susan Walsh. *Land Reform in Mexico, 1910–1980.* Orlando: Academic Press, 1984.

Sánchez Rodríguez, Martín. "Mexico's Breadbasket: Agriculture and Environment in the Bajío." In *A Land between Waters*, ed. Christopher Boyer, 50–72. Tucson: University of Arizona Press, 2012.

Santiago, Myrna I. *The Ecology of Oil: Environment, Labor, and the Mexican Revolution, 1900–1938.* Cambridge: Cambridge University Press, 2006.

Saravia, Atanasio G. "Minucias de historia de Durango: Algodón, lana, moreras y colmenas." *Memorias de la Academia Mexicana de la Historia Correspondiente de la Real de Madrid* 15, no. 3 (July–September 1956): 271–85.

Saucedo Galindo, Mario. "Informe y estudio médico social de campamento y pueblo de El Palmito, Dgo." Tesis que se presenta para su examen profesional de médico cirujano,

Universidad Nacional Autónoma de México, Facultad Nacional de Medicina, Mexico City, 1942.

Sauer, Jonathan D. *Historical Geography of Crop Plants: A Select Roster.* Boca Raton, FL: CRC Press, 1993.

Schuler, Friedrich E. *Mexico between Hitler and Roosevelt: Mexican Foreign Relations in the Age of Lázaro Cárdenas, 1934–1940.* Albuquerque: University of New Mexico Press, 1999.

Scott, James C. *Seeing like a State: How Certain Schemes to Improve the Human Condition Have Failed.* New Haven, CT: Yale University Press, 1998.

Senior, Clarence Ollson. *Democracy Comes to a Cotton Kingdom: The Story of Mexico's La Laguna.* Mexico City: Centro de Estudios Pedagógicos e Hispanoamericanos, 1940.

Shapiro, Judith. *Mao's War against Nature: Politics and the Environment in Revolutionary China.* Cambridge: Cambridge University Press, 2001.

Silva Herzog, Jesús, ed. *El agrarismo mexicano y la reforma agraria: Exposición y crítica.* Mexico City: Fondo de Cultura Económica, 1964.

Simon, Joel. *Endangered Mexico: An Environment on the Edge.* San Francisco: Sierra Club Books, 1997.

Simonian, Lane. *Defending the Land of the Jaguar: A History of Conservation in Mexico.* Austin: University of Texas Press, 1995.

Simpson, Eyler N. *The Ejido: Mexico's Way Out.* Chapel Hill: University of North Carolina Press, 1937.

Smith, C. Wayne, and Joe Tom Cothren, eds. *Cotton: Origin, History, Technology, and Production.* New York: Wiley, 1999.

Smith, Merritt Roe, and Leo Marx, eds. *Does Technology Drive History? The Dilemma of Technological Determinism.* Cambridge, MA: MIT Press, 1994.

Soto Laveaga, Gabriela. "Bringing the Revolution to Medical Schools: Social Service and a Rural Health Emphasis in 1930s Mexico." *Mexican Studies/Estudios Mexicanos* 29, no. 2 (2013): 397–427.

Spenser, Daniela. *The Impossible Triangle: Mexico, Soviet Russia, and the United States in the 1920s.* Durham, NC: Duke University Press, 1999.

Stark, Barbara, Lynette Heller, and Michael A. Ohnersorgen. "People with Cloth: Mesoamerican Economic Change from the Perspective of Cotton in South-Central Veracruz." *Latin American Antiquity* 9, no. 1 (1998): 7–36.

Suárez Cortez, Blanca Estela. *Historia de los usos del agua en México: Oligarquías, empresas y ayuntamientos (1840–1940).* Mexico City: Comisión Nacional del Agua, Centro de Investigaciones y Estudios Superiores en Antropología Social and Instituto Mexicano de Tecnología del Agua, 1998.

Suárez Cortez, Blanca Estela, and Diana Birrichaga Gardida. *Dos estudios sobre usos del agua en México (siglos XIX y XX).* Mexico City: Centro de Investigaciones y Estudios Superiores en Antropología Social and Instituto Mexicano de Tecnología del Agua, 1997.

Summerhill, William. "The Development of Infrastructure." In *The Cambridge Economic History of Latin America, Volume 2: The Long Twentieth Century*, ed. Victor Bulmer-Thomas, John Coatsworth, and Roberto Cortes-Condes, 293–326.

Tebar Hurtado, Javier. *Reforma, revolución y contrarrevolución agrarias: Conflicto social y lucha política en el campo (1931–1939).* Barcelona, Spain: Flor del Viento Ediciones, 2006.

Toledo, Víctor M. "The Ecological Consequences of the 1992 Agrarian Law of Mexico." In *Reforming Mexico's Agrarian Reform,* ed. Laura Randall, 247–60. Armonk, NY: M. E. Sharpe, 1996.

Tortolero Villaseñor, Alejandro, ed. *Tierra, agua y bosques: Historia y medio ambiente en el México central.* Mexico City: Universidad de Guadalajara, 1996.

Tortolero Villaseñor, Alejandro. "Water and Revolution in Morelos, 1850–1915." In *A Land between Waters: Environmental Histories of Modern Mexico,* ed. Christopher Boyer, 124–49. Tucson: University of Arizona Press, 2012.

Valdés, Carlos Manuel. *La gente del mezquite: Los nómadas del noreste en la colonia.* Mexico City: Centro de Investigaciones y Estudios Superiores en Antropología Social and Instituto Nacional Indigenista, 1995.

Valencia Vargas, Juan C., Juan J. Díaz Nigenda, and Héctor J. Ibarrola Reyes. "La gestión integrada de los recursos hídricos en México: Nuevo paradigma en el manejo del agua," 2007. http://www2.inecc.gob.mx/publicaciones/libros/452/valencia.html.

Vargas-Lobsinger, María. *La Comarca Lagunera: De la Revolución a la expropiación de las haciendas, 1910–1940.* Mexico City: Universidad Nacional Autónoma de México, 1999.

———. *La hacienda de "La Concha": Una empresa algodonera de la Laguna, 1883–1917.* Mexico City: Instituto de Investigaciones Históricas, Universidad Nacional Autónoma de México, 1984.

Vaughan, Mary K. *Cultural Politics in Revolution: Teachers, Peasants, and Schools in Mexico, 1930–1940.* Tucson: University of Arizona Press, 1997.

Viesca, Francisco, ed. *Refutación a la demanda de la Compañía Agrícola Industrial Colonizadora del Tlahualilo, S.A., contra el Gobierno Federal de la República Mexicana sobre aguas del Río Nazas presentada ante la Tercera Sala de la Suprema Corte de Justicia de la Nación.* Mexico City: Imprenta y Fototipia de la Secretaría de Fomento, 1909.

Villa Guerrero, Guadalupe. "Una mina de oro blanco: La compañía agrícola del Tlahualilo." In *Durango (1840–1915): Banca, transportes, tierra e industria,* ed. María Guadalupe Rodríguez, 111–36. Durango, Mexico: Instituto de Investigacions Históricas, Universidad Juárez del Estado de Durango, 1995.

Villarello, Juan D. "Algunos datos acerca de las aguas subterráneas de la Comarca Lagunera de Torreón, Coahuila." *Revista Mexicana de Ingeniería y Arqitectura* 3, no. 12 (December 15, 1925): 738–54.

Vitz, Matthew. "'The Lands with Which We Shall Struggle': Land Reclamation, Revolution, and Development in Mexico's Lake Texcoco Basin, 1910–1950." *Hispanic American Historical Review* 92, no. 1 (2012): 41–71.

Vivar, Gonzalo. "Recursos de agua de la hacienda de Hornos, municipio de Viesca, estado de Coahuila." *Irrigación en México* 8, no. 4 (1934): 207–28.

Waitz, Paul. "Algunos datos sobre el agua subterránea y su aprovechamiento." *Irrigación en México,* 1, no. 1 (1930): 30–35.

Wakild, Emily. *Revolutionary Parks: Conservation, Social Justice, and Mexico's National Parks, 1910–1940.* Tucson: University of Arizona Press, 2011.

Walsh, Casey. *Building the Borderlands: A Transnational History of Irrigated Cotton along the Mexico-Texas Border.* College Station: Texas A&M University Press, 2008.

Wendel, Jonathan F., and Corrinne E. Grover. "Taxonomy and Evolution of the Cotton Genus." In *Cotton,* ed. David Fang and Richard Percy, 25–44. Agronomy Monograph 57. Madison, WI: American Society of Agronomy, Crop Science Society of America, and Soil Science Society of America, 2015.

White, Richard. *The Organic Machine: The Remaking of the Columbia River.* New York: Hill and Wang, 1995.

Wilkie, James Wallace. *The Mexican Revolution: Federal Expenditure and Social Change since 1910,* 2d ed. Berkeley: University of California Press, 1970.

Wilkie, James Wallace, and Edna Monzón de Wilkie. *México visto en el siglo XX: Entrevistas de historia oral.* Mexico City: Instituto Mexicano de Investigaciones Económicas, 1969.

Wilkie, Raymond. *San Miguel: A Mexican Collective Ejido.* Stanford, CA: Stanford University Press, 1971.

Wislizenus, Frank A. *Memoir of a Tour to Northern Mexico, Connected with Colonel Doniphan's Expedition, in 1846 and 1847.* Washington, DC: Tippin and Streeper, 1848.

Woelfle-Erskine, Cleo, July Oskar Cole, and Laura Allen, eds. *Dam Nation: Dispatches from the Water Underground.* New York: Soft Skull, 2007.

Wolaver, Brad D., John M. Sharp, Jr., Juan M. Rodriguez, and Juan Carlos Ibarra Flores. "Delineation of Regional Arid Karstic Aquifers: An Integrative Data Approach." *Ground Water* 46, no. 3 (2008): 396–413.

Wolfe, Mikael. "El Agua de la Revolución: The Historical Evolution and Devolution of a Socio-environmental Right in Mexico." In *Mexico in Focus: Social, Political and Environmental Issues,* ed. José Galindo, 289–306. New York: Nova Science, 2014.

———. "Bringing the Revolution to the Dam Site: How Technology, Labor and Nature Converged in the Microcosm of a Northern Mexican Company Town, 1936–1946." *Journal of the Southwest* 53, no. 1 (2011): 1–31.

———. "The Sociolegal Redesignation of Ejido Land Use, 1856–1912." In *Mexico in Transition: New Perspectives on Mexican Agrarian History, Nineteenth and Twentieth Centuries/ México y sus transiciones: reconsideraciones sobre la historia agraria mexicana, siglos XIX y XX.,* ed. Antonio Escobar Ohmstede and Matthew Butler, 291–318. Austin: Lozano Long Institute of Latin American Studies, University of Texas, Austin, and Centro de Investigaciones y Estudios Superiores en Antropologia Social, 2013.

World Commission on Dams. *Dams and Development: A New Framework for Decision-Making.* London: Earthscan, 2000.

Worster, Donald. *Dust Bowl: The Southern Plains in the 1930s.* New York: Oxford University Press, 2004.

———. *Nature's Economy: A History of Ecological Ideas,* 2d ed. Cambridge: Cambridge University Press, 1994.

————. *Rivers of Empire: Water, Aridity, and the Growth of the American West.* New York: Pantheon, 1985.

Worthington Pump and Machinery Corporation. *100 Years, 1840–1940, Worthington.* Harrison, NJ: Worthington Pump and Machinery, 1940.

Wright, Angus Lindsay. *The Death of Ramón González: The Modern Agricultural Dilemma.* Austin: University of Texas Press, 2005.

Index

Page references in italics indicate an illustration and *t* refers to a table

Aboites, Luis: *El agua de la nación*, 16–17; *La decadencia del agua de la nación*, 17
Agrarian Code (1934), 115
Agrarian Dept., 95, 162
agrarian reforms. *See also* Article 27; Cardenista reform; Rehabilitation Plan: Agrarian Law (1915), 52–53; Agrarian Law of the Sovereign Revolutionary Convention (1915), 254n101; Carrancista agrarian law (1915), 54–55, 60, 254n100; continuity across administrations, 131–32; General Agrarian Law (1915), 54–55; importance of, 244n41; Law of Irrigation (1926), 72–74, 88; Law on the Use of Waters under Federal Jurisdiction (1910), 17–18, 51, 56, 87–88; Plan of Ayala (1911), 52, 222–23, 254n100; role of revolutionaries in, 53–54; *vs.* Spanish reform, 105, 264n33; Water Law (1929), 87–88
Agricultural Association of Durango, 195
agricultural education, 189
El agua de la nación (Aboites), 16–17
Aguanaval River, 5, 25–27, 227, 239n6
Águila ejido, 118–19
AHA (Historical Water Archive), 16, 47
Alamán, Lucas, 31–32
Aldaco Jurado, Francisco, 157–58
Alemán, Miguel: agrarian reforms of, 169; corruption under, 191; ISI policy of, 174–75, 178–79; politics of, 222; SRH created by, 164; on the vedas, 184; water distribution to

ejidos by, 180; and Worthington de México, 176–77
alfalfa, 120*t*, 260n80
Allen, Francisco, 75–76, 83, 112, 113
Álvarez y Álvarez, Máximo, 162, 273n83
Amaya Brondo, Abelardo, 209
American Bridge, 143
American Colorado River Land Company, 121
American Medical Association, 200
Amigos del Suelo (Friends of the Soil), 195
Ana ejido, 202
Anderson Clayton Company, 121–23, 198, 203–4
Angostura Dam, 132, 148, 269n2
aniego method (flood-farming irrigation), *40*; compatibility with the dam, 140, 208, 282n35; criticisms of, 50; definition of, 2; effects of the Nazas River flow on, 248n45; inefficiency of, 40, 169; *vs.* semi-aniego method, 168; SRH *vs.* ejidatarios on, 168–70, 274n15; sustainability of, 3, 171; use in Laguna region, 34–40, 252–53n91
anthropologists, 193–94
anti-environmentalism, 241n23
A. O. Smith, 176
apisonado (pest control by trampling), 35
Archivo Histórico del Agua (AHA), 16, 47
Arocena, Rafael, 33, 247–48n42
Arreguín Mañón, José P., 81
arsenic, 190, 195, 216, 260n79

Article 27 (of Constitution of 1917). *See also* Cardenista reform; reparto de aguas: on agricultural development, 15; on conservation, 15, 18, 57, 75, 192; mandate of, 2; on national waters, 87; revision of (1945), 174, 180–81, 220; revision of (1992), 5, 222–23; on traditional and historic rights to ejidos, 54–55; on water access/ownership, 17–18, 56, 64, 87, 180–81; on water resources, 15–16

Article 75 (National Property Water Law), 180

artwork representing natural and technical (envirotechnical) harmony, *8, 9, 12, 13*

Association to Promote the Nazas River Dam, 74–75, 83

Ávila Camacho, Manuel, 126; agrarian policies of, 131, 170; campamento workers' complaints to, 151, 271n46; Palmito/Lázaro Cárdenas Dam dedicated by, 163–64; soil conservation efforts of, 165; water distribution decree by, 172–73, 175, 180, 275n24

Ayluardo, Román, 102

Aymes, Adolfo, 86, 260–61n85

Azúcar Dam, 132, 148, 269n2

Bach y Dorsch, 143

Bank of Mexico, 189

Bartlett, John, 248n45

Becerril Colín, Alfredo, 136

Belausteguigoitia, Ramón de, 86

Beteta, Ramón, 91, 96

Biestro, Ernesto, 139, 141–42

Bistráin, Pablo, 168–69

Blake, Jorge, 136–38, 137*t*, 270n14

Blázquez, Mario, 98, 99–100

Bombas Laguna, 179

Bombas Nacionales, 179

Bombas Peerless Tisa, 179

bonanceros, 103

Bonavía y Zapata, Bernando, 246–47n33

Bonilla, José, 86–87, 281n26

Borlaug, Norman, 188

Boulder City, 145

Boyer, Christopher, 13

braceros (guest workers), 182, 278n61

Braña, Rogelio, 273n71

Brazilian drought industry, 185

British companies' struggle with Mexican government, 69–70, 257–58n38

Brittingham, Juan F., 74, 86, 175, 251–52n85, 260–61n85

Brown Knox and Company, 143

Brundtland Report (United Nations; 1987), 195

Bucareli Accords (1923), 257–58n38

Bundesen, Herman N., 200

Cabrera, Luis, 54

Calderón, Felipe, 219

Calderón R., Enrique, 102

California, 73

Calles. *See* Elías Calles, Plutarco

Callista Law of Dotation and Restitution of Lands and Waters, 88

campamentos (encampments), 132, 148, 151, 192–93, 272n53. *See also under* Lázaro Cárdenas/El Palmito Dam; Nazas River Dam

Campos, Cheche, 53–54

Caraveo, Marcelo, 134–35

Cárdenas, Lázaro: and Álvarez y Álvarez, 162, 273n83; CNI influence on, 95; commitment to radical agrarian reform, 131; departure from office, 159; and ejidos, creation of, 43, 95–97, 263n8; on irrigation goals for Palmito, 170; meeting with Blázquez, 99–100; modern equipment approved by, 139; and the Nazas River Dam, 100–101, 104; oil companies nationalized by, 142–43, 149, 276n33; Palmito Dam dedicated by, 163–64; political shift to the right, 131–32; politics of, 222; presidency of, 97–104; prosperity promised by, 156; relationship with Anderson Clayton Company, 267n73; reparto de tierras completion announced by, 141; sculpture of, 164, *165*; soil conservation efforts of, 165; supervision of reparto de tierras, 96, 106; veneration of, 95, 262n1; on water scarcity in the ejidos, 162

Cardenista reform (1936; reparto de tierras), 2, 47, 59, 64–65, 96, 262n4; *vs.* Alemán's reform, 169; Ávila Camacho's support of, 170; completion of, 104, 141, 157; critique of, 106 (*see* Rehabilitation Plan); ejidatarios' reactions to, 157; engineers' role in, 220; inconsistencies within, 114; reactions to, 105–6; as a social experiment, 3–4; social justice as ethos of, 160; tenth anniversary of, 167; termination of, 227; unsustainability of, 5; *vs.* water distribution, 5, 111 (*see also* reparto de aguas)

Carey, Mark, 10–11

Carney, Henry, 178

Carranza, Venustiano, 18, 54–55, 67–68

Carson, Rachel: *Silent Spring*, 188, 200

Carvajal, René, 181

Castillón, Juan, 79

Castro Bernal, Francisco, 225, 226

CCM (Mexican Peasant Confederation), 99

Cedillo, Saturnino, 96

Cementos Hidalgo (Cementos Mexicanos; CEMEX), 74

Central Union (of ejidos), 282n29, 282n39

Cháirez Araiza, Carlos, 34, 260n79

Chávez, Eduardo, 194

chemical pesticides. *See* pesticides

Civil Code of Mexico (1884), 181, 277n56; (1932), 181

class divisions in postrevolutionary Laguna, 63–64

Clayton, William, 121, 267n73

CNA (National Water Commission), 224–25, 227–28

CNC (National Confederation of Peasants), 205–6, 211, 278n67

CNI (National Irrigation Commission). *See also* engineers; SRH: campamentos (encampments) built by, 132, 145, 148 (*see also under* Lázaro Cárdenas/El Palmito Dam; Nazas River Dam); Cárdenas influenced by, 95; Cárdenas's changes to, 109; Cárdenas sculpture unveiled by, 164, *165*; compensation paid to landholders by, 115; dam building by, 153–54, 270n7 (*see also* Lázaro Cárdenas/El Palmito Dam); Dept. of Social Action founded by, 150; expansion of, 164; irrigated lands redistributed by, 180; Laguna Irrigation District demarcated by, 172–73, 275n24; local water boards organized by, 125–26; management of ejidos–small landholders conflict, 126–27; medical students hired by, 151–52; mission of, 88; Nazas River regime managed by, 110–12, 115–16; on the Palmito Dam site selection, 140; Palmito Dam water distribution

controlled by, 166–67; preliminary water regulation decreed by, 115–16, 118; replaced by Ministry of Hydraulic Resources, 16; road building by, 138; social services for workers provided by, 148, *149*, 151–54; surveys ordered by, 87, 112, 135–36; water management fee charged by, 173

Cobián, Feliciano, 46–47, 251n75

Colizza, Agustín, 36

Collective Ejido Associations/Societies, 117, 175

La Colonia (former Tlajualilo Company land), 124

Comisión Nacional de Irrigación. *See* CNI

Comisión Nacional del Agua (CNA), 224–25, 227–28

Committee of Petitioners for Urban Land, 155

Communist Party, 63

La Concordia (property), 140

Confederación Campesina Mexicana (CCM), 99

Confederación de Trabajadores de México (CTM), 99

Confederación Nacional Campesina (CNC), 206, 211, 278n67

Confederación Regional Obrera Mexicana (CROM), 63

Confederación Revolucionaria de Obreros y Campesinos de la Región Lagunera (CROC), 282n31

conservation: cost of, 241n22; definition of, 14; and global competitiveness, 241n22; laws for, 14–15; *vs.* preservation, 14, 242n26–27; and scarcity of resources, 13–14, 240–41n17, 241n23; Soil and Water Conservation Law (1946), 165, 174, 189, 195, 275n27; técnicos' role in, 2, 13–20; urgency of need for, 12; of water, 2, 19, 174, 224

Constitution of Mexico: (1857), 15; (1917), 15, 159, 180–82, 220, 242n30. *See also* Article 27

contamination of groundwater, 260n79. *See also* arsenic

Contreras, Calixto, 253n93

Convention of Workers and Peasants of Durango, 91–92

cooperative farming, 262n3

Coria, Antonio, 171, 207

Corona Páez, Sergio, 41

Cotter, Joseph, 188, 276n40
cotton: botanical diversity of, 30–32; chin-
    chilla variety, 33; cultivation of, 30–31, 144,
    214, 246n28; evolution of, 29; historical
    overview of, 29–34; infestations in, 199*t*
    (*see also* pink bollworm); irrigation meth-
    ods for, 31, 33; planting of, 32–33, 247n40;
    pricing volatility of, 62, 205, 264n31
Cotton Association, 204–5, 281n28
cotton handicraft industry, 29
cotton industry: American financing of,
    121–23; *vs.* dairy industry, 186, 214, 217;
    dam's effect on, 162; drought's effect on, 158;
    in Laguna, 2–3, 28, 213–14, 246–47n33; in
    Matamoros, 214; in Mexicali, 214; Mexican
    vs. U.S. production, 201; production levels,
    82*t*, 119–20, 120*t*, 231*t*, 233–36*t*, 237*t*; under
    the Rehabilitation Plan, 213–14; reliance
    on the Nazas River flow, 54; success of,
    24, 28–29, 75, 245–46n15, 246–47n33,
    251–52n85; use in trade, 29–30, 246n28
credit: cooperative arrangements for, 148–49;
    for dairy farms, 186; informal, 192; limited
    access to, 161, 167, 190; through Ejido Bank,
    158, 173, 185, 200, 202, 204; through U.S.
    Export-Import Bank, 179
CROC (Revolutionary Confederation of
    Workers and Campesinos of the Laguna
    Region), 282n31
CROM (Regional Mexican Labor Confedera-
    tion), 63
CTM (Workers' Confederation of Mexico), 99
Cuatro Ciénegas, 26–27, 228, 281n24
El Cuije ejido, 187, 202

dairy industry: *vs.* cotton industry, 186, 214,
    217; and groundwater pumping, 186–90,
    278–79n70; production levels, 237*t*; success
    of, 3, 217–18, 281n28
Davis, Mike, 165
DDT (dichlorodiphenyltrichloroethane), 188,
    190, 199–200, 226, 279n75
La decadencia del agua de la nación (Aboites), 17
decentralization policies, 275n24
deforestation, 78, 282n31
Delgado, Luciano, 150
Democratic Union of Mexican Women of the
    Comarca Lagunera, 193

Dept. of Agrarian and Colonization Affairs,
    211
Dept. of Social Action, 150
Depression (global), 89
desagüe, 18–19
desiccation theory, 18, 259n62, 282n31
Díaz, Porfirio, 3, 4, 252n86
Díaz Ordaz, Gustavo, 211
División del Norte, 53, 253n93
Does Technology Drive History? (Marx and
    Smith), 10
Don Martín Dam, 139, 168, 274n13
downriver *vs.* upriver zones, 107–8
drought industry, 185, 193, 200
droughts, 5, 66, 158, 164–66, 191–94, 274n6,
    280n5. *See also* mini–Dust Bowl
Duffield, Paul C., 279n81
Durango's ecological landscape, 138
Dust Bowl (U.S.), 164–65

Eckstein, Salomón, 119
Ejido Bank, 117, 162, 185–86, 193, 204, 273n71,
    278n67. *See also under* credit
Ejido Medical Service, 160
ejidos: agricultural practices of, 120, 267n71;
    American financing of, 121–23; autonomy
    of, 205; as central institutions of agrarian
    reform, 95, 104–5; *vs.* commercial agricul-
    ture, 207; definition of, 2, 254n100;
    demands for water from Palmito Dam's
    reservoir, 166–67; drinking/gambling
    in, 161–62; ejidatarios' fatalism about
    water supply, 187, 225, 279n71; ejidatarios'
    inability to rent or sell land, 284n8;
    ejidatarios' reactions to the reparto, 157;
    films about, 159; governance of, 132, 139;
    vs. haciendas, 95–96, 105, 114–15, 262n3,
    263n6, 265n37; landlessness in, 201
    (*see also* libres); machinery used in, 201,
    283n44; quality of land in, 114–15; reloca-
    tion of, 209, 211, 213, 217; responsibilities
    and roles played in, 96–97; *vs.* small
    landholders, 117–19, 126–27, 194–95;
    socioeconomic decline in (1950s), 170;
    subsistence agriculture in, 202; water
    access in, 116–18, 119, 158, 192, 225, 273n71;
    working/living conditions, 117, 156–62,
    201, 267n64, 273n71

Electric Industries of Mexico, 178
Electric Material, 178
Elías Calles, Plutarco: agrarian reform under, 69; CNI founded by, 16; concessions granted by, 257n32; dam building ordered by, 270n7; Engineering Commission of, 269n6; irrigation works built by, 72–74; Laguna regional study called for by, 80; lobbied by pro-dammers, 88; meeting with Brittingham and Fairburn (1925), 74; on the Nazas River Dam, 88–90, 261n90; presidency of, 263n9
Emiliano Zapata of Viesca (ejido), 186–87
employment, 192–93
Encinas, Dionisio, 99
engineers. See also López Zamora, Emilio: in artwork, 7–10, 8, 11, 12; on canals, 209, 217; as conservationists, 2, 13–20; on damming's effects on aniego irrigation, 140; definition of, 1; on the ecological impact of a second dam, 207; equipment needed by, 136–38, 143–44; flow-data gauges installed by, 134–35, 269–70n6; importance of, 7, 219–20; lives of, 5; on the Rehabilitation Plan's failures, 215–16; relationship with nature, 11–12; reports on Nazas River and Laguna, 139, 142; role in state mediation, 1–2, 10–11; on soils, 140; surveys by, 135–36; training and education of, 7; transportation problems of, 137–38, 143–44; U.S.–Mexican collaboration of, 198, 281n14; workers' relationship with, 148–49, 157
Enríquez, Celso A., 75
entomologists, 198–99
environmental history, definition of, 239n7
environmentalism, 224, 242n30
envirotechnical history, 6–13
Equipos Mecánicos de La Laguna (Mechanical Equipment of the Laguna), 166, 175, 190, 280nn83–84
Escobar, Gonzalo, 72, 98, 258n44
Escobar, Rómulo, 15
Espinosa Mireles, Gustavo, 55, 63
E. Viñedo ejido, 119

Fabricación de Máquinas, 179
Fairbanks Morse, 179

Fairburn, T.M., 69–70, 74, 105–6
Favela, Manuel, 133
Federal Committee for School Construction, 159
Federal Confederation of Work, 98
Federal Water Law (1934), 110, 181, 217, 265n46
Federal Zones along Nazas River., 66–67
Federation of Worker and Campesino Unions of the Comarca Lagunera, 98
Fernández Aguirre, Braulio, 225
Fernández Canyon, 50, 140
Fiege, Mark, 248n46
flood-farming. See aniego method
Flores, José Leonardo, 31
Flores, Juan Nepomuceno, 42, 44, 250n69
flow-gauging stations, 134–35, 269–70nn6–7
Fox, Vicente, 219, 228
Franco Ugarte, Pedro, 60, 76
Franklin, Benjamin (Mexican engineer), 166
Fuente, José de la, 75, 83, 90

García, J. Isabel, 102
García, Pastor, 173
García, Rolando Víctor, 165–66
García de la Cadena, Gumaro, 70, 72
Gayol, Roberto, 50–51
General Cable, 143
General Credit Bureau (Treasury Ministry), 132
General Electric, 178
geohydrological knowledge vs. pumping business, 170–86, 172. See also vedas; Worthington de México; corruption in the pumping business, 175; Ejido Bank's corruption/power, 185–86, 278n67; engineer Ojeda on, 170–71; feasibility studies for a second dam, 173; geohydrology, definition of, 81; Gómez on, 170–71; groundwater laws' history, 180–81, 277n55; groundwater overexploitation, 173–74, 187; pump types, 176; Soil and Water Conservation Law (1946), 165, 174, 189, 195, 275n27; water depletion/salinization, 171, 180, 187, 194–95, 217; water distribution order of preference, 180; water distribution regulation (1941), 172–73, 175, 180, 275n24; water management fee, 173

Gómez, Marte R.: as an alleged Henriquista,
276n45; Equipos Mecánicos de La Laguna
established by, 166; on geohydrological
knowledge *vs.* pumping business, 170–71;
Green Revolution under, 189; on López
Zamora, 283n55; Palmito Dam dedicated
by, 163–64; pump-business connections
of, 175–76, 191, 273n71, 275n29, 276n38
(*see also* Worthington de México); support
for agrarian reform, 261n95; support for
Nazas River Dam, 87; wealth of, 196
Gómez Morín, Manuel, 103–4, 264n31
Gómez Palacio, 84
González Fariño, Carlos, 76
González Fariño, Fernando, 72
Grandin, Greg, 242n30
Green Revolution, 182, 188–89, 191, 223
groundwater conservation, 174. *See also*
conservation
groundwater pumping. *See also* geohydrological knowledge *vs.* pumping business;
vedas: and the dairy industry, 186–90,
278–79n70; effect on water levels, 19,
112–14, 226; expense of, 117; importance
to Laguna irrigation, 171; invasiveness of,
219–20; regulation of, 112–14, 172–73, 220,
284n4; reliance on, 5, 78–83; technology,
109; unsustainability of, 219–20
groundwater *vs.* surface water, 19–20
Group of Small Colonists of the Tlahualilo
Perimeter, 126–27
Gruson, Sydney, 183
Guadalupe dam, 72, 111
guayule farming, 250–51n73
Guerrero, Guadalupe, 134–35
Gutiérrez, Antonio, 92–93
Gutiérrez, Dionisio, 27
Gutiérrez, Donato, 32–33, 39

Hail, Marshall, 3–4, 105
Hellman, Judith Adler, 214, 282n29
Henríquez Guzmán, Miguel, 276n45
Hernández, A. Porfirio, 199, 213
Herrera y Lasso, José, 73, 258n47
Hessel, W.S., 83, 260n78
Hispano-Tlaxcalans, 41–42, 257n31
historical revisionism, 257n31
Historical Water Archive (AHA), 16, 47

Holby, John, 106
Hool, Alan E., 198
Hoover Dam, 145
housing, 152–55, 160–61
Huerta, Adolfo de la, 65
Huerta, Eduardo de la, 35
Huerta, Victoriano, 67, 257n33
Humboldt, Alexander von, 28
hydraulic technology, 222–29
hydrological drought, 165
hydrometric stations, 135, 269–70n6

Ibarrola, J. Ramón de, 35–36
import substitution industrialization (ISI),
174–75, 178–79
Indé (Durango), 150–51
INE (National Institute of Ecology), 228
Ingeniería Hidráulica en México, 181
Institutional Revolutionary Party (PRI), 185,
207, 223
insurgency and repression, 185, 278n65
Irrigación en México, 81
Irrigation District, 124–26, 170, 172–73, 187,
193, 215–17, 275n24
ISI (import substitution industrialization),
174–75, 178–79

Jaramillo insurgency, 278n65
Jefe Máximo. *See* Elías Calles, Plutarco
Jiménez, César, 7
Jiménez, Juan Ignacio, 42
Johnston Pump Company de México, 179
Juambelz, Antonio, 105
Juárez, Benito, 42

Kelly, Isabel, 187–88, 193, 201–2
King, J. Paul, 121
Kisch, Egon Erwin, 157, 160
Knight, Alan, 244n41

labor rights, 63
Laguna Ejido Unión, 103
Laguna Loan Bank (Banco Refaccionario de
La Laguna), 89
Laguna region, 2–3; agricultural success in,
25, 27–28, 47–48; apathy of land owners
toward damming Nazas in, 23–24; canals
in, 36–39, *37, 38*, 200–201, 209, 217, 249n51

(*see also* tunnels and diversion canals); climate and geography of, 25–29, 200, 245n8; drought in, 225; ecological history of, 4; environmental awareness in, 228–29; exemption from agrarian reform, 261n93; hydraulic works in, 71–72; instability of, 134; irrigation used in, 25, 70–71; land distribution, 71*t*; naming of, 25; plea for exemption from agrarian reform, 66–67, 257n32; population of, 42–43, 87, 281n23; poverty in, 254n102; soil fertility of, 36; as a strategic location in the Revolution, 53; wildlife in, 26, 35, 245n11, 248n46

Laguna Strike Committee, 101

LALA (La Laguna Dairy Company), 3, 217–18, 228

land distribution. *See* Cardenista reform

Latour, Bruno, 11

Law on General Means of Communications (1888), 41, 44–45, 66

Law on the Use of Waters under Federal Jurisdiction (1910), 51, 252–53n91

Law to Promote Industry (Ley de Fomento de Industria de Transformación), 177

Layne and Bowler Pump Company, 81

Lázaro Cárdenas/El Palmito Dam: campamento at, 144–55, *146–47, 149,* 271nn45–46; completed dam, *156*; construction of, 114, 138–42, *142,* 154–55, 226; cost of, 142, 155, 271n25; dedication of, 144, 162, 163–64, 166–67; ejidatarios' visits to/ work on, 156–57; ejidos' demands for water from reservoir, 4, 166–67; as a flagship dam, 3, 132, 164; flood-control capability of, 167–68, 206; foreign visitors to, 139; funding for, 143, 269n2; gauging stations for, 134–36, 269–70n6; groundbreaking for, 106; hydroelectric plant for, 140–41, 274n11; irrigation goals/expectations for, 164, 167–70; local workforce for, 156–57, 162; naming of, 98; propaganda about, 156; site selection for, 50–51, 70, 88–89, 140–41, 252n90; working/living conditions at the site, 144–45, 148–55, *149,* 161, 271n45

League of Agrarian Communities, 98

League of Socialist Agronomists, 191

Legion of Veterans of the Revolution, 123–24

Lerdo (Durango), 68, 266n58

Lerdo Law, 52

Ley de Educación Agrícola (Agricultural Education Law), 189

Ley de Fomento de Industria de Transformación (Law to Promote Industry), 177

libres (landless ejidatarios), 161, 201, 267n64, 281n24

Ligas Femeniles (Women's Leagues), 161

limestone, 138

Lomas Coloradas Dam ("Las Tórtolas"), 206–7, 214

Lombardo Toledano, Vicente, 99

López Bancalari, Ignacio, 70

López Mateos, Adolfo, 192–93, 202–5, 209, 211

López Zamora, Emilio, 167, 170, 191–92, 209, 211–14, 217–18, 273n71, 283n55. *See also* Rehabilitation Plan

Lorenzo Pardo, Manuel, 76–77, 83, 167–68, 170, 274n11

Madero, Francisco I.: care for workers, 49; and the Nazas River Dam, 3, 4, 23–25, 42–44, 47–51, 221, 251n81; and the Nazas River Inspection Commission, 24; on the Palmito Dam site selection, 140, 173, 206

Madero family, 250–51n73

Maeda, Luis, 226, 279n75

Mallet Prevost, Sergio, 249n59, 250n71, 251n74

Marroquín y Rivera, Manuel, 35–36, 39, 41, 50–51, 86–87

Martínez, Benigno, 101

Marx, Leo: *Does Technology Drive History?* 10

Matos, José de, 31

Maximato period, 88

medical students, 151–52

Medina, Gregorio, 135

Menéndez, A., 122–23

meteorological stations, 269–70nn6–7

Mexican Agriculture Dept., 188

Mexican-American Agricultural Commission, 189–90, 279n81

Mexican-American Convention on the Pink Bollworm (1953), 198, 281n14

Mexican Cement Company (CEMEX), 74

Mexican Cotton Estates of Tlahualilo, Ltd. *See* Tlahualilo Company

Mexican Loan Bank, 122–23
Mexican National Confederation of Cotton
    Producers, 198
Mexican Peasant Confederation (CCM), 99
Mexican Revolution (1910–1917), 51, 244n41.
    See also Water of the Revolution
Meyers, William K., 42
Midgett, R. R., 158
Mijares, Manuel, 157
milk production, 237t. See also dairy industry
mini–Dust Bowl (Mexico), 164, 166, 170,
    182–85, 190, 278n60
Mining Code of Mexico (1884), 277n56
Ministry of Agriculture and Colonization,
    52–53
Ministry of Agriculture and Livestock.
    See SAG
Ministry of Hydraulic Resources (SRH).
    See SRH
Ministry of Industry and Development
    (SF), 32
Ministry of Public Education (SEP), 153, 159
Ministry of the Environment, Natural
    Resources, and Fisheries (SEMARNAP/
    SEMARNAT), 224
Mitchell, Timothy, 6, 10, 240–41n17
Mixed Regulatory Commission, 112
Mixed Waters Commission, 109
Molina, Olegario, 46, 50, 107
Molina Enríquez, Andrés, 54
molinos (corn mills), 161–62
Montes de Oca, Luis, 121
Mottier, Nicole, 273n71
Muir, John, 242n26
Muñoz, Emilia, 124

Nacional Financiera, 177, 276n38
NAFTA (North American Free Trade Agree-
    ment), 189
Nájera, Enrique, 269n6
Narro, Rafael B., 86–87, 281n26
National Action Party (PAN), 223, 227–28
National Agrarian Commission, 95
National Agricultural Chambers of Mexico,
    60–61
National Agricultural Credit Bank, 95
National Autonomous University of Mexico
    (UNAM), 151

National Committee of Proletarian Defense
    in Mexico, 98
National Confederation of
    Campesinos(CNC), 206, 211, 278n67
National Convention of Engineers, 74, 258n50
National Cotton Associations of Mexico, 204
National Institute of Ecology (INE), 228
National Institute of Nutrition, 216
National Iron and Steel Works, 178
National Irrigation Commission. See CNI
National Livestock Program (Programa
    Nacional de Ganadería), 214
National Property Water Law (Article 75 of),
    180
National Revolutionary Party (PNR), 99,
    109, 132
National Union of Agriculture and Develop-
    ment workers, 151
National Water Commission (CNA), 224–25,
    227–28
natural resources, ownership of, 15–18, 243n33
nature vs. technology ("illusory boundary"
    between), 6
Nazas River, flow of. See also aniego method
    (flood-farming irrigation): alternating
    routes of, 245n13, 248n45; attention from
    engineers, 259n59; capacity, 108t; and
    construction progress on dams, 153–54;
    diversion dams for, 249n51; equipment and
    transportation affected by, 137; fertilizing
    sediments from, 138–40, 208, 281n26
    (see also aniego method); illustrations of,
    28, 37; importance to agriculture, 2, 36, 133,
    226, 249n49; influence on Mexican water
    law, 18, 41; inland drainage of, 244–45n5;
    instability of, 133–34; Laguneros' joyous re-
    action to, 133–34; largest (1944), 167; mea-
    surements of, 41, 231t; rainfall's effect on,
    25–27, 154; reverence for, 133–34; taming of
    (1936–1940), 138–44, 142, 163; tunnels and
    diversion canals for, 141, 142, 154, 167, 209,
    217; variability of, 40, 52, 54, 62, 253n99;
    water conflicts over, 33–34, 51–57
Nazas River Dam: alternative site choices,
    50–51, 70, 77, 88–89, 252n90; construction
    site as an exemplary "company town," 5, 132;
    effect on surrounding lands, 49, 86, 244n3,
    263n18; environmental instability of the

site, 133–38, 269–70nn6–7; estimated effect on agricultural success, 49–50, 75; federalization of, 83–93; flow data for, 134–35; funding for, 100; groundbreaking for, 132; as incomplete, 131–32; investigation by engineers, 96–97, 101–2; lobbying for, 83–84, 90–91, 221, 260n80; Madero's involvement in, 3, 47–51, 221, 251n81; opposition to, 70, 76–77, 84–86, 98–100, 220–21, 254–55n2; public fears regarding, 48; revival of the project, 4–5, 134; scope of, 48–49, 251n81; support for, 74–75, 91–93, 221, 258n50; water distribution changes caused by, 48–49

Nazas River Inspection Commission, 24, 25, 35–36, 37, 66, 103, 110, 134, 244n3

New Deal, 164–65

North American Free Trade Agreement (NAFTA), 189

North American Natural Resource Conservation Convention (1909), 14–15

Núñez de Esquivel, Melchor, 28

Obregón, Álvaro, 57, 64–66

oil companies, 142–43, 149, 276n33

Ojeda O., Donaciano, 170–71

Olcott, Jocelyn, 161–62

Olsson, Tore, 189

La Opinión, 83–84, 100

Ornelas, Gil, 36, 108, 249n51, 265n39, 265n44

Oropeza, Jesús, 168–69

Oros River, 134

Ortiz Garza, Nazario S., 92

Ortiz Rubio, Pascual, 88, 89, 261n95, 263n9

Othón, Manuel José, 24

El Pabellón Dam, 139

Pacheco, Carlos, 44, 45

Padilla, Mariano, 101

Palmers, Edward, 61

El Palmito Dam. See Lázaro Cárdenas/El Palmito Dam; Nazas River Dam

Pamanes, Jesús, 76

PAN (National Action Party), 223, 227–28

Pan American Union, 275n27

Pardo, Manuel. See Lorenzo Pardo, Manuel

Parras, 27

Parres, José G., 112, 116, 126

Partido Acción Nacional (PAN), 223, 227–28

Partido de la Revolución Democrática (PRD), 223

Partido Nacional Revolucionario (PNR), 99, 109, 132

Partido Revolucionario Institucional (PRI), 185, 207, 223

Pedro Rodríguez Triana Ejido Credit Society, 185

Peña Nieto, Enrique, 219

peons: health care for, 160; housing for, 152–53; persuasion to join ejidos, 96; profit-sharing for, 104; wages for, 135; working conditions of, 157

Pequeña Propiedad Agrícola de la Comarca Lagunera (PPAC), 116, 268n90

Peralta, Carlos, 96, 115, 156

Pereyra, Orestes, 253n93

Pérez Treviño, Manuel, 87

pesticides: advertisements for, 198; biological alternatives to, 200; chemical, 5, 188; DDT, 188, 190, 199–200, 226, 279n75; defiant use of, 198–200, 199t; effectiveness of, 187, 198–200, 204, 281n26; lack of regulations re, 198; natural/organic, 188; spraying of, 188, 190, 279nn74–75; unhealthy levels of, 216

Pinchot, Gifford, 15, 241n23

pink bollworm, 264n31; vs. boll weevil, 61; climate's effect on, 85, 158; entomologists on, 198, 281n14; percentage of cotton infested with, 199t; pesticides used on, 188, 190, 199; spread of, 61–62

plagas (scourges) of Laguna landowners, 60–64, 66, 85, 255n6, 264n31

Plana, Manuel, 42, 43

Plan de Rehabilitación. See Rehabilitation Plan

PNR (National Revolutionary Party), 99, 109, 132

Porfiriato period, 39–40, 42

Portes Gil, Emilio, 87, 88

PPACL (Small Landholders of the Laguna Region), 116, 268n90

Prats, Alardo, 200–202

PRD (Revolutionary Democratic Party), 223

PRI (Institutional Revolutionary Party), 185, 207, 223

Programa Nacional de Ganadería (National Livestock Program), 214
protests, 193, 205, 282n29
publicizing of water laws of foreign countries, 251n74
Pules García, José, 157
pumping. *See* geohydrological knowledge *vs.* pumping business; groundwater pumping; vedas

Quadri, Gabriel, 286n25
Quevedo, Miguel Ángel de, 14–15, 18–19, 57, 75, 77–78, 83, 282n31
Quiñones, Simón, 157

railroads, 39–40, 143–44
rainfall figures, 182–83
Ramos River, 134
Rangel Carrillo, J. Trinidad, 102
red *vs.* white unions, 98
reforestation, 282n31
Regional Mexican Labor Confederation (CROM), 63
Rehabilitation Plan (Plan de Rehabilitación; 1960s), 191–218; and amount of water in the aquifer, 209, 215–16, 280n2; Central Union's role in, 282n29, 282n39; classification of agricultural property, 212*t*; compaction's role in, 206, 209, *210*, 211, 213–14, 217; creation/unveiling of, 191, 202; and defiant pesticide use, 198–200, *199t*; and defiant pumping, 192–98, *195–96tt*, *197*; diversification of economy by, 225; ejidatarios' acceptance of, 211–13; environmental crisis due to, 192, 202–6, *203*; funding for, 209; goals of, 192, 203, 211; hydraulic technology's use in, 192, 214, 280n2; from reform to rehabilitation, 202–9, *203*, 281n28; relocation of ejidos, 209, 211, 213, 217; as a second agrarian reform, 192, 209, *210*, 211–18, 212*t*; successes/failures of, 213–18; Tlahualilo ejidos affected by, 209, *210*
Remington Rand, 178
reparto de aguas (water distribution): engineers' role in, 220; as integral to the reparto de tierras (land distribution), 109–10, 132, 163–64, 192; termination of, 227; urgent need for, 110, 111–12

reparto de tierras (land distribution). *See* Cardenista reform
repression and insurgency, 185, 278n65
Restrepo, Iván, 119
Revolutionary Confederation of Workers and Campesinos of the Laguna Region (CROC), 282n31
Revolutionary Democratic Party (PRD), 223
Reyes Pimentel, José, 156
Reynolds, Steve, 191
rhyolite, 138
Riemann, Armando, 139, 141–42
Rincón de Ramos station (El Palmito), 134–35, 269–70n6
Río Grande/Bravo, 259n59
Río Lerma, 259n59
Ríos de Mendoza, Josefina, 217
Rivera, Diego, 7, *8*, *9*, 131, 269 (epigraph)
Rivers of Empire (Worster), 14
roads: Bermejillo–Palmito, 141; Mapimí–Palmito, 138
Rockefeller Foundation, 188–89
Rodríguez, Abelardo, 90–91, 261n93, 263n9
Rodríguez, Álvaro, 35
Rodríguez Cruz, Arturo, 163
Rodríguez Triana, Pedro V., 102–3, 113, 264n27
Rojas Miranda, E., 102
Rojas Tamez, Joel, 155
Roosevelt, Franklin D., 164–65
Rouaix, Pastor, 14, 59, 67, 257n34
Ruiz Martínez, Ignacio, 78

Sacramento Canal, 209
SAG (Ministry of Agriculture and Livestock), 177, 184, 186, 198, 205, 209, 211
Sahagún, Bernardino de, 30
Salas Álvarez, Francisco, 139, 148
Salazar, José Inés, 57
Salinas (de Gortari), Raúl, 225, 279n71
Salinas de Gortari, Carlos, 5, 222–24, 285n12
Salt River Project (Arizona), 171
Sanalona Dam, 132
Sánchez Mejorada, Javier, 258n50
Sandoval, Arturo, 139
Sandoval, Froylán, 124
San Ignacio, 140
San Juan de Tlahualilo, 123–24

San Miguel ejido (Matamoros), 159–60, 193–94
San Román, José de, 84–85
Santoyo, Francisco, 157
Sanz, Susana, 165–66
Saucedo, Canuto, 149
Saucedo Galindo, Mario, 151–53
Scott, James C.: *Seeing Like a State*, 10
Searle, Clarence E., 176
Secretaría de Agricultura y Ganadería. *See* SAG
Secretaría de Educación Pública (SEP), 153, 159
Secretaría de Fomento (SF), 32
Secretaría de Recursos Hidráulicos (SRH). *See* SRH
Seeing Like a State (Scott), 10
SEMARNAP/SEMARNAT (Ministry of the Environment, Natural Resources, and Fisheries), 224
semi-aniego technique (embankment irrigation), 168
SEP (Ministry of Public Education), 153, 159
Serrano, Joaquín, 111, 112, 113–14, 124, 126
Serrato, Manuel, 35
Servicio Nacional de Irrigación y Construcciones, 52–53
SF (Ministry of Industry and Development), 32
Sierra Madre Occidental, 138
Sifuentes Dozal, Enrique, 144–45
El Siglo de Torreón, 78–79, 83, 84, 91–92, 100, 119, 166, 186, 190
Silent Spring (Carson), 188, 200
Six-Year Plan (1934), 59, 90–91, 132
Small Landholders of the Laguna Region (PPAC), 116, 268n90
smallpox, 160
Smith, F. F., 76–77, 87, 140–41
Smith, H. T., 158
Smith, Merritt Roe: *Does Technology Drive History?* 10
Socialist League of San Pedro, 92
social *vs.* political revolution, 18, 244n41
Soil and Water Conservation Law (1946), 165, 174, 189, 195, 275n27
soil conservation districts, 164–65
El Sol de México, 215
Solís Dam, 132
Spanish water law, 277n55
S. Pearson and Son, 50, 140, 252n86

SRH (Ministry of Hydraulic Resources; *formerly* CNI): on the commission on relocation of ejidos, 211; compacting by, 209, *210* (*see also* Rehabilitation Plan); creation of, 164; Department of Subterranean Hydrology, 215–16; emergency drought-relief program of (1952), 184–85; groundwater extraction regulated and encouraged by, 181–82, 187; on overhauling the irrigation system, 206 (*see also* Rehabilitation Plan); on traditional irrigation methods, 168–70, 274n15; vedas decreed by (*see* vedas)
Statute for Workers at the Service of the State, 150
strikes in Laguna, 99, 101, 102–3, 264n27
Suárez, Eduardo, 132, 269n2
Suinaga Luján, Pedro, 101
Supreme Court (Mexico), 180
surface water *vs.* groundwater, 19–20
sustainability, 2, 224
symbolism *vs.* functionality (of Lázaro Cárdenas/El Palmito Dam), 167
Syndical Confederation of Workers and Peasants, 92

Talleres Industriales, 179
tandas (allocated water rounds), 107, 167
tariffs on cotton, 75, 259n52
technical training, 189–90, 279n81
technopolitics, definition of, 10, 240–41n17
Técnica del Norte, 83
técnicos. *See* engineers; López Zamora, Emilio
Ten Tragic Days mutiny, 56
Tepalcatepec Commission, 267n72
Teresa y Miranda, José de, 250n67
Theis, Charles V., 81
Thorne, Henry Van Rosenthal, 138–39, 143–44, 148–49, 155, 164
Tlahualilo Canal, *68*
Tlahualilo Company: colonization by, 44, 250n66; complaints against, 46–47; expansion of, 46; focus on water rights over land rights, 67–70; labor used by, 250n66; liquidation of and redistribution of lands, 123–27; *vs.* Mexican government, 44–47, 51, 67–70, 123; on the Nazas River Dam, 252n87; Rehabilitation Plan's effects on former lands (ejidos) of, 209, *210*; renaming

Tlahualilo Company (*continued*)
    of, 46; soil and irrigation in, 140; water
    concessions received by, 33, 67, 257n33
Torreón, *12, 13, 38,* 71*t*; battles fought in,
    51, 55; convention of engineers held in,
    77; dairy industry in, 186 (*see also* dairy
    industry); medical care available in, 160;
    population of, 43, 75; as a principal city of
    Laguna, 24, 31, 43, 84; and the reparto de
    tierras, completion of, 141 (*see also under*
    Cardenista reform); strikes in, 99; water
    levels around, 113
Torres Cordera, Guillermo, 190
Townsend, C. H. T., 255n9
Trasquila Dam, 108, 265n39
tunnels and diversion canals, 141, *142,* 154, 167,
    209, 217
typhoid epidemic (1946), 160

Unified Socialist Confederation of Mexico, 98
Unión Central, 185
unionization, 62–63, 99
United Nations Brundtland Commission, 224
United Nations Conference (1992), 224
United Nations Research Institute for Social
    Development, 218
U.S. aid to Mexico, 144
U.S. Dept. of Agriculture, 144, 188, 190, 198
U.S. National Drought Mitigation Center,
    274n6
U.S. Weather Bureau, 270n7
El Universal, 205–6
Universidad Nacional Autónoma de México
    (UNAM), 151
Uranga, Esteban, 198
Usumacinta project, 285n12

Valencia, Salvador, 75
Vargas, Plácido, 75, 80, 83, 88–90, 98
Vázquez, Gabino, 96, 113
Vázquez Ávila, Enrique, 225, 226–27
Vázquez del Mercado, Francisco, 137, 148
Vázquez del Mercado, Gabino, 96, 110, 113
Vázquez Gómez, Emilio, 56–57
vedas (pumping prohibitions): based on geo-
    hydrological knowledge of aquifers, 166;
    emergency program re, 184–85; enforce-
    ment of, 179, 194, 218; noncompliance with,

190, 192–98, 195–96*tt, 197*; total number of,
    278n58; zoning of, 182, *183,* 184*t,* 194, 195*t*
Velázquez, Elpidio, 151
Vera, Manuel, 50–51
Viesca, 257n32
Villa, Pancho, 51, 53–54, 253n95, 254n101
Villista Law, 54–55, 254n100. See also agrarian
    reforms
Vivar, Gonzalo, 82–83
Vogt, William, 173–74, 275n27

Waitz, Paul, 81–82, 83, 112–13, 136–37, 140
Wakild, Emily, 13
Warman, Arturo, 223
"water apartheid," 4
water distribution. *See* reparto de aguas
Water Law (1972), 284n4
Water of the Revolution (El agua de la Revolu-
    ción), 13, 17–18, 51, 57, 60, 192
water regulation (1895), 47, 111, 266n48
water regulation (1909), 47, 106–7, 107*t,* 111,
    116–17, 123, 132, 180, 266n48
water regulation (1938), 123, 124–26, 132, 180,
    268n90
water regulation (1941), 172–73, 175, 180,
    275n24
water rights: arguments for equity in, 116–17;
    and federal authority, 44–45, 51, 55–56,
    250n69, 252–53n91; *vs.* land rights, 64–67;
    of small landholders, 124–25, 268n90
water waste (haciendas *vs.* campesinos),
    102–3
Weckmann, Bernardo, 124
Weckmann, Luis, 124
Weiss, Andrew, 76–77, 139, 143, 171
wells, 81, 158–59, 170–71, 194, 194–95*tt,*
    248n45, 273n71. *See also* geohydrological
    knowledge *vs.* pumping business; ground-
    water pumping; vedas
wheat, 82*t,* 119–20, 188; production levels,
    120*t*
White, Richard, 11
White Engineering, 73, 138–40
white *vs.* red unions, 98
Whitney, Eli, 28
Wilkie, Raymond, 159–61, 193–94, 280n5
windlasses, 134–35
Wislizenus, Frank, 248n45

Workers' Confederation of Mexico (CTM), 99
Workers' Federation of the Laguna Region, 101
Workers' Union of El Palmito, 148–49
World Bank, 209
World Health Organization, 216
World War II, 143–44, 188
Worster, Donald: *Rivers of Empire*, 14
Worthington, Henry R., 176
Worthington de México, 5, 166, 177–80, 190, 196, *197*, 198, 276–77n46, 276n40

Worthington Pump and Machinery, 81, 83, 166, 175–76, 179–80, 276n33
Wright, Angus, 200
Wulff, Frederico, 265n39

Zapata, Emiliano, 2, 18, 52, 222–23, 253n95, 254n101
Zapatistas' agricultural constraints on politico-military power, 52
Zarzosa, Agustín, 116, 117, 171
Zuloaga, Leonardo, 42